ARCO GOLD MCAT SAMPLE EXAMS

5th Edition

Stefan Bosworth, Ph.D.
Marion A. Brisk, Ph.D.
Ronald P. Drucker, Ph.D.
Denise Garland, Ph.D.
Edgar M. Schnebel, Ph.D.
Rosie M. Soy, M.A.

THOMSON
＿＿＿＊＿＿＿ TM
PETERSON'S

Australia • Canada • Mexico • Singapore • Spain • United Kingdom • United States

An ARCO Book

ARCO is a registered trademark of Thomson Learning, Inc., and is used herein under license by Peterson's.

About Thomson Peterson's

Thomson Peterson's (www.petersons.com) is a leading provider of education information and advice, with books and online resources focusing on education search, test preparation, and financial aid. Its Web site offers searchable databases and interactive tools for contacting educational institutions, online practice tests and instruction, and planning tools for securing financial aid. Thomson Peterson's serves 110 million education consumers annually.

Petersons.com/publishing

Check out our Web site at www.petersons.com/publishing to see if there is any new information regarding the rest and any revisions or corrections to the content of this book. We've made sure the information in this book is accurate and up-to-date; however, the test format or content may have changed since the time of publication.

For more information, contact Thomson Peterson's, 2000 Lenox Drive, Lawrenceville, NJ 08648; 800-338-3282; or find us on the World Wide Web at: www.petersons.com/about

Editor: Mandie Rosenberg; Production Editor: Joe Ziegler; Composition Manager: Linda M. Williams; Manufacturing Manager: Ray Golaszewski

ISBN 0-7689-1478-7

Printed in the United States of America

10 9 8 7 6 5 4 3 2 1   06 05 04

Fifth Edition

CONTENTS

Periodic Table of the Elements

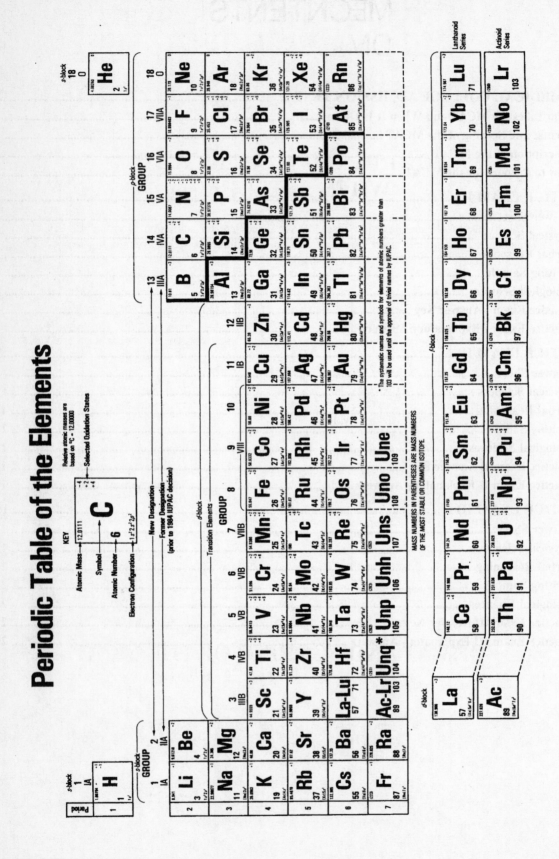

THE MEDICAL COLLEGE ADMISSION TEST

WHO TAKES THE MCAT AND WHEN IT IS GIVEN

The Medical College Admission Test (MCAT) is required for admission to virtually every medical school in the United States and Canada. In addition, it is either required or recommended by many schools of veterinary medicine.

The MCAT is used as one means of evaluating an applicant's chances of success in medical school. Admission committees also review grades, letters of reference, and the medical school application essay before deciding which candidates will be called for an interview for medical school admission. Success on the MCAT will greatly enhance your chances of being accepted to medical school.

The MCAT exam is given twice a year: once in April and once in August. Registration materials are available at the premed office of most colleges, or you can write to the MCAT Program Office at P.O. Box 4056, Iowa City, Iowa 52243.

You may take the MCAT as many times as you like. However, scores from previous MCATs will be furnished to the medical schools you apply to and may affect your chances of being accepted. If you want to take the exam more than three times, you must request permission in writing from the American Association of Medical Colleges.

The MCAT score you receive is good for five years. After that, you will be required to take the exam again. Candidates are encouraged to take the MCAT in the spring of their junior year in order to meet medical school application deadlines. However, you may take the MCAT at any time during your academic career.

FORMAT AND SCORING OF THE MCAT

The MCAT exam is divided into four sections, which are administered as follows:

Section 1   Physical Sciences—77 questions, 100 minutes
(60-minute lunch break)
Section 2   Verbal Reasoning—60 questions, 85 minutes
(10-minute break)
Section 3   Writing Sample—2 essays, 60 minutes
(10-minute break)
Section 4   Biological Sciences—77 questions, 100 minutes

The exam begins at 8 a.m. and ends at approximately 5:30 p.m.

You will receive four separate scores for your MCAT exam, one score for each section. The Physical Sciences, Verbal Reasoning, and Biological Sciences scores are reported on a scale ranging from 1 to 15, with 1 being the lowest and 15 the highest. The Writing Sample score is converted to an alphabetic scale ranging from a low of J to a high of T. Each letter represents the sum of two separate scores for each Writing Sample item.

The range of acceptable scores varies greatly from school to school. Some schools consider a score of 7 acceptable and others consider only scores of 10 or more acceptable. In a recent survey of medical school admission officers, the average response for the lowest acceptable score was 7.

DESCRIPTION OF THE MCAT

The four sections of the MCAT are quite different from past MCAT exams and are quite different from each other. Let's examine them one by one.

Physical Sciences. The Physical Sciences section of the MCAT covers inorganic chemistry and physics. The knowledge required for this section of the exam includes the basic concepts covered in first-year courses in general chemistry and physics. The problem-solving questions require math knowledge up to and including pre-calculus as well as some basic statistics.

The Physical Science test consists of 10 to 11 problem sets with 4 to 8 questions based on each set. In addition, the test includes 15 questions that are independent of any passage and independent of each other.

The specific concepts covered include the following: acids and bases, atomic and nuclear structure, bonding, electrochemistry, electronic circuits, electrostatics and electromagnetism, electronic structure and the periodic table, equilibrium and momentum, fluids and solids, force and motion, gravitation, light and geometrical optics, phases and phase equilibria, rate processes in chemical reactions, kinetics and equilibrium, solution chemistry, sound, stoichiometry, thermodynamics and thermochemistry, translational motion, wave characteristics and periodic motion, and work and energy.

While there is no longer a quantitative section on the MCAT exam, many of the concepts that were covered in the quantitative section are now included in the physical and biological sciences sections.

Verbal Reasoning. The Verbal Reasoning section of the MCAT is similar to the reading section of the old exam, but both the articles and the questions cover a broader range of topics and skills. The Verbal Reasoning test consists of 500- to 750-word passages taken from the humanities, the social sciences, and the natural sciences. Each passage is followed by 6 or 7 multiple-choice questions based on the information presented. All the information necessary to answer the questions is found in the passages. No prior subject matter knowledge is needed to answer any questions in this test.

Verbal reasoning questions are designed to measure your ability to understand, evaluate, and apply information presented in prose passages. You may be asked to recognize information that supports a writer's thesis and to evaluate additional information that does not support the writer's argument. You may be asked to evaluate the strengths and weaknesses of a particular author's arguments or to use information given in a passage to solve other, similar problems. You may be asked what effect new information might have on the conclusions of specific passages and how broad conclusions, explanations, and hypotheses can be applied.

Writing Sample. The Writing Sample section of the MCAT is based on the experimental writing section that has been used on previous MCATs. This section of the MCAT consists of two 30-minute essays on specific topics presented on the test. Each writing sample item consists of a statement followed by three writing tasks. The first task is to explain the statement. The second task is to provide an example illustrating a viewpoint opposite to the statement given. And the third task is to discuss how the conflict between these two opposing statements might be resolved.

Your essays will be reviewed by two readers who look for your ability to organize an answer, explain the statement, develop a central concept, synthesize conflicting concepts and ideas, and express yourself clearly and correctly.

The essay topics will not cover controversial subjects such as religion or politics, nor will they be medical topics or topics that require prior knowledge.

Any school to which you send your MCAT scores will receive your writing score. Copies of your essays will be sent to any medical school that requests them.

Biological Sciences. The Biological Sciences section tests the basic concepts covered in first-year biology and genetics as well as concepts covered in the first semester of organic chemistry. In addition, the problem-solving questions may require knowledge of statistics, particularly as it applies to genetics and environmental concepts.

Like the Physical Sciences test, the Biological Sciences test consists of 10 to 11 problem sets with 4 to 8 questions based on each set. Each test also includes 15 independent multiple-choice questions.

The specific concepts covered include the following: amines; biological molecules; circulatory, lymphatic, and immune systems; digestive and excretory systems; evolution; generalized eukaryotic cell; genetics; hydrocarbons; microbiology; molecular biology; enzymes and cellular metabolism; DNA and protein synthesis; muscle and skeletal systems; nervous and endocrine systems; organic covalent bonding; oxygen-containing compounds; reproductive systems; respiration systems; separations and purifications; skin systems; specialized eukaryotic cells; and the use of spectroscopy in structural identification.

HOW TO PREPARE FOR THE MCAT

The best preparation for the MCAT starts months before the exam and follows a rigorous course of review and study. For those who wish to begin by seeing what the exam is like and perhaps trying a practice test, this book provides the three full-length practice exams complete with explanatory answers. Visit www.petersons.com bookstore to find more Arco and Peterson's MCAT review books.

Use the scoring guide on the next page to give yourself some indication as to how well you have done on the practice exams. The guide should help you to identify your areas of weakness so that you can direct your study where it will do you the most good. You might also want to highlight your score on each successive practice exam to keep track of your increasing expertise on the MCAT. Do be aware, however, that this guide is only an approximation. This is NOT the actual scoring mechanism used on the MCAT. The range of raw scores contributing to each scaled score is adjusted with each administration of the MCAT to take into account variations in difficulty of questions.

Physical Sciences		Verbal Reasoning		Biological Sciences	
Raw Score	Scaled Score	Raw Score	Scaled Score	Raw Score	Scaled Score
0-9	1	0-6	1	0-8	1
10-17	2	7-13	2	9-17	2
18-28	3	14-19	3	18-29	3
29-34	4	20-25	4	30-34	4
35-39	5	26-30	5	35-40	5
40-45	6	31-34	6	41-46	6
46-49	7	35-39	7	47-51	7
50-56	8	40-43	8	52-58	8
57-61	9	44-48	9	59-64	9
62-65	10	49-51	10	65-68	10
66-69	11	52-54	11	69-70	11
70-72	12	55-56	12	71-72	12
73-74	13	57-58	13	62-63	13
75-76	14	59	14	74-76	14
77	15	60	15	77	15

PRACTICE EXAM I

	Time
Physical Sciences Questions 1–77	**100** minutes
Verbal Reasoning Questions 78–137	**85** minutes
Writing Sample 2 Essays	**60** minutes
Biological Sciences Questions 138–214	**100** minutes

ANSWER SHEET
PRACTICE EXAM I

Physical Sciences	Verbal Reasoning	Biological Sciences

Physical Sciences

1. Ⓐ Ⓑ Ⓒ Ⓓ
2. Ⓐ Ⓑ Ⓒ Ⓓ
3. Ⓐ Ⓑ Ⓒ Ⓓ
4. Ⓐ Ⓑ Ⓒ Ⓓ
5. Ⓐ Ⓑ Ⓒ Ⓓ
6. Ⓐ Ⓑ Ⓒ Ⓓ
7. Ⓐ Ⓑ Ⓒ Ⓓ
8. Ⓐ Ⓑ Ⓒ Ⓓ
9. Ⓐ Ⓑ Ⓒ Ⓓ
10. Ⓐ Ⓑ Ⓒ Ⓓ
11. Ⓐ Ⓑ Ⓒ Ⓓ
12. Ⓐ Ⓑ Ⓒ Ⓓ
13. Ⓐ Ⓑ Ⓒ Ⓓ
14. Ⓐ Ⓑ Ⓒ Ⓓ
15. Ⓐ Ⓑ Ⓒ Ⓓ
16. Ⓐ Ⓑ Ⓒ Ⓓ
17. Ⓐ Ⓑ Ⓒ Ⓓ
18. Ⓐ Ⓑ Ⓒ Ⓓ
19. Ⓐ Ⓑ Ⓒ Ⓓ
20. Ⓐ Ⓑ Ⓒ Ⓓ
21. Ⓐ Ⓑ Ⓒ Ⓓ
22. Ⓐ Ⓑ Ⓒ Ⓓ
23. Ⓐ Ⓑ Ⓒ Ⓓ
24. Ⓐ Ⓑ Ⓒ Ⓓ
25. Ⓐ Ⓑ Ⓒ Ⓓ
26. Ⓐ Ⓑ Ⓒ Ⓓ
27. Ⓐ Ⓑ Ⓒ Ⓓ
28. Ⓐ Ⓑ Ⓒ Ⓓ
29. Ⓐ Ⓑ Ⓒ Ⓓ
30. Ⓐ Ⓑ Ⓒ Ⓓ
31. Ⓐ Ⓑ Ⓒ Ⓓ
32. Ⓐ Ⓑ Ⓒ Ⓓ
33. Ⓐ Ⓑ Ⓒ Ⓓ
34. Ⓐ Ⓑ Ⓒ Ⓓ
35. Ⓐ Ⓑ Ⓒ Ⓓ
36. Ⓐ Ⓑ Ⓒ Ⓓ
37. Ⓐ Ⓑ Ⓒ Ⓓ
38. Ⓐ Ⓑ Ⓒ Ⓓ
39. Ⓐ Ⓑ Ⓒ Ⓓ

40. Ⓐ Ⓑ Ⓒ Ⓓ
41. Ⓐ Ⓑ Ⓒ Ⓓ
42. Ⓐ Ⓑ Ⓒ Ⓓ
43. Ⓐ Ⓑ Ⓒ Ⓓ
44. Ⓐ Ⓑ Ⓒ Ⓓ
45. Ⓐ Ⓑ Ⓒ Ⓓ
46. Ⓐ Ⓑ Ⓒ Ⓓ
47. Ⓐ Ⓑ Ⓒ Ⓓ
48. Ⓐ Ⓑ Ⓒ Ⓓ
49. Ⓐ Ⓑ Ⓒ Ⓓ
50. Ⓐ Ⓑ Ⓒ Ⓓ
51. Ⓐ Ⓑ Ⓒ Ⓓ
52. Ⓐ Ⓑ Ⓒ Ⓓ
53. Ⓐ Ⓑ Ⓒ Ⓓ
54. Ⓐ Ⓑ Ⓒ Ⓓ
55. Ⓐ Ⓑ Ⓒ Ⓓ
56. Ⓐ Ⓑ Ⓒ Ⓓ
57. Ⓐ Ⓑ Ⓒ Ⓓ
58. Ⓐ Ⓑ Ⓒ Ⓓ
59. Ⓐ Ⓑ Ⓒ Ⓓ
60. Ⓐ Ⓑ Ⓒ Ⓓ
61. Ⓐ Ⓑ Ⓒ Ⓓ
62. Ⓐ Ⓑ Ⓒ Ⓓ
63. Ⓐ Ⓑ Ⓒ Ⓓ
64. Ⓐ Ⓑ Ⓒ Ⓓ
65. Ⓐ Ⓑ Ⓒ Ⓓ
66. Ⓐ Ⓑ Ⓒ Ⓓ
67. Ⓐ Ⓑ Ⓒ Ⓓ
68. Ⓐ Ⓑ Ⓒ Ⓓ
69. Ⓐ Ⓑ Ⓒ Ⓓ
70. Ⓐ Ⓑ Ⓒ Ⓓ
71. Ⓐ Ⓑ Ⓒ Ⓓ
72. Ⓐ Ⓑ Ⓒ Ⓓ
73. Ⓐ Ⓑ Ⓒ Ⓓ
74. Ⓐ Ⓑ Ⓒ Ⓓ
75. Ⓐ Ⓑ Ⓒ Ⓓ
76. Ⓐ Ⓑ Ⓒ Ⓓ
77. Ⓐ Ⓑ Ⓒ Ⓓ

Verbal Reasoning

78. Ⓐ Ⓑ Ⓒ Ⓓ
79. Ⓐ Ⓑ Ⓒ Ⓓ
80. Ⓐ Ⓑ Ⓒ Ⓓ
81. Ⓐ Ⓑ Ⓒ Ⓓ
82. Ⓐ Ⓑ Ⓒ Ⓓ
83. Ⓐ Ⓑ Ⓒ Ⓓ
84. Ⓐ Ⓑ Ⓒ Ⓓ
85. Ⓐ Ⓑ Ⓒ Ⓓ
86. Ⓐ Ⓑ Ⓒ Ⓓ
87. Ⓐ Ⓑ Ⓒ Ⓓ
88. Ⓐ Ⓑ Ⓒ Ⓓ
89. Ⓐ Ⓑ Ⓒ Ⓓ
90. Ⓐ Ⓑ Ⓒ Ⓓ
91. Ⓐ Ⓑ Ⓒ Ⓓ
92. Ⓐ Ⓑ Ⓒ Ⓓ
93. Ⓐ Ⓑ Ⓒ Ⓓ
94. Ⓐ Ⓑ Ⓒ Ⓓ
95. Ⓐ Ⓑ Ⓒ Ⓓ
96. Ⓐ Ⓑ Ⓒ Ⓓ
97. Ⓐ Ⓑ Ⓒ Ⓓ
98. Ⓐ Ⓑ Ⓒ Ⓓ
99. Ⓐ Ⓑ Ⓒ Ⓓ
100. Ⓐ Ⓑ Ⓒ Ⓓ
101. Ⓐ Ⓑ Ⓒ Ⓓ
102. Ⓐ Ⓑ Ⓒ Ⓓ
103. Ⓐ Ⓑ Ⓒ Ⓓ
104. Ⓐ Ⓑ Ⓒ Ⓓ
105. Ⓐ Ⓑ Ⓒ Ⓓ
106. Ⓐ Ⓑ Ⓒ Ⓓ
107. Ⓐ Ⓑ Ⓒ Ⓓ

108. Ⓐ Ⓑ Ⓒ Ⓓ
109. Ⓐ Ⓑ Ⓒ Ⓓ
110. Ⓐ Ⓑ Ⓒ Ⓓ
111. Ⓐ Ⓑ Ⓒ Ⓓ
112. Ⓐ Ⓑ Ⓒ Ⓓ
113. Ⓐ Ⓑ Ⓒ Ⓓ
114. Ⓐ Ⓑ Ⓒ Ⓓ
115. Ⓐ Ⓑ Ⓒ Ⓓ
116. Ⓐ Ⓑ Ⓒ Ⓓ
117. Ⓐ Ⓑ Ⓒ Ⓓ
118. Ⓐ Ⓑ Ⓒ Ⓓ
119. Ⓐ Ⓑ Ⓒ Ⓓ
120. Ⓐ Ⓑ Ⓒ Ⓓ
121. Ⓐ Ⓑ Ⓒ Ⓓ
122. Ⓐ Ⓑ Ⓒ Ⓓ
123. Ⓐ Ⓑ Ⓒ Ⓓ
124. Ⓐ Ⓑ Ⓒ Ⓓ
125. Ⓐ Ⓑ Ⓒ Ⓓ
126. Ⓐ Ⓑ Ⓒ Ⓓ
127. Ⓐ Ⓑ Ⓒ Ⓓ
128. Ⓐ Ⓑ Ⓒ Ⓓ
129. Ⓐ Ⓑ Ⓒ Ⓓ
130. Ⓐ Ⓑ Ⓒ Ⓓ
131. Ⓐ Ⓑ Ⓒ Ⓓ
132. Ⓐ Ⓑ Ⓒ Ⓓ
133. Ⓐ Ⓑ Ⓒ Ⓓ
134. Ⓐ Ⓑ Ⓒ Ⓓ
135. Ⓐ Ⓑ Ⓒ Ⓓ
136. Ⓐ Ⓑ Ⓒ Ⓓ
137. Ⓐ Ⓑ Ⓒ Ⓓ

Biological Sciences

138. Ⓐ Ⓑ Ⓒ Ⓓ
139. Ⓐ Ⓑ Ⓒ Ⓓ
140. Ⓐ Ⓑ Ⓒ Ⓓ
141. Ⓐ Ⓑ Ⓒ Ⓓ
142. Ⓐ Ⓑ Ⓒ Ⓓ
143. Ⓐ Ⓑ Ⓒ Ⓓ
144. Ⓐ Ⓑ Ⓒ Ⓓ
145. Ⓐ Ⓑ Ⓒ Ⓓ
146. Ⓐ Ⓑ Ⓒ Ⓓ
147. Ⓐ Ⓑ Ⓒ Ⓓ
148. Ⓐ Ⓑ Ⓒ Ⓓ
149. Ⓐ Ⓑ Ⓒ Ⓓ
150. Ⓐ Ⓑ Ⓒ Ⓓ
151. Ⓐ Ⓑ Ⓒ Ⓓ
152. Ⓐ Ⓑ Ⓒ Ⓓ
153. Ⓐ Ⓑ Ⓒ Ⓓ
154. Ⓐ Ⓑ Ⓒ Ⓓ
155. Ⓐ Ⓑ Ⓒ Ⓓ
156. Ⓐ Ⓑ Ⓒ Ⓓ
157. Ⓐ Ⓑ Ⓒ Ⓓ
158. Ⓐ Ⓑ Ⓒ Ⓓ
159. Ⓐ Ⓑ Ⓒ Ⓓ
160. Ⓐ Ⓑ Ⓒ Ⓓ
161. Ⓐ Ⓑ Ⓒ Ⓓ
162. Ⓐ Ⓑ Ⓒ Ⓓ
163. Ⓐ Ⓑ Ⓒ Ⓓ
164. Ⓐ Ⓑ Ⓒ Ⓓ
165. Ⓐ Ⓑ Ⓒ Ⓓ
166. Ⓐ Ⓑ Ⓒ Ⓓ
167. Ⓐ Ⓑ Ⓒ Ⓓ
168. Ⓐ Ⓑ Ⓒ Ⓓ
169. Ⓐ Ⓑ Ⓒ Ⓓ
170. Ⓐ Ⓑ Ⓒ Ⓓ
171. Ⓐ Ⓑ Ⓒ Ⓓ
172. Ⓐ Ⓑ Ⓒ Ⓓ
173. Ⓐ Ⓑ Ⓒ Ⓓ
174. Ⓐ Ⓑ Ⓒ Ⓓ
175. Ⓐ Ⓑ Ⓒ Ⓓ
176. Ⓐ Ⓑ Ⓒ Ⓓ

177. Ⓐ Ⓑ Ⓒ Ⓓ
178. Ⓐ Ⓑ Ⓒ Ⓓ
179. Ⓐ Ⓑ Ⓒ Ⓓ
180. Ⓐ Ⓑ Ⓒ Ⓓ
181. Ⓐ Ⓑ Ⓒ Ⓓ
182. Ⓐ Ⓑ Ⓒ Ⓓ
183. Ⓐ Ⓑ Ⓒ Ⓓ
184. Ⓐ Ⓑ Ⓒ Ⓓ
185. Ⓐ Ⓑ Ⓒ Ⓓ
186. Ⓐ Ⓑ Ⓒ Ⓓ
187. Ⓐ Ⓑ Ⓒ Ⓓ
188. Ⓐ Ⓑ Ⓒ Ⓓ
189. Ⓐ Ⓑ Ⓒ Ⓓ
190. Ⓐ Ⓑ Ⓒ Ⓓ
191. Ⓐ Ⓑ Ⓒ Ⓓ
192. Ⓐ Ⓑ Ⓒ Ⓓ
193. Ⓐ Ⓑ Ⓒ Ⓓ
194. Ⓐ Ⓑ Ⓒ Ⓓ
195. Ⓐ Ⓑ Ⓒ Ⓓ
196. Ⓐ Ⓑ Ⓒ Ⓓ
197. Ⓐ Ⓑ Ⓒ Ⓓ
198. Ⓐ Ⓑ Ⓒ Ⓓ
199. Ⓐ Ⓑ Ⓒ Ⓓ
200. Ⓐ Ⓑ Ⓒ Ⓓ
201. Ⓐ Ⓑ Ⓒ Ⓓ
202. Ⓐ Ⓑ Ⓒ Ⓓ
203. Ⓐ Ⓑ Ⓒ Ⓓ
204. Ⓐ Ⓑ Ⓒ Ⓓ
205. Ⓐ Ⓑ Ⓒ Ⓓ
206. Ⓐ Ⓑ Ⓒ Ⓓ
207. Ⓐ Ⓑ Ⓒ Ⓓ
208. Ⓐ Ⓑ Ⓒ Ⓓ
209. Ⓐ Ⓑ Ⓒ Ⓓ
210. Ⓐ Ⓑ Ⓒ Ⓓ
211. Ⓐ Ⓑ Ⓒ Ⓓ
212. Ⓐ Ⓑ Ⓒ Ⓓ
213. Ⓐ Ⓑ Ⓒ Ⓓ
214. Ⓐ Ⓑ Ⓒ Ⓓ

Writing Sample 1

_____

_____

_____

_____

_____

_____

_____

_____

_____

_____

_____

_____

_____

_____

_____

_____

_____

_____

_____

_____

_____

_____

END OF PART 1

Writing Sample 2

_____

_____

_____

_____

_____

_____

_____

_____

_____

_____

_____

_____

_____

_____

_____

_____

_____

_____

_____

_____

_____

_____

END OF PART 2

PHYSICAL SCIENCES

Time: 100 Minutes
Questions 1–77

Directions: This test contains 77 questions. Most of the questions consist of a descriptive passage followed by a group of questions related to the passage. For these questions, study the passage carefully and then choose the best answer to each question in the group. Some questions in this test stand alone. These questions are independent of any passage and independent of each other. For these questions, too, you must select the one best answer. Indicate all your answers by blackening the corresponding circles on your answer sheet.

A periodic table is provided at the beginning of this book. You may consult it whenever you feel it's necessary.

Passage I (Questions 1–7)

Archimedes is probably most remembered for an anecdote that claims he ran naked through the streets yelling "Eureka!" after discovering the principle that bears his name. The story goes that while soaking in a bathtub and trying to solve the problem of how to tell if a gold crown had been adulterated with less valuable metals such as copper or silver, he noticed that a body wholly or partially immersed in a fluid appears to weigh less.

This apparent loss of weight equals the weight of the fluid displaced by the body and can be thought of as an upward buoyant force, F_B, supplied by the fluid. If the body is completely submerged, the volume of water displaced equals the volume of the body.

Essentially, Archimedes was trying to find a technique that would allow him to determine the density of an irregularly shaped object. Density, ρ, and weight, w, are related through the acceleration due to gravity, g:

$$\rho = (m/V)(g/g) = mg/gV = w/gV$$

1. A 60-kg swimmer pulls himself onto a 2m × 2m raft moored in the middle of a small lake. By how much does the raft sink when the swimmer climbs onto it?

   A. 1.5 cm
   B. 3.0 cm
   C. 4.5 cm
   D. 6.0 cm

2. A clever student needs to determine the density of liquid X. She has at her disposal a spring balance and an irregularly shaped object of unknown material that is inert in air, water, and liquid X. In air the object weighs 2.00 N. In water it weighs 1.60 N. And in liquid X it weighs 1.70 N. The density of liquid X is

   A. 250 kg/m³
   B. 500 kg/m³
   C. 750 kg/m³
   D. 1250 kg/m³

3. A 10^5 m³ ship weighing 10^4 N floats next to a loading dock. If V_s and W_s are the volume and weight of the ship, and V_w and W_w are the volume and weight of the displaced water, which statement is most accurate?

   A. $V_s = V_w$ and $W_s = W_w$
   B. $V_s > V_w$ and $W_s = W_w$
   C. $V_s > V_w$ and $W_s > W_w$
   D. $V_s = V_w$ and $W_s < W_w$

4. A layer of oil 4 meters deep floats on a layer of water that is 8 meters deep. The density of the oil is 300 kg/m³. A cube with a volume of 2 m³ floats at the oil-water interface with exactly half of its volume in the water. What is the density of the cube?

   A. 375 kg/m³
   B. 500 kg/m³
   C. 650 kg/m³
   D. 1300 kg/m³

5. A barge filled with garbage has a density of 800 kg/m^3. What percent of the barge's volume is above the water line? The volume below the water line is called the draft of the ship.

   A. 22%
   B. 33%
   C. 67%
   D. 78%

6. A high altitude hot air balloon is made of a durable but lightweight material. It is filled with hot air at a density of 1.0 kg/m^3 until it expands to a volume of 4.5×10^3 m^3. If the balloon floats at an altitude where the outside air density is 1.5 kg/m^3, what is the maximum load the balloon can carry?

   A. 1.5×10^4 N
   B. 9.8×10^3 N
   C. 1.5×10^3 N
   D. Problem can't be solved without being told the mass of the balloon.

7. While constructing a commercial riverfront pier engineers discover a 300-kg boulder submerged near the position for one of the pier's supports. Examination of a sample from the boulder shows it has a density of 2400 kg/m^3. They decide to use a large marine crane to lift the boulder vertically out of the water. What is the tension of the crane's cable just before the boulder is lifted? Assume the cable is taut and the boulder is not yet in motion.

   A. 1225 N
   B. 1715 N
   C. 2940 N
   D. 4165 N

Passage II (Questions 8–13)

Transverse and longitudinal standing waves are easily represented by sine waves. Positions of maximum displacement from equilibrium are called antinodes, A. Positions of zero displacement are called nodes, N.

For a complete cycle of a wave of wavelength λ the distance between any two consecutive nodes (N-A-N) or any two consecutive antinodes (A-N-A) is half of the wavelength, $\lambda/2$. The distance between an adjacent node and antinode (N-A) is a quarter of the wavelength, $\lambda/4$.

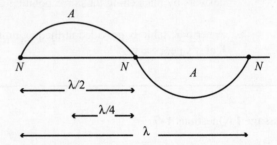

Longitudinal standing waves can be produced in columns of air in pipes. The closed end of a pipe is always a node. The open end of a pipe is always an antinode.

Wavelength, λ, and frequency, ν, of mechanical waves are related to the speed of the wave through the given medium: $\lambda\nu = v$

For room temperature air, the speed of sound, v, is 340 m/s.

The lowest natural frequency is called the fundamental frequency, ν_o, and has wavelength λ_o. A harmonic is an integer multiple of the fundamental frequency, $n\nu_o$, with $n = 1, 2, 3, \ldots$. So the fundamental frequency is the first harmonic. The harmonics that occur naturally are called overtones.

I. Fundamental and first overtone for a pipe open at both ends.

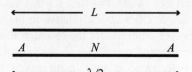

$\lambda/2 = L$
Therefore, $\lambda_o = 2L$ and $v_o = v/2L$
Overtones are multiples of v_o:
$$n\, v_o = n[v/2L]$$

$\lambda/2 = L/2$
Therefore, $\lambda_1 = 2(L/2)$ and $v_1 = 2[v/2L]$
For the first overtone $n = 2$, the second harmonic. This implies that the ratio of natural frequencies is $n = 1:2:3:\ldots..$

II. Fundamental and first overtone for a pipe closed at one end.

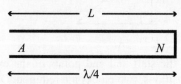

$\lambda/4 = L$
Therefore, $\lambda_o = 4L$ and $v_o = v/4L$

Overtones are multiples of v_o:
$$n\, v_o = n[v/4L]$$

$\lambda/4 = L/3$
Therefore, $\lambda_1 = 4(L/3)$ and
$\lambda_1 = v/(4L/3) = 3[v/4L]$

For the first overtone $n = 3$, the third harmonic. This implies that the ratio of natural frequencies is $n = 1:3:5:\ldots..$

8. The auditory canal of the outer ear is essentially a 3.0-cm pipe closed at one end by the eardrum. What is the fundamental frequency in air associated with the ear?

   A. 1.1×10^{-2} mHz
   B. 2.8×10^{-3} mHz
   C. 5.6×10^{-3} mHz
   D. 1.7×10^{-5} mHz

9. When an organ pipe is open at both ends, it resonates with a fundamental frequency of 240 Hz. What is the fundamental frequency of the same pipe if it is closed at one end?

   A. 60 Hz
   B. 120 Hz
   C. 360 Hz
   D. 480 Hz

10. A pipe resonates at 60 Hz, 100 Hz, and 140 Hz. How long is the pipe?

    A. 1.4 m
    B. 2.8 m
    C. 4.3 m
    D. 8.5 m

11. A flutist plays a note with a fundamental wavelength of 170 cm. How many compression regions reach a nearby listener per second?

    A. 170
    B. 200
    C. 500
    D. Can't be determined without knowing distance between flutist and listener.

12. For an organ pipe closed at its top end, the second overtone is

    A. second harmonic.
    B. third harmonic.
    C. fourth harmonic.
    D. fifth harmonic.

13. A pipe of length L is closed at *both* ends. What is its fundamental wavelength?

    A. L/2
    B. L
    C. 2L
    D. 4L

Passage III (Questions 14–18)

The two fundamental postulates of Einstein's special theory of relativity are:

1. The laws of physics are identical in all inertial frames of reference. An inertial frame is a set of coordinate axes that is at rest or moving with constant speed; it is not undergoing any acceleration. An observer in the frame has a clock that sits at rest relative to the observer and is used to measure the time it takes for an event to occur.
2. The speed of light in vacuum is always 3.00×10^8 m/s. This value is independent of both the motion of the observer and the source of the light.

One consequence of the postulates is that events that are simultaneous in one frame of reference are not, in general, simultaneous in any frame of reference that is moving relative to the first frame.

A person, say, Observer A, measuring an interval of time between events in his own reference frame (the one moving at the same speed as Observer A), measures what is called the proper time of the interval, Δt_o. The proper time will be shorter than the interval, Δt, measured by any other observer in motion relative to Observer A.

For a given event the two time intervals are related by:

$$\Delta t = \Delta t_o/(1 - v^2/c^2)$$

Where c is the speed of light and v is the speed associated with the event being observed. Since v^2/c^2 is always less than 1, Δt is always greater than Δt_o.

A way to picture this is with the following thought experiment. A spaceship traveling at speed v sends a beam of light from a source to a mirror. This is event 1. The beam is reflected to a detector sitting next to the source. This is event 2.

Figure 1 is for an observer on the spaceship. The light travels a distance of 2D. The time for this travel is measured by a single clock at rest relative to the ship. This gives the proper time, Δt_o, for the complete event.
$$\Delta t_o = 2D/c$$
Figure 2 is for an observer on earth watching the spaceship fly by.

While the light is going to and from the mirror, the ship travels a distance of $v\Delta t$. Therefore, the light looks like it has traveled a greater distance, 2L.

From the right triangle relationship, $D^2 + (v\Delta t/2)^2 = L^2$. Therefore, $L > D$.

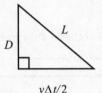

And since the start and end points of the events have different positions, two clocks are required. One at the start position to measure when the beam leaves the source and one at the end position when the beam returns to the detector.

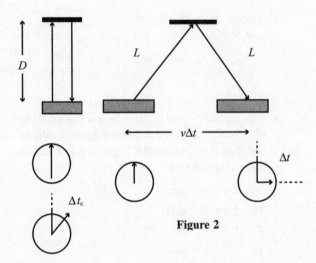

Figure 2

Figure 1

14. An observatory monitors the speed of a passing spaceship by recording flashes of laser light emitted by the ship. The ship is traveling at a constant speed of 2.0×10^8 m/s and its onboard computers are programmed to emit a laser pulse every 10 seconds. What is the time between flashes recorded at the observatory?

A. 7.5 s
B. 13.4 s
C. 17.3 s
D. 90.0 s

15. An observer on a spaceship sees ten flashes of light in 10 seconds. An observer on the ground sees the same ten flashes in 20 seconds. What is the speed of the spaceship?

A. 2.0×10^8 m/s
B. 2.3×10^8 m/s
C. 2.6×10^8 m/s
D. 2.9×10^8 m/s

16. In a particular experiment unstable particles called muons are created in a linear accelerator and then ejected at a constant speed of $0.99c$. The observed average lifetime for these particles was 16 μs. What is the average half-life of a muon?

A. 2.2 μs
B. 7.8 μs
C. 15.6 μs
D. 110 μs

17. A space probe travels 20 light years at a constant speed of $0.9950c$. How long does the trip take in the frame of reference of an observer on the earth?

A. 2 years
B. 5 years
C. 20 years
D. 50 years

18. A massless particle is traveling at the speed c parallel to a beam of light. If an observer could travel on the particle, the light beam would appear to:

A. be at rest relative to the particle traveling beside it at the speed c.
B. travel away from the observer at a speed less than c.
C. travel away from the observer at a speed equal to c.
D. have a non-inertial frame of reference.

Passage IV (Questions 19–25)

When a battery is used to charge a capacitor in series with a resistor, the charge q on the capacitor doesn't instantly rise to its final value. As charge builds up on the capacitor plates, it opposes the flow of additional charge. As a result the build up of charge is exponential. The time constant τ describes how the charge varies with time and is equal to the product of the capacitance C and the resistance R of the circuit:

$$\tau = RC$$

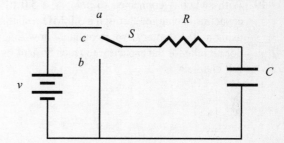

When the switch S is in position a:
1. The charge q on the capacitor increases exponentially with time until it reaches its maximum value of $q_o = CV$.
   The voltage across the capacitor increases with the charge. Its maximum value is that of the voltage source (battery).
2. The current i flowing through the resistor decreases exponentially with time from its maximum value of $i_o = V/R$.

When the switch S is in position b:
1. The charge on the capacitor decreases exponentially with time.
2. As the charge on the capacitor decreases, the current through the resistor again decreases.

When the switch is in position *c*, the charge on the capacitor is held constant.

The exponential values for *RC* circuit are summarized on Table I.

Table I.		
Time constant	Charge	Current
τ	q	i
RC	$0.63q_f$	$0.37i_o$
$2RC$	$0.86q_f$	$0.14i_o$
$3RC$	$0.95q_f$	$0.05i_o$
$3RC$	$0.98q_f$	$0.02i_o$
$5RC$	$0.993q_f$	$0.007i_o$

Decreasing charge follows the values in column 3.

Increasing current follows the values in column 2.

After one time constant the capacitor has reached ~ 63% of its full charge and the current has decreased to 37% of its maximum value.

After five time constants the capacitor has reached over 99% of its charged or discharged value. Effectively, the charge or the current has reached its final value after five time constants.

19. With switch *S* connected to point *a*, a 5.0 µF capacitor is charged through a 3.0 MΩ resistor using a 30-V battery. Approximately how long does it take for the capacitor to reach 86% of its full charge?

    A. 12 s
    B. 15 s
    C. 30 s
    D. 37 s

20. What is the value of the charging resistance for a 100 µF capacitor in a *RC* circuit with a 10 s time constant?

    A. 10 Ω
    B. 1 kΩ
    C. 10 kΩ
    D. 100 kΩ

21. With switch *S* in position *a*, the capacitor is fully charged by an applied voltage of 200V. The switch is changed to position *b* and the capacitor discharges to 1 V in approximately 40 seconds. At what time was the voltage across the capacitor 74 V?

    A. 8 s
    B. 10 s
    C. 37 s
    D. 63 s

22. A 2.0 µF capacitor in series with a 6.0 MΩ resistor is charged using a 50-V battery. What is the most likely charge on the capacitor after 6 seconds?

    A. 25 µC
    B. 31 µC
    C. 39 µC
    D. 63 µC

23. Doubling the capacitance in a given *RC* circuit will:

    A. decrease the maximum current through the circuit.
    B. decrease the time required to fully charge the capacitor.
    C. increase the maximum current through the circuit.
    D. increase the time required to fully charge the capacitor.

24. Referring to the figure in the passage, the battery is V, the resistor is Ω and the time constant is 6 seconds. At time *t* = 0 the switch *S* is connected to point *a*. What is the current through the resistor at *t* = 40 seconds?

    A. 0 A
    B. 1 A
    C. 2 A
    D. 4 A

25. Referring to the figure in the passage, after the capacitor is fully charged the switch *S* is moved from point *a* to point *b* at *t* = 0. The time constant for the *RC* circuit is 10 seconds. What is the charge on the capacitor at *t* = 20 seconds?

A. q_{max}

B. $0.86\ q_{max}$

C. $0.14\ q_{max}$

D. 0

Passage V (Questions 26–31)

Thin films, including soap bubbles and oil slicks, show patterns of alternating dark and bright regions resulting from interference among the reflected light waves. If two waves are in phase their crest and troughs will coincide. The interference will be constructive and the amplitude of the resultant wave will be greater than the amplitude of either constituent wave. If the two waves are out of phase by ½ a wavelength (180°), the crests of one wave will coincide with the troughs of the other wave. The interference will be destructive and the amplitude of the resultant wave will be less than that of either constituent wave.

At the interface between two transparent media, some light is reflected and some light is refracted.

1. When incident light, I, reaches the surface at point *a*, some of the light is reflected as ray R_a and some is refracted following the path *ab* to the back of the film.
2. At point *b* some of the light is refracted out of the film and part is reflected back through the film along path *bc*. At point *c* some of the light is reflected back into the film and part is refracted out of the film as ray R_c.

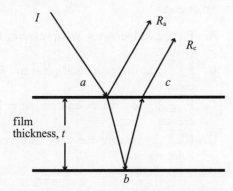

R_a and R_c are parallel. However, R_c has traveled the extra distance within the film of *abc*. If the angle of incidence is small, then *abc* is approximately twice the film's thickness.

If R_a and R_c are in phase, they will undergo constructive interference and the region *ac* will be bright. If R_a and R_c are out of phase, they will undergo destructive interference and the region *ac* will be dark.

The thickness of the film and the refractive indices of the media at each interface determine the final phase relationship between R_a and R_c.

    I. Refraction at an interface never changes the phase of the wave.

    II. For reflection at the interface between two media 1 and 2. If $n_1 < n_2$ the reflected wave will change phase. If $n_1 > n_2$ the reflected wave will not undergo a phase change.

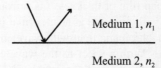

For reference, $n_{air} = 1.00$.

    III. If the waves are in phase after reflection at all interfaces, then the effects of path length in the film are:

        Constructive interference occurs when:
        $2t = m\lambda/n$ m = 0, 1, 2, 3……

        Destructive interference occurs when:
        $2t = (m + ½)\lambda/n$ m = 0, 1, 2, 3……

    If the waves are 180° out of phase after reflection at all interfaces then the effects of path length in the film are:

        Constructive interference occurs when:
        $2t = (m + ½)\lambda/n$ m = 0, 1, 2, 3……

        Destructive interference occurs when:
        $2t = m\lambda/n$ m = 0, 1, 2, 3……

26. A thin film with index of refraction 1.50 coats a glass lens with index of refraction 1.80. What is the minimum thickness of the thin film that will strongly reflect light with wavelength 600 nm?

A. 150 nm

B. 200 nm

C. 300 nm

D. 450 nm

27. A thin film with index of refraction 1.33 coats a glass lens with index of refraction 1.50. Which of the following choices is the smallest film thicknesses that will not reflect light with wavelength 640 nm?

A. 160 nm
B. 240 nm
C. 360 nm
D. 480 nm

28. A soap film of thickness t is surrounded by air and is illuminated at near normal incidence by monochromatic light with wavelength λ in the film. With respect to the wavelength of the monochromatic light in the film, what film thickness will produce maximum constructive interference?

A. ¼ λ
B. ½ λ
C. 1 λ
D. 2 λ

29. The average human eye sees colors with wavelengths between ~ 430 nm to 680 nm. For what visible wavelength(s) will a 350-nm thick $n = 1.35$ soap film produce maximum destructive interference?

A. 945 nm
B. 473 nm
C. 315 nm
D. None of these choices

30. A 600-nm light is perpendicularly incident on a soap film suspended in air. The film is 1.00 µm thick with $n = 1.35$. Which statement most accurately describes the interference of the light reflected by the two surfaces of the film?

A. The waves are close to destructive interference.
B. The waves are close to constructive interference.
C. The waves show complete destructive interference.
D. The waves show complete constructive interference.

31. A thin film of liquid polymer $n = 1.25$ coats a slab of Pyrex, $n = 1.50$. White light is incident perpendicularly to the film. In the reflections full destructive interference occurs for λ 600 nm and full constructive interference occurs for $\lambda = 700$ nm. What is the thickness of the polymer film?

A. 120 nm
B. 280 nm
C. 460 nm
D. 840 nm

Questions 32–39 are not based on any passage.

---

32. What is the magnitude of the acceleration experienced by a particle of mass $m = 1.67 \times 10^{-27}$ kg and charge $q = +1.6 \times 10^{-19}$ C placed in an electric field $E = 0.010$ N/C?

A. 9.6×10^9 m/s^2
B. 9.6×10^8 m/s^2
C. 9.6×10^7 m/s^2
D. 9.6×10^6 m/s^2

33. In Case A, when an 80-kg skydiver falls with arms and legs fully extended to maximize his surface area, his terminal velocity is 60 m/s. In Case B, when the same skydiver falls with arms and legs pulled in and body angled downward to minimize his surface area, his terminal velocity increases to 80 m/s. In going from Case A to Case B, which of the following statements most accurately describes what the skydiver experiences?

A. $F_{air\ resistance}$ increases and pressure, P, increases
B. $F_{air\ resistance}$ increases and pressure, P, decreases
C. $F_{air\ resistance}$ decreases and pressure, P, increases
D. $F_{air\ resistance}$ remains the same and pressure, P, increases

34. What is the electric resistance of the filament in a 60-W light bulb connected to a 120V potential difference?

    A. 2 Ω
    B. 30 Ω
    C. 240 Ω
    D. 7.2×10^2 Ω

35. Two blocks A and B of masses M_A and M_B respectively, are located 1.0 m apart on a horizontal surface. The coefficient of static friction μ_s between the blocks and the surface is 0.50. Block A is secured to the surface and cannot move. What is the minimum mass of Block A that provides enough gravitational attraction to move Block B? The universal gravitation constant is 6.67×10^{-11} Nm^2/kg^2.

    A. 7.5×10^9 kg
    B. 7.3×10^{10} kg
    C. 14.7×10^{11} kg
    D. The problem cannot be solved without knowing the mass of Block B.

36. Block A is moving with acceleration A along a frictionless horizontal surface. When a second block, B, is placed on top of Block A the acceleration of the combined blocks drops to 1/5 the original value. What is the ratio of the mass of A to the mass of B?

    A. 5:1
    B. 4:1
    C. 3:1
    D. 2:1

37. If you were to throw a ball vertically upward with an initial velocity of 50 m/s, approximately how long would it take for the ball to return to your hand? Assume air resistance is negligible.

    A. 2.5 s
    B. 5.0 s
    C. 7.5 s
    D. 10 s

38. Johnny and his sister Jane race up a hill. Johnny weighs twice as much as Jane and takes twice as long as Jane to reach the top. Compared to Jane:

    A. Johnny did more work and delivered more power.
    B. Johnny did more work and delivered the same amount of power.
    C. Johnny did more work and delivered less power.
    D. Johnny did less work and Johnny delivered less power.

39. An 80-kg skydiver jumps from an altitude of 3000 m. Assuming air resistance is negligible, estimate the skydiver's velocity at an altitude of 1000 m?

    A. 50 m/s
    B. 100 m/s
    C. 200 m/s
    D. 300 m/s

Passage VI (Questions 40–45)

A student must analyze a colored solution of compound Y, whose concentration is designated as "X" mol/L. She also has a solution that is 1.00 M in compound Y.

Experiment 1: At the outset, no instruments are available to her, so she makes up color standards in test tubes, holds them up to a light bulb, and arranges them in order from lightest to darkest, as in Figure 1 below.

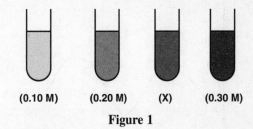

(0.10 M)   (0.20 M)   (X)   (0.30 M)

Figure 1

Experiment 2: The student gains access to a simple spectrophotometer, which allows her to measure the absorbance of the solutions that she prepared in Experiment 1 at a visible wavelength of her choice. The measurements, all at 520 nm, are shown in Figure 2 below:

Concentration (M)	Absorbance
0.240	0.186
0.390	0.298
×	0.389
0.588	0.462

Figure 2

The student plots her data of absorbed light at 520 nm in Figure 3 below.

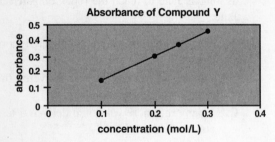

Figure 3

The student has learned that by the Beer-Lambert Law, absorbance, A, has a straightforward relation to the molar absorptivity, a, which depends on the nature of the absorbing species and varies with wavelength; the path length, b, which, for this instance, is the diameter of the test tube; and the concentration, c, of the absorbing species:

$$A = abc$$

The transmittance, T, is defined as:

$$T = I_{out}/I_{in} =$$

where I_{in} is the intensity of the light that enters the sample tube, and I_{out} is the intensity of the light that leaves the tube. T is related to the absorbance A by the relation

$$A = -\log T$$

She then uses the spectrophotometer to obtain the visible absorption spectrum of compound Y in aqueous solution as shown in Figure 4.

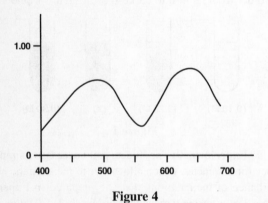

Figure 4

Experiment 3: The student finds that compound Y is sparingly soluble in hexane. She repeats the study of absorbance versus concentration in this new solvent, as shown in Figure 5.

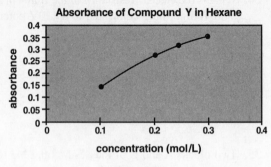

Figure 5

40. Which of the following is the most reasonable conclusion that the student can draw from the data of Experiment 1?

A. The concentration of solution X is 0.25 M.

B. The concentration of solution X is 0.250 M.

C. The concentration of solution X is between 0.3 and 0.4.

D. The concentration of solution X is between 0.2 and 0.3.

41. The student decides to repeat Experiment 1, taking additional measurements in order to get better accuracy. What is likely to be the chief limitation in the sensitivity of this method?

A. Errors in the measuring device used to measure solution volumes as dilutions are made

B. The uncertainty in the concentration of the original solution of compound Y

C. The student's ability to judge the degree of color intensity in the test tubes

D. Evaporation of the solvent

42. In Experiment 2, for approximately what wavelength of light is the *transmittance* the greatest?

A. 450 nm

B. 490 nm

C. 560 nm

D. 640 nm

43. Which of the following is closest to the *frequency* of light that is most likely to be absorbed by compound Y?

    A. 6.4×10^{-7} m
    B. 1.9×10^{11} s^{-1}
    C. 4.7×10^{14} s^{-1}
    D. 6.0×10^{19} s^{-1}

44. Judging from the results of Experiment 2, what is the concentration of solution X?

    A. 0.20 M
    B. 0.25 M
    C. 0.30 M
    D. 0.38 M

45. Which of the following might best explain the difference in the *shape* of the curve showing absorbance *v* concentration in water and in hexane?

    A. Compound Y is less soluble in hexane than in water.
    B. Compound Y may tend to hydrolyze at high concentrations in water.
    C. Compound Y may dimerize (i.e., form Y$_2$ molecules) in hexane according to the equation $2Y \rightarrow Y_2$.
    D. At high concentrations, hexane may absorb some of the incoming light.

Passage VII (Questions 46–50)

A fuel cell may be thought of as a battery whose reactants are supplied continuously from the outside. The figure below shows the essential components of a fuel cell.

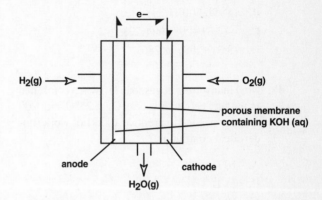

From the figure, one can see that oxygen and hydrogen gases are supplied to the cell. Hydrogen molecules supplied at the anode side are split into H$^+$ ions and electrons by a metal catalyst. The hydrogen ions migrate through the electrode while the electrons travel through the external circuit. At the cathode the electrons and hydrogen ions combine with O$_2$ molecules to form water.

When a fuel cell uses an alkaline medium, the half-reactions are

cathode: $4e^- + O_2(g) + 2H_2O(l) \rightarrow 4OH^-(aq)$

anode: $2H_2(g) + 4OH^-(aq) \rightarrow 4H_2O(l) + 4e^-$

$$2H_2(g) + O_2(g) \rightarrow 4H_2O(l)$$

The overall cell reaction has a value of $\Delta H° = -285.8$ kJ and $\Delta G° = -237.2$ kJ at 25°C.

46. If the overall cell voltage for the fuel cell reaction is 1.23 V, and the potential for the half reaction below is as indicated,

    $4e^- + O_2(g) + 2H_2O(l) \rightarrow 4OH^-(aq)$
    $E° = 0.40$ V

    what is E° for the half reaction $2H_2O(l) + 2e^- \rightarrow H_2(g) + 2OH^-(aq)$?

    A. 0.41 V
    B. 0.83 V
    C. −0.41 V
    D. −0.83 V

47. Which of the following expressions (with units omitted) can be used to obtain $\Delta G°$ at 25°C for the reaction from the cell voltage? (Note that F, Faraday's constant = 96,500 JV^{-1} mol^{-1} and R, the gas constant, = 8.31 JK^{-1} mol^{-1})

    A. $-$ (4)(96,500)(1.23)
    B. (4)(96,500)(1.23)
    C. $-$ (8.31)(298) ln(1.23)
    D. (8.31)(298) ln(286)

48. How many liters of gaseous H_2, when combined in the fuel cell with excess O_2 at 25°C and 1.00 atm, are needed to produce 100 kJ of work (under ideal conditions)?

    A. 10 L
    B. 21 L
    C. 18 L
    D. 41 L

49. Suppose that the concentration of hydroxide ion in the cell membrane is doubled. What effect will this change have on the measured cell voltage?

    A. It will be reduced by ½.
    B. It will be increased by a factor of 2.
    C. It will be increased by a factor of 4.
    D. It will be unchanged.

50. What is the approximate value of $\Delta S°$ for the fuel cell reaction at 25°C?

    A. -1600 J/K
    B. -160 J/K
    C. 160 J/K
    D. 1600 J/K

Passage VIII (Questions 51–56)

The figure below shows three chambers that are connected by valves. At the outset of an experiment, the valves are closed and the contents of the chambers are detailed on the diagram. The temperature of all of the chambers is held at 300 K throughout. The pressure outside of the chambers is held at 1.00 atm.

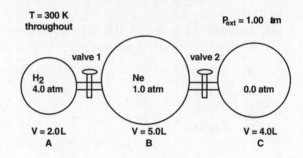

51. Which of the following describes the root-mean-square velocity of gas molecules in chambers A and B before valve 1 is opened?

    A. $v_A < v_B$
    B. $v_A = v_B$
    C. $v_A > v_B$
    D. There is not sufficient information to determine the answer.

52. What is the total pressure in chamber A after valve 1 is opened?

    A. 1.00 atm
    B. 1.14 atm
    C. 1.86 atm
    D. 3.20 atm

53. Assume that the initial state of the system is that shown in the diagram. Which of the following describes the *work* done on the Ne atoms when valve 2 is opened, with valve 1 remaining shut?

    A. 0
    B. 3.00 L atm
    C. -3.00 L atm
    D. -8.00 L atm

54. Suppose that the volume of chamber C were to be doubled, with other initial conditions held the same. Which of the following would *not* be affected by this change?

    A. The final pressure in the apparatus after both valves are opened

    B. The initial rate of effusion of gas from chamber B into chamber C as valve 2 is opened, with valve 1 left closed

    C. The final moles of gas in chamber A after both valves are opened

    D. DS, the change in entropy, of the Ne atoms, after valve 2 is opened, with valve 1 left closed

55. What is the total kinetic energy of all gas molecules after both valves are opened?

    A. 760 J
    B. 1220 J
    C. 1980 J
    D. 3740 J

56. Suppose that after both valves are opened, the entire apparatus is cooled sufficiently to lower the total internal pressure to 0.0100 atm. What is the partial pressure of H_2?

    A. 0.0029 atm
    B. 0.0062 atm
    C. 0.0080 atm
    D. 0.0100 atm

Passage IX (Questions 57–63)

Transition metals have the ability to form a wide variety of complex ions in which other atoms or groups of atoms (called ligands) surround them in well-defined geometric shapes. When the central metal ions have partially filled *d* orbitals, colors are often seen in the crystalline compounds or in their solutions. (Figure 1 shows three common shapes of complex ions.)

octahedral complex

tetrahedral complex

square planar complex

Figure 1

Crystal field theory, and its subsequent extension ligand field theory, shows that for a metal ion surrounded by six ligands in a square bipyramidal (or octahedral) arrangement, the highest occupied *d* orbitals of the metal have energies in the "3 and 2" arrangement, as shown in Figure 2.

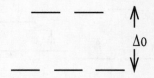

d-orbitals after ligand-field splitting

Figure 2

When determining the electronic configuration of a transition metal ion, recall that the uppermost 4s—

electrons, for example—are removed before the 3d electrons in first-row transition metals, and that a similar relationship holds for later rows of transition metals.

Note that some ligands (described as bidentate) are large enough that they can bond to the central atom at two sites. An important example is ethylenediamine, $H_2NCH_2CH_2NH_2$, abbreviated *en*, which can bond to a central metal ion at each of its two nitrogen atoms. (See Figure 3).

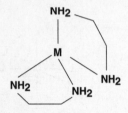

M(en)₂ tetrahedral complex

Figure 3

The value of the splitting factor, Δ_O, can be determined by measuring λ_{max} for absorption and converting to energy units. The magnitude of Δ_O depends not only upon the nature of the metal ion, but also upon the ligand, as the following list shows:

Partial "Spectroscopic Series"
$I^- < Cl^- < OH^- < H_2O < NH_3 < NO_2^- < CO < CN^-$
ß "weak-field" ligands→ ß "strong-field" ligands→

In the case of mixed ligands (e.g., the $FeCl_3(CN)_3^{3+}$ ion), Δ_O is determined by the additive contributions of the ligand strengths.

The size of Δ_O is critically important in determining how the energy levels are filled. An ion with five *d* electrons may exhibit the configuration shown in Figure 2 (a) below ("low spin")—characteristic of large values of Δ_O. But, surprisingly, a low value for Δ_O will lead to the "high spin" configuration shown in Figure 4 (b). In the latter case, the extra energy needed to promote two electrons to the upper level is exceeded by the gain in stability that results when electrons move to separate orbitals.

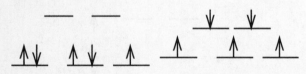

a. low-spin (due to strong-field ligands)　　**b. high-spin (due to weak-field ligands)**

Figure 4

Although octahedral geometry is extremely common in transition metal complexes, it is not the only possibility. Figure 3 shows the ordering of energy levels in tetrahedral and square planar complexes.

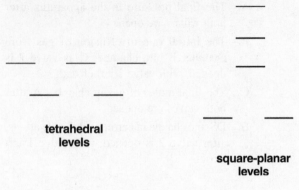

tetrahedral levels

square-planar levels

Figure 5

Generally the ligand field splitting is low in tetrahedral complexes, which usually display high-spin configurations. The situation is reversed for square planar complexes, which display low-spin configurations.

57. Given the following data about the absorption maxima of several complex ions, what is the order of Δ_O for these ions?

compound	λ_{max}
$[CrCl_6]^{3+}$	758
$[Cr(NH_3)_6]^{3+}$	465
$[Cr(H_2O)_6]^{3+}$	694

A. $\Delta_O([CrCl_6]^{3+}) < \Delta_O([Cr(NH_3)_6]^{3+}) < \Delta_O([Cr(H_2O)_6]^{3+})$

B. $\Delta_O([Cr(NH_3)_6]^{3+}) < \Delta_O([Cr(H_2O)_6^{3+}] < \Delta_O([CrCl_6]^3)$

C. $\Delta_O([CrCl_6]^3) < \Delta_O([Cr(H_2O)_6]^{3+}) < \Delta_O([Cr(NH_3)_6]^{3+})$

D. $\Delta_O([Cr(H_2O)_6]^{3+}) < \Delta_O([Cr(NH_3)_6]^{3+}) < \Delta_O([CrCl_6]^3)$

58. Predict the order of Δ_O for the following compounds:

   I. $[Fe(H_2O)_6]^{2+}$
   II. $[Fe(CN)_2(H_2O)_4]^{2+}$
   III. $[Fe(CN)_4(H_2O)_2]^{2+}$

A. $\Delta_O(I) < \Delta_O(II) < \Delta_O(III)$
B. $\Delta_O(II) < \Delta_O(I) < \Delta_O(III)$
C. $\Delta_O(III) < \Delta_O(II) < \Delta_O(I)$
D. $\Delta_O(I) < \Delta_O(II) < \Delta_O(III)$

59. From the information given in the passage, what is the most likely configuration of the cobalt *d* electrons for the species $CoCl_6^{3-}$ and $Co(NO_2)_6^{3-}$?

   A. $CoCl_6^{3-}$: low spin; $Co(NO_2)_6^{3-}$: low spin
   B. $CoCl_6^{3-}$: high spin; $Co(NO_2)_6^{3-}$: low spin
   C. $CoCl_6^{3-}$: low spin; $Co(NO_2)_6^{3-}$: high spin
   D. $CoCl_6^{3-}$: high spin; $Co(NO_2)_6^{3-}$: high spin

60. A chemist wants to determine the molecular geometry of the $[CoCl_4]^{2-}$ ion. Which of the following gives the best suggestion for a measurement and for the interpretation of that measurement?

   A. Using absorption spectroscopy, measure λ_{max} then calculate Δ_O for octahedral geometry.
   B. Measure the molecule's magnetic moment and use the result to estimate the number of unpaired spins in the molecule. If this number is low, the geometry is likely to be square planar; otherwise, it is likely to be tetrahedral.
   C. Measure the molecule's magnetic moment and use the result to estimate the number of unpaired spins in the molecule. If this number is low, the geometry is likely to be tetrahedral; otherwise, it is likely to be square planar.
   D. Measure the molecule's magnetic moment and use the result to estimate the number of unpaired spins in the molecule. If this number is low, the geometry is likely to be tetrahedral; otherwise, it is likely to be octahedral.

61. Iron forms complexes such as $[Fe(CN)_4(H_2O)_2]^{2+}$ when it is reacted with water and cyanide ions as ligands. If ligand X is bidentate, which of the following describes its reaction to form an octahedral complex with Fe^{2+} in water?

   A. $Fe^{2+}(aq) + X(aq) \rightarrow FeX^{2+}(aq)$
   B. $Fe^{2+}(aq) + 2X(aq) \rightarrow FeX_2^{2+}(aq)$
   C. $Fe^{2+}(aq) + 3X(aq) \rightarrow FeX_3^{2+}(aq)$
   D. $Fe^{2+}(aq) + 6X(aq) \rightarrow FeX_6^{2+}(aq)$

62. The equilibrium constant describing the formation of an aqueous transition metal complex containing bidentate ligands is usually much larger than the corresponding constant for a complex containing "monodentate" ligands (such as Cl^- or H_2O). Which of the following best explains this generalization, taking the particular example of octahedral coordination?

   A. Since a bidentate ligand binds to two sites, the stabilizing enthalpy per ligand is about twice that which is expected for a monodentate ligand.
   B. When the bidentate ligands leave the solution to bind to the metal, entropy is reduced.
   C. When the six monodentate ligands leave the solution to bind to the metal, entropy is reduced, but is roughly balanced by the entropy increase due to the release of six water molecules previously bound to the metal ion, keeping it in solution.
   D. When the six monodentate ligands leave the solution to bind to the metal, entropy is reduced, but is roughly balanced by the entropy increase due to the six water molecules previously bound to the metal ion, keeping it in solution. When the three bidentate ligands leave the solution to bind to the metal, entropy is reduced as well, but this reduction is more than counterbalanced by the entropy increase due to the six water molecules previously bound to the metal ion.

63. The oxygen-carrying compound hemoglobin contains "heme" groups, each of which bind to Fe^{2+} through nitrogen atoms at four of its coordination sites. A nitrogen atom on the surrounding protein occupies the fifth site, leaving space for an O_2 molecule to bind to the iron atom at the sixth site in the octahedral geometry. Which of the following is the most reasonable in light of the information presented in the passage?

A. The CO molecule may be dangerous to humans because its position on the spectrochemical series indicates that it might bind strongly to Fe^{2+} and prevent other ligands from attaching.

B. The CN^- ion may be dangerous to humans because it participates in high-spin complexes.

C. The SCN^- ion may be dangerous to humans because its position on the spectrochemical series indicates that it might bind strongly to Fe^{2+} and prevent other ligands from attaching.

D. Humans could be protected from the toxic effect of CO by high concentrations of chloride ion.

Passage X (Questions 64–69)

The Gibbs phase rule is often written as

$$F = C - P + 2$$

where C is the number of components and P is the number of phases present. The number 2 is used when both pressure and temperature are allowed to vary. F is the number of degrees of freedom—which generally include variables such as temperature, pressure, and composition—that can change independently without a change in the number of phases in equilibrium.

The phase rule can be applied in a straightforward manner to the pure substance whose phase diagram is given below in Figure 1.

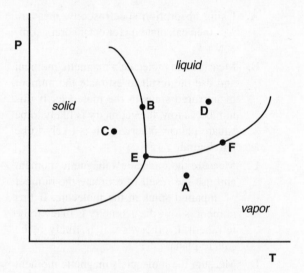

Figure 1

For point A, C = 1 (there is only one component), and P = 1 (the system is a gas), so F = 1 − 1 + 2 = 2.

The system has two degrees of freedom: both pressure and temperature may vary within the limits that define a gas on the diagram.

When a system contains two components, we may have a *solution* in the liquid phase (a familiar situation) but also in the solid phase. Solid solutions of unlimited composition may form from pure elements under a special set of conditions known as the *Hume-Rothery rules*:

1. The atoms must have atomic radii that differ by no more than 15%.
2. The elements must have the same crystal structure.
3. The elements must have the same ionic charge.
4. The elements must have approximately the same electronegativity.

Values of the quantities needed to verify the Hume-Rothery rules for representative elements are given in Figure 2.

Element	at. Radius (nm)	electro-negativity	crystal structure
Al	0.143	1.90	diamond cubic
Au	0.144	2.54	fcc
Cu	0.128	1.90	fcc
Fe	0.124	1.83	hcp
Li	1.52	1.57	hcp
Mn	0.112	1.55	cubic
Ni	0.125	1.91	fcc
Zn	0.133	1.65	hcp

Figure 2

When a pair of elements (or compounds) shows unlimited mutual solubility, its phase behavior can be described in a diagram similar to that shown below in Figure 3.

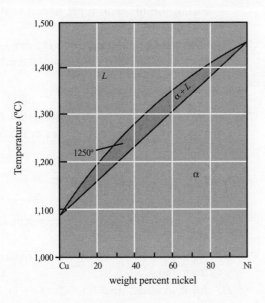

Figure 3

On this diagram, which describes the Ni/Cu system, pressure is fixed at 1.00 atm, and the free variables are temperature and composition. At high temperatures, a liquid solution of the metals is found; at low temperatures, a solid solution of the metals, indicated as "α" occurs; and in the middle region, there is a mixture of the liquid and solid.

Two phase boundaries, the liquidus and the solidus, are labeled in Figure 3. The figure shows an example of a "tie line," a horizontal line drawn from the liquidus to the solidus at a particular temperature. The point on the horizontal axis where the tie line intersects the liquidus gives the composition of the pure liquid at the temperature specified. The point of intersection of the tie line with the solidus gives the composition of the pure solid.

On this diagram, pressure is fixed at 1.00 atm. This constraint leads to a change in the phase rule, which is appropriately stated here as

$$F = C - P + 1$$

64. For Figure 1, which of the following best describes what the phase rule predicts for the number of degrees of freedom at point B?

A. If the temperature is fixed, then the pressure is determined.
B. Both temperature and pressure are free to vary.
C. Both temperature and pressure are fixed.
D. Neither the temperature nor the pressure can be fixed.

65. At which point on the diagram are both temperature and pressure required to be fixed in order to maintain the phase(s) shown?

A. Point C
B. Point D
C. Point E
D. Point F

66. Which of the following elements would be expected to be soluble over the greatest range of composition?

A. Mn and Al
B. Li and F
C. Zn and Au
D. Ni and Cu

67. Which of the following alloys of nickel and copper could be melted for casting at 1370°C but would not melt in a 1270°C environment?

A. 25% Ni
B. 45% Ni
C. 60% Ni
D. 80% Ni

68. How many degrees of freedom are found at 1250°C for a nickel-copper alloy containing 30% nickel?

   A. 0

   B. 1

   C. 2

   D. 3

69. Which of the following best describes the relative composition of the liquid and solid phases of the Cu/Ni system at 1250°C?

   A. The liquid has a higher percentage of Ni than the solid.

   B. The liquid has the same percentage of Ni as the solid.

   C. The liquid has a lower percentage of Ni than the solid.

   D. Only solid exists at this temperature.

INDIVIDUAL QUESTIONS

70. Solid AgCl (formula wt. = 143.3 g/mol) was added to distilled water, stirred, and filtered to remove excess solid. 1.00 L of the resulting solution was then heated to evaporate the liquid, resulting in 1.92 mg of solid AgCl. According to the experiment, which of the following is the value of K_{sp} for AgCl?

   A. $1.3 \ 10^{-5}$

   B. $1.8 \ 10^{-10}$

   C. $1.9 \ 10^{-3}$

   D. 0.0438

71. Write the net ionic equation for the complete reaction of sodium acetate ($NaC_2H_3O_2$) with excess sulfuric acid (H_2SO_4).

   A. $2NaC_2H_3O_2(aq) + H_2SO_4 \rightarrow Na_2SO_4(aq) + 2HC_2H_3O_2(aq)$

   B. $2C_2H_3O_2^-(aq) + H_2SO_4(aq) \rightarrow SO_4^{2-}(aq) + 2HC_2H_3O_2(aq)$

   C. $2C_2H_3O_2^-(aq) + H^+(aq) + HSO_4^-(aq) \rightarrow SO_4^{2-}(aq) + 2HC_2H_3O_2(aq)$

   D. $C_2H_3O_2^-(aq) + H^+(aq) \rightarrow HC_2H_3O_2(aq)$

72. You are given four bottles containing the following solutions:

   (1) 0.10 M HCl

   (2) 0.10 M NaOH

   (3) 0.10 M formic acid, HCH_2O_2 ($K_a = 1.8 \times 10^{-4}$)

   (4) 0.10 M ammonia, NH_3 ($K_b = 1.8 \times 10^{-5}$)

You also have access to water. Which of the following procedures would be most effective at producing a solution that will maintain a pH of 9.0?

   A. Add HCl to a sample of NaOH, monitoring the pH with a pH meter until it reaches 9.0.

   B. Add HCl to a sample of NH_3, monitoring the pH with a pH meter until it reaches 9.0.

   C. Add NaOH to a sample of HCH_2O_2, monitoring the pH with a pH meter until it reaches 9.0.

   D. Add NaOH to a sample of NH_3, monitoring the pH with a pH meter until it reaches 9.0.

73. Which of the following best describes the change (if any) in oxidation states in the following reaction?

$$4\,Au(s) + 8\,CN^-(aq) + O_2(g) + 2H_2O(l) \rightarrow 4[Au(CN)_2]^- (aq)^- + 4OH^-(aq)$$

   A. No oxidation or reduction occurs in this reaction.

   B. Au is reduced from 0 to –1; O is oxidized from 0 to +2.

   C. Au is oxidized from 0 to +2; O (in O_2) is reduced from 0 to –2.

   D. Au is oxidized from 0 to +1; O (in O_2) is reduced from 0 to –2.

74. An aluminum atom is found to exist in the atomic configuration $1s^2 2s^1 2p^6 3s^2 3p^2$. The atom is best described as being in:

   A. its ground state.

   B. an excited state.

   C. a steady state.

   D. an ionized state.

75. The table below shows average bond dissociation enthalpies (symbolized as "D_{H-H}", etc.) determined from a broad sampling of molecules. It is found that the C=O bond in CO_2 is not well described by bond enthalpies found in other compounds. Use the information for the reaction below to determine the answer that best estimates the enthalpy of the C=O bond in CO_2.

$$CH_4(g) + 2O_2(g) \rightarrow CO_2(g) + 2H_2O(\ell)\Delta H = -890 \text{ kJ}$$

bond	bond dissociation enthalpy (kJ/mol)
C–H	414
O=O	498
O–H	464

- **A.** 600 kJ/mol
- **B.** 700 kJ/mol
- **C.** 800 kJ/mol
- **D.** 900 kJ/mol

76. List the following molecules according to the expected value of their "N-to-O" bond lengths, from shortest to longest.

$$NO_2^-, NO_3^-, ONO^+$$

- **A.** $NO_2^- < NO_3^- < ONO^+$
- **B.** $ONO^+ < NO_2^- < NO_3^-$
- **C.** $NO_3^- < NO_2^- < ONO^+$
- **D.** $ONO^+ < NO_3^- < NO_2^-$

77. Which of the following diatomic molecules or ions of the general form X_2 will have the *greatest* bond length when each is ionized by losing one electron?

$$N_2, C_2^-, CN^{2+}$$

Assume that the energy levels for the molecular orbitals for all are as follows:

σ*2p   _____

π*2p   _____ _____

σ2p   _____

π2p   _____ _____

σ*2s   _____

σ2s   _____

- **A.** N_2
- **B.** C_2^-
- **C.** CN^{2+}
- **D.** N_2 and C_2^- will be the same.

END OF TEST 1.

**IF YOU FINISH BEFORE THE TIME IS UP, YOU MAY
CHECK YOUR WORK ON THIS TEST ONLY.**

VERBAL REASONING

Time: 85 Minutes
Questions 78–137

Directions: There are nine passages in this test. Each passage is followed by questions based on its content. After reading a passage, choose the one best answer to each question and indicate your selection by blackening the corresponding space on your answer sheet.

Passage I (Questions 78–84)

The Civil War was the most disastrous war in American history. There were more than 650,000 casualties, which was far more than in any other war we have fought. In fact, the casualty count was greater than
(5) all our other wars combined. The question is, why was the war fought and what were the long-term effects of the war?

Any high school student could tell you that the Civil War was fought to end slavery, an issue that clearly
(10) divided the North and South. Unfortunately, this is only partly true. The big issue was not slavery, but states' rights versus the powers of the central government. This issue had plagued the country since its formation. The Articles of Confederation were specifically designed
(15) to keep the 13 original states semi-autonomous. The central government only had power when the states agreed on a specific issue to give the central government power. At the Constitutional Convention of 1787, this issue was one of the most important issues that was
(20) resolved. While the states recognized that the Articles of Confederation were a failure and the central government had to be strengthened, many of the states still wanted a central government with limited powers. The issue was resolved by creating the first federal system
(25) of government, which reserved certain powers for the central government but left a large number of powers for the states. The issue continued to pop up throughout the first half of the nineteenth century, with some southern states arguing that since they entered the
(30) United States voluntarily, they could secede from the nation and form their own nation if they so choose, and in fact, South Carolina voted to secede in the 1820s, but the issue was defused through a compromise that kept South Carolina in the Union.

(35) With the election of Abraham Lincoln, many southern states felt the issue of the central government's

power had come to a head. Although Lincoln did not oppose slavery, he was against further expansion of slavery. For many slave states, the idea that slavery
(40) could not expand further and the ultimate end of slavery were synonymous. Many southern states claimed a right to secede from the Union. They said the Constitution of the United States was not a binding document, but a voluntary agreement that could be terminated at
(45) any time by any state. In December of 1860 South Carolina seceded from the Union. Within three months of Lincoln's election, six other southern states seceded. They were Mississippi, Florida, Alabama, Georgia, Louisiana, and Texas. These seven states were followed
(50) by four more states: Virginia, Arkansas, Tennessee, and North Carolina. These final four states took a much longer time to decide on secession. Of course, Lincoln and the central government disagreed with this interpretation of the Constitution as a voluntary union. Lin-
(55) coln also tried to reassure the slave states that he did not plan to end slavery but only limit its spread. In fact, several slave states believed the president and did not secede. States such as Maryland, Delaware, Kentucky, Missouri, and western Virginia remained part of the
(60) United States. Western Virginia became the separate state of West Virginia because it did not secede from the Union. Had these states also seceded, particularly Maryland and Delaware, which were industrial states, the course of the war might have been different.

(65) When the states did secede, the federal government moved quickly to end the secession. War broke out soon after the announcement of secession when southern troops fired on Fort Sumter, which was a federal fort. When the war broke out, the issue of slavery
(70) was only one of the issues that were discussed. The central government was quick to state that it was not fighting to end slavery but to establish the power of the central government and to make it clear that the Constitution that bound the states together was not a volun-

(75) tary agreement. Obviously, the states that had seceded from the United States made a strong argument in the opposite direction. The fact that slavery was a secondary issue is made clear by the fact that the Emancipation Proclamation freeing slaves was not made until *(80)* 1863, two years into the war and even then was thought of as a war tactic to weaken the South and only affected those states that were in rebellion. The final ending of slavery in the United States did not come until the conclusion of the war with the passage of the Thir- *(85)* teenth Amendment to the Constitution.

With the conclusion of the war and the victory of the North, for the first time the central government was clearly more powerful than the state governments. The question of secession from the United States would *(90)* never be raised in a serious way again. From this point on, the power of the central government grew and the power of the state governments diminished. This process has continued through the twentieth century and into the twenty-first century. No one could look at our *(95)* system of government today and question where the main power lies. Everything from drinking ages to decisions about welfare are made either exclusively or mostly at the federal level. The issue that had haunted the country since the end of the Revolutionary War had *(100)* been finally resolved in the bloodiest war in American history by the victory of the North in the Civil War. A second result of the Civil War was that the South developed after the war as a significantly poorer region of the country than either the North or the West. The *(105)* South remained largely an agricultural economy for the next 100 years, which was heavily exploited by the North. This economic inequality was further enhanced by the fact that most of the destruction of the Civil War was done in those states that seceded. Even today there *(110)* is a significant economic difference between the North and particularly the Deep South.

78. According to the article, the Civil War was fought mainly over the issue of

    A. slavery.

    B. states' rights versus federal authority.

    C. the South's dislike of Abraham Lincoln.

    D. All of the above

79. According to the article, a number of the southern states disputed that the U.S. Constitution was a binding document, as the issue

    A. could be argued that the Constitution was a voluntary agreement and any state had the right to withdraw from it.

    B. of power between the federal government and the power of the state governments was never tested.

    C. of secession was a voluntary right of each southern state.

    D. over slavery became one reason a state could leave the Union.

80. According to the article, many southern states feared the election of Abraham Lincoln as president because they believed

    A. they held more power than that of the central government as represented by the newly-elected president.

    B. he opposed slavery.

    C. he would initiate a law ending slavery.

    D. he would exercise further power over individual states.

81. The passage notes that when Lincoln was elected president, he

    A. was committed to ending slavery in the South.

    B. did not see slavery as an important issue.

    C. wanted to limit the expansion of slavery.

    D. None of the above

82. Based on the article, the significance of Maryland and Delaware not seceding from the Union at the outset of the Civil War was

    A. that their presence did not diminish the central government's power.

    B. their belief that slavery had to be ended.

    C. that they accepted the central government's authority over the states' powers.

    D. that as industrial states, their products would be instrumental in the North's success to win the Civil War.

83. A primary result of the Civil War was

    A. the passing of the Thirteenth Amendment ending slavery.

    B. the apologies of secession states to the central government.

    C. establishing the central government's power over that of state governments.

    D. an agreement from both sides that such a war would not occur again.

84. After the Civil War, the South

    A. was unable to establish itself as an industrial region since it was primarily an agricultural area.

    B. lost a sizeable number in population as it remained agricultural, forcing people to move to the West for better prospects.

    C. was forced to rely heavily on the North for its economic support in recovering from the Civil War.

    D. remained a poorer section of the country due to its agriculturally based economy.

Passage II (Questions 85–91)

Music during the Renaissance, roughly 1350–1600, was primarily religious. It gave way to a different style of music that reflected a period of time in Europe, from about 1600 to 1750, that was referred to as
(5) the Baroque music. Baroque music was an expression of order—of the fundamental order of the universe. The Baroque period was also a period of exuberance in contrast to the assuredness and self-reliance of the Renaissance, which preceded the Baroque period. At the base
(10) of Baroque society was the accepted concept of absolute monarchy. The King and Queen had all-powerful status in their country, resulting in an increasing separation between classes. As the power of the nobility grew larger as a class, in order to continue with the
(15) King's power, tradesmen created their own class, the *bourgeoisie.* The Baroque period was also seen as the age of reason, where scientific inquiry was developing and increasing by the scientific method developed by Isaac Newton. Scientists were exploring their surround-
(20) ings both on Earth and in the heavens.

The term "baroque" had several origins depending on which country the music developed. In Italy, the word originally meant a logical process that was contorted or involuted. The French used it to mean a disre-
(25) gard of rules of proportion, allowing the artist to create works that reflected whatever caught his attention. In Portuguese, *perola barroca* were the words used by jewelers to describe a rough or irregularly shaped pear. The last description was an appropriate one for the Baroque
(30) period, which included the production of what is considered some of the greatest music of all time.

Prior to the development of Baroque music, religious music was played with whatever instrument was at hand. Instrumental music began appearing that al-
(35) lowed parts of the music to be played with specific instruments. Virtuoso instrumentalists were emerging playing the music that highlighted their technical abilities. Three major composers of Baroque music, also considered to be the pillars of Baroque music, were An-
(40) tonio Vivaldi, Johann Sebastian Bach, and George Frideric Handel. Vivaldi and Bach were brilliant virtuoso instrumentalists as well. Vivaldi composed music for the violin that he intentionally made difficult to play so that when he performed before audiences, he
(45) was emphasizing that he was one of the greatest violin soloists. Bach not only composed volumes of music but was a master organ player. Handel composed *The Messiah*, a musical interpretation of the life of Christ, and which is played today as an annual Christmas event
(50) in major cities around the world. He also created what is considered the masterpiece of his music, *Hallelujah Chorus.*

Baroque music developed four forms: The *opera,* the *cantata,* the *oratorio,* and the *concerto. Opera*
(55) flourished in the early Baroque period in two major centers: Italy and England. Claudio Monteverdi dominated Italian opera with his first opera, *Orfio,* presented in 1607. The *opera* in England was based on an early music tradition known as the *masque,* an aristocratic
(60) entertainment that combined instrumental music with poetry and dance. Henry Purcell, considered the first major English opera composer, created music at a time when many saw the theater as the devil's work and theatrical performances were forbidden. However, *opera*
(65) music was allowed. By the late Baroque period the opera had become refined, combining beautiful melodies from Italy, a sense of refinement from France, orderly technique from Germany, and the choral traditions from England.

(70) The *cantata* was based on a narrative of sacred or secular origins put to music for vocalists, a chorus, and instrumentalists. The origin of the word is from the Italian "cantare" which means to sing. In Lutheran tradition, *cantatas*, or "sacred music," were sung in church
(75) every Sunday. The texts for the *cantatas* were based on gospel readings chosen for the day by the cleric. *Cantatas* were to be brief, personal combinations of both vocalists and instrumentalists. Johann Sebastian Bach was a prolific composer creating over 200 *cantatas* as
(80) an organist for his church.

The *oratorio* was mostly religious with texts based on religious stories. One can compare it to an opera but without props, scenery, or costume. The story is told with a narrator and the use of the aria, chorus,
(85) and recitative. The best known composer of this form was Frideric Handel, whose oratorios—*The Messiah* and the *Hallelujah Chorus*—are just two of the many he wrote.

During the Baroque period, the use of only in-
(90) strumental music was primary. However, more music that had previously been played for any instrument at hand were being written for virtuoso instrumentalists. This music or *concerto* highlighted their technical abilities. *Concerto* also had specific solo *cadenza* passages
(95) where a player was able to show off his technical ability as well.

Thus, the Baroque period not only created a wide variety of forms and techniques, it also was responsible for the development of the *opera*, the *oratorio*,
(100) the *cantata,* and the *concerto.* One can say that as an art form, Baroque music was an important development that eventually evolved into what is considered classical music.

85. Baroque music can be associated with a society that

- **A.** believed strongly in three classes: the aristocracy, the middle class, and the poor.
- **B.** was ruled by a king's divine rights.
- **C.** balanced exuberance with restraint in living.
- **D.** accepted piety as a ruling force in life.

86. According to the article, Baroque music can be

- **A.** spiritual, religious music.
- **B.** remnants of music sung in Latin during church ceremonies.
- **C.** stately and orderly.
- **D.** the brief music flowing out from the Renaissance period.

87. Baroque music involved the playing of

- **A.** any musical instrument.
- **B.** a cello, a violin, and the piano.
- **C.** instrumentalists using techniques to emphasize their mastery of the instrument being used.
- **D.** a combination of the organ and a choir in a church setting.

88. The author states the origin of the word *Baroque* is attributed to

- **A.** the Portuguese words, *perola barroca.*
- **B.** an Italian logical process that was contorted.
- **C.** eighteenth-century French artists' works that did not observe accepted rules of proportion.
- **D.** All of the above

89. The passage states that one of the composers below was considered a major composer of Baroque music.

- **A.** Wolfgang Amadeus Mozart
- **B.** Claudio Monteverdi
- **C.** Johann Sebastian Bach
- **D.** Henry Purcell

90. Based on the article, one can assume that Baroque music reflected

- **A.** European taste in music.
- **B.** a transitional period between late Renaissance music and early classical music.
- **C.** early forms of operatic music.
- **D.** only the works of the major composers.

91. One can interpret from the passage's tone that Baroque music was significant in

- **A.** nurturing music that could be played by only one instrumentalist.
- **B.** nurturing music played by virtuoso instrumentalists.
- **C.** developing the three forms of Baroque music: the *opera,* the *oratorio,* and the *concerto.*
- **D.** fusing religious music with secular music.

Passage III (Questions 92–98)

The question of whether there is or has been life on Mars has been part of the imagination of humans for centuries. Astronomers used to think they saw canals on the planets' surface. H.G. Wells wrote of a war (5) between Earth and Mars in his story *War of the Worlds*. Now we may have the opportunity to find out whether life has ever existed on Mars. Based on prior research by unmanned spaceships, studies of life which exist in unusual places on Earth, and a wave of new missions (10) to Mars, at long last we may answer the question of whether there is or was life on Mars and what form it might take or have taken. Taking advantage of the closest distance between Mars and Earth in 66,000 years or approximately 33,000,000 miles, five rockets have been (15) sent to explore Mars. The United States has sent three exploration vehicles and the European Union has sent two exploration vehicles. Some of these vehicles are orbiting the planet, while others are landing robots on the surface of the planet to explore and take samples. (20) Only a third of the vehicles sent to land on Mars have been successful, so how much information we receive will depend on how many of the spaceships arrive in tact. One mission has already been lost. The Beagle II which was a joint venture of Great Britain and the Eu- (25) ropean Union has been lost after entering the atmosphere of Mars. However, another mission, the Spirit Rover, has landed safely and is already sending back pictures.

As to the possibility of life on Mars in the past, (30) there is already some evidence of its existence. Meteorites presumed to have originated on Mars have been closely studied. Though no fossils have been found, organic molecules have been. Like water, these are a basic building block of life. Though some scientists ar- (35) gue that the organic molecules result from contamination on Earth, others argue that the molecules come from Mars. In addition, the current theories on the development of Mars would suggest that early in the planet's history, the environment was much more (40) favorable to the development of life, possibly even complex life. It is believed that more than a billion years ago, the planet was similar to Earth with an atmosphere high in oxygen and dense enough to produce rain, which in turn produced streams and rivers. Satellite pictures (45) show evidence of what appear to be river beds. Unfortunately, because the gravitational pull from Mars is smaller than Earth's, Mars was not able to hold the atmosphere and the environment of the planet became steadily less conducive to life. The thinner atmosphere (50) meant more exposure to radiation, a much colder planet and the loss of rainfall. These conditions probably turned most of the planet into a lifeless waterless desert. However, at the north and south poles it appears that the water froze rather than disappeared, leaving the possibility of current life.

(55) While those who speculated about life in the past usually thought of humanoid life, it is clear that if there is life, it will most likely be of the one-cell variety. Bacteria particularly have been shown to live and even thrive in extremely inhospitable and diverse environ- (60) ments on Earth and similar life forms may have adapted to the Martian environment. The vast amounts of water might prove to be an ideal environment for the development of life and the thick layer of ice would provide protection from external sources of radiation and the (65) severe cold. If life does exist on Mars, it should show some similarities to life on Earth. Certainly it would be carbon based and some of the life processes would be similar. On Earth, life adjusts to the environment that it occupies, and on Mars, life has likely done the same. (70) Therefore, there would be many interesting differences and no doubt numerous surprises in how life adapted to this hostile environment. If we bring back samples, we will have to be very careful not to contaminate Earth's ecosystem. The results of this contamination could be (75) catostrophic.

These exciting possibilities will open up in the next few years as new information comes in from the Mars missions. It will take more exploration before we will know for certain whether life ever existed. If life (80) does exist on Mars, it will take further missions to understand the ecological system under which this life exists. If there is or was life on Mars, the discovery that life is more flexible than once thought will open up the possibilities that life might also exist in many other (85) places in the universe. Finally, it is likely that we will only develop a more complete understanding of Mars through manned exploration, which both the United States and China have recently committed themselves to, with the hope of a Mars landing by 2020.

92. The author believes that

   A. speculation of life on Mars has been highly imaginative.
   B. the possibility of life on Mars has been based on scientific studies of meteorites from Mars and the likelihood of the presence of water on the planet.
   C. conclusive evidence of life on Mars has been found on meteorites from Mars.
   D. the gradual deterioration of the planet's atmosphere and environment was caused by the inhabitants of Mars.

93. According to the article, the exploration of Mars by the United States and the European Union has

 A. been a cooperative effort.
 B. caused a competitive endeavor for each in reaching Mars first.
 C. demonstrated that the use of several space vehicles for each is extremely costly.
 D. been the impetus for each to use various space vehicles to learn about life on Mars.

94. One of the following statements is NOT referred to in the article:

 A. It is possible that life developed on Mars through an environment and atmosphere remarkably like that of Earth.
 B. The life likely to be found on Mars is not humanoid.
 C. The unwillingness of the United States and the European Union to share information about their explorations of Mars has caused an irrevocable rift between the two parties.
 D. The likelihood of abundant water below the ice at the north and south poles of Mars would be beneficial to the growth of bacteria on the planet.

95. Which of the following is true?

 I. Hydrogen has been found at both the south and north poles in large quantities
 II. It is unreasonable to assume that some form of life could exist below the ice level on Mars.
 III. If life does exist on Mars, it would be hydrogen based.
 IV. Thick layers of ice on Mars would allow life to develop and protect it from radiation.

 A. I and IV
 B. II
 C. II and III
 D. I and III

96. The most likely form of life on Mars is

 A. humanoid.
 B. viral.
 C. bacterial.
 A. aquatic.

97. The passage states that some of these specific environmental conditions on the planet's surface could prevent the existence of life:

 A. Lack of sufficient rainfall and the decrease of streams and rivers
 B. The thin atmosphere, lack of sufficient oxygen, and high levels of solar radiation
 C. Severe cold, low rainfall, and increased exposure to radiation
 D. Hydrogen-based atmosphere, poor rainfall, and severe cold

98. The tone of the article implies that the author is

 A. highly enthusiastic about the possibilities of life on Mars.
 B. guarded in his statements since actual space exploration vehicles have not provided samples to prove the existence of life on Mars.
 C. hopeful that the United States and the European Union will form a productive alliance in exploring space together.
 D. emphatically factual about the knowledge on the existence of life on Mars.

Passage IV (Questions 99–104)

For more than 60 years, inflation has been the number one danger to the economy. Prices have gone up slowly during some periods and more rapidly during others. People complained that their money could
(5) not buy much. The government tried several policies to control runaway inflation, including trying to slow the rate of economic growth, reducing government spending, reducing government debt, controlling wages and prices, and keeping interest rates high. Nobody consid-
(10) ered deflation even a possibility much less a potential problem.

Ask anyone if he would like prices to go down and most likely, the response would be positive. It sounds like a bargain to spend less for an item. How-
(15) ever, few remember the last period of significant deflation, which we now call the Great Depression. From 1929 to 1940 the government fought hard not to control inflation but to create it. Prices went down dramatically from 1929 to 1933 and the consequences were
(20) devastating. When prices go down, either worker productivity goes up or wages go down or both. In the case of the Great Depression, wages fell as companies desperate to sell their over supply of goods cut wages so that they could cut prices. In addition to cutting wages,
(25) companies eliminated as many jobs as possible, helping unemployment levels to reach 25%. Of course, as people earned less or nothing at all, they found it increasingly difficult to pay their bills. Suddenly payments on mortgages, cars, and other consumer debt became
(30) impossible for many people to make. When wages decline, the relative cost of individual and corporate debt increase. Banks trying to recoup their losses and stave off bankruptcy foreclosed on many houses and farms, driving thousands of people from their homes and lead-
(35) ing to a migration of the homeless. When the banks would try to resell the property, they were forced to sell for a pittance of what they were owed. Also, decreasing profits and outright loss made corporations increasingly unable to pay their debts. Numerous com-
(40) panies folded, further worsening the economic situation for the banks. The massive deflation forced banks to begin closing their doors to millions of Americans, who in turn, lost their savings. This action created a sense of panic and led to runs on the banks, even sound
(45) ones, and further bank closures. Unlike past periods of deflation, such as during the depression of the 1870s and the panic of the 1890s, the government stepped in, but not before significant damage had been done to the economy and only after a new president was elected.
(50) With people having less and less money, prices and wages continued to decline. What began to slow the process of deflation was massive government spending, based on debt with the conscious decision to try to

create inflationary pressures. In fact, only with the start
(55) of World War II in Europe did deflation turn into rapid inflation and the economy finally recovered.

Today our society may face deflation again. There is already a severe deflation in the electronics industry and little price rise in many other areas of the economy.
(60) In fact overall inflation at the retail level is running at two to three percent and at the wholesale level even less. The best example of current deflation is the electronics industry where consumers have learned not to buy products when they first come out, but to wait as
(65) they will inevitably come down in price. This awareness of the constant drop in prices and the unwillingness of consumers to rush and buy new products have caused significant profit losses, with some companies folding and others moving much of their operations to
(70) countries where wages are lower, in effect, reducing wages. The federal government is so concerned about this phenomena, it has set federal interest rates lower than they have been in over 40 years to encourage spending which hopefully would lead to a greater inflation.
(75) Having done this and with a massive federal deficit, deflation may seem to be kept at bay. While no economist would advocate runaway inflation or eliminate the possibility that this could still occur, most economists are at least as concerned and maybe more concerned
(80) about deflation as a threat to the economy.

One reason that economists worry about runaway deflation is that the United States, though the largest economy in the world, is still part of a world market. Price competition and the need to sell not only comes
(85) from home but also from abroad, where wages are often much lower and productivity is much higher. Increasingly, companies must learn to produce at the lowest possible cost and sell at the lowest cost. Of course, the effect of this practice is like the one used in the
(90) 1930s. It pushes both prices and wages down, while trying to reduce the work force by increasing use of technology. If this practice were to spread to other industries and also to real estate, which up to this point has been untouched by deflationary pressures, the re-
(95) sults could be catastrophic.

No economist can tell what the future will bring or whether the real economic danger will be inflation or deflation, but for the first time in years the threat of deflation is being taken seriously by economists and
(100) by the federal government. This is one of the reasons why the federal government has allowed a huge federal deficit to develop and has chosen the inflationary policy of keeping the price of borrowing money cheap rather than the deflationary policy of making the cost
(105) of borrowing expensive.

99. According to the article, the government tried all but one of the following approaches to controlling inflation.

    A. Wage and price controls

    B. Reduction of government spending

    C. Keeping interest rates high

    D. Reducing military expenditures

100. Deflation can be as dangerous as inflation, according to the author, because of all but one of the following.

    A. When prices go down, wages often go down.

    B. When wages go down, relative debt increases.

    C. When wages go down, people have less money to buy things.

    D. When prices go down, there is little incentive to produce items that are needed by the public.

101. One example the article gives of an industry where deflation is already a major factor is

    A. petroleum.

    B. electronics.

    C. food.

    D. textiles.

102. According to the article, inflation at the retail level is currently running at

    A. 1% to 2%.

    B. 2% to 3%.

    C. 3% to 4%.

    D. 4% to 5%.

103. The last time deflation was a major problem for the economy was during

    A. the depression of the 1870s.

    B. the panic of the 1890s.

    C. the period 1929 through 1933.

    D. World War II.

104. The author summarizes the article by stating that

    A. neither inflation nor deflation can be seen as truly dangerous economically.

    B. the federal government's history in facing deflation has been one of neglect and misunderstanding which it will rectify through creating a deficit and a policy of making the cost of borrowing expensive.

    C. finally the federal government realizes the dangers of deflation and in response has developed a deficit and is following an inflationary policy of borrowing money at an inexpensive rate.

    D. the federal government is aggressively engaging in a program to counteract the threat of deflation through creating an enormous deficit and borrowing money cheaply at the deflationary rate.

Passage V (Questions 105–110)

    An amazing discovery has been made in the last quarter of a century. Life can exist without the need to breathe oxygen or to use the Sun as a source of energy. The main energy source in this newly discovered envi-
(5) ronment seems to be sulfur compounds, particularly hydrogen sulfide produced by microbes. These microbes appear to play the same role as plants do in other ecological systems. A group of microbes called hyperthermophiles breathe iron instead of oxygen and
(10) live in an environment that one would assume life could not survive in. These microbes have been shown to live at temperatures of more than 112 degrees centigrade, well above the boiling point of water. The idea that microbes can live at such high temperatures and breathe
(15) iron opens up a world of possibilities. First, the fact of life in this environment expands our concept of suitable environments for the development of life and increases the likelihood that satellites such as Europa and planets such as Mars could contain life as well as plan-
(20) ets in other solar systems and galaxies. While these extraterrestrial bodies lack enough atmospheric oxygen to support oxygen-breathing organisms above ground, we believe they may have water below ground and we know that many of these planets and satellites have
(25) volcanic activity. These would be the two ingredients that would create a suitable environment for life to develop. If there is volcanic activity under what is now assumed to be vast bodies of water, then the environment would be ideal for the development of life similar
(30) to hyperthermophiles' life on Earth. It is possible that some variance of this type of life could exist even without water inside volcanoes.

The knowledge that life can flourish in these conditions also may give scientists a better understanding
(35) of evolution. These life forms may have been among
the earliest to develop. The early environment of Earth
would have been well suited for the development of
these first life forms as there was extensive volcanic
action and soon thereafter large bodies of water. Fur-
(40) ther study will be needed to better understand how these
microbes survive, and their relationship to the evolutionary chain.

The more surprising part of the discovery of life
in this environment is the quantity and diversity of that
(45) life. It is possible that more life lives under the surface
of the earth than on top of it. A whole ecological system may exist as much as a mile beneath the surface of
the earth, a system that has developed in tremendous
heat and that is not based on the energy of the Sun. The
(50) hyperthermophiles appear to be the basis of this diverse
ecological system. Not only do they breathe iron but
they produce deposits of other metals such as magne-
tite which other species feed on. Of further interest is
that in this environment a number of species long
(55) thought to be extinct have in fact thrived. New species
are being discovered all the time and these species range
from giant clams to six-foot tube worms, all of which
have evolved differently from their relatives that live
in less extreme environments.
(60)   A final area that has exciting potential is the possibilities of commercial uses for these microbes and
also the other life forms discovered in this environment.
One of the first things that comes to mind is the pharmaceutical potential. How many new cures for currently
(65) incurable diseases lie at these depths? Research is only
just beginning on this exciting front. Also there are likely
industrial uses for hyperthermophiles and possibly for
the other species of life found in this environment. Researchers have already begun to look at possible appli-
(70) cations that might make certain processes, which are
currently not economical to develop, become profitable.
Hyperthermophiles might also be useful in breaking
down industrial pollutants to substances that are not
dangerous for the environment. Clearly we are only at
(75) the beginning of acquiring a better understanding of
these life forms and their potential applications and there
is much more to learn. With each new discovery our
understanding of how life develops will be expanded.

105. According to the author, all but one of the following makes the discovery of hypermophiles
exciting.

A. Their abundance
B. They breathe sulfur rather than oxygen.
C. They live in an environment that was pre-
viously thought to be too hot for life to
exist.
D. They exist deep in the water.

106. The reason that the discovery of hyperthermophiles increases the likelihood that life
might exist on other planets is because

A. if life can exist in such a hostile environment on Earth, it might also exist in similarly hostile environments on other planets.
B. this discovery suggests that life forms
might be able to develop that can breathe
virtually anything.
C. there may be no limits to the amount of
heat that some life forms can sustain and
still survive.
D. we have discovered similar environments
on other planets and satellites.

107. In order to develop suitable environmental
conditions for the development of hyperthermophiles' life, the following are necessary:

A. oxygen and an extremely high tempera-
ture.
B. sulfur compounds.
C. microbe-producing hydrogen sulfide.
D. water above ground and volcanic activ-
ity.

108. The article surmises that this environment

A. has been able to sustain species considered to have died out.
B. is still dependent upon the Sun's energy.
C. maintains the lives of species without their
evolving.
D. stimulates hyperthermophiles to breathe
iron at twice the rate one expects.

109. The discovery of the hyperthermophiles raises its potential for

   A. diluting chemical contaminants to non-threatening elements in the environment.

   B. research on economical operations that can become profitable.

   C. treating incurable illnesses.

   D. All of the above

110. The main idea of the article is

   A. that the discovery of other human-like species, the hyperthermophiles, can survive without oxygen or sunlight.

   B. the discovery of plant-like microbes called hyperthermophilies that breathe iron and can survive in extremely high temperatures.

   C. the discovery of hyperthermophilies, microbes, that breathe iron and live in temperatures above the boiling point of water.

   D. that the discovery of hyperthermophilies, microbes, will provide potential research subjects for commercial purposes.

Passage VI (Questions 111–117)

     The Cold War has finally ended. As we look back on the period of time between 1946 and 1990, what are the lessons to be learned? Before we can look at the outcomes, we must first have a quick review of some
(5) of the major events of the Cold War.

     With the end of World War II, the world was changed. Two countries emerged from the rubble of war as superpowers, the United States and the Soviet Union. In some ways the United States and the Soviet Union
(10) were bound to clash. The friction began almost immediately after the war ended over the fate of the eastern European countries. While Franklin Roosevelt had acceded to the Soviet demand after the war that its sphere of influence would cover most of Eastern Europe with
(15) the exceptions of Austria and Greece, the United States regretted this decision. The United States realized that control of Eastern Europe by the Soviets gave their government enormous power which threatened the stability of Western Europe. In addition, the Soviet Union
(20) had strong communist parties in at least two western countries, France and Italy. The United States quickly developed an alliance known as NATO which was designed to limit Soviet expansion. The Soviet Union responded with the alliance known as the Warsaw Pact,
(25) which was developed to protect Soviet influence in Eastern Europe. These actions meant that Europe had been divided neatly in half, with the West being aligned with the United States and the East with the Soviet Union. With this development we can say that the Cold
(30) War had begun.

     The first major issue of the Cold War was access to Berlin. At the end of the war Berlin had been divided by the victorious allies. Berlin was well within the Soviet jurisdiction of East Germany and increasingly, the
(35) Soviets believed that they had the right to control access to it. The Western powers did not agree. Finally, the Soviets closed all western access to what had become known as West Berlin. The United States and its allies responded with an airlift during which the needed
(40) goods were flown into West Berlin. The fear was that a hot war might break out, but as with much of the Cold War a compromise saved the situation from getting out of hand. While the world lived on the edge of nuclear war throughout the Cold War, what was referred to as a
(45) balance of terror was kept and usually at the last minute compromises were worked out between the two sides. This balance of terror was based on an enormous arms race that cost both economies of the East and West much of their productivity. Unless the balance of terror was
(50) kept equal, it was feared that war would break out. Both sides feared the other's intent.

     While direct confrontations were infrequent, indirect confrontations were common. The beginning was the loss of China to the Communists in 1949 and this
(55) confrontation was continued with the Korean War in 1950. In the Korean War the United States and some of its allies sent troops to defend South Korea, but the Soviets only sent weapons through the Chinese. Afraid their own border was threatened by the U.S. presence,
(60) North Korea sent troops across the border and in part fought a proxy war for the Soviet Union. Ultimately the first major conflict that clearly pit the troops of one side against the weapons of the other ended in a draw. The next major arena was Vietnam which was a colony
(65) of France. At first the French were involved in the war to keep their colonial empire. However, despite increased involvement from the United States, the French lost the war to a communist insurgency. After the French were defeated, the United States and some of its allies
(70) first sent aid to the government of South Vietnam to help it fight a new communist insurgency in the south. Next, the United States and some of its allies sent troops, while the Soviets sent aid to the other side. Though the war dragged on, it ultimately lead to a communist vic-
(75) tory. There were several other arenas for this proxy war, including the Congo and Cuba. In the Congo the Soviets lost but in Cuba they won.

     Direct confrontations were the exceptions and were limited to West Berlin and the Cuban Missile Cri-

(80) sis. Only in these circumstances did the risk of war seem dangerously close because one side or the other had to back down to avoid war. These near catastrophies kept the world on edge. Of the two close calls to war, the Cuban missile crisis was the closer. We now know that
(85) President John F. Kennedy was fully prepared for a nuclear confrontation over Cuba and it was only the last-minute decision by the Soviet premier, Nikita Khruschev, to withdraw the missiles that saved the world from nuclear annihilation.
(90) In addition to the arms race that the Cold War precipitated, it also precipitated an economic race in other areas, from consumer goods to space travel. If one side took the lead in an area, the other side was quick to respond. When the Soviets sent the first satel-
(95) lite into space in 1958, the United States responded with a massive space program that eventually led to the first human exploration of the Moon.

What finally brought the Cold War to an end and led to the breakup of the Soviet Union was a massive
(100) military buildup by the United States in the 1980s. The Soviets could keep up, but only by sacrificing consumer products. This drastic action in turn created significant unhappiness among the Soviet population. First, the Eastern European countries became restive and then
(105) populations inside the Soviet Union became increasingly dissatisfied. A second factor that played into the hands of the United States was that the Soviet Union became involved in a civil war in Afganistan that proved both economically and politically costly. Finally, in
(110) 1990 the Soviet Union collapsed with Eastern Europe gaining its independence and eventually many areas of the former Soviet Union also gained independence. Finally, the Communist party lost control.

If lessons are to be learned from the Cold War,
(115) clearly one is that economic might ultimately proved key to victory. Another lesson that has become clear only after the end of the Cold War is that with rare exceptions both sides believed they could not afford to use their ultimate weapons and therefore, hot war be-
(120) tween the two power giants was not an option. The third lesson that can be learned from the Cold War was that it was enormously costly both in lives and to the economies of both countries, creating huge national deficits. The final effect of the Cold War is that a generation of
(125) people lived under constant threat of nuclear annihilation. Living with the possibility of nuclear annihilation affected this generation in ways that we as yet don't fully know.

111. Conflict began almost immediately after World War II between which of the following sets of countries?

   A. The United States and China
   B. The United States and Vietnam
   C. The United States and North Korea
   D. The United States and the Soviet Union

112. According to the passage, access to West Berlin was the first major issue of the Cold War that would precipitate:

   A. further friction over the right to control it.
   B. another war but between the U.S. and the U.S.S.R.
   C. a show of force by the Soviets to frighten the United States.
   D. a retaliation by two major European countries, Great Britain and France.

113. The author stated that one of the key factors to the United States' victory in the Cold War was

   A. its scientific edge over the Soviet Union.
   B. the support of its allies.
   C. its ability to produce consumer goods.
   D. its economic strength.

114. The phrase "balance of terror" used in the passage meant

   A. both American and Soviet cooperation against future wars.
   B. the mutual fear of the consequences of a nuclear war between the U.S. and the U.S.S.R. encouraged the two powers to make last-minute compromises.
   C. the use of nuclear weapons in a final battle between the U.S. and the U.S.S.R.
   D. the use of fear to keep in check other countries planning to become a major power.

115. During the Cold War, two major indirect confrontations occurred with the assistance of the U.S. and the U.S.S.R. between which of the following countries?

   A. China and Cuba

   B. China and Vietnam

   C. Korea and the Congo

   D. Korea and Vietnam

116. Which of the following were factors responsible for the end of the Cold War and the breakup of the U.S.S.R.?

   I. Sacrificing consumer products and unrest in the Eastern European countries inside the U.S.S.R.

   II. U.S.S.R. involvement in Africa being costly economically and politically

   III. The massive military buildup in the U.S.S.R. that was a drastic economic action

   IV. None of the above

   A. IV

   B. II and III

   C. I

   D. I and III

117. By the end of the passage, the author is concerned about one particular lesson learned from the Cold War.

   A. The consequences of living with the possibility of nuclear annihilation and its effects on one generation

   B. The consequences of the enormous costs in lives and economies for both the U.S. and U.S.S.R. in order that one nation emerges as victorious

   C. The consequences of military warfare between both nations without the use of nuclear weapons

   D. The consequences nuclear warfare would have on the environment worldwide

Passage VII (Questions 118–124)

Two thousand years ago the ancient Athenians created drama, or western theater as it has become known. Creating its form, techniques, and terminology are still considered of major literary importance. The
(5) Athenians had invented many of the greatest works, drama and comedy, in theater two thousand years before Shakespeare. There have been only two other periods in western theater history that come close to the importance of ancient Athens—Elizabethan England
(10) and the twentieth century. Shakespeare was the great playwright of Elizabethan England but it was Athens that produced at least five great playwrights. Although the twentieth century produced thousands of excellent plays and films, their form and often their content were
(15) based on the innovations of these ancient Athenians. The Athenians considered theatergoing a festive occasion but more importantly, believed it to be an important role in a citizen's education. Athenian theatergoers would spend a whole day viewing this form of enter-
(20) tainment.

As far back as 1200 B.C. religious rites in Ancient Greece were practiced and these rites became the foundation of the theater. Throughout Greece were living primitive tribes. One tribe in particular that lived in the
(25) northern area of Greece, in an area called Thrace, created a cult. This cult began practicing the worship of Dionysus, the god of human and agricultural fertility. During the cult's ritual celebrations, members would celebrate by getting intoxicated, participating in orgies,
(30) sacrificing humans and animals, and experiencing hysterical rampages by women known as *maenads*. A particular controversial custom that the cult also practiced involved uninhibited dancing and emotional displays that created an altered state known as *ecstasis* from
(35) which the word *ecstasy* is derived. Among the Greeks *ecstasy* was an important concept as it provided within drama in the theater a way of releasing powerful emotions. The cult spread south through the tribes of Greece over the next six centuries and over this period of time
(40) the rites of Dionysus became part of the mainstream and more civilized. By 600 B.C. the rites were practiced every Spring throughout much of Greece. Greece was divided by this time into city-states, separate nations centered around major cities and regions. The most
(45) prominent city-state was Athens where the Rites of Dionysus evolved into what we know today as theater.

Drama competitions, which changed the Dionysian Festivals, were started by Pisistratus, ruler of Athens, in 532 B.C. These competitions became popu-
(50) lar annual events for the next 50 years. The *archon*, a government authority, would choose the competitors while wealthy patrons, the *choregos,* financed the productions. At the festival of Dionysus, *tragedies* and

comedies, besides other theatrical events, were per-
(55) formed annually. Tragedy told a story that was intended
to teach religious lessons. Similar to biblical parables,
tragedies were written to show the right and wrong paths
of life. They were not simply plays with bad endings or
pathos, meaning pitiable people or events. Tragedies
(60) presented people who made their own choices, which
ran afoul of society's rules, life's rules, or simply fate.
A major character was the tragic protagonist who refused to accept fate or life's rules, either out of character weakness or strength. The protagonist's main fault
(65) would most often be *hubris*, a Greek (and modern English) word meaning arrogance. In *Oedipus Rex* it could
be the arrogance of not accepting what life intends as
in fate; in *Agamemnon*, it is the arrogance of assuming
the right to kill, or in *Orestes,* the arrogance of assum-
(70) ing the right to seek vengeance. Whatever the root, the
protagonist's ultimate collision with fate, reality, or
society is inevitable and irrevocable. Classical tragedy
showed that a belief in the dignity and greatness of human beings was not incompatible with a full awareness
(75) of their limitations. If tragedy, according to the philosopher Aristotle, provided a release for the emotions
of pity and terror, theatergoers would feel pity for the
unfortunate protagonist and would fear that they might
also undergo a disaster allowing themselves to be purged
(80) of these emotions. Thus, the festival of Dionysus offered an opportunity for Athenians to release pent-up
feelings. Since the festival meant all business activities
ceased, Athenians would throw themselves into drinking, feasting, and carousing. The plays were the means
(85) for them to participate emotionally as spectators rather
than merely to view the plays passively.

Comedies, on the other hand, allowed Athenians
to be able to laugh at their own and at others' short-
comings and to remember that life is not all earnest-
(90) ness and work. The exact origins of comedy are not
known although the word *comedy* comes from *komos,*
which means a revel. It seems probable that fertility
rituals and celebrations are at the origins of comedy.
From the earliest days of Greece, groups of men, or
(95) revelers, would go from village to village, wearing high,
artificial phalluses, telling often-obscene jokes, and
singing and dancing. The community would participate
in these revels. How comedy as an art form grew from
these revels is unknown, but it was recognized as such
(100) at the festival of Dionysus in Athens around 486 B.C.,
much later than tragedy. The only Greek classical comic
author whose work survived, Aristophanes, composed
what are considered "old comedies." His comedies used
many of the old ritual features of the *komos*: the big
(105) phalluses, padding, animal costumes, grotesque masks,
and obscene jokes. But the purpose was no longer to
promote fertility, but to entertain people by making fun
of real people or institutions through overt satire. Ap-

proximately a hundred years later, "new comedy" had
(110) evolved that resembled today's modern farces where
ordinary people were involved through the use of mistaken identities, ironic situations, and wit. Menander,
the more significant practitioner of new comedy, con-
tributed a comedy model that greatly influenced com-
(115) edy. The style of comedy Menander created with its
emphasis on mistaken identity, romance, and situational
humor, would become the model for subsequent comedy, from the Romans to Shakespeare and to Broad-
way.
(120)   By 406 B.C., 128 years after the first Athenian
drama competition, the golden era of Greek drama was
declining. The free-thinking culture of Athens that gave
birth to theater would be overrun by the Spartans and
would later be torn apart by constant warring with other
(125) city-states. Despite the continuation of theater in
Greece, it would not rise again to the same creativity.

118. The passage states that ancient Greece created
drama

    A. 3,000 years ago.

    B. 2,000 years ago.

    C. in 532. B.C.

    D. in 486 B.C.

119. One of the first reasons that comedy developed was to

    A. celebrate fertility rituals.

    B. give people the opportunity to celebrate.

    C. make people laugh.

    D. vent emotions that otherwise might be a
danger to society.

120. According to the passage, religious rites practiced in the cult of Dionysus

    A. were ceremonies held in an atmosphere
of calmness and tranquility.

    B. relied only on animal sacrifices.

    C. would involve women who whipped
themselves into hysteria.

    D. required members to refrain from intoxi-
cation.

121. For the Greeks the concept of *ecstasis,* an altered state of emotion,

    A. was acceptable as a means to loosen up inhibitions.

    B. was an important element in drama as it allowed individuals to freely indulge in strong emotions.

    C. was a result of unrestrained dancing and passions.

    D. All of the above

122. The festival of Dionysus allowed Athenians

    A. a period of days to observe religious rites.

    B. to celebrate with abandon.

    C. to view numerous plays of tragedy and comedy by well-known writers of the time.

    D. to fast in order to prepare themselves for emotional involvement in watching plays.

123. According to the passage, Aristotle's definition of tragedy was

    A. a means to learn a religious reason.

    B. watching the major character making the wrong choice because he cannot accept fate.

    C. the means by which the observers of the play feel sorry for the main character in the situation he has created and are afraid they would do the same.

    D. having a major character become a tragic protagonist whose fault was pride.

124. The difference between old comedy and new comedy in ancient Greece was that

    A. old comedy relied on rituals using vulgar props and shameful jokes, while new comedy used people from everyday life in various situations of confused identities, ironic situations, and cleverness.

    B. old comedy relied on rituals using various props and entertaining jokes, while new comedy involved people from everyday life in awkward situations they eventually resolve.

    C. old comedy relied on rituals using vulgar props and entertaining jokes, while new comedy used ordinary people caught in humorous situations that are similar to real life.

    D. old comedy relied on rituals using what the Greeks called *komos,* along with witty jokes, while new comedy used ordinary people from all walks of life caught in embarrassing situations.

Passage VIII (Questions 125–131)

Attention Deficit Hyperactivity Disorder (ADHD) is a commonly diagnosed disorder in both children and adults. It is characterized by inattention, hyperactivity, and impulsiveness. According to the
(5) DSM-IV, symptoms of inattention include being easily distracted, not noticing details, making careless mistakes, having difficulty following instructions, and losing objects frequently. Symptoms of hyperactivity and impulsiveness and feelings of restlessness are often
(10) characterized by an inability to stay seated or constant roaming around, answering questions prematurely, and having difficulty waiting in lines or going out of turn. These symptoms can be associated with numerous other conditions. There is as yet no clearly defined cause for
(15) ADHD and diagnosis is symptomatic.

There have been many theories about the cause or causes of ADHD. Some scientists thought that perhaps too much sugar might cause the condition. Others thought the cause might be environmental, having to
(20) do with conditions in the home. Still other scientists have believed that the cause might be found in minor injuries to the brain. A new theory is that the level of brain activity in certain key areas may be lower among those with ADHD than those who do not have it. Lev-
(25) els of brain activity can be measured by the brain's use of glucose. It has been found that those people who had been diagnosed with ADHD used less glucose in areas of the brains that control attention. This would indicate

less activity in these regions of the brain. If further stud-
(30) ies indicate that this is true, this could lead to a way to
test for ADHD and also possible new treatments. There
is some research to suggest that toxins taken during
pregnancy, such as cigarette smoke and crack cocaine,
for example, may increase the likelihood of offspring
(35) developing ADHD. Finally, there is evidence that
ADHD runs in families, which may indicate a genetic
component to the disease, which if true could lead to
being able to diagnose the disease even before it occurs and to develop genetic treatments for the disease.
(40) It should be added that though biological causes are
considered of major importance in the development of
the condition, the environment that children grow up
in may also be an important contributing factor at least
in some cases of ADHD.

(45) There are many aspects to treatment. Medications
such as Ritalin, Dexedrine, and Cylert can be used. All
three of these drugs are stimulants. But when used by
ADHD sufferers, they help the child or adult to control
the symptoms of ADHD. Antidepressants are often used
(50) to treat the anxiety and depression that frequently accompanies the disease. The use of stimulants for treatment of
ADHD, particularly among children, has been heavily debated. There are potential serious side effects that must be
weighed into any decision to use these medications and
(55) the medications should be closely monitored. These drugs
should not be used until other illnesses that have similar
symptoms have been ruled out as possible causes of the
behavior. Because we have not developed a biological test
for ADHD, doctors must be very careful with their diag-
(60) noses. A new non-stimulant drug for the treatment of
ADHD has recently been approved. The drug brand name
Strattera has been shown in clinical tests to be as effective
as Ritalin. This drug will give doctors an effective alternative to the use of stimulants and may ease the worries of
(65) many parents.

While ADHD people can lead normal productive
lives if diagnosed and treated, many adults who have
the disease are misdiagnosed. It was assumed until recently that ADHD was largely a children's disease that
(70) disappeared with the onset of adulthood. Therefore,
when adults exhibited similar symptoms, they were
often misdiagnosed with depression or anxiety disorder. We now know that many people will live a lifetime
with ADHD and that many people who were not diag-
(75) nosed in childhood will be diagnosed as adults. Treatment for adults varies but often includes psychotherapy,
cognitive therapy, support groups, and social skills train-
ing. The most important thing for an adult with this
disease is to learn how to compensate for the disease.
(80) This means changing behavior in a way that takes the
disease into account. The first step is to recognize that
much of one's behavior that has caused frustration in
the past can be modified by learning to view tasks, and

activities differently. This approach in turn can lead to
(85) a more positive attitude that can improve functioning
and possibly reduce depression associated with the
disease.

In the future it is likely that better diagnostic techniques will be developed and that better treatments for
(90) both children and adults will be created. Improved diagnostic tools will lead to more rapid treatment, and
improved medications will help to make the treatment
more successful. In the more distant future as a better
understanding of the disease is developed, creating tech-
(95) niques for prevention and/or cures involving genetic
manipulation is possible.

125. All of the following are symptoms of ADHD
EXCEPT

   A. restlessness.
   B. answering out of turn.
   C. constant roaming around.
   D. violent behavior.

126. All but one of the following have been suggested as causes for ADHD.

   A. Genetic defect
   B. External environment
   C. Too much sugar in the diets of children
   D. Below-average intelligence

127. The passage points out that ADHD has symptoms that

   A. can be quickly diagnosed.
   B. can be linked to several other conditions.
   C. include lethargy and difficulty in talking.
   D. may cause self-inflicted injury.

128. The author discusses that the treatment of
ADHD has relied on useful stimulants and

   A. should be continued indefinitely due to
their effectiveness in controlling the
symptoms.
   B. tranquilizers such as Valium that can be
used to counteract feelings of nervousness
and despondency.
   C. warns that those given to children should
be considered carefully and supervised
closely.
   D. such medications should be used while
other diseases with similar symptoms are
being dismissed as possible causes of the
behavior.

129. Among the various theories presented in the passage on how ADHD is caused, one of the following is NOT referred to:

A. It can be a hereditary illness that runs in families through a genetic component.

B. People with ADHD use less glucose in those areas of their brains that affect attention span.

C. Cigarette smoking and the use of crack cocaine by pregnant women may likely cause ADHD in infants.

D. Constant injury to the brain would make an individual exhibit the symptoms of AHDH.

130. The author recognizes that adults who are diagnosed with ADHD

A. must learn how to balance their lives using behavioral approaches that promote feeling positive and reducing anxiety.

B. have refused treatment believing that the disorder will eventually disappear with age.

C. assume that they cannot have healthy, useful lives.

D. are continuously depressed or anxious.

131. The passage ends with the prediction that

A. ultimately ADHD is not a curable disorder.

B. in the future it is possible that science will create better treatments for ADHD that provide immediate help and improved medicines.

C. improved diagnostic techniques and treatments will slightly improve chances for being cured.

D. despite improved diagnostic techniques and treatments, ADHD will continue to exist.

Passage IX (Questions 132–137)

Much folklore around the world has a traditional trickster figure who is the primary character in folk stories. His importance is underlined by his cleverness and in some cultures he is seen as a god, while in other (5) cultures, the trickster figure can be foolish and destructive. As a god he can intercede on behalf of man or lead man astray. The trickster tales for many people in different cultures are entertaining and amusing. Stories of a small and often weak trickster who is able to outwit a (10) larger and more powerful enemy are common in folk literature. Sometimes the trickster is presented as being greedy, imitative, stupid, bombastic, and dishonest. The trickster can also be seen as quick-witted, shrewd, and artful. He is seen as Loki, the wolf, in north- (15) ern Europe and Kitsune the fox in Japan. In West Africa the trickster is the cunning spider, Anansi, who is also found in tales throughout the Caribbean due to the transportation of slaves from West Africa to various islands. The trickster, who can also be a divine fool or (20) sacred clown, is a powerful creature in the legends of most Native American tribes. He takes on various shapes, such as the raven, crow, blue jay, and the coyote. In the American south, various animals such as the rabbit, fox, bear, wolf, turtle, and possum are the more (25) popular trickster figures used in oral folktales. Brer or Bruh Rabbit is a favorite of the African-American storytellers. In all folk stories, the trickster survives by his wits but he does more than stay alive. The word itself refers to his forever playing tricks on larger, stron- (30) ger animals around him that gets the trickster out of trouble but may vigorously deceive them when there is no danger. While enjoying duping his adversaries, the trickster is not always victorious. Occasionally he overreaches himself and finds that he has been too sharp for (35) his own good.

In West African folktales the major trickster figure is Anansi, the spider trickster. He figures largely in tales from the West coast of Africa in the countries of Liberia, Sierra Leone, and on the Gold Coast. Anansi is (40) foolish, entertaining, or even indolent but he always provides a lesson to learn through his stories. Anansi stories are told by skilled storytellers who memorize their stories to capture the interests of an audience. These oral traditional tales have morals or lessons for (45) one to learn. One Anansi story, for example, has Anansi being outwitted by Turtle in a story of sharing food. Anansi takes advantage of Turtle by telling Turtle to wash his hands in the river to clean up before eating the meal of yams. Each time Turtle returns to the table, (50) Anansi yells at him for having dirty hands since Turtle has to walk in the dirt from the river back to Anansi's table and thus continues to become dirty. Turtle figures out to walk on the grass which keeps his hands clean

but Anansi has already finished the whole meal. Turtle
(55) says nothing in reproach to Anansi and instead, thanks
him for sharing the meal and offers Anansi a free meal
should the spider find himself near Turtle's home. When
Anansi decides to visit Turtle for the meal, he has to eat
the meal in Turtle's house which is underwater. But since
(60) Anansi is so light, he needs to fill his jacket pockets
with stones and rocks to keep him from popping back
up to the surface. However, each time Anansi is about
to start eating, Turtle tells Anansi that he cannot wear
his jacket while eating as it is not customary to do so.
(65) Anansi has noticed that Turtle already has removed his
jacket. When Anansi takes off his jacket, he zooms back
to the surface, popping out of the riverbank. Putting his
head down into the water, he watches Turtle slowly
enjoying the free meal. Audiences are told that the moral
(70) of this story is: *When you try to outsmart someone, you
may find that you're the one outsmarted.*

Tales of Anansi were brought to the Caribbean
when enslaved Africans would share with one another
stories from their countries. These tales continued the
(75) oral tradition of folklore in the West Indies. But in the
Caribbean Anansi is the West Indian folk hero. In West
Indian stories Anansi can be a spider trickster or a spider with some human features. As a character he balances between being an insect, animal, and human fig-
(80) ure. He is able to move easily between both the human
and animal worlds. The story of Anansi and his family
riding in a car or going to the supermarket would seem
normal for West Indians. Folktales in the West Indies
are referred to as "Anansi stories" and such a collec-
(85) tion always has Anansi as the prominent figure. He is
heroic in being able to overcome what may seem to be
impossibly challenging obstacles or societal pressures.
Yet he is also greedy and reckless.

In some North American traditions the trickster
(90) figure has been called Coyote, Coyote Man, and Old
Man Coyote. A few stories depict Coyote as pretending to be the Creator, who fashions mankind out of mud
and creates animals such as the buffalo, elk, deer, antelope, and bear. In these traditions, however, Coyote-
(95) Creator is never referred to as an animal although he
does meet his animal counterpart, coyote. In these myths
both walk together and talk together, calling one "elder
brother" and the other "younger brother." Thus both
the spiritual and the body are brothers who always talk
(100) and walk together. However, the stories told of Old Man
Coyote as a trickster figure are many. In them, he is a
teacher, survivor, and a fool as well as a hero. He is
always traveling, being stupid, outrageous, cunning,
wise, and mischievous and often doing good in spite of
(105) himself. In stories Old Man Coyote never dies but gets
up and comes to life again.

African-American folktales were born when black
slaves, forcibly brought from Africa to this new world,
began sharing stories from their cultures and home
(110) countries. Africans brought their religious beliefs, music, and cultural customs. They also brought the oral
storytelling tradition which changed as it reflected the
life experiences of these captives and their descendants
in response to their new conditions in America. Since
(115) trickster stories with animal figures dominated African
oral storytelling, slaves were able to adapt them to fit
their enslavement. Contacts that plantation slaves made
with one another in their new world, combined with
memories and habits from the old world of Africa,
(120) helped them create a body of folk expressions about
themselves and their experiences. The slaves created
tales in which various animals such as the rabbit, fox,
bear, wolf, and possum took on the characteristics of
the people on the plantation. The trickster figure of the
(125) rabbit, known as Brer, Bruh or Buh Rabbit, became a
particular favorite of the slave storytellers. Although
Rabbit was small and seemingly helpless compared to
the powerful bear, the wily fox, and the ferocious wolf,
he was made smart, clever, and shrewd as told by the
(130) slave storyteller.

Clearly, the trickster figure assumes different
forms in many cultures and remains a primary character in folklore literature. His attributes often emphasize
the paradox in his character: He can be a sacred cre-
(135) ator, making mankind and animals; he can be a clown
in which he makes his audience laugh at his foolishness or greediness; or he can be an animal with heroic
characteristics of cleverness and wit. As a trickster figure, he is a reflection for his audiences of their own
(140) cultural foibles and nuances.

132. According to the passage, the trickster figure
around the world assumes all of the following
shapes EXCEPT a(n):

   A. animal.

   B. insect.

   C. bird.

   D. turtle.

133. The trickster figure is NOT a figure who:

   A. is often outwitted in African-American
folktales.

   B. despite his small size, can outwit a larger
adversary.

   C. is able to inhabit the insect and human
worlds in the Caribbean.

   D. can be reborn after death in Native American folklore.

134. Based on the passage, the trickster figure can be found in all but one of the following:

    A. oral traditional storytelling.

    B. written folklore.

    C. collection of stories.

    D. poetry.

135. Among various cultures, the trickster does NOT serve as:

    A. a figure who learns a lesson.

    B. a figure who repeatedly fails to outwit his enemy.

    C. someone who is smart and cunning.

    D. a creator of men and animals.

136. In the brief story included in the passage about Anansi, the spider, from West Africa, the parable learned by Anansi can also be interpreted as:

    A. Be careful of those you invite to your home.

    B. There is always someone else who is brighter than you.

    C. Being greedy can bring you trouble.

    D. If you think with your stomach, your head will learn nothing.

137. One can infer from the passage that the trickster figure

    A. is far more admired than feared in many cultures.

    B. allowed people to vent their anger.

    C. represented the morals of a culture.

    D. was more often a figment of people's imagination.

WRITING SAMPLE

Time: 60 Minutes
2 Essays

Directions: This test consists of two parts. You will have 30 minutes to complete each part. During the first 30 minutes, you may work on Part 1 only. During the second 30 minutes, you may work on Part 2 only. You will have three pages for each essay answer (see pages 9–14), but you do not have to fill all three pages. Be sure to write legibly; illegible essays will not be scored.

Part 1

Consider this statement:

If you play with fire, you might get burned.

Write a unified essay in which you perform the following tasks: Explain what you think the above statement means. Describe a specific situation in which you do not get burned playing with fire. Discuss what you think determines whether or not getting burned when playing with fire is dangerous.

Part 2

Consider this statement:

When a lawyer defends himself, he has a fool for a client.

Write a unified essay in which you perform the following tasks: Explain what you think the above statement means. Describe a specific situation in which a lawyer is not a fool if he defends himself. Discuss what you think determines whether or not a lawyer who has to defend himself is being foolish.

BIOLOGICAL SCIENCES

Time: 100 Minutes
Questions 138–214

Directions: This test contains 77 questions. Most of the questions consist of a descriptive passage followed by a group of questions related to the passage. For these questions, study the passage carefully and then choose the best answer to each question in the group. Some questions in this test stand alone. These questions are independent of any passage and independent of each other. For these questions, too, you must select the one best answer. Indicate all of your answers by blackening the corresponding circles on your answer sheet.

A periodic table is provided at the beginning of the book. You may consult it whenever you feel it's necessary.

Passage I (Questions 138–144)

Nobel laureates Joshua Lederberg and Edward Tatum discovered genetic recombination in bacteria in the mid-1940s. Using two strains of *E. coli* with different nutritional deficiencies, they were able to determine that an exchange of genetic material can occur during conjugation between bacterial cells grown together in the same culture medium.

Each strain had three different wild-type (+) genes and three different mutations in genes that normally synthesize the nutrients biotin, cysteine, leucine, phenylalanine, thiamine, threonine, or tyrosine. The genotype of strain Y10 was +, +, leu, +, thi, thr, while that of strain Y24 was bio, cys, +, phe, +, +. In order to survive alone, strain Y10 needed leucine, thiamine, and threonine added to its culture medium, whereas strain Y24 required biotin, cysteine, and phenylalanine.

In the experiment, both strains were grown together in a culture medium containing all six nutrients. Subsequently, a variety of new cell types (recombinants) were recovered, including some that could grow on a minimal medium that lacked all six nutrients.

138. What was the genotype of the recombinant cells that could grow on minimal medium?

A. bio, cys, leu, phe, thi, thr
B. bio, cys, leu, +, +, +
C. +, +, +, phe, thi, thr
D. +, +, +, +, +, +

139. What structures enable the exchange of genetic material between bacterial cells?

A. Cilia
B. Protein coats
C. Pili
D. Peptidoglycans

140. In a control experiment, strains Y10 and Y24 were grown in separate cultures. What result in the control setups would support the idea that genetic exchange between strains was occurring in the experimental setup?

A. In the control experiment, the only cells recovered were cells that could grow on a minimal medium.
B. In the control experiment, no cells were recovered that could grow on a minimal medium.
C. In the control experiment, some cells from strain Y10 were recovered that could grow without leucine added to the medium.
D. In the control experiment, some cells from strain Y24 were recovered that could not grow unless threonine was added to the medium.

141. The technique called interrupted conjugation can be used to map genes located along the length of a bacterial chromosome. Strains of donor cell A containing genes X, Y, and Z, and strains of recipient cell B lacking these genes are grown together in such a way that conjugation occurs. Twenty identical cultures are maintained, and each is vigorously shaken to interrupt conjugation at a different time. One culture is shaken after 2 minutes, another culture is shaken after 4 minutes, a third culture is shaken after 6 minutes, and so on, until the 20th culture is shaken after 40 minutes. B cells with gene Z were found in all cultures shaken after the 18-minute mark; B cells with gene Y were found in all cultures shaken after the 8-minute mark; and B cells with gene X were found in only those cultures shaken after the 38-minute mark. What is the order of the three genes along the bacterial chromosome?

A. Z, Y, X
B. X, Z, Y
C. Y, X, Z
D. Y, Z, X

142. In question 141, which two genes are closer together along the bacterial chromosome?

A. X and Y
B. Z and X
C. Y and Z
D. All three genes are equidistant.

143. In addition to conjugation, other methods of sexual reproduction in bacteria include:

A. transition and transversion.
B. transduction and transition.
C. transformation and transduction.
D. transversion and transformation.

144. The method of sexual reproduction in bacteria that utilizes a virus is called:

A. transition.
B. transversion.
C. transformation.
D. transduction.

Passage II (Questions 145–151)

Glucose homeostasis is essential in that the ability to carry out cellular respiration and continuously produce adequate amounts of ATP is a matter of life and death for all cells. As shown in the figure below, the pancreas plays a central role in maintaining appropriate glucose levels.

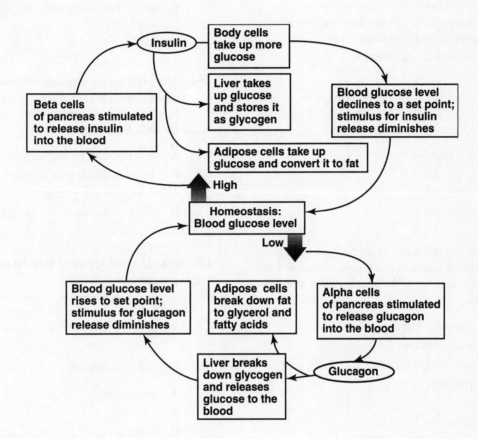

145. What is the primary stimulus to the pancreas for release of more insulin?

   A. A hormone from the anterior pituitary gland

   B. A releasing hormone from the hypothalamus

   C. A neurotransmitter from the autonomic nervous system

   D. High glucose levels in the blood

146. Under which condition would the release of insulin most likely occur?

   A. Absorptive state

   B. Post-absorptive state

   C. Fight-or-flight response

   D. All of the above

147. Glucagon does not act alone in raising glucose levels when they fall. Which of the following hormones can also be considered hyperglycemic?

   A. Cortisol

   B. Growth hormone

   C. Epinephrine

   D. All of the above

148. Hyperglycemic hormones also increase blood levels of alternative molecules that can be used by most cells as substitutes for glucose in cellular respiration. The process that provides these alternative molecules is called:

   A. glycogenesis.

   B. glycolysis.

   C. gluconeogenesis.

   D. glycogenolysis.

149. What role does the sympathetic nervous system play in raising glucose levels?

   A. It stimulates the pancreas to release glucagon.
   B. It stimulates the adrenal medulla to release epinephrine and norepinephrine.
   C. It stimulates the adrenal cortex to release cortisol and cortisone.
   D. It slows down digestion.

150. Before amino acids can be utilized by cells in cellular respiration, they must first be modified in the liver. This process is called:

   A. deamination.
   B. beta oxidation.
   C. mobilization.
   D. nitrification.

151. When glucose levels drop, fats can be utilized in cellular respiration. The conversion of fatty acids to ketones in the liver is part of a process called:

   A. anaerobic respiration.
   B. beta oxidation.
   C. coenzymization.
   D. deacidification.

Passage III (Questions 152–157)

   The chain-initiating and chain-propagating steps for the chlorination of methane are:

   (1) $Cl_2 \xrightarrow{\text{Heat or light}} 2Cl$
   (2) $Cl + CH_4 \rightarrow HCl + CH_3$
   (3) $CH_3 + Cl_2 \rightarrow CH_3Cl + Cl$

   Chain-terminating steps follow to produce chlorine gas, ethane, and methyl chloride.

152. Chain-propagating steps:

   A. absorb energy and produce reactive species.
   B. consume reactive species and generate different reactive species.
   C. do not produce reactive species.
   D. are not part of chain-reaction mechanisms.

153. All chain reactions involve:

   A. chain-initiating and chain-terminating steps only.
   B. chain-initiating, chain-propagating, and chain-terminating steps.
   C. chain-initiating and chain-propagating steps only.
   D. inhibitors.

154. Although the chlorination of methane to form methyl chloride is exothermic, the reaction occurs only at high temperature. The best explanation is that the:

   A. heat of reaction is negative.
   B. chain-initiating step is endothermic.
   C. activation energy is low.
   D. chain-terminating step is endothermic.

Questions 155 and 156 are based on the following statement.

   The addition of O_2 causes the formation of CH_3OO which temporarily slows down the reaction.

155. Oxygen is called a(n):

   A. terminator.
   B. inhibitor.
   C. catalyst.
   D. enzyme.

156. The best explanation for this temporary slow down is that:

   A. CH_3OO is less reactive than CH_3.
   B. CH_3OO is very unstable and decomposes.
   C. CH_3OO is more reactive than the reactive species generated in the chain reaction.
   D. oxygen does not form free radicals.

157. If reaction (2) involves Br it is more endothermic. Which of the following is an explanation?

   A. Forming the H-X bond is more exothermic for H-Cl.

   B. Forming the H-X bond is more endothermic for H-Cl.

   C. Breaking the CH_3-H bond is more endothermic when Br is in the reaction.

   D. Breaking the CH_3-H bond is more endothermic when Cl is in the reaction.

Questions 158 through 162 are NOT based on a descriptive passage.

---

158. A gene includes the following DNA sequence:
…GTTCAGGATTCC…

What is the anticodon on the tRNA molecule that is responsible for bringing the third amino acid in this sequence to the ribosomes during translation?

   A. CUA

   B. GAT

   C. CAU

   D. GAU

159. The return of the resting potential to the neuron membrane during the first part of repolarization is primarily the result of:

   A. sodium ions flowing in.

   B. potassium ions flowing out.

   C. the sodium-potassium ATP pump.

   D. All of the above

160. Aldehydes react with alcohols in acidic solution to form:

   A. hemiacetals and acetals.

   B. hemiacetals only.

   C. ketals only.

   D. hemiketals only.

161. Mutualistic associations between fungi and plant roots are called:

   A. lichens.

   B. leguminous nodules.

   C. mycorrhizae.

   D. endosymbionts.

162. Iron (Fe) is an important mineral needed in trace amounts. Which of the following cells require iron?

   A. Developing red blood cells

   B. Liver cells

   C. Developing red blood cells and liver cells

   D. All cells

Passage IV (Questions 163–169)

The normal maintenance of balance and equilibrium involves a complex combination of ascending and descending neuronal pathways that include both central and peripheral circuits. Peripherally, some cranial nerves deliver sensory input from receptors in the eyes, maculae, and ampullae, while others carry motor signals to the muscles controlling eye movements. In addition, spinal nerves continuously send sensory information into the central nervous system from muscles, tendons, and joints. Central nervous system structures that are part of the balance and equilibrium pathways are found in all major regions of the brain, including the brain stem, diencephalon, cerebrum, and cerebellum. Tracts such as the vestibulospinal and the spinocerebellars are involved as well.

163. The receptors that detect changes in position and tension within muscles, tendons, and joints are called:

   A. nociceptors.

   B. baroreceptors.

   C. visceroreceptors.

   D. proprioceptors.

164. In motion sickness, visual signals from inside the vehicle indicate the body is fixed, while signals originating with the movement of fluids in the ampullae indicate that the body is in motion. This produces a sensory input "mismatch" that can result in subsequent stimulation of the vomiting center. The respective locations of the ampullae and the vomiting center are the:

A. middle ear and the midbrain.

B. inner ear and midbrain.

C. middle ear and medulla oblongata.

D. inner ear and medulla oblongata.

165. Balance signals, like most sensory inputs, synapse in a major relay center of the brain before reaching their final destinations. This major sensory relay center is in the:

A. thalamus.

B. basal ganglia (nuclei).

C. cerebellum.

D. hypothalamus.

166. The maculae contain small calcium carbonate stones (otoconia or otoliths) that stimulate hair-cell receptors involved in the maintenance of static equilibrium. They are located in the:

A. middle ear.

B. saccule and utricle.

C. cochlea.

D. semicircular canals.

167. The cranial nerves that control the extrinsic muscles that move the eyes are the:

A. optic (II), oculomotor (III), and trochlear (IV).

B. optic (II), trochlear (IV), and abducens (VI).

C. oculomotor (III), trochlear (IV), and abducens (VI).

D. optic (II), oculomotor (III), trochlear (IV), and abducens (VI).

168. Vertigo, an inappropriate sense of motion, can result from abnormal stimulation of the balance receptors or from dysfunction elsewhere along the equilibrium pathway, including sites inside the central nervous system. Which of the following is LEAST likely to be a cause of vertigo?

A. Viral infection of the vestibulocochlear nerve (VIII)

B. The influence of alcohol on cerebellar neurons

C. Abnormal fluid pressures in the vestibule

D. Disruption of signals between the cochlea and the cerebellum

169. The vestibulospinal and spinocerebellar tracts are primarily:

A. gray matter in the spinal cord.

B. white matter in the spinal cord.

C. cranial nerves.

D. spinal nerves.

Passage V (Questions 170–175)

The skin is a highly complex organ with functions that include protection, detecting changes in the environment, and various aspects of homeostatic regulation. It ranges in thickness from approximately 0.5mm (eyelids) to 6mm (soles of the feet). Its numerous accessory structures work as coordinated units in what is described as an integrated organ system, the integumentary system.

The Skin

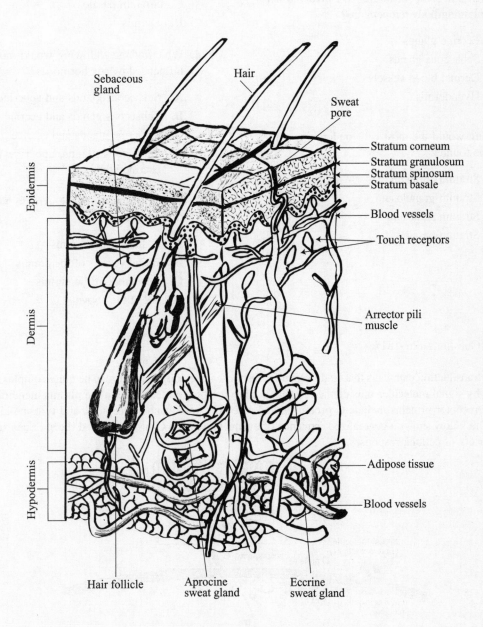

170. Which structures are NOT regulated by autonomic neurons?

A. Eccrine glands

B. Arrector pili muscles

C. Dermal blood vessels

D. Touch receptors

171. Which skin components are NOT involved with maintaining body temperature?

A. Eccrine glands

B. Sebaceous glands

C. Dermal blood vessels

D. Hypodermis

172. Where would the most cells undergoing mitosis be found?

A. Stratum corneum

B. Stratum granulosum

C. Stratum spinosum

D. Stratum basale

173. Malignant melanoma, the most dangerous form of skin cancer, arises from melanocytes, which can metastasize (spread to other parts of the body) rapidly if the condition is not diagnosed and treated early. In which specific region would such cancerous cells originate?

A. Stratum corneum

B. Stratum granulosum

C. Stratum basale

D. Dermis

174. Which of the following would most likely be influenced by sex hormones?

A. Sebaceous glands and apocrine glands

B. Sebaceous glands and eccrine glands

C. Apocrine glands and eccrine glands

D. Sebaceous glands, apocrine glands, and eccrine glands

175. Which structures of the skin do NOT develop from ectoderm?

A. Glands of the dermis

B. Blood vessels of the dermis

C. Receptors of the dermis

D. All of the above

Passage VI (Questions 176–181)

Signal-transduction pathways that lead to specific responses in eukaryotic cells can be quite complex. They often are activated by signal molecules outside the cell that bind to receptor proteins within the plasma membrane. Various categories of receptor proteins include G-protein-linked receptors, ion-channel receptors, and tyrosine-kinase receptors. The figure below shows a generalized sequence of events in which a G-protein-linked receptor can subsequently produce a variety of cellular responses.

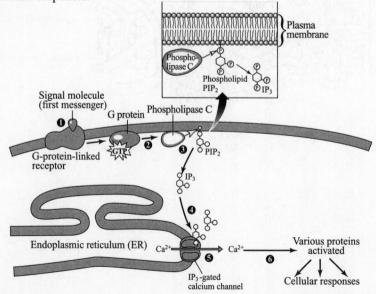

176. The signal molecule that binds to the G-protein-linked receptor in Step 1 is usually referred to as a(n):

A. enzyme.

B. substrate.

C. ligand.

D. moderator.

177. In this particular sequence, the substances IP_3 and Ca^{2+} are important components essential in producing a cellular response. In signal-transduction nomenclature, such components are called:

A. initiators.

B. metabolic intermediates.

C. humoral factors.

D. second messengers.

178. The figure indicates that phospholipase C is an enzyme that:

A. converts a cytoplasmic component to a membrane component.

B. converts a membrane component to a cytoplasmic component.

C. acts as a competitive inhibitor in the cytoplasm.

D. acts as a competitive inhibitor in the membrane.

179. In its inactive form, the G protein is bound to a GDP molecule (guanosine diphosphate). When activated (between Step 1 and Step 2), the GDP is displaced by GTP (guanosine triphosphate), allowing the G protein to bind to and activate phospholipase C. The G protein can also act as a catalyst in the hydrolysis of its GTP to GDP. What will result from this action?

A. Deactivation of the G protein

B. Deactivation of phospholipase C

C. Both A and B

D. Neither A nor B

180. Signal receptors are not always found within the plasma membrane. The receptor for testosterone is an intracellular receptor. When activated by testosterone, this receptor can turn on genes associated with male sex characteristics. The main reason that the receptor can be intracellular is because testosterone is:

A. water soluble.

B. a protein.

C. a lipid.

D. a hormone.

181. In addition to being part of specific signal-transduction pathways, calcium is vital in numerous other bodily functions. Which of the following specific processes is NOT influenced by calcium?

A. Binding of troponin within myofibrils

B. Activation of renin-angiotensin system in renal corpuscles

C. Release of neurotransmitters at axon endings

D. Activation of prothrombin and fibrinogen during coagulation

Passage VII (Questions 182–187)

Phosphates, sulfonates, and carboxylates are all esters:

Carboxylate   Sulfonate   Phosphate

Inorganic esters like carboxylates undergo hydrolysis to form the parent acid and the alcohol. In basic solution, the hydroxide anion attacks the acyl carbon in carboxylates while it attacks the alkyl carbon in sulfonates leading to a difference in the site of cleavage. Phosphate esters are somewhere in between carboxylates and sulfonates in that cleavage can occur in either direction.

182. The best explanation for the different site of attack of nucleophiles on carboxylates and sulfonates is that:

A. the carboxylate anion is strongly basic and therefore a poor cleaving group.

B. the sulfonate anion is weakly basic and therefore a good cleaving group.

C. A and B are correct.

D. Neither A nor B is correct.

183. The best explanation for why nucleophilic attack at phosphorus competes with attack at the alkyl carbon is that:

A. phosphorus can accept a fifth group.

B. phosphoric acid is between carboxylic acid and sulfonic acid.

C. in acidic solution phosphate esters readily form phosphoric acid.

D. None of the explanations are correct.

Questions 184 through 187 are based on the following statement.

Because phosphoric acid contains three hydroxyl groups, three types of esters can form: monoalkyl, dialkyl, and trialkyl phosphates. In acidic solution, all phosphate esters are cleaved to form phosphoric acid, while only trialkyl phosphates undergo hydrolysis in basic solution with only one alkoxy group being removed.

184. As pH rises, the rate of hydrolysis of monoalkyl phosphates, $ROPO(OH)_2$, tends to:

A. increase.

B. decrease.

C. remain the same.

D. Not enough information is provided to predict the outcome.

185. As pH rises, the rate of hydrolysis of dialkyl phosphates tends to:

A. increase.

B. remain the same.

C. decrease.

D. None of the above

186. A monoalky phosphate ester could exist in many forms in aqueous solution. They include the:

A. monoanion and dianion.

B. monoanion, dianion, and protonated ester.

C. dianion only.

D. monoanion, dianion, neutral ester, and protonated ester.

187. In acidic solution, one expects that phosphate esters are:

A. inert.

B. partially cleaved.

C. readily cleaved to form phosphoric acid.

D. involved in an elimination reaction.

Questions 188 through 192 are NOT based on a descriptive passage.

188. Which organ can interconvert the monosaccharides fructose, galactose, and glucose, as well as transaminate the various nonessential amino acids?

    A. The pancreas
    B. The kidney
    C. The small intestine
    D. The liver

189. Which radioactive isotopes can be used to label which macromolecules?

    A. Radioactive phosphorus and nitrogen can be used to label DNA, RNA, and proteins.
    B. Radioactive phosphorus and nitrogen can be used to label DNA and RNA only.
    C. Radioactive phosphorus and nitrogen can be used to label DNA only.
    D. Radioactive phosphorus only can be used to label DNA, RNA, and proteins.

190. Chromatography can be used to:

    A. separate nonvolatile liquids.
    B. separate volatile liquids.
    C. separate a nonvolatile liquid from a volatile liquid.
    D. All of the above

191. When closely related species exhibit mechanical isolation, this represents a:

    A. form of adaptive radiation.
    B. pre-zygotic reproductive barrier.
    C. form of convergence.
    D. reduction in hybrid viability.

192. Which of the following responses will result from increased levels of calcitonin in the blood?

    A. Increased osteoblast activity and decreased osteoclast activity
    B. Increased osteoblast activity and increased osteoclast activity
    C. Decreased osteoblast activity and decreased osteoclast activity
    D. Decreased osteoblast activity and increased osteoclast activity

Passage VIII (Questions 193–197)

In order to identify and understand the structure of a particular mutation, specific mutagens can be used to revert that mutation to normal wild-type. Proflavin is an intercalating agent that can enter the double helix and disrupt DNA metabolism, causing the addition or deletion of a base pair. In contrast, ultraviolet (UV) radiation "excites" purines and pyrimidines, which can result in single-base substitutions. The alkylating agent ethylmethane sulfonate (EMS) can add an ethyl group to guanine, giving it a structure similar to that of adenine. This causes it to pair with thymine instead of cytosine.

Cultures of *E. coli* mutants unable to synthesize the amino acid leucine (leu⁻) were separately treated with the above three mutagens and plated out on media lacking leucine in order to isolate any cultures that may have reverted to wild-type (leu⁺). The results were as follows:

Mutant Culture	Mutagen Treatment		
	Proflavin	UV	EMS
1	+	−	−
2	−	+	−
3	−	+	+
4	−	−	−

193. Culture 1 contains a mutation that is most likely:

    A. any substitution.
    B. an addition of a base pair.
    C. a deletion of a base pair.
    D. either an addition or a deletion of a base pair.

194. Culture 3 contains a mutation that is most likely:

    A. any substitution.
    B. a transition.
    C. a transversion.
    D. either an addition or a deletion of a base pair.

195. Culture 2 contains a mutation that is most likely:

    A. any substitution.
    B. a transition.
    C. a transversion.
    D. any frameshift mutation.

196. Which statement is correct about the original mutation in Culture 4?

    A. It could be a single-base substitution.

    B. It could be an addition of a base pair.

    C. It could be a deletion of a base pair.

    D. None of the above statements are correct.

197. The base analog 5-bromouracil has a structure similar to that of thymine, and in its most stable conformation binds to adenine. However, it can undergo a tautomeric shift so that it binds to guanine instead. Thus, the type of mutation that can be caused by 5-bromouracil is:

    A. any substitution.

    B. a transition.

    C. a transversion.

    D. either an addition or a deletion of a base pair.

Passage IX (Questions 198–203)

    Regulation of stomach activity involves a combination of neural and hormonal mechanisms that include events occurring in the head (cephalic phase), in the stomach (gastric phase), and in the small intestine (intestinal phase). Both stimulatory and inhibitory events can occur in all three locations.

    During the cephalic phase, the sight, smell, and taste of food can lead to neural signals in the hunger center and then along the vagus nerve to stomach glands and muscles, thereby increasing their activity. By contrast, loss of appetite or depression can be inhibitory during the cephalic phase. Within the stomach and small intestine, the presence of certain foods, the level of muscular distention and stretch, and the pH of the food mixture all influence responses associated with the gastric and intestinal phases.

198. During the cephalic phase, which part of the brain is LEAST likely to be part of the pathway that leads to an increase in gastric activity?

    A. Cerebrum

    B. Hypothalamus

    C. Pons

    D. Medulla oblongata

199. The vagus nerve, as well as the hormones, gastrin, and intestinal gastrin, all stimulate gastric activity, including the production of HCl by parietal cells in the gastric mucosa. HCl production is accomplished with the help of the enzyme carbonic anhydrase, which catalyzes the dissociation of carbonic acid into bicarbonate ions and hydrogen ions. The hydrogen ions subsequently combine with chloride ions in the stomach lumen after the latter have gone through a sequence of exchange reactions with the bicarbonate ions. This exchange between chloride and bicarbonate ions, as well as the associated catalytic activity of carbonic anhydrase, also occur during:

    A. carbon dioxide transport between tissues and lungs.

    B. blood pressure corrections carried out by the renin-angiotensin system.

    C. reabsorption in the proximal convoluted tubule.

    D. cerebrospinal fluid formation in the ventricles of the brain.

200. Distention of the duodenum, as well as the presence of fatty, acidic chyme causes intestinal endocrine cells to release the hormones GIP, CCK, and secretin, which combine to inhibit further gastric activity. CCK and secretin have concurrent effects that help alter intestinal conditions. Which of the following most likely represents the concurrent effects of these hormones?

    A. Stimulation of sodium bicarbonate and digestive enzymes from the pancreas and inhibition of bile from the liver and gallbladder

    B. Inhibition of sodium bicarbonate and digestive enzymes from the pancreas and stimulation of bile from the liver and gallbladder

    C. Stimulation of sodium bicarbonate and digestive enzymes from the pancreas and stimulation of bile from the liver and gallbladder

    D. Inhibition of sodium bicarbonate and digestive enzymes from the pancreas and inhibition of bile from the liver and gallbladder

201. As absorption proceeds and space becomes available in the small intestine, how is the remainder of the food that is stored in the stomach released for processing?

    A. Stimulation by the vagus nerve and stimulation by intestinal gastrin
    B. Stimulation by the vagus nerve and inhibition by intestinal gastrin
    C. Inhibition by the vagus nerve and stimulation by intestinal gastrin
    D. Inhibition by the vagus nerve and inhibition by intestinal gastrin

202. Which statement is MOST correct about the hormones released by the small intestine to regulate the activities of the stomach?

    A. To reach their target cells, the hormones must first pass through the liver.
    B. The hormones can reach their target cells via the direct connection through the sphincter between the lumens of the small intestine and the stomach.
    C. To reach their target cells, the hormones must first pass through the liver and the heart.
    D. The hormones reach their target cells via ducts that connect the small intestine and the stomach.

203. During an emergency "fight-or-flight" situation, neural signals will cause gastric activity to:

    A. speed up via acetylcholine.
    B. speed up via norepinephrine.
    C. slow down via acetylcholine.
    D. slow down via norepinephrine.

Passage X (Questions 204–209)

The Grignard reagent has the formula RMgX and is formed when an alkyl halide reacts with Mg:

$$RX + Mg \rightarrow RMgX$$

It is a very useful synthetic reagent because carbon is bound to a more electropositive element, thus giving it carbanion-like character. The negatively charged carbon in the Grignard reagent can thus act as a nucleophile attacking a variety of carbonyl compounds to form alcohols. Its reactivity, however, limits its usefulness; any compound containing hydrogen attached to an electronegative or even a triply bonded carbon is sufficiently acidic to decompose a Grignard reagent.

204. The Grignard reagent that could be reacted with acetone to form 2-methyl-2-pentanol is:

    A. n-propylmagnesium bromide.
    B. n-butylmagnesium chloride.
    C. isopropylmagnesium bromide.
    D. None of the above

205. Grignard reagents also combine with inorganic compounds like CO_2, H_2O, and O_2. The carbonation of t-butylmagnesium chloride produces the salt of:

    A. dimethylacetic acid.
    B. trimethylacetic acid.
    C. methylacetic acid.
    D. acetone.

206. Grignard reactions generally occur in dry ether because:

    A. the stronger acid H_2O will displace the weaker RH acid from its salt.
    B. the stronger acid diethyl ether will displace the weaker RH acid from its salt.
    C. water slows down the reaction.
    D. water reacts with ethers.

207. Which of the following statements about Grignard reagents is correct?

    A. Grignard reagents react with formaldehyde.
    B. Grignard reagents can be formed from all organic compounds containing a halide.
    C. Grignard reagents react with carboxylic esters to form ketones.
    D. None of the above

208. Grignard reagents cannot be prepared from:

    A. $HO(CH_2)_3Br$.
    B. chlorobenzene.
    C. t-butylchloride.
    D. o-dichlorobenzene.

209. Carboxylic esters react with Grignard reagents to form:

    A. diols.
    B. carboxylic acid.
    C. alkanes.
    D. tertiary alcohols.

Questions 210 through 214 are NOT based on a descriptive passage.

210. Lesch-Nyhan syndrome is an X-linked genetic disorder that affects neurological function, metabolism of purines, behavior, and viability. Therefore, this disorder can be described as:

A. pleiotropic.

B. polygenic.

C. polycistronic.

D. multiple allelic.

211. In which of the following peripheral locations are connections found for the autonomic motor neurons that regulate heart rate?

A. Aortic arch

B. Aortic semi-lunar valve

C. Tricuspid valve

D. Sino-atrial node

212. The Hardy-Weinberg principle supports the idea that populations will not evolve and, instead, will remain in equilibrium as long as certain conditions are met. One of these conditions is that:

A. populations remain relatively small.

B. migration can occur.

C. mating is random.

D. mutation occurs on a regular basis.

213. The dehydration of

$$CH_3-CH_2-\underset{\underset{OH}{|}}{\overset{\overset{CH_3}{|}}{C}}-CH_3$$

yields mostly which of the following?

A. $CH_2{=}CH-\underset{\underset{OH}{|}}{\overset{\overset{CH_3}{|}}{C}}-CH_3$

B. $CH_3-CH{=}\overset{\overset{CH_3}{|}}{C}-CH_3$

C. $CH_3-CH_2-\overset{\overset{CH_3}{|}}{C}{=}CH_2$

D. $CH_3-CH_2-\overset{\overset{CH_2}{\|}}{C}-CH_3$

214. Which statement is correct concerning aerobic and anaerobic respiration in muscle cells?

A. The final electron acceptor in both aerobic and anaerobic respiration is organic.

B. The final electron acceptor in both aerobic and anaerobic respiration is inorganic.

C. The final electron acceptor in aerobic respiration is organic, whereas the final electron acceptor in anaerobic respiration is inorganic.

D. The final electron acceptor in aerobic respiration is inorganic, whereas the final electron acceptor in anaerobic respiration is organic.

PRACTICE EXAM I ANSWER KEY

PHYSICAL SCIENCES

1. A	40. D
2. C	41. C
3. B	42. C
4. C	43. C
5. A	44. B
6. A	45. C
7. B	46. D
8. B	47. A
9. B	48. B
10. C	49. D
11. B	50. B
12. D	51. C
13. C	52. C
14. B	53. A
15. C	54. B
16. A	55. C
17. C	56. B
18. C	57. C
19. C	58. A
20. D	59. B
21. A	60. B
22. C	61. C
23. D	62. D
24. A	63. A
25. C	64. A
26. B	65. C
27. C	66. D
28. A	67. C
29. B	68. B
30. D	69. C
31. D	70. B
32. D	71. C
33. D	72. B
34. C	73. D
35. B	74. B
36. B	75. C
37. D	76. B
38. B	77. C
39. C	

VERBAL REASONING

78. B	109. D
79. A	110. C
80. B	111. D
81. C	112. B
82. D	113. D
83. C	114. B
84. D	115. D
85. B	116. C
86. C	117. A
87. C	118. B
88. A	119. A
89. C	120. C
90. B	121. D
91. B	122. B
92. B	123. C
93. D	124. A
94. C	125. D
95. A	126. D
96. C	127. B
97. B	128. C
98. A	129. D
99. D	130. A
100. A	131. B
101. B	132. D
102. B	133. A
103. C	134. D
104. C	135. B
105. C	136. B
106. A	137. A
107. D	
108. A	

BIOLOGICAL SCIENCES

138. D	177. D
139. C	178. B
140. B	179. C
141. D	180. C
142. C	181. B
143. C	182. C
144. D	183. A
145. D	184. B
146. A	185. C
147. D	186. D
148. C	187. C
149. B	188. D
150. A	189. B
151. B	190. D
152. B	191. B
153. B	192. A
154. B	193. D
155. B	194. B
156. A	195. C
157. A	196. D
158. D	197. B
159. B	198. C
160. A	199. A
161. C	200. C
162. D	201. A
163. D	202. C
164. D	203. D
165. A	204. A
166. B	205. B
167. C	206. A
168. D	207. A
169. B	208. A
170. D	209. D
171. B	210. A
172. D	211. D
173. C	212. C
174. A	213. B
175. B	214. D
176. C	

PRACTICE EXAM I EXPLANATORY ANSWERS

PHYSICAL SCIENCES

1. **The correct answer is (A).** The volume of water that the raft must displace to support the swimmer is:

    $V = m_{swimmer}/r_{water} = 60$ kg/1000 kg/m^3 = 0.060 m^3

    The area of the raft is 2m × 2m = 4m^2

    Therefore, the height of the raft changes by: h = V/A = 0.060m^3/4m^3 = 0.015m = 1.5 cm.

2. **The correct answer is (C).** w_X and w_w are the apparent weight losses of the object in liquid X and in water, respectively. The equation to solve is: $\rho_X = w_X/gV_X$ but this has two unknowns, ρ_X and V_X. However, because the object is immersed in the fluids:

    $V_X = V_w = V = w_w/g\rho_w = w_X/ g\rho_X$

    This gives:

    $\rho_X = w_X\rho_w/w_X = (0.30$ N)(1000 kg/m^3)/0.40 N = 750 kg/m^3

3. **The correct answer is (B).** The explanation is in paragraph 2 of the passage. The weight of the ship equals the weight of the fluid it displaces. The volumes aren't equal because the ship isn't completely immersed in the fluid, it's floating.

4. **The correct answer is (C).** If the cube floats with half of its volume in the water and the other half in the oil, then logically its density must equal the average of the densities of the oil and the water.

    Here's the proof. The upward buoyant force equals the weight of the displaced oil and the displaced water:
    $F_B = m_{oil}g + m_{water}g$

    Since the cube is in equilibrium at the oil-water interface, F_B also equals the downward force of the cube's weight: $F_B = m_{cube}g$

    This gives: $m_{cube} = m_{oil} + m_{water} = \rho_{oil}V_{oil} + \rho_{water}V_{water}$
    $= (300$ kg/m^3)(2 m^3) + (1000 kg/m^3)(2 m^3) = 600 kg + 2000 kg
    $= 2600$ kg

    Remember: $V_{oil} = V_{water} = ½ V_{cube} = ½ (4$ m^3) = 2 m^3

    $\rho_{cube} = m_{cube}/V_{cube} = 2600$ kg/4 m^3 = 650 kg/m^3

5. **The correct answer is (A).** The weight of the floating barge is:

    $w_{barge} = \rho_{barge}V_{barge}g$

    This is balanced by F_B which is the weight of the water displaced by the barge. If V_{draft} is the volume of barge submerged below the water line, then the weight of the water displaced is:

    $w_{water} = \rho_{water}V_{draft}g$

    Therefore:

    $\rho_{barge}V_{barge}g = \rho_{water}V_{draft}g \rightarrow V_{draft}/V_{barge} = \rho_{barge}/\rho_{water}$
    $= (800$ kg/m^3)/(1030 kg/m^3) = 0.78 = 78%

    78% of the barge's volume is below the water line. Therefore, 22% is above the water line.

6. **The correct answer is (A).** The cold air displaced by the balloon is:

$$w_{\text{cold air}} = V_{\text{balloon}}\rho_{\text{cold air}}g = (3.0 \times 10^3 \text{ m}^3)(1.5 \text{ kg/m}^3)g = 4500g \text{ N} = F_B$$

The buoyance force, F_B, must support the weight of hot air in the balloon and its load.

The weight of the hot air in the balloon is:

$$W_{\text{hot air}} = V_{\text{balloon}}\rho_{\text{hot air}}g = (3.0 \times 10^3 \text{ m}^3)(1. \text{ kg/m}^3)g = 3000g \text{ N}$$

The maximum load the balloon can support is:

$$4500g \text{ N} - 3000g \text{ N} = 1500g \text{ N} = 14700 \text{ N} \sim 1.5 \times 10^4 \text{ N}$$

Note: This answer is based on the presumption that the mass of the balloon is negligible.

7. **The correct answer is (B).** First find the weight and the volume of the boulder:

$$w_{\text{boulder}} = (300 \text{ kg})(9.8 \text{ kg/m}^3) = 2940 \text{ N}$$

$$V_{\text{boulder}} = m_{\text{boulder}}/\rho_{\text{boulder}} = 300 \text{ kg}/2400 \text{ kg/m}^3 = 0.125 \text{ m}^3$$

$$V_{\text{boulder}} = V_{\text{water displaced by boulder}}$$

The weight of the displaced water is:

$$w_{\text{water}} = \rho_{\text{water}}Vg = (1000 \text{ kg/m}^3)(0.125 \text{ m}^3)(9.8 \text{ kg/m}^3) = 1225 \text{ N} = F_B$$

Since the boulder hasn't started moving, it is in equilibrium. The tension T on the taut cable is found from Newton's second law:

$$\Sigma F_y = F_B + T + (-w_{\text{boulder}}) = 0$$

$$T = w_{\text{boulder}} - F_B = 2940 \text{ N} - 1225 \text{ N} = 1715 \text{ N}$$

8. **The correct answer is (B).** For a pipe closed at one end, $v_o = v/4L = (340 \text{ m/s})/4(0.030 \text{ m}) = 2800 \text{ s}^{-1} = 2.8 \times 10^{-3}$ Hz. Remember, a reciprocal second, s^{-1}, equals a hertz, Hz.

9. **The correct answer is (B).** For a pipe open at both ends: $v_o = v/2L$. For a pipe closed at one end: $v_o = v/4L$. Therefore, the fundamental frequency for the open pipe is twice that of the pipe closed at one end.

10. **The correct answer is (C).** Since overtones are multiples of the fundamental frequency, the difference between successive overtones is constant. In this case each overtone differs by 40 Hz. Working backwards the fundamental frequency must be 20 Hz. Then:

$$3(20 \text{ Hz}) = 60 \text{ Hz} \qquad 5(20 \text{ Hz}) = 100 \text{ Hz} \qquad 7(20 \text{ Hz}) = 140 \text{ Hz}$$

The overtones are odd multiples of the fundamental, therefore, the pipe is closed at one end and $v_o = v/4L$.

The length of the pipe is: $L = v/4v_o = (340 \text{ m/s})/4(20 \text{ s}^{-1}) = 4.25 \text{ m} \sim 4.3 \text{ m}$

11. **The correct answer is (B).** The compression regions are 170 cm apart and the rate at which they reach the listener is the frequency of the wave:

$$v = v/\lambda = (340 \text{ m/s})/1.70 \text{ m} = 200 \text{ s}^{-1}$$

12. **The correct answer is (D).** For closed pipes the overtones are in the ratio $n = 1:3:5:7:\ldots\ldots$

$n = 1$ is the fundamental, $n = 3$ is the first overtone, $n = 5$ is the second overtone.

13. **The correct answer is (C).** A pipe closed at both ends has nodes at both ends and for its fundamental tone only one antinode. This is exactly the same situation found in pipes open at both ends.

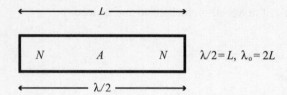

$\lambda/2 = L$, $\lambda_o = 2L$

14. **The correct answer is (B).** Be careful in determining which site is the proper frame of reference, the spaceship or the observatory. Obviously the ship moves during the interval between flashes. An observer on Earth sees the ship move and the flashes occurring at different points in the sky. However, an observer on the ship is at rest relative to the ship and would record the flashes as occurring at the same location (inside the ship). Therefore, the ship is the proper frame of reference and the time interval measured at the observatory is:

$$\Delta t = \Delta t_o/(1 - v^2/c^2)^{1/2} = 10s/(1 - [(2.00 \times 10^8 m/s)^2/(3.00 \times 10^8 m/s)^2]^{1/2}$$

$$\Delta t = 10s/[1 - (2/3)^2]^{1/2} = 10s/(5/9)^{1/2} = 10s(3)/(5)^{1/2} = 30s/5^{1/2}$$

To estimate, find the value of a square root. Find two perfect squares that bracket the number you want to evaluate.

$4^{1/2} < 5^{1/2} < 9^{1/2}$, therefore, $2 < 5^{1/2} < 3$.

Since the square root of 5 lies between 2 and 3, Δt must lie between $30s/2 = 15s$ and $30s/3 = 10s$. Choice (B) falls in this range.

$\Delta t = 30s/2.24 = 13.4s$

15. **The correct answer is (C).** The flashes originate on the spaceship, so 10s is the proper time interval, Δt_o and 20s is Δt.

$$\Delta t = \Delta t_o/(1 - v^2/c^2)^{1/2} \text{ rearranges to:}$$

$$1 - v^2/c^2 = (\Delta t_o/\Delta t)^2$$

$$v^2 = c^2(1 - (\Delta t_o/\Delta t)^2) = (3.00 \times 10^8 m/s)^2(1 - 100/400)$$

$$= 9.00 \times 10^{16} m^2/s^2(0.75)$$

$$v = (6.75 \times 10^{16} m^2/s^2)^{1/2} = 2.6 \times 10^8 \text{ m/s}$$

Estimate the value of $(6.75 \times 10^{16})^{1/2}$: $(6.75)^{1/2}(10^{16})^{1/2}$

$(10^{16})^{1/2} = 10^8$

$4^{1/2} < 6.75^{1/2} < 9^{1/2} \rightarrow 2 < 6.75^{1/2} < 3$

The velocity lies between $2.00 \times 10^8 m/s$ and $3.00 \times 10^8 m/2$. This only eliminates choice (A).

Evaluate choice (C) since its value is halfway between those of choices (B) and (D). $(2.6 \times 10^8)^2$ will either be greater than, less than, or equal to 6.75×10^{16}.

16. **The correct answer is (A).** The muons are moving relative to the laboratory, therefore, 16 μs is Δt and the true half-life is Δt_o.

$$\Delta t_o = \Delta t(1 - v^2/c^2)^{1/2} = (16 \text{ μs})(1 - 0.99^2)^{1/2} = (16 \text{ μs})(1 - 0.98)^{1/2}$$

$$= (16 \text{ μs})(0.02)^{1/2} = 2.2 \text{ μs}$$

To estimate the value of $(0.02)^{1/2}$ rewrite it as $(2 \times 10^{-2})^{1/2}$ and evaluate the character and the exponent separately:

$1^{1/2} < 2^{1/2} < 4^{1/2} \rightarrow 1 < 2^{1/2} < 2$

$(10^{-2})^{1/2} = 10^{-1}$

Therefore, $(0.02)^{1/2}$ lies between .1 and .2 and Δt_o lies between:

(16 μs)(.1) = 1.6 μs and (16 μs)(.2) = 3.2 μs

Choice (A) is the only value in this range.

17. **The correct answer is (C).** 20 light years is the distance light travels in 20 Earth years. The observer on Earth always measures a longer time than an observer traveling with the probe and nothing can travel faster than the speed of light.

18. **The correct answer is (C).** The second postulate.

19. **The correct answer is (C).** From Table I a capacitor reaches 86% of its final charge after two time constants, $t = 2RC$.

$$t = 2(3.0 \times 10^6 \, \Omega)(5.0 \times 10^{-6} F) = 30 \text{ s}$$

20. **The correct answer is (D).** Solve $\tau = RC$ for $R = \tau/C = 10s/100 \times 10^{-6}F = 10^5 \, \Omega = 100 \text{ k}\Omega$

21. **The correct answer is (A).** The capacitance C of the capacitor is fixed. Since $q = CV$, the voltage across the capacitor must follow the same exponential growth curve as the charge. After 40 s only $1/200 \sim 0.5\%$ of the original voltage drop remains which means that only $\sim 0.5\%$ of the original charge remains. Effectively the capacitor is completely discharged. Therefore, the time constant is 8 seconds.

$40 \text{ s} = 5RC$ and $RC = 40 \text{ s}/5 = 8 \text{ s}$

When the voltage drop is 74 V, only $74/200 \sim 37\%$ of the original voltage is present which means that 37% of the full charge remains. According to Table I this decrease occurs after one time constant.

22. **The correct answer is (C).** Find the time constant for the circuit and the charge on the fully charged capacitor:

$$\tau = RC = (6.0 \times 10^6 \text{ M}\Omega)(2.0 \times 10^{-6} \text{ F}) = 12 \text{ s}$$

$$q_o = CV = (2.0 \times 10^{-6} \text{ F})(50 \text{ V}) = 100 \times 10^{-6} \text{ C} = 100 \text{ μC}$$

Since $t = 6$ s is half of one time constant, the charge at $\tau = RC$ is an upper bound on the q: $q < 0.63q_o = 63$ μC

Since the growth rate is exponential, then q is greater than half the percentage change for one time constant: $q > (0.63/2)q_o = 0.315q_o = 31.5$ μC

Therefore, 31.5 μC < q < 63 μC and the best choice is (C).

23. **The correct answer is (D).** The time required to charge the capacitor is given by the time constant $\tau = RC$. With R held constant, τ increases if C increases and it takes longer to charge the capacitor.

Incidentally, the maximum current is given by Ohm's law: $i_o = V/R$. Since only C changes, the value of i_o remains the same.

24. **The correct answer is (A).** The capacitor is fully charged after $\sim 5RC = 30$ seconds. Current can only flow through the resistor while the capacitor is charging or discharging. Once q reaches a constant value, the current i becomes zero.

25. **The correct answer is (C).** Referring to Table I after two time constants, the charge has decreased to 14% of its maximum value.

26. The correct answer is (B). $n_{air} < n_{film} < n_{glass}$. Reflection with phase change of $\lambda/2$ occurs for ray a at the air-film interface and for ray b at the film-glass interface. Therefore, reflections alone keep both rays in phase.

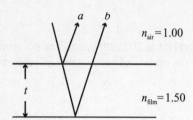

Constructive interference then depends on making the path length difference, $2t$, within the film a multiple of λ.

$2t = m\lambda/n$ $t = $ m $(600$ nm$)/2(1.50) = $ m200 nm

For m = 1, $t = 200$.

27. The correct answer is (C). The ratio of the refractive indices is $n_{air} < n_{film} < n_{glass}$. Reflections at the interfaces do not produce a net phase difference between rays a and b. (See diagram from Answer 26 above.)

Destructive interference requires that the optical path length through the film, $2t$, be an odd multiple of $\lambda/2$:

$2t = (m + \frac{1}{2})\lambda/n$ $t = (m + \frac{1}{2})(640$ nm$)/2(1.33) \rightarrow t = (m + \frac{1}{2})240$ nm

For m = 0, $t = 120$ nm which is not one of the choices.

For m = 1, $t = 360$ nm.

28. The correct answer is (A). It isn't necessary to know if $n_{air} < n_{soap}$ or $n_{air} > n_{soap}$.

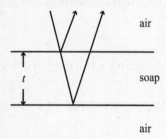

Either ray a or ray b will undergo a phase change during reflection. Therefore the two rays will be out of phase. For constructive interference to occur, the optical path difference must provide a 180° phase change for ray b. This happens if $2t$ is an odd multiple of $\lambda/2$. Since $2t = \lambda/2$, $t = \lambda/4$.

29. The correct answer is (B). Choices (A) and (C) are eliminated immediately since they are outside the visible range. For soap $n_{air} > n_{soap}$. The reflected wave, ray$_a$, undergoes a phase change at the air-soapy water interface. Ray R_b doesn't change phase at the soapy water-air interface. Based on interface reflections, the two rays are out of phase. To maintain this, the optical path difference, $2t$, must not produce a phase change in R_b. Therefore the path must be an integer multiple of λ.

$2t = m\lambda/n$ $\lambda = 2tn/m = 2(350$ nm$)(1.35)/$m $= 945$ nm/m

For m = 1, $\lambda = 945$ nm

For m = 2, $\lambda = 473$ nm   [this is choice (B)]

For m = 3, $\lambda = 315$ nm

Choice (B), $\lambda = 473$ nm, is the only choice in the visible range.

30. The correct answer is (D). Again, ray R_a is reflected with phase change and ray R_b isn't. For the two reflected waves to interact:

$2t = M\lambda/n$ where M is either m or m + ½

$M = 2tn/\lambda = 2(1.00 \times 10^{-6}\text{m})(1.35)/600 \times 10^{-9}$ nm = 4.5

$M = m + \frac{1}{2}$ for m = 4. This describes the complete constructive interaction.

31. The correct answer is (D). Both rays R_a and R_b are reflected with a change of phase. Therefore the net change of phase with reflection is zero. For constructive interference, $2t = m\lambda/n$ and for destructive interference $2t = (m + \frac{1}{2})\lambda/n$.

$t = (m + \frac{1}{2})(600 \text{ nm})/2(1.25) = m700/2(1.25)$

$600m + 300 = 700m \quad 300 = 100m \quad m = 3$

Solve either equation for t: $t = 3(700 \text{ nm})/2(1.25) = 840$ nm

32. The correct answer is (D). The force on the charged particle due to the electric field is: $F_{Electric} = qE$. And from Newton's second law: $a = F_{Electric}/m$.

$a = qE/m = (1.6 \times 10^{-19}\text{ C})(0.010\text{ N/C})/1.67 \times 10^{-27}\text{ kg} = 9.6 \times 10^{6}\text{ m/s}^2$

This is an easy problem to estimate the answer on:

$a \sim (2 \times 10^{-19}\text{ C})(10^{-2}\text{ N/C})/ 2 \times 10^{-27}\text{ kg} = 10^{-19} \times 10^{-2} \times 10^{27} = 10^{6}\text{ m/s}^2$

$a \sim 10 \times 10^{5}\text{ m/s}^2$

33. The correct answer is (D). For the first part of the question, remember that terminal velocity means the acceleration experienced becomes zero.

Since $a = 0$ m/s^2, then, $\Sigma F_y = F_{air\ resistance} - F_W = 0$

$F_{air\ resistance} = F_W\ mg$

For the second part of the question, while the velocity is higher, the acceleration is still zero. Therefore, the $F_{air\ resistance}$ is still equal to the skydiver's weight.

$F_{air\ resistance\ Case\ A} = F_{air\ resistance\ Case\ B}$

What has changed is the surface area of the skydiver. Since pressure is $P = F/A$, as A decreases, the pressure experienced increases.

$P_A A_A = P_B A_B = mg$

Since $A_A > A_B$, then $P_A < P_B$

34. The correct answer is (C). Electric power $P = IV = I^2R = V^2/R$. For the information given, use $P = V^2/R$.

Therefore $R = V^2/P = (120V)^2/60$ W = 240 V^2/W = 240 Ω

35. **The correct answer is (B).** We need to determine the maximum force that static friction exerts on Block B. This is the force that must be overcome by the gravitational force between Blocks A and B.

Forces acting on Block B

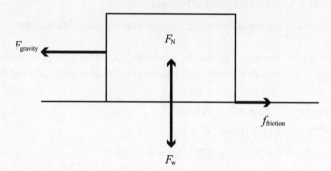

Since motion is only along the x direction, $\sum F_y = 0$. For Block B:

$\sum F_y = 0 = F_N - F_W$ gives $F_N = F_W = M_B g$

By definition the frictional force is: $f_{friction} = \mu_s F_N = \mu_s M_B g$

From $F_{gravity} = f_{friction}$ we get: $G M_A M_B / r^2 = \mu_s M_B g$ and $M_A = \mu_s M_B g r^2 / G M_B = \mu_s g r^2 / G$

$M_A = 0.5(9.8 \text{ m/s}^2)(1.0 \text{ m})^2 / 6.67 \times 10^{-11} \text{ Nm}^2/\text{kg}^2 = 7.3 \times 10^{10} \text{ kg}$

M_A can be estimated as:

$M_A \sim (5 \times 10^{-1})(10 \text{ m/s}^2)(1.0 \text{ m}^2) / 7 \times 10^{-11} \text{ Nm}^2/\text{kg}^2 \sim (5/7) \times 10^{11} \text{kg}$

$\sim 0.7 \times 10^{11} \text{kg} \sim 7 \times 10^{10} \text{kg}$

36. **The correct answer is (B).** Apply Newton's second law: $F_A = F_{AB}$, therefore:

$m_A a_A = (m_A + m_B)a_{AB}$ and $a_{AB} = a_A/5$

therefore: $m_A a_A = (m_A + m_B)a_A/5$ which reduces to $4m_A = m_B$ or 4:1

37. **The correct answer is (D).** The only force acting on the ball is gravity. The ball will ascend until gravity reduces its velocity to zero and then it will descend. Find the time it takes for the ball to reach its maximum height and then double the time to cover the round trip.

Using $v_{\text{at maximum height}} = v_0 + at = v_0 - gt$, we get:

$0 \text{ m/s} = 50 \text{ m/s} - (9.8 \text{ m/s}^2)t$

Therefore, $t = (50 \text{ m/s})/(9.8 \text{ m/s}^2) \sim (50 \text{ m/s})/(10 \text{ m/s}^2) \sim 5 \text{ s}$

This is the time it takes the ball to reach its maximum height. The total round trip time is $2t \sim 10 \text{ s}$.

38. **The correct answer is (B).** The work is done against gravity so it is equal to the change in potential energy.

$W = E_p = mgh$

For a fixed height, work is proportional to weight lifted. Since Johnny weighs twice as much as Jane he works twice as hard to get up the hill.

Power is work done per unit time. For Johnny this is $W/\Delta t$. Jane did half the work in half the time, $(1/2 \text{ W})/(1/2 \Delta t.) = W/\Delta t$ which is the same power delivered by Johnny.

39. **The correct answer is (C).** The skydiver has an initial vertical velocity of zero, and falls through a distance of 2000 m under the acceleration due to gravity.

From: $2gy = v^2 - v_o^2$

We get:

$v = (2gy - v_o^2)^{1/2} = [2(9.8 \text{ m/s}^2)(2000 \text{ m}) - 0]^{1/2} = [39200 \text{ m}^2/\text{s}^2]^{1/2} \sim 198 \text{ m/s}$

which is closest to answer (C).

40. The correct answer is (D). This is a crude experiment that simply relies on perceived color differences. Choices (A) and (B) presume that the concentration of the unknown lies precisely halfway between the bracketing standard test tubes, but this presumption is unwarranted. Choice (C) would result from misreading the diagram.

41. The correct answer is (C). The method is as good as the student's eye, but it must fail at some small color difference that is too small to see.

42. The correct answer is (C). The transmittance is greatest when the absorbance is lowest. This can be seen from the equation relating T to A, or to the fact that the absorbance in the series of test tubes rose in the same order as the color intensity rose.

43. The correct answer is (C). Use $v = c/\lambda_{max}$, where λ_{max} is the wavelength where A is a maximum.

$$v = c/\lambda_{max} = (3.00 \times 10^8 \text{ m/s})/(6.40 \times 10^{-7} \text{ m})$$
$$= 4.69 \times 10^{14} \text{ s}^{-1}$$

44. The correct answer is (B). Read down to the horizontal axis from point X (the third point from the right) on the concentration/absorption curve in Experiment 2.

45. The correct answer is (C). If a dimerization reaction were to occur,

$$2\,Y \rightarrow Y_2$$

then Le Chatelier's Principle predicts that it would be favored at high concentrations of Y, which would drive the reaction to equilibrium farther to the right. Since dimerization will remove Compound Y from the solution, its absorption curve will drop below the linear function that we would otherwise expect.

46. The correct answer is (D). Here are the half reactions and overall reactions, as written in the passage.

cathode: $4e^- + O_2(g) + 2H_2O(l) \rightarrow 4OH–(aq)$ 0.40 V

anode: $2H_2(g) + 4OH^-(aq) \rightarrow 4H_2O(l) + 4e^-$? V

$2H_2(g) + O_2(g) \rightarrow 2H_2O(l)$ 1.23 V

$E_{cell} = E_{cathode} - E_{anode}$

$E_{anode} = E_{cathode} - E_{cell}$

$= (0.40 \text{ V}) - (1.23 \text{ V})$

$= -0.83 \text{ V}$

The question asks for E° for a different half-reaction, one whose coefficients are smaller than the anode by a factor of 2. But when we divide (or multiply) a half reaction by a constant, we don't change the value of E°, which is an "intensive" property.

47. The correct answer is (A). $\Delta G = -nFE° = - (4 \text{ mol})(96,500 \text{ JV}^{-1} \text{ mol}^{-1})(1.23 \text{ V})$

48. The correct answer is (B). The overall cell reaction is

$2H_2(g) + O_2(g) \rightarrow 4H_2O(l)$ $\Delta G = -237.2 \text{ kJ}$

The value of ΔG was given in the passage. But ΔG is the maximum work that can be done by the system.

$-100 \text{ kJ} (2 \text{ mol } H_2 / -237.2 \text{ kJ}) = 0.84 \text{ mol } H_2$

$V = nRT/P = (0.84 \text{ mol})(0.08206 \text{ L atm K}^{-1} \text{ mol}^{-1})(298 \text{ K})/(1.00 \text{ atm})$

$= 21 \text{ L}$

49. The correct answer is (D). Since the [OH⁻] terms in each of the half reactions cancel out when the overall cell reaction is written, the overall voltage does not depend on [OH⁻].

50. **The correct answer is (B).** We might guess that $\Delta S°$ will be negative, since the overall reaction shows three reactant molecules converting to two products. To calculate $\Delta S°$, we use the definition of G:

$$\Delta G° = \Delta H° - T\,\Delta S°$$

$$\Delta S° = (\Delta H° - \Delta G°)/T$$

$$= [-285.8 \text{ kJ} - (-237.2 \text{ kJ})]/(298 \text{ K})$$

$$= -0.16 \text{ kJ/K} = -160 \text{ J/K}$$

51. **The correct answer is (C).** The gas molecules have the same initial temperature: 300 K. But since the H_2 molecules are lighter, they will have a higher rms speed.

52. **The correct answer is (C).** We can use Boyle's Law for each gas, then find the total pressure by adding:

$$(P_{H2})_{final} = (P_{H2})_{initial}\,(V_{initial}/V_{final}) = (4.0 \text{ atm})(2.0 \text{ L}/(2.0 + 5.0)\text{L})$$

$$= 1.14 \text{ atm}$$

$$(P_{Ne})_{final} = (P_{Ne})_{initial}\,(V_{initial}/V_{final}) = (1.0 \text{ atm})(5.0 \text{ L}/(2.0 + 5.0)\text{L})$$

$$= 0.714 \text{ atm}$$

$$P_{total} = 1.142 \text{ atm} + 0.714 \text{ atm} = 1.856 \text{ atm} \approx 1.86 \text{ atm}$$

53. **The correct answer is (A).** Work is given by $w = -P_{ext}\Delta V$, where P_{ext} is the pressure against which the expanding Ne must push, and ΔV is the change in the volume of the Ne. But since the pressure in chamber C is zero, then P_{ext} is zero as well. (The fact that the pressure outside the apparatus is 1.00 atm is immaterial, since this pressure does not act on the Ne atoms as they expand.)

54. **The correct answer is (B).** The effusion rate for Ne atoms depends on the rms average speed of the atoms, not the volume into which they are expanding. But an increase in volume for chamber C will lower the final pressure, causing choice (A) to be incorrect. It will also lower the final number of moles of gas in chamber A, causing choice (C) to be incorrect. As for choice (D), the entropy of an expanding gas increases as the final volume is made to be larger, since the larger the volume, the greater the number of microstates available to the gas molecules.

55. **The correct answer is (C).** The average kinetic energy of one mole of a gas is given by 3/2RT, so the average kinetic energy of a sample containing *n* moles is given by 3/2*n*RT. In this problem, we can solve for the initial number of moles in chambers A and B before the valve is opened, then calculate the kinetic energy in each. Since T is constant, the kinetic energy will also remain constant.

For chamber A, $n = PV/RT = (4.00 \text{ atm})(2.0 \text{ L})/(0.08206 \text{ L atm/K mol})(300 \text{ K}) = 0.325 \text{ mol}$

For chamber B, $n = PV/RT = (1.00 \text{ atm})(5.0 \text{ L})/(0.08206 \text{ L atm/K mol})(300 \text{ K}) = 0.203 \text{ mol}$

$n_{total} = (0.325 \text{ mol} + 0.203 \text{ mol}) = 0.528 \text{ mol}$

K.E. $= 3/2(0.528 \text{ mol})(8.3145 \text{ J/K mol})(300 \text{ K})$

$= 1980 \text{ J}$

56. **The correct answer is (B).** Partial pressure is defined as

$$P_{H2} = X_{H2}P_{tot} = (n_{H2}/n_{tot})P_{tot}$$

We can calculate the moles of each gas using initial conditions, as in the previous problem, getting $n_{H2} = 0.325$ mol, $n_{Ne} = 0.203$ mol, and $n_{tot} = (0.325 \text{ mol} + 0.203 \text{ mol}) = 0.528$ mol.

$$P_{H2} = (0.325 \text{ mol}/0.528 \text{ mol})(0.0100 \text{ atm})$$

$$= 0.0062 \text{ atm}$$

57. **The correct answer is (C).** The splitting factors, Δ_O, lie in the reverse order of wavelength, since $E_{photon} = hc/\lambda$.

58. **The correct answer is (A).** Since CN⁻ is a stronger ligand than H_2O, the splitting factor increases as more CN⁻ ligands are added to the compound.

59. **The correct answer is (B).** Cl⁻ is a weak-field ligand, while NO_3^- is a high-field ligand. The passage points out that in the case of weak-field ligands, Δ_O is small, so promotion to a high-field complex is favorable. This is not the case for a strong-field ligand.

60. **The correct answer is (B).** Since there are four ligands, not six, the choices are between square planar and tetrahedral geometries. The passage points out that tetrahedral splittings tend to be lower than square planar ones, producing high-spin states for tetrahedral geometries and low-spin states for square planar geometries.

61. **The correct answer is (C).** Evidently Fe^{2+} undergoes octahedral coordination, i.e., coordination with six ligand sites. A bidentate ligand has two sites per molecule, so three such ligands will coordinate to one Fe^{2+} ion.

62. **The correct answer is (D).** Unlike the previous questions, this one requires an evaluation of arguments that lie outside the direct content of the passage. Choices (A), (B), and (C) do not address the paradox that a bidentate ligand should bind more strongly, despite involving the same number of metal/ligand bonds. The key is in the explanation provided in choice (D), that the entropy increases as water declines levee.

63. **The correct answer is (A).** CO is a strong-field ligand and would be expected to be difficult to dislodge from the iron atom in the heme group.

64. **The correct answer is (A).** The number of degrees of freedom, F, is found by setting P equal to 2, since both solid and liquid coexist at point B:

    $$F = 1 - 2 + 2 = 1$$

    With one degree of freedom, we can allow either the temperature or the pressure to vary, but the other will then be determined by the phase boundary line on the diagram.

65. **The correct answer is (C).** At point E (the "triple point"), three phases are in equilibrium, so P = 3:

    $$F = 1 - 3 + 2 = 0$$

    Because there are zero degrees of freedom, neither temperature nor pressure is free to vary.

66. **The correct answer is (D).** There is close agreement in the radii and electronegativity of Ni and Cu, they each crystallize in the fcc class, and each can have an ionic charge of +2. None of the other pairs show such close agreement.

67. **The correct answer is (C).** A value is required for the *x*-axis of Figure 2 such that the higher temperature lies above the liquidus and the lower temperature lies below the solidus.

68. **The correct answer is (B).** Since two phases are present, P = 2, and the phase rule predicts

    $$F = C - P + 1$$
    $$= 2 - 2 + 1 = 1$$

    Thus, once the temperature is specified, the composition of the phases is determined.

69. **The correct answer is (C).** That the solid contains a greater percentage of Ni than the liquid can be seen by noting that the intersection of the 1250°C tie line with the liquidus comes at a lower percentage of Ni than does the intersection of the 1250°C tie line with the solidus. There is an intuitive explanation for this result as well: pure Ni is higher-melting than pure Cu, as seen by the extremes of the solidus and liquidus. Therefore, as the solid solution begins to melt, the liquid formed is mostly Cu, since Cu has a lower melting point.

70. The correct answer is (B). The experiment tells us the mass of AgCl that had been dissolved in 1.00 L of water; let's convert this solubility from g/L to mol/L:

$$(1.92 \times 10^{-3} \text{ g/L})/(143.3 \text{ g/mol}) = 1.34 \times 10^{-5} \text{ mol/L}$$

When this quantity of AgCl was in solution, there were 1.34×10^{-5} mol/L of both Ag^+ and Cl^-.

To determine K_{sp}, we calculate

$$K_{sp} = [Ag^+][Cl^-] = (1.34 \times 10^{-5})^2 = 1.8 \times 10^{-10}$$

71. The correct answer is (C). This is the only choice to correctly show sulfuric acid dissociating as $H^+(aq) + HSO_4^-(aq)$.

72. The correct answer is (B). By acidifying some of the NH_3, we create a mixture of NH_3 and NH_4^+ which will have buffer properties. We calculate K_a for NH_4^+ using the relationship

$$K_a = K_w/K_b = (1 \times 10^{-14})/(1.8 \times 10^{-5})$$
$$= 5.56 \times 10^{-10}$$

Since $[H^+] = K_a [NH_4^+]/[NH_3]$, for a pH 9.0 solution we have

$$(1.00 \times 10^{-9}) = (5.56 \times 10^{-10})[NH_4^+]/[NH_3]$$
$$[NH_4^+]/[NH_3] = 1.80$$

This is a reasonable ratio to achieve. By contrast, a buffer solution made by adding NaOH to formic acid [Choice (C)] would require an impractically low ratio of HCH_2O_2 to $CH_2O_2^-$ that would not have buffer properties:

$$(1.00 \times 10^{-9}) = (1.8 \times 10^{-4})[HCH_2O_2]/[CH_2O_2^-]$$
$$[HCH_2O_2]/[CH_2O_2^-] = 5.6 \times 10^{-6}$$

73. The correct answer is (D). The reaction is unusual in that two states of O are found on the left—only O_2 is reduced—and in that the Au on the right exists as part of a "complex ion" in which Au^+ combines with two CN^- ions to form a charged, soluble complex.

74. The correct answer is (B). The ground state of Al is $1s^2 2s^2 2p^6 3s^2 3p^1$. The state that is described differs from the ground state by having one 1s electron raised to the valence 3p level. This is an "excited state" that will only exist for a short time. To be an "ionized state," the configuration would have to show the gain or loss of one or more of aluminum's 13 electrons.

75. The correct answer is (C). We use the following expression:

$$\Delta H = \Sigma \text{ (enthalpy of bonds broken)} - \Sigma \text{ (enthalpy of bonds formed)}$$
$$-890 \text{ kJ} = (4 \text{ mol})(414 \text{ kJ/mol}) + 2(498 \text{ kJ/mol}) - 2 D_{C=O} - (4 \text{ mol})(464 \text{ kJ/mol})$$
$$D_{C=O} = 799 \text{ kJ/mol}$$

76. The correct answer is (B). We write resonance structures for each compound and find that in ONO^+ the average ON bond is a double bond—in molecular orbital language, the bond order is 2. In contrast, in NO_2^- the average bond has a bond order of 1.5, and in NO_3^- the average bond order is 1.3. As the bond order decreases, the bond length increases.

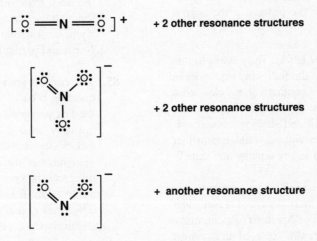

+ 2 other resonance structures

+ 2 other resonance structures

+ another resonance structure

77. The correct answer is (C). As the diagrams below illustrate, by inserting the number of valence electrons from the two original atoms, then correcting for the net charge, the bond order, calculated as b.o. = 1/2(# of bonding e's – # of antibonding e's) is 3.0 for N_2, 2.5 for C_2^-, and just 1.5 for CN^{2+}. As bond order decreases, bond length increases, so CN^{2+} has the greatest bond length.

N_2

σ^*_{2p}	_____
π^*_{2p}	_____ _____
σ_{2p}	⇅
π_{2p}	⇅ ⇅
σ^*_{2s}	⇅
σ_{2s}	⇅

C_2^-

σ^*_{2p}	_____
π^*_{2p}	_____ _____
σ_{2p}	↑
π_{2p}	⇅ ⇅
σ^*_{2s}	⇅
σ_{2s}	⇅

CN^{2+}

σ^*2p	_____
π^*2p	_____ _____
$\sigma2p$	_____
$\pi2p$	⇅ ↑
σ^*2s	⇅
$\sigma2s$	⇅

VERBAL REASONING

78. The correct answer is (B). The answer to this question is based on the following sentence in paragraph 2: "The big issue was not slavery but states' rights versus the powers of the central government."

79. The correct answer is (A). The answer to this question is based on the following sentences in paragraph 3: "Many southern states claimed a right to secede from the Union. They said the Constitution of the United States was not a binding document, but a voluntary agreement that could be terminated at any time by any state."

80. The correct answer is (B). The answer to this question is based on these sentences in paragraph 3: "With the election of Abraham Lincoln, many southern states felt the issue of the central government's power had come to a head. . . . [He] was against further expansion of slavery. For many slave states, the idea that slavery could not expand further and the ultimate end of slavery were synonymous."

81. The correct answer is (C). The answer to this question is based on these sentences in paragraph 3: "Lincoln . . . was against further expansion of slavery."

82. The correct answer is (D). The answer to this question is based on the following sentence and what it implies in paragraph 3: "Had these states also seceded, particularly Maryland and Delaware, which were industrial states, the course of the war might have been different."

83. The correct answer is (C). The answer to this question is based on this sentence in paragraph 5: "With the conclusion of the war and the victory of the North, for the first time the central government was clearly more powerful than the state governments. The question of secession from the United States would never be raised in a serious way again. From this point on, the power of the central government grew and the power of the state governments diminished."

84. The correct answer is (D). The answer to this question is based on the following statements in the last paragraph: "A second result of the Civil War was that the South developed after the war as a significantly poorer region of the country than either the North or the West. The South remained largely an agricultural economy for the next 100 years, which was heavily exploited by the North. This economic inequality was further enhanced by the fact that most of the destruction of the Civil War was done in those states that seceded. Even today there is a significant economic difference between the North and particularly the Deep South."

85. The correct answer is (B). The answer to this question is based on the following statement in the last paragraph: "Thus, the Baroque period not only created a wide variety of forms and techniques, it also was responsible for the development of the *opera*, the *oratorio*, the *cantata*, and the *concerto*." One could say that as an art form, Baroque music was an important development that eventually evolved into what is considered classical music.

86. The correct answer is (C). The answer to this question is based on the following statement in paragraph 1: "Baroque music was an expression of order—of the fundamental order of the universe."

87. The correct answer is (C). The answer to this question is based on the following statements in paragraph 3: "Prior to the development of Baroque music, religious music was played with whatever instrument was at hand. Instrumental music began appearing that allowed parts of the music to be played with specific instruments. Virtuoso instrumentalists were emerging playing the music that highlighted their technical abilities."

88. The correct answer is (A). The answer to this question is based on the following statement in paragraph 2: "In Portuguese, *perola barroca* were the words used by jewelers to describe a rough or irregularly shaped pear."

89. The correct answer is (C). The answer to this question is based on the following statement in paragraph 3: "Three major composers of Baroque music, also considered the pillars of Baroque music, were Antonio Vivaldi, Johann Sebastian Bach, and George Frideric Handel."

90. The correct answer is (B). The answer to this question is based on the following statement in the last paragraph: "One can say that as an art form, Baroque music was an important development that eventually evolved into what is considered classical music."

91. The correct answer is (B). The answer to this question is found through the process of elimination. Choice (A) is incorrect as Baroque music was created to be played by more than one instrumentalist. Choice (C) ignores the fact that Baroque music developed four forms: the *opera,* the *oratorio,* the *concerto,* and the *cantata.* Choice (D) is incorrect according to the following statement from paragraph 1: "Music during the Renaissance, roughly 1350–1600, was primarily religious. It gave way to a different style of music that reflected a period of time in Europe, from about 1600 to 1750, that was referred to as the Baroque music."

92. The correct answer is (B). The answer to this question is based on the statement in paragraph 2: "As to the possibility of life on Mars in the past, there is already some evidence of its existence. Meteorites presumed to have originated on Mars have been closely studied. Though no fossils have been found, organic molecules have been . . . " And the statement in paragraph 3:"The vast amounts of water might prove to be an ideal environment for the development of life and the thick layer of ice would provide protection from external sources of radiation and the severe cold."

93. The correct answer is (D). The answer to this question is based on the following statements in paragraph 1: " . . . five rockets have been sent to explore Mars. The United States has sent three and the European Union has sent two exploration vehicles. Some of these vehicles will orbit the planet, while others are landing robots on the surface of the planet to explore and take samples."

94. The correct answer is (C). There is no reference to this statement anywhere in the article. Choice (A) is stated in paragraph 2 in the following statement: "It is believed that more than a billion years ago, the planet was similar to Earth with an atmosphere high in oxygen and dense enough to produce rain, which in turn produced streams and rivers." Choice (B) is supported by this statement in paragraph 3: "While those who speculated about life in the past usually thought of humanoid life, it is clear that if there is life, it will most likely be of the one-cell variety." Choice (D) is stated in the following statements in paragraph 3: "Bacteria particularly have been shown to live and even thrive in extremely inhospitable and diverse environments on Earth and similar life forms may have adapted to the Martian environment."

95. The correct answer is (A). Statement I can be found in paragraph 3. Statement IV is supported by paragraph 3: "The vast amounts of water might prove to be an ideal environment for the development of life and the thick layer of ice would provide protection from external sources of radiation and the severe cold." Choice (B) is a false statement according to this sentence in paragraph 3: "The vast amounts of water might prove to be an ideal environment for the development of life and the thick layer of ice would provide protection from external sources of radiation and the severe cold." Choice (C) is incorrect because both statements are false, based on the following sentences in paragraph 3: "The vast amounts of water might prove to be an ideal environment for the development of life and the thick layer of ice would provide protection from external sources of radiation and the severe cold." Statement III is contradicted by the following sentence in paragraph 3: "If life does exist on Mars, it should show some similarities to life on Earth. Certainly it would be carbon based and some of the life processes would be similar." Choice (D) has two contradictions. However, statement III is false based on this statement in paragraph 3: "If life does exist on Mars, it should show some similarities to life on Earth. Certainly it would be carbon based and some of the life processes would be similar."

96. The correct answer is (C). The answer to this question is based on the following statements in paragraph 3: "While those who speculated about life in the past usually thought of humanoid life, it is clear that if there is life, it will most likely be of the one-cell variety. Bacteria particularly have been shown to live and even thrive in extremely inhospitable and diverse environments on Earth and similar life forms may have adapted to the Martian environment."

97. The correct answer is (B). The answer to this question is based on this statement in paragraph 3: "Because of the very thin atmosphere, severe cold, lack of sufficient oxygen and high levels of solar radiation, it is extremely unlikely that life would exist on the surface of the planet."

98. The correct answer is (A). The answer to this question is based on these statements in paragraph 4: "These exciting possibilities will open up in the next few years as new information comes in from the Mars missions" and "If there is or was life on Mars, the discovery that life is more flexible than once thought will open up the possibilities that life might also exist in many other places in the universe."

99. The correct answer is (D). Choices (A), (B), and (C) are referred to in the first paragraph: "For more than 60 years, inflation has been the number one danger to the economy. Prices have gone up slowly during some periods and more rapidly during others. People complained that their money could not buy much. The government tried several policies to control runaway inflation, including trying to slow the rate of economic growth, reducing government spending, reducing government debt, controlling wages and prices, and keeping interest rates high. Nobody considered deflation even a possibility much less a potential problem." Choice (D) is not stated as a choice in the passage.

100. The correct answer is (A). The answer to this question is based on the sentences in paragraph 4: "One reason that economists worry about runaway deflation is that the United States, though the largest economy in the world, is still part of a world market. Price competition and the need to sell not only comes from home but also from abroad, where wages are often much lower and productivity is much higher. Increasingly, companies must learn to produce at the lowest possible cost and sell at the lowest cost. Of course, the effect of this practice is like the one used in the 1930s. It pushes both prices and wages down, while trying to reduce the work force by increasing use of technology."

101. The correct answer is (B). The answer to this question is based on these sentences in paragraph 3: "The best example of current deflation is the electronics industry where consumers have learned not to buy products when they first come out, but to wait as they will inevitably come down in price. This awareness of the constant drop in prices and the unwillingness of consumers to rush and buy new products have caused significant profit losses, with some companies folding and others moving much of their operations to countries where wages are lower, in effect, reducing wages."

102. The correct answer is (B). The answer to this question is based on this sentence in paragraph 3: "In fact overall inflation at the retail level is running at two to three percent and at the wholesale level even less."

103. The correct answer is (C). The answer to this question is based on these sentences in paragraph 2: "However, few remember the last period of significant deflation which we now call the Great Depression. From 1929 to 1940 the government fought hard not to control inflation but to create it. Prices went down dramatically from 1929 to 1933 and the consequences were devastating."

104. The correct answer is (C). The answer to this question is based on the last paragraph: "No economist can tell what the future will bring or whether the real economic danger will be inflation or deflation, but for the first time in years the threat of deflation is being taken seriously by economists and by the federal government. This is one of the reasons why the federal government has allowed a huge federal deficit to develop and has chosen the inflationary policy of keeping the price of borrowing money cheap rather than the deflationary policy of making the cost of borrowing expensive."

105. The correct answer is (C). The answer to this question is based on these sentences in paragraph 1: "An amazing discovery has been made in the last quarter of a century. Life can exist without the need to breathe oxygen or to use the Sun as a source of energy. The main energy source in this newly discovered environment seems to be sulfur compounds, particularly hydrogen sulfide produced by microbes. These microbes appear to play the same role as plants do in other ecological systems. A group of microbes called hyperthermophiles breathe iron instead of oxygen and live in an environment that one would assume life could not survive in. These microbes have been shown to live at temperatures of more than 112 degrees centigrade, well above the boiling point of water. The idea that microbes can live at such high temperatures and breathe iron opens up a world of possibilities."

106. The correct answer is (A). The answer to this question is based on the following sentences in paragraph 1: "An amazing discovery has been made in the last quarter of a century. Life can exist without the need to breathe oxygen or to use the Sun as a source of energy. The main energy source in this newly discovered environment seems to be sulfur compounds, particularly hydrogen sulfide produced by microbes. These microbes appear to play the same role as plants do in other ecological systems. A group of microbes called hyperthermophiles breathe iron instead of oxygen and live in an environment that one would assume life could not survive in. These microbes have been shown to live at temperatures of more than 112 degrees centigrade, well above the boiling point of water. The idea that microbes can live at such high temperatures and breathe iron opens up a world of possibilities. First, the fact of life in this environment expands our concept of suitable environments for the development of life and increases the likelihood that satellites such as Europa and planets such as Mars could contain life as well as planets in other solar systems and galaxies."

107. The correct answer is (D). The answer to this question is based on these sentences in paragraph 1: "While these extraterrestrial bodies lack enough atmospheric oxygen to support oxygen-breathing organisms above ground, we believe they may have water below ground and we know that many of these planets and satellites have volcanic activity. These would be the two ingredients that would create a suitable environment for life to develop."

108. The correct answer is (A). The answer to this question is based on these sentences in paragraph 4: "Of further interest is that in this environment a number of species long thought to be extinct have in fact thrived. New species are being discovered all the time and these species range from giant clams to six-foot tube worms."

109. The correct answer is (D). The answer to this question is based on these sentences in paragraph 4: "A final area that has exciting potential is the possibilities of commercial uses for these microbes. . . . One of the first things that comes to mind is the pharmaceutical potential. How many new cures for currently incurable diseases lie at these depths? Research is only just beginning on this exciting front. Also there are likely industrial uses for hyperthermophiles. Researchers have already begun to look at possible applications that might make certain processes, which are currently not economical to develop, become profitable.

Hyperthermophiles might also be useful in breaking down industrial pollutants to substances that are not dangerous for the environment."

110. The correct answer is (C). The answer to this question is found in paragraph 1, based on these sentences: "A group of microbes called hyperthermophiles breathe iron instead of oxygen and live in an environment that one would assume life could not survive in. These microbes have been shown to live at temperatures of more than 112 degrees centigrade, well above the boiling point of water."

111. The correct answer is (D). The answer to this question is based on the following sentences in paragraph 2: "Two countries emerged from the rubble of war as superpowers, the United States and the Soviet Union. In some ways the United States and the Soviet Union were bound to clash. The friction began almost immediately after the war ended over the fate of the eastern European countries."

112. The correct answer is (B). The answer to this question is based on this sentence in paragraph 3: "The fear was that a hot war might break out, but as with much of the Cold War a compromise saved the situation from getting out of hand."

113. The correct answer is (D). The answer to this question is based on the sentences in paragraphs 6, 7, and 8. Paragraph 6 points out that both sides were involved in an economic race such as in the space program for both countries in the following sentences: "In addition to the arms race that the Cold War precipitated, it also precipitated an economic race in other areas, from consumer goods to space travel. If one side took the lead in an area, the other side was quick to respond. When the Soviets sent the first satellite into space in 1958, the United States responded with a massive space program that eventually led to the first human exploration of the Moon." Paragraph 7 has sentences implying that the U.S.S.R. was unable to provide economic stability, therefore causing its eventual collapse: "What finally brought the Cold War to an end and led to the breakup of the Soviet Union was a massive military buildup by the United States in the 1980s. The Soviets could keep up, but only by sacrificing consumer products. This drastic action in turn created significant unhappiness among the Soviet population. First, the Eastern European countries became restive and then populations inside the Soviet Union became increasingly dissatisfied. A second factor that played into the hands of the United States was that the Soviet Union became involved in a civil war in Afghanistan that proved both economically and politically costly. Finally, in 1990 the Soviet Union collapsed with Eastern Europe gaining its independence and eventually many areas of the former Soviet Union also gained independence. Finally, the Communist party lost control." In paragraph 8 the following sentence further reinforced the point that the U.S. economy ultimately was victorious over the U.S.S.R. in the Cold War: " If lessons are to be learned from the Cold War, clearly one is that economic might ultimately proved key to victory."

114. **The correct answer is (B).** The answer to this question is based on the following sentences in paragraph 3: "The fear was that a hot war might break out, but as with much of the Cold War a compromise saved the situation from getting out of hand. While the world lived on the edge of nuclear war throughout the Cold War, what was referred to as a balance of terror was kept and usually at the last minute compromises were worked out between the two sides. This balance of terror was based on an enormous arms race that cost both economies of the East and West much of their productivity. Unless the balance of terror was kept equal, it was feared that war would break out. Both sides feared the other's intent."

115. **The correct answer is (D).** The answer to this question is in paragraph 4 based on the following sentences: "While direct confrontations were infrequent, indirect confrontations were common. The beginning was the loss of China to the Communists in 1949 and continued with the Korean War in 1950. In the Korean War the United States and some of its allies sent troops to defend South Korea, but the Soviets only sent weapons through the Chinese. Afraid their own border was threatened by the U.S. presence, North Korea sent troops across the border and in part fought a proxy war for the Soviet Union. Ultimately the first major conflict that clearly pit the troops of one side against the weapons of the other ended in a draw. The next major arena was Vietnam which was a colony of France. At first the French were involved in the

war to keep their colonial empire. However, despite increased involvement from the United States, the French lost the war to a communist insurgency. After the French were defeated, the United States and some of its allies first sent aid to the government of South Vietnam to help it fight a new communist insurgency in the south."

116. **The correct answer is (C).** The answer to this question is based on these sentences in paragraph 7: "What finally brought the Cold War to an end and led to the breakup of the Soviet Union was a massive military buildup by the United States in the 1980s. The Soviets could keep up, but only by sacrificing consumer products. This drastic action in turn created significant unhappiness among the Soviet population. First, the Eastern European countries became restive and then populations inside the Soviet Union became increasingly dissatisfied."

117. **The correct answer is (A).** The answer to this question is based on the following sentences in the last paragraph: "If lessons are to be learned from the Cold War, clearly one is that economic might ultimately proved key to victory. Another lesson that has become clear only after the end of the Cold War, is that with rare exceptions both sides believed they could not afford to use their ultimate weapons and therefore, hot war between the two power giants was not an option. The third lesson that can be learned from the cold war was that it was enormously costly both in lives and to the economies of both countries, creating huge national deficits. The final effect of the Cold War is that a generation of people lived under constant threat of nuclear annihilation. Living with the possibility of nuclear annihilation affected this generation in ways that we as yet don't fully know."

118. **The correct answer is (B)** The answer to this question is based on the statement in paragraph 1: "Two thousand years ago the ancient Athenians created drama, or western theater as it has become known."

119. **The correct answer is (A).** The answer to this question is based on this statement in paragraph 4: "It seems probable that fertility rituals and celebrations are at the origins of comedy."

120. **The correct answer is (C).** The answer to this question is based on this statement in paragraph

2: "During the cult's ritual celebrations, members would celebrate by getting intoxicated, participating in orgies, sacrificing humans and animals, and experiencing hysterical rampages by women known as *maenads*."

121. The correct answer is (D). The answer to this question is based on these statements in paragraph 2: "A particular controversial custom that the cult also practiced involved uninhibited dancing and emotional displays that created an altered state known as *ecstasis* from which the word *ecstasy* is derived. Among the Greeks *ecstasy* was an important concept as it provided within drama in the theater a way of releasing powerful emotions."

122. The correct answer is (B). The answer to this question is based on the following statements in paragraph 3: "Thus, the festival of Dionysus offered an opportunity for Athenians to release pent-up feelings. Since the festival meant all business activities ceased, Athenians would throw themselves into drinking, feasting, and carousing."

123. The correct answer is (C). The answer to this question is based on this statement in paragraph 3: "If tragedy, according to the philosopher Aristotle, provided a release for the emotions of pity and terror, theatergoers would feel pity for the unfortunate protagonist and would fear that they might also undergo a disaster allowing themselves to be purged of these emotions."

124. The correct answer is (A). The answer to this question is based on these statements in paragraph 4: "His comedies used many of the old ritual features of the *komos*: the big phalluses, padding, animal costumes, grotesque masks, and obscene jokes." "Approximately a hundred years later, 'new comedy' had evolved that resembled today's modern farces where ordinary people were involved through the use of mistaken identities, ironic situations, and wit."

125. The correct answer is (D). When symptoms are discussed in the first paragraph, violent behavior is not mentioned.

126. The correct answer is (D). Intelligence is not referred to throughout the passage.

127. The correct answer is (B). The answer to this question is based on the following sentences in paragraph 1: "These symptoms can be associated with numerous other conditions. There is as yet no clearly defined cause for ADHD and diagnosis is symptomatic."

128. The correct answer is (C). The answer to this question is based on the following sentences in paragraph 3: "The use of stimulants for treatment of ADHD, particularly among children, has been heavily debated. There are potential serious side effects that must be weighed into any decision to use these medications and the medications should be closely monitored." Choices (A), (B), and (D) are not accurate statements.

129. The correct answer is (D). It is the only sentence that is incorrect in paragraph 2 if one looks at the following: "Still other scientists have believed that the cause might be found in minor injuries to the brain." Choices (A), (B), and (C) are stated in the paragraph.

130. The correct answer is (A). The answer to this question is based on the following sentences in paragraph 4: "The most important thing for an adult with this disease is to learn how to compensate for the disease. This means changing behavior in a way that takes the disease into account. The first step is to recognize that much of one's behavior that has caused frustration in the past can be modified by learning to view tasks and activities differently. This approach in turn can lead to a more positive attitude that can improve functioning and possibly reduce depression associated with the disease."

131. The correct answer is (B). According to sentences in the last paragraph: "In the future it is likely that better diagnostic techniques will be developed and that better treatments for both children and adults will be created. Improved diagnostic tools will lead to more rapid treatment, and improved medications will help to make the treatment more successful. In the more distant future as a better understanding of the disease is developed, creating techniques for prevention and/or cures involving genetic manipulation is possible."

132. The correct answer is (D). The answer to this question is based on the following statements in paragraph 1: "He is seen as Loki, the wolf, in northern Europe and Kitsune the fox in Japan. In west Africa the trickster is the cunning spider, Anansi, who is also found in tales throughout the Caribbean due to the transportation of slaves from West Africa to various islands. The trickster, who can also be a divine fool or sacred clown, is a powerful creature in the legends of most Native American tribes. He takes on various shapes, such as the raven, crow, blue jay, and the coyote. In the American south, various animals such as the rabbit, fox, bear, wolf, turtle, and possum are the more popular trickster figures used in oral folktales. Brer or Bruh Rabbit is a favorite of African-American storytellers."

133. **The correct answer is (A).** The answer to this question is based on the following statements in paragraph 5: "The trickster figure of the rabbit, known as Brer, Buh Bruh Rabbit, became a particular favorite of the slave storytellers. Although Rabbit was small and seemingly helpless compared to the powerful bear, the wily fox, and the ferocious wolf, he was made smart, clever, and shrewd as told by the slave storyteller." Choice (A) is the opposite of the above statements.

134. **The correct answer is (D).** You can answer this by the process of elimination. Choices (A), (B), and (C) are referred to throughout the passage as sources in learning about the trickster figure. For example, paragraph 1 has the statements "Much folklore around the world has a traditional trickster figure who is the primary character in folk stories" and "The trickster tales for many people in different cultures are entertaining and amusing. Stories of a smaller and often weaker trickster who is able to outwit a larger and more powerful enemy are common in folk literature." Also are the statements ". . . in the legends of most Native American tribes . . . He takes on various shapes, such as the raven, crow, blue jay, and the coyote" and "In West Africa the trickster is the cunning spider, Anansi, who is also found in tales throughout the Caribbean due to the transportation of slaves from West Africa to various islands. In the American south, various animals such as the rabbit, fox, bear, wolf, turtle, and possum are the more popular trickster figures used in oral folktales." There is no reference in the article to poetry as a source in telling about the trickster figure.

135. **The correct answer is (B).** It is a contradiction of what has been stressed about the characteristics of the trickster figure. The following statements in paragraph 1 point out that: "In all folk stories, the trickster survives by his wits but he does more than stay alive. The word itself refers to his forever playing tricks on larger, stronger animals around him that gets the trickster out of trouble." In paragraph 2 is the statement: "In West African folktales the major trickster figure is Anansi, the spider trickster . . . (who) always provides a lesson to learn through his stories." In paragraph 4 it is stated that "In some North American traditions the trickster figure has been called Coyote, Coyote Man, and Old Man Coyote. A few stories depict Coyote as pretending to be the Creator, who fashions mankind out of mud and creates animals such as the buffalo, elk, deer, antelope, and bear."

136. **The correct answer is (B).** If one reads the story carefully, this choice seems to be the most logical answer in contrast to Choices (A), (C), and (D).

137. **The correct answer is (A).** You can answer this by process of elimination. Throughout the passage is the emphasis that the trickster figure in cultural folklore was admired rather than feared. In the last paragraph are these statements that reinforce that point: "Clearly, the trickster figure assumes different forms in many cultures and remains a primary character in folklore literature. His attributes often emphasize the paradox in his character: He can be a sacred creator, making mankind and animals; he can be a clown in which he makes his audience laugh at his foolishness or greediness; or he can be an animal with heroic characteristics of cleverness and wit. As a trickster figure, he is a reflection for his audiences of their own cultural foibles and nuances."

BIOLOGICAL SCIENCES

138. The correct answer is (D). If the recombinant cells can grow on minimal medium, they must be able to synthesize all six nutrients. They must be wild-type (+) at each locus.

139. The correct answer is (C). The pilus or sex pilus is the structure that allows the transfer of DNA between bacterial cells during conjugation. Peptidoglycans are molecules found in bacterial cell walls, while protein coats are viral structures.

140. The correct answer is (B). Choices (A), (C), and (D) would all suggest that genetic change took place in the control setups while strains were grown separately.

141. The correct answer is (D). The data suggest that gene Y entered the recipient cells first (8 min.), followed by gene Z (18 min.) and gene X (38 min.).

142. The correct answer is (C). Loci for genes Z and Y are "10 minutes apart" (18-8); loci for genes X and Y are "30 minutes apart" (38-18); and loci for genes X and Z are "20 minutes apart."

143. The correct answer is (C). Transformation takes place when exogenous genetic material from one bacterial cell is assimilated into another bacterial cell. Transduction involves a bacterial cell picking up new genetic material from a bacteriophage (virus) that had previously infected another bacterial cell. Transitions and transversions are two types of substitution point mutations.

144. The correct answer is (D). Transduction involves a bacteriophage.

145. The correct answer is (D). Insulin is regulated by a negative feedback system based on blood glucose levels. Neither the anterior pituitary gland nor the hypothalamic releasing hormones directly affect insulin release by the pancreas.

146. The correct answer is (A). Directly after a meal during the absorptive state, blood glucose levels are usually highest. Choices (B) and (C) would be associated with the release of glucagon and the need to increase blood glucose levels.

147. The correct answer is (D). Cortisol, growth hormone, and epinephrine all help raise glucose levels when needed.

148. The correct answer is (C). Gluconeogenesis includes the utilization of glycerol and fatty acids from fats as well as the utilization of amino acids for ATP production. Glycogenolysis breaks glycogen down to glucose, not into alternative molecules.

149. The correct answer is (B). During stress or emergency situations, the sympathetic nervous system stimulates many "fight-or-flight" responses, including the release of epinephrine and norepinephrine from the adrenal medulla into the blood. These hormones then help fulfill the energy requirements of cells via glycogenolysis and gluconeogenesis.

150. The correct answer is (A). The amino group must be removed (deamination) from amino acids before they can be used for cellular respiration. Some amino acids can then be converted to pyruvic acid, some to acetyl-CoA, and others to Krebs cycle intermediates.

151. The correct answer is (B). The entire process of converting fatty acids to ketones in the liver so that these molecules can be delivered to cells for the production of acetyl-CoA is called beta oxidation.

152. The correct answer is (B). In chain reactions there must be one or more chain-propagating steps in which a reactive species is consumed and another is generated so that new reactions will follow.

153. The correct answer is (B). All chain reactions have the three fundamental series of steps.

154. The correct answer is (B). The chain-initiating step involving the homolytic breaking of the Cl_2 bond is highly endothermic (DH = +58 kcal/mol) and therefore occurs significantly only at elevated temperatures.

155. The correct answer is (B). Any substance that slows down or stops a reaction is called an inhibitor. It may be present in small amounts, and after it is consumed the reaction proceeds normally.

156. The correct answer is (A). Oxygen is thought to react with the methyl radical:

$$CH_3 + O_2 \rightarrow CH_3\text{-O-O}$$

CH_3OO is markedly less reactive than CH_3 and therefore drastically slows down the chain reaction.

157. The correct answer is (A). More energy is released when HCl is formed than HBr. The HCl bond is stronger.

158. The correct answer is (D). The anticodon on the tRNA molecule responsible for bringing the third amino acid during translation must be complementary to the third mRNA codon transcribed from the original DNA. The third "triplet" along the DNA is GAT. This will be transcribed as the mRNA codon CUA. Therefore, the anticodon must be GAU.

159. The correct answer is (B). The inflow of sodium ions causes the inside of the membrane to become positive during depolarization. The outflow of potassium ions at the onset of repolarization returns the resting potential to the membrane (positive outside, negative inside). The sodium-potassium ATP pump then returns the proper ion concentrations to both sides of the membrane.

160. The correct answer is (A).

161. The correct answer is (C). Lichens are organisms that are the result of symbiotic relationships between fungi and photosynthetic algae. The root nodules of legumes contain nitrogen-fixing bacteria. The term *endosymbiosis* relates to the prokaryotic origin of mitochondria and chloroplasts before they became eukaryotic organelles.

162. The correct answer is (D). Iron is a vital part of the heme portion of hemoglobin, as well as the cytochromes of the electron transport chain. Although the former function is relevant only in developing RBCs, the latter function is relevant to all cells.

163. The correct answer is (D). Baroreceptors are blood pressure detectors, nociceptors are for pain, and visceroreceptors are generally associated with the internal organs.

164. The correct answer is (D). The ampullae are found at the bases of each semicircular canal in the inner ear. These structures are of primary importance in dynamic and rotational equilibrium. The vomiting center, like other centers for basic life functions (cardiac, vasomotor, respiratory, swallowing, etc.) is in the medulla oblongata.

165. The correct answer is (A). The thalamus is the main sensory relay center for signals reaching the cerebrum. It is also part of the balance pathway that includes connections between the cerebrum and cerebellum.

166. The correct answer is (B). The saccule and utricle in the vestibule of the inner ear contain the otoconia that respond to gravity and head position for the maintenance of static equilibrium.

167. The correct answer is (C). Cranial nerves III, IV, and VI control the six extrinsic eye muscles. The optic nerve (II) is primarily a sensory nerve carrying visual signals.

168. The correct answer is (D). Cochlear receptors send signals concerned with hearing to the cerebrum (not the cerebellum).

169. The correct answer is (B). The vestibulospinal and spinocerebellar tracts are descending and ascending spinal tracts of white matter, respectively.

170. The correct answer is (D). Touch receptors detect changes due to mechanical forces exerted on the skin, and, together with their sensory neurons, are components of the somatic nervous system. Eccrine glands, arrector pili muscles (smooth muscles), and the smooth muscles in the walls of dermal blood vessels are all involuntary effectors innervated by motor neurons of the autonomic nervous system.

171. The correct answer is (B). Sebaceous glands release the oily secretion, sebum, into hair follicles, which helps prevent hair and the surface of the epidermis from drying out. Eccrine glands (through their release of sweat), dermal blood vessels (through vasodilation when body temperature is too high and vasoconstriction when body temperature is too low), and the hypodermis (through the insulating properties of adipose tissue) all directly contribute to thermoregulation.

172. **The correct answer is (D).** The stratum basale (stratum germinativum) rests on the non-living basement membrane separating the epidermis from the dermis. It is here that mitosis takes place to produce new cells, while older cells are pushed closer to the surface. Although some mitotic activity takes place in the stratum spinosum, [choice (C)], most occurs in the stratum basale.

173. **The correct answer is (C).** The stratum basale is also the site of melanocytes, the melanin-producing cells in which melanoma arises. The dark appearance of the stratum granulosum, [choice (B)] is due to an accumulation of the protein keratin which helps "waterproof" the skin.

174. **The correct answer is (A).** The secretory activities of both sebaceous glands and apocrine glands are influenced by sex hormones. Excessive sebaceous secretions starting at puberty can lead to blocked sebaceous ducts, subsequent bacterial infections, and the associated symptoms of acne. Apocrine glands, found primarily in the axillary and pubic regions, begin secreting odorous sweat at puberty (it may serve as a sex attractant!).

175. **The correct answer is (B).** Blood vessels and all components of the cardiovascular system arise from mesoderm.

176. **The correct answer is (C).** A ligand is defined as a molecule that binds to a receptor.

177. **The correct answer is (D).** The signal molecules that bind to receptors are considered "first messengers," while those molecules that relay the signal to the interior of the cell are "second messengers."

178. **The correct answer is (B).** Phospholipase C breaks a bond within the membrane phospholipid PIP_2 to form inositol triphosphate (IP_3), one of the system's cytoplasmic second messengers. Competitive inhibition is not an issue in this system.

179. **The correct answer is (C).** The replacement of GTP by GDP causes the deactivation of the G protein and its separation from phospholipase C. When the G protein dissociates from the enzyme, the enzyme itself becomes inactive again.

180. **The correct answer is (C).** Testosterone can have an intracellular receptor because it is a lipid-soluble steroid (lipid) that can freely pass through the membrane's phospholipid bilayer.

181. **The correct answer is (B).** Calcium binds to troponin, causing the troponin-tropomyosin complex to shift so that actin and myosin can interact during muscle contraction. Calcium also plays a role in both the release of neurotransmitters from synaptic vesicles and in the activation of plasma proteins needed for coagulation.

182. **The correct answer is (C).** It is difficult to break the alkyl-O bond in carboxylates because the anion is strongly basic, while the bond cleaves readily in sulfonates because the anion is weakly basic.

183. **The correct answer is (A).** P forms stable pentacovalent compounds because it can expand its octet.

184. **The correct answer is (B).** Monoalkyl and dialkyl phosphate esters do not undergo basic hydrolysis because they contain acidic –OH groups. These groups in basic solution form anions that repel ⁻OH.

185. **The correct answer is (C).** See explanation for Question 184.

186. **The correct answer is (D).** Because acidic phosphate acids ionize, all of these are possible.

187. **The correct answer is (C).** Acid hydrolysis of an ester produces the parent acid and alcohol.

188. **The correct answer is (D).** These are just two of many vital functions carried out by the liver.

189. **The correct answer is (B).** Nitrogen is a component of the nitrogenous bases in DNA and RNA nucleotides as well as the amino acids in proteins. However, phosphorus is only a component of the phosphate groups in DNA and RNA nucleotides. It is not usually found in proteins.

190. The correct answer is (D).

191. The correct answer is (B). Pre-zygotic reproductive isolation mechanisms prevent mating and/or the successful formation of a viable zygote. Mechanical isolation refers to the anatomical incompatibility of mating structures.

192. The correct answer is (A). Calcitonin causes a decrease in blood calcium. This is accomplished, in part, by the increased activity of osteoblasts, cells that remove calcium from the blood for new bone tissue formation. Calcitonin also reduces the activity of osteoclasts, cells that increase the movement of calcium from bones to blood.

193. The correct answer is (D). Since Culture 1 is reverted to leu$^+$ by proflavin, the original mutation must have been either an addition or a deletion.

194. The correct answer is (B). Culture 3 is reverted by EMS, which causes transitions. Confirming this possibility is the fact that UV also reverted Culture 3, while proflavin did not.

195. The correct answer is (C). The fact that Culture 2 is reverted by UV radiation suggests that the original mutation could be any substitution. However, since EMS *did not* revert the mutation, Culture 2 must originally have had the transversion type of substitution.

196. The correct answer is (D). Because Culture 4 was *not reverted* by any of the three mutagens, it *could not* have contained a single-base substitution, and it *could not* have contained an addition or a deletion of a base pair.

197. The correct answer is (B). In its most stable conformation, 5-bromouracil binds to the purine adenine. In its alternate conformation, it combines with guanine. Such purine-purine substitutions (as well as pyrimidine-pyrimidine substitutions) are transitions.

198. The correct answer is (C). During the cephalic phase, perception associated with the sight, smell, and taste of food takes place in the cerebral cortex. The hunger/satiety centers are in the hypothalamus, and signals along the vagus nerve leave the brain from the medulla.

199. The correct answer is (A). Carbonic anhydrase and the exchange of bicarbonate and chloride ions are integral parts of the "chloride shift" that occurs during carbon dioxide transport.

200. The correct answer is (C). To reduce distension of the intestinal wall, as well as the amount of fats and other food molecules in the acidic chyme arriving from the stomach, secretions from the pancreas, liver, and gallbladder are all needed. Sodium bicarbonate from the pancreas neutralizes the acidic chyme and establishes the correct pH for pancreatic and intestinal digestive enzymes. Bile from the liver and gallbladder helps emulsify fats in preparation for their subsequent digestion.

201. The correct answer is (A). As stated in Question 199, the vagus nerve, gastrin, and intestinal gastrin stimulate gastric activity. This leads to the further processing of food and subsequent release into the small intestine.

202. The correct answer is (C). Hormones, by definition, are endocrine secretions that travel in the blood. Blood from the small intestine (superior mesenteric vein) travels to the liver via the hepatic portal vein, and then to the heart via the hepatic vein and inferior vena cava. Only then does the heart pump this blood throughout the body (first to the lungs via pulmonary circulation, and then to all areas via aorta and systemic circulation).

203. The correct answer is (D). The sympathetic nervous system slows down digestive activity with norepinephrine. When the "emergency" is over, the parasympathetic system (vagus nerve) will speed up digestive activity back to normal with acetylcholine.

204. The correct answer is (A). The nucleophilic carbon adds to the carbonyl carbon.

205. The correct answer is (B). The nucleophilic carbon of the Grignard reagent adds to the doubly bonded carbon as in aldehydes and ketones leading to the –OH group. The presence of the other –C=O group, however, gives the carboxylic acid.

206. **The correct answer is (A).** Grignard reagents will not even form in the presence of water due to the fact that water is a stronger acid than the alkane. Water will thus displace the alkane from its salt.

207. **The correct answer is (A).** A Gignard reagent cannot be prepared from a molecule that in addition to a halide contains a group like –OH or –COOH with which it will react. In general, any group that has a hydrogen bonded to an O or N will react with a Grignard reagent to form the corresponding alkane.

208. **The correct answer is (A).** See the explanation to Question 207.

209. **The correct answer is (D).** The nucleophilic carbon of the Grignard reagent attaches to the electron-deficient carbonyl carbon ejecting the alkoxide group. The resulting ketone, however, reacts with another Grignard reactant to form a tertiary alcohol.

210. **The correct answer is (A).** When an allele at a single locus influences many aspects of an individual's phenotype, it is described as having pleiotropic effects.

211. **The correct answer is (D).** Both sympathetic and parasympathetic motor neurons form neuromuscular junctions at the SA node (the heart's pacemaker) in the right atrium.

212. **The correct answer is (C).** Hardy-Weinberg equilibrium conditions include no mutations, no migration, no selection, large populations, and random mating.

213. **The correct answer is (B).** The most substituted alkene is favored in elimination reactions.

214. **The correct answer is (D).** The final electron acceptor in aerobic respiration is oxygen (inorganic), resulting in the formation of water. The final electron acceptor in anaerobic respiration is pyruvic acid (organic), resulting in the formation of lactic acid.

PRACTICE EXAM II

	Time
Physical Sciences Questions 1–77	100 minutes
Verbal Reasoning Questions 78–137	85 minutes
Writing Sample 2 Essays	60 minutes
Biological Sciences Questions 138–214	100 minutes

ANSWER SHEET
PRACTICE EXAM II

Physical Sciences		Verbal Reasoning		Biological Sciences	
1. Ⓐ Ⓑ Ⓒ Ⓓ	40. Ⓐ Ⓑ Ⓒ Ⓓ	78. Ⓐ Ⓑ Ⓒ Ⓓ	108. Ⓐ Ⓑ Ⓒ Ⓓ	138. Ⓐ Ⓑ Ⓒ Ⓓ	177. Ⓐ Ⓑ Ⓒ Ⓓ
2. Ⓐ Ⓑ Ⓒ Ⓓ	41. Ⓐ Ⓑ Ⓒ Ⓓ	79. Ⓐ Ⓑ Ⓒ Ⓓ	109. Ⓐ Ⓑ Ⓒ Ⓓ	139. Ⓐ Ⓑ Ⓒ Ⓓ	178. Ⓐ Ⓑ Ⓒ Ⓓ
3. Ⓐ Ⓑ Ⓒ Ⓓ	42. Ⓐ Ⓑ Ⓒ Ⓓ	80. Ⓐ Ⓑ Ⓒ Ⓓ	110. Ⓐ Ⓑ Ⓒ Ⓓ	140. Ⓐ Ⓑ Ⓒ Ⓓ	179. Ⓐ Ⓑ Ⓒ Ⓓ
4. Ⓐ Ⓑ Ⓒ Ⓓ	43. Ⓐ Ⓑ Ⓒ Ⓓ	81. Ⓐ Ⓑ Ⓒ Ⓓ	111. Ⓐ Ⓑ Ⓒ Ⓓ	141. Ⓐ Ⓑ Ⓒ Ⓓ	180. Ⓐ Ⓑ Ⓒ Ⓓ
5. Ⓐ Ⓑ Ⓒ Ⓓ	44. Ⓐ Ⓑ Ⓒ Ⓓ	82. Ⓐ Ⓑ Ⓒ Ⓓ	112. Ⓐ Ⓑ Ⓒ Ⓓ	142. Ⓐ Ⓑ Ⓒ Ⓓ	181. Ⓐ Ⓑ Ⓒ Ⓓ
6. Ⓐ Ⓑ Ⓒ Ⓓ	45. Ⓐ Ⓑ Ⓒ Ⓓ	83. Ⓐ Ⓑ Ⓒ Ⓓ	113. Ⓐ Ⓑ Ⓒ Ⓓ	143. Ⓐ Ⓑ Ⓒ Ⓓ	182. Ⓐ Ⓑ Ⓒ Ⓓ
7. Ⓐ Ⓑ Ⓒ Ⓓ	46. Ⓐ Ⓑ Ⓒ Ⓓ	84. Ⓐ Ⓑ Ⓒ Ⓓ	114. Ⓐ Ⓑ Ⓒ Ⓓ	144. Ⓐ Ⓑ Ⓒ Ⓓ	183. Ⓐ Ⓑ Ⓒ Ⓓ
8. Ⓐ Ⓑ Ⓒ Ⓓ	47. Ⓐ Ⓑ Ⓒ Ⓓ	85. Ⓐ Ⓑ Ⓒ Ⓓ	115. Ⓐ Ⓑ Ⓒ Ⓓ	145. Ⓐ Ⓑ Ⓒ Ⓓ	184. Ⓐ Ⓑ Ⓒ Ⓓ
9. Ⓐ Ⓑ Ⓒ Ⓓ	48. Ⓐ Ⓑ Ⓒ Ⓓ	86. Ⓐ Ⓑ Ⓒ Ⓓ	116. Ⓐ Ⓑ Ⓒ Ⓓ	146. Ⓐ Ⓑ Ⓒ Ⓓ	185. Ⓐ Ⓑ Ⓒ Ⓓ
10. Ⓐ Ⓑ Ⓒ Ⓓ	49. Ⓐ Ⓑ Ⓒ Ⓓ	87. Ⓐ Ⓑ Ⓒ Ⓓ	117. Ⓐ Ⓑ Ⓒ Ⓓ	147. Ⓐ Ⓑ Ⓒ Ⓓ	186. Ⓐ Ⓑ Ⓒ Ⓓ
11. Ⓐ Ⓑ Ⓒ Ⓓ	50. Ⓐ Ⓑ Ⓒ Ⓓ	88. Ⓐ Ⓑ Ⓒ Ⓓ	118. Ⓐ Ⓑ Ⓒ Ⓓ	148. Ⓐ Ⓑ Ⓒ Ⓓ	187. Ⓐ Ⓑ Ⓒ Ⓓ
12. Ⓐ Ⓑ Ⓒ Ⓓ	51. Ⓐ Ⓑ Ⓒ Ⓓ	89. Ⓐ Ⓑ Ⓒ Ⓓ	119. Ⓐ Ⓑ Ⓒ Ⓓ	149. Ⓐ Ⓑ Ⓒ Ⓓ	188. Ⓐ Ⓑ Ⓒ Ⓓ
13. Ⓐ Ⓑ Ⓒ Ⓓ	52. Ⓐ Ⓑ Ⓒ Ⓓ	90. Ⓐ Ⓑ Ⓒ Ⓓ	120. Ⓐ Ⓑ Ⓒ Ⓓ	150. Ⓐ Ⓑ Ⓒ Ⓓ	189. Ⓐ Ⓑ Ⓒ Ⓓ
14. Ⓐ Ⓑ Ⓒ Ⓓ	53. Ⓐ Ⓑ Ⓒ Ⓓ	91. Ⓐ Ⓑ Ⓒ Ⓓ	121. Ⓐ Ⓑ Ⓒ Ⓓ	151. Ⓐ Ⓑ Ⓒ Ⓓ	190. Ⓐ Ⓑ Ⓒ Ⓓ
15. Ⓐ Ⓑ Ⓒ Ⓓ	54. Ⓐ Ⓑ Ⓒ Ⓓ	92. Ⓐ Ⓑ Ⓒ Ⓓ	122. Ⓐ Ⓑ Ⓒ Ⓓ	152. Ⓐ Ⓑ Ⓒ Ⓓ	191. Ⓐ Ⓑ Ⓒ Ⓓ
16. Ⓐ Ⓑ Ⓒ Ⓓ	55. Ⓐ Ⓑ Ⓒ Ⓓ	93. Ⓐ Ⓑ Ⓒ Ⓓ	123. Ⓐ Ⓑ Ⓒ Ⓓ	153. Ⓐ Ⓑ Ⓒ Ⓓ	192. Ⓐ Ⓑ Ⓒ Ⓓ
17. Ⓐ Ⓑ Ⓒ Ⓓ	56. Ⓐ Ⓑ Ⓒ Ⓓ	94. Ⓐ Ⓑ Ⓒ Ⓓ	124. Ⓐ Ⓑ Ⓒ Ⓓ	154. Ⓐ Ⓑ Ⓒ Ⓓ	193. Ⓐ Ⓑ Ⓒ Ⓓ
18. Ⓐ Ⓑ Ⓒ Ⓓ	57. Ⓐ Ⓑ Ⓒ Ⓓ	95. Ⓐ Ⓑ Ⓒ Ⓓ	125. Ⓐ Ⓑ Ⓒ Ⓓ	155. Ⓐ Ⓑ Ⓒ Ⓓ	194. Ⓐ Ⓑ Ⓒ Ⓓ
19. Ⓐ Ⓑ Ⓒ Ⓓ	58. Ⓐ Ⓑ Ⓒ Ⓓ	96. Ⓐ Ⓑ Ⓒ Ⓓ	126. Ⓐ Ⓑ Ⓒ Ⓓ	156. Ⓐ Ⓑ Ⓒ Ⓓ	195. Ⓐ Ⓑ Ⓒ Ⓓ
20. Ⓐ Ⓑ Ⓒ Ⓓ	59. Ⓐ Ⓑ Ⓒ Ⓓ	97. Ⓐ Ⓑ Ⓒ Ⓓ	127. Ⓐ Ⓑ Ⓒ Ⓓ	157. Ⓐ Ⓑ Ⓒ Ⓓ	196. Ⓐ Ⓑ Ⓒ Ⓓ
21. Ⓐ Ⓑ Ⓒ Ⓓ	60. Ⓐ Ⓑ Ⓒ Ⓓ	98. Ⓐ Ⓑ Ⓒ Ⓓ	128. Ⓐ Ⓑ Ⓒ Ⓓ	158. Ⓐ Ⓑ Ⓒ Ⓓ	197. Ⓐ Ⓑ Ⓒ Ⓓ
22. Ⓐ Ⓑ Ⓒ Ⓓ	61. Ⓐ Ⓑ Ⓒ Ⓓ	99. Ⓐ Ⓑ Ⓒ Ⓓ	129. Ⓐ Ⓑ Ⓒ Ⓓ	159. Ⓐ Ⓑ Ⓒ Ⓓ	198. Ⓐ Ⓑ Ⓒ Ⓓ
23. Ⓐ Ⓑ Ⓒ Ⓓ	62. Ⓐ Ⓑ Ⓒ Ⓓ	100. Ⓐ Ⓑ Ⓒ Ⓓ	130. Ⓐ Ⓑ Ⓒ Ⓓ	160. Ⓐ Ⓑ Ⓒ Ⓓ	199. Ⓐ Ⓑ Ⓒ Ⓓ
24. Ⓐ Ⓑ Ⓒ Ⓓ	63. Ⓐ Ⓑ Ⓒ Ⓓ	101. Ⓐ Ⓑ Ⓒ Ⓓ	131. Ⓐ Ⓑ Ⓒ Ⓓ	161. Ⓐ Ⓑ Ⓒ Ⓓ	200. Ⓐ Ⓑ Ⓒ Ⓓ
25. Ⓐ Ⓑ Ⓒ Ⓓ	64. Ⓐ Ⓑ Ⓒ Ⓓ	102. Ⓐ Ⓑ Ⓒ Ⓓ	132. Ⓐ Ⓑ Ⓒ Ⓓ	162. Ⓐ Ⓑ Ⓒ Ⓓ	201. Ⓐ Ⓑ Ⓒ Ⓓ
26. Ⓐ Ⓑ Ⓒ Ⓓ	65. Ⓐ Ⓑ Ⓒ Ⓓ	103. Ⓐ Ⓑ Ⓒ Ⓓ	133. Ⓐ Ⓑ Ⓒ Ⓓ	163. Ⓐ Ⓑ Ⓒ Ⓓ	202. Ⓐ Ⓑ Ⓒ Ⓓ
27. Ⓐ Ⓑ Ⓒ Ⓓ	66. Ⓐ Ⓑ Ⓒ Ⓓ	104. Ⓐ Ⓑ Ⓒ Ⓓ	134. Ⓐ Ⓑ Ⓒ Ⓓ	164. Ⓐ Ⓑ Ⓒ Ⓓ	203. Ⓐ Ⓑ Ⓒ Ⓓ
28. Ⓐ Ⓑ Ⓒ Ⓓ	67. Ⓐ Ⓑ Ⓒ Ⓓ	105. Ⓐ Ⓑ Ⓒ Ⓓ	135. Ⓐ Ⓑ Ⓒ Ⓓ	165. Ⓐ Ⓑ Ⓒ Ⓓ	204. Ⓐ Ⓑ Ⓒ Ⓓ
29. Ⓐ Ⓑ Ⓒ Ⓓ	68. Ⓐ Ⓑ Ⓒ Ⓓ	106. Ⓐ Ⓑ Ⓒ Ⓓ	136. Ⓐ Ⓑ Ⓒ Ⓓ	166. Ⓐ Ⓑ Ⓒ Ⓓ	205. Ⓐ Ⓑ Ⓒ Ⓓ
30. Ⓐ Ⓑ Ⓒ Ⓓ	69. Ⓐ Ⓑ Ⓒ Ⓓ	107. Ⓐ Ⓑ Ⓒ Ⓓ	137. Ⓐ Ⓑ Ⓒ Ⓓ	167. Ⓐ Ⓑ Ⓒ Ⓓ	206. Ⓐ Ⓑ Ⓒ Ⓓ
31. Ⓐ Ⓑ Ⓒ Ⓓ	70. Ⓐ Ⓑ Ⓒ Ⓓ			168. Ⓐ Ⓑ Ⓒ Ⓓ	207. Ⓐ Ⓑ Ⓒ Ⓓ
32. Ⓐ Ⓑ Ⓒ Ⓓ	71. Ⓐ Ⓑ Ⓒ Ⓓ			169. Ⓐ Ⓑ Ⓒ Ⓓ	208. Ⓐ Ⓑ Ⓒ Ⓓ
33. Ⓐ Ⓑ Ⓒ Ⓓ	72. Ⓐ Ⓑ Ⓒ Ⓓ			170. Ⓐ Ⓑ Ⓒ Ⓓ	209. Ⓐ Ⓑ Ⓒ Ⓓ
34. Ⓐ Ⓑ Ⓒ Ⓓ	73. Ⓐ Ⓑ Ⓒ Ⓓ			171. Ⓐ Ⓑ Ⓒ Ⓓ	210. Ⓐ Ⓑ Ⓒ Ⓓ
35. Ⓐ Ⓑ Ⓒ Ⓓ	74. Ⓐ Ⓑ Ⓒ Ⓓ			172. Ⓐ Ⓑ Ⓒ Ⓓ	211. Ⓐ Ⓑ Ⓒ Ⓓ
36. Ⓐ Ⓑ Ⓒ Ⓓ	75. Ⓐ Ⓑ Ⓒ Ⓓ			173. Ⓐ Ⓑ Ⓒ Ⓓ	212. Ⓐ Ⓑ Ⓒ Ⓓ
37. Ⓐ Ⓑ Ⓒ Ⓓ	76. Ⓐ Ⓑ Ⓒ Ⓓ			174. Ⓐ Ⓑ Ⓒ Ⓓ	213. Ⓐ Ⓑ Ⓒ Ⓓ
38. Ⓐ Ⓑ Ⓒ Ⓓ	77. Ⓐ Ⓑ Ⓒ Ⓓ			175. Ⓐ Ⓑ Ⓒ Ⓓ	214. Ⓐ Ⓑ Ⓒ Ⓓ
39. Ⓐ Ⓑ Ⓒ Ⓓ				176. Ⓐ Ⓑ Ⓒ Ⓓ	

Writing Sample 1

_____
_____
_____
_____
_____
_____
_____
_____
_____
_____
_____
_____
_____
_____
_____
_____
_____
_____
_____
_____
_____
_____
_____

END OF PART 1

Writing Sample 2

_____

_____

_____

_____

_____

_____

_____

_____

_____

_____

_____

_____

_____

_____

_____

_____

_____

_____

_____

_____

END OF PART 2

PHYSICAL SCIENCES

Time: 100 Minutes
Questions 1–77

Directions: This test contains 77 questions. Most of the questions consist of a descriptive passage followed by a group of questions related to the passage. For these questions, study the passage carefully and then choose the best answer to each question in the group. Some questions in this test stand alone. These questions are independent of any passage and independent of each other. For these questions, too, you must select the one best answer. Indicate all your answers by blackening the corresponding circles on your answer sheet.

A periodic table is provided at the beginning of this book. You may consult it whenever you feel it's necessary.

Passage I (Questions 1–7)

In its simplest form a capacitor consists of two parallel plates of conducting material separated by an insulator called a dielectric. When the conductors are connected to the terminals of a voltage source, electrons move to one plate, giving it a net negative charge. This forces electrons to leave the opposite plate, giving it a net positive charge. When the capacitor is removed from the power source, charge can't leave the plate. The capacitor stores the electric energy in the dielectric.

Capacitance indicates the amount of charge a particular capacitor can store per volt of potential difference across its plates.

I. In terms of the charge, stored capacitance is the ratio of the charge q on either plate to the potential difference V between the plates.

$$C = q/V$$

Capacitance is measured in the unit farad = coulomb/volt, F = C/V.

II. In terms of the geometry of the capacitor,

$$C = 8.85 \times 10^{-15} \, KA/d$$

where A is the area on one of the plates and d is the separation between the plates.

K is the unitless dielectric constant of the insulating material between the plates. The total charge on the plates increases by the factor K:

$$q = KC_oV$$

C_o is the capacitance when the plates are separated by air. For air, K = 1.

For capacitors connected in series, the reciprocal of the total capacitance is equal to the sum of the reciprocals of all the separate capacitances. For capacitors connected in parallel, the total capacitance is the sum of the individual capacitances.

1. A particular parallel plate capacitor has square plates separated by an air gap 0.012 mm wide. If the length of the sides of the plates are tripled, what is the separation required to keep the capacitance the same?

   A. 0.0013 mm
   B. 0.004 mm
   C. 0.036 mm
   D. 0.108 mm

2. A 10 V power source charges a 5 μF capacitor with air as its dielectric. The power source is removed and the air gap is carefully replaced with a material of dielectric constant K = 5. What is the final charge on the capacitor?

   A. 250 μC
   B. 50 μC
   C. 25 μC
   D. 5 μC

107

3. A 6000 V power supply charges a 10 μF capacitor, C_1. The power supply is removed and C_1 is connected to an uncharged capacitor C_2 of capacitance 5 μF as shown. What is the final potential difference V_{ab} across the combination of C_1 and C_2?

A. 3000 V
B. 4000 V
C. 5000 V
D. 6000 V

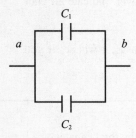

4. Three identical capacitors are connected in three patterns shown below. List the circuits in order of increasing capacitance.

A. I < II, III
B. III < II < I
C. I < III < II
D. II < I < III

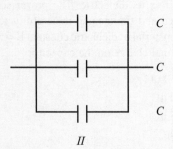

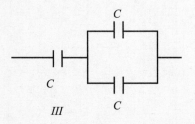

5. The constant in the equation $C = 8.85 \times 10^{-15}$ KA/d comes from $C = KA/(4\pi k)d$ where k is the Coulomb constant, 9×10^9 Nm^2/C^2. Which of the following is equivalent to the unit F?

A. C^2/Nm^2
B. C^2/J
C. V/C
D. Nm^2/C^2

6. A parallel plate capacitor has a capacitance of 19.2 μF when the insulator between the plates is glass, K = 8.0. When the glass is replaced with rubber, the capacitance becomes 6.0 μF. What is the dielectric constant of the rubber?

A. 2.5
B. 4.7
C. 7.5
D. 12.0

7. A parallel plate capacitor is charged to a given voltage by a battery. While the battery is still connected, the plates are pulled farther apart. Which statement most accurately describes what happens?

A. The capacitance increases and the charge on each plate decreases.
B. The capacitance increases and the charge on each plate increases.
C. The capacitance decreases and the charge on each plate decreases.
D. The capacitance decreases and the charge on each plate increases.

Physical Sciences

Passage II (Questions 8–13)

An enterprising physics student has developed a software package that calculates gravity-based parameters for actual and theoretical planets and satellites. The program is based on the following simple principles and approximations:

a. Newton's second law, F = ma, applies.

b. Newton's law of universal gravitation states that every body attracts every other body with a force of magnitude $F_{gravity} = GMm/r^2$, where M and m are the masses of two interacting bodies, r is the distance between their centers of mass, and G is the gravitational constant.

c. For a pair of interacting bodies if one is significantly more massive than the other, the heavier body is considered stationary with the smaller body orbiting around it.

d. The orbit of the smaller body is a circle. The smaller body experiences a centripetal force, $F_{centripetal} = mv^2/r$, directed towards the center of the more massive body.

e. For bodies on or near the surface of a planet, r is simply the planet's radius, R.

f. Planets are spheres with volume, $V = (4/3)\pi R^3$.

g. The total mechanical energy of a satellite is the sum of its kinetic and gravitational potential energy. $E = E_k + E_p = mv^2/2 - GMm/r = $ constant.

   • Since the more massive planet is stationary, E_k depends only on the motion of the satellite.

   • The potential gravitational energy increases from a large negative value to zero as the distance increases to infinity.

The speed needed for a projectile to completely escape the pull of the planet is called the escape velocity. A projectile that is completely beyond the gravity of a planet has a total mechanical energy of zero with respect to that planet. Conservation of energy requires that the total mechanical energy of the projectile when it was at the planet's surface must also equal zero.

8. Two commercial satellites, Seeker I and Seeker II, have circular orbits of R and 2R, respectively, about the same planet. What is the orbital velocity of Seeker II if the orbital velocity of Seeker I is v?

   A. v/2
   B. $v/(2)^{1/2}$
   C. $v(2)^{1/2}$
   D. 2v

9. Two boxes of negligible mass are placed 2 meters apart on the surface of Planet X. Initially 15 identical steel ball bearings are placed in each box. Which statement is most accurate if 10 of the ball bearings are transferred from box 1 to box 2?

   A. The force of gravity between the two boxes remains the same.
   B. The force of gravity between the two boxes increases.
   C. The force of gravity between the two boxes decreases.
   D. Any change in $F_{gravity}$ between the boxes cannot be determined without knowing the mass of the steel ball bearings.

10. Planet Y has density D, and surface gravitational acceleration, g. The radius of Planet Y is suddenly doubled while its density remains the same. Compared to the original g, the new value of the surface gravitational acceleration would be which of the following?

    A. $4g$
    B. $2g$
    C. g
    D. $g/2$

11. Which expression is an accurate description of the kinetic energy for a satellite of mass m in a circular orbit of radius r around a planet of mass M?

    A. $2GMm/r$
    B. GMm/r
    C. $GMm/2r$
    D. GM/r^2

12. Which expression is an accurate description of the total mechanical energy of a satellite of mass m in a circular orbit of radius *r* around a planet of mass M?

    A. GMm/*r*

    B. –GMM/*r*

    C. GMm/2*r*

    D. –GMm/2*r*

13. What is the minimum velocity required to launch a rocket from the surface of Planet Z? The planet has a mass of M and a radius of R.

    A. $(2GM/R^2)^{1/2}$

    B. $(2GM/R)^{1/2}$

    C. $(GM/R^2)^{1/2}$

    D. $(GM/R)^{1/2}$

Passage III (Questions 14–18)

    A freshman physics lab is designed to study the transfer of electrical energy from one circuit to another by means of a magnetic field using simple transformers. Each transformer has two coils of wire electrically insulated from each other but wound around a common core of ferromagnetic material. The two wires are close together but do not touch each other.

    The primary (1°) coil is connected to a source of alternating (AC) current. The secondary (2°) coil is connected to a resistor such as a light bulb. The AC source produces an oscillating voltage and current in the primary coil that produces an oscillating magnetic field in the core material. This in turn induces an oscillating voltage and AC current in the secondary coil.

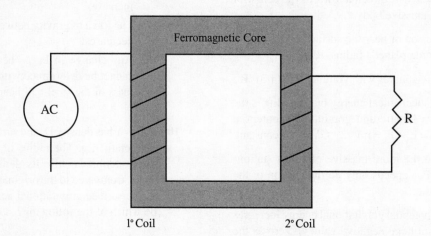

1° Coil   2° Coil

    Students collected the following data comparing the number of turns per coil (N), the voltage (V), and the current (I) in the coils of three transformers.

	Primary Coil				**Secondary Coil**		
	$N_{1°}$	$V_{1°}$	$I_{1°}$		$N_{2°}$	$V_{2°}$	$I_{2°}$
Transformer 1	100	10 V	10 A		200	20 V	5 A
Transformer 2	100	10 V	10 A		50	5 V	20 A
Transformer 3	200	10 V	10 A		100	5 V	20 A

14. The primary coil of a transformer has 100 turns and is connected to a 120 V AC source. How many turns are in the secondary coil if there's a 2400 V across it?

    A. 5

    B. 50

    C. 200

    D. 2000

15. The primary coil of a given transformer has 1/3 as many turns as its secondary coil. What primary current is required to provide a secondary current of 3.0 mA?

    A. 1.0 mA

    B. 6.0 mA

    C. 9.0 mA

    D. 12.0 mA

16. A transformer with 40 turns in its primary coil is connected to a 120 V AC source. If 20 watts of power is supplied to the primary coil, how much power is developed in the secondary coil?

A. 10 W
B. 20 W
C. 80 W
D. 160 W

17. Which of the following is a correct expression for R, the resistance of the load connected to the secondary coil?

A. $(V_{1^\circ}/I_{1^\circ})(N_{2^\circ}/N_{1^\circ})$
B. $(V_{1^\circ}/I_{1^\circ})(N_{2^\circ}/N_{1^\circ})^2$
C. $(V_{1^\circ}/I_{1^\circ})(N_{1^\circ}/N_{2^\circ})$
D. $(V_{1^\circ}/I_{1^\circ})(N_{1^\circ}/N_{2^\circ})^2$

18. A 12 V battery is used to supply 2.0 mA of current to the 300 turns in the primary coil of a given transformer. What is the current in the secondary coil if N_{2° = 150 turns?

A. 0 A
B. 1.0 mA
C. 2.0 mA
D. 4.0 A

Passage IV (Questions 19–25)

The moment of inertia, *I*, measures an object's resistance to rotational motion about a specific axis. The observed value depends on the object's mass, M; distance of the mass from the axis of rotation, R; and a parameter, β, that depends on the object's shape.

I depends on the location and orientation of the axis of rotation. In general, but not necessarily, this axis passes through the object's center of mass. When it does:

$$I_{cm} = \beta MR^2$$

Moments of Inertia for Some Common Shapes
Thin hoop, axis through center
R is radius

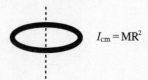

$I_{cm} = MR^2$

Solid uniform disk or cylinder, axis through center
R is radius

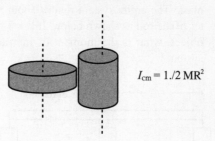

$I_{cm} = 1./2\,MR^2$

Thin uniform rod, axis through center
L is length

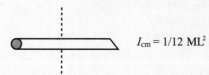

$I_{cm} = 1/12\,ML^2$

Uniform solid sphere, axis through center
R is radius

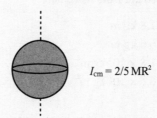

$I_{cm} = 2/5\,MR^2$

Two important rules for manipulating moments of inertia are:

I. *Moments of inertia add.* If two bodies are rigidly connected, the total moment of inertia is the sum of the two individual moments of inertia.

II. *Parallel Axis Theorem.* If I_{cm}, the moment of inertia of an object about any axis through its center of mass is known, then the moment of inertia about any axis parallel to this axis and a distance *d* away is:

$$I_{new} = I_{cm} + Md^2$$

Finally, if the object rolls as well as rotates then it has translational kinetic energy as well as rotational kinetic energy. The fraction of the kinetic energy that will be rotational depends on the moment of inertia and is given by: β/(1+ β).

19. Three objects of identical shape and mass, M, are attached to a rod of length L and negligible mass. The entire system rotates about the center of the rod as shown below. If $\beta = 1$ for each object, what is the moment of inertia of the system?

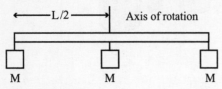

A. $\frac{1}{2}\,ML^2$

B. ML^2

C. $2\,ML^2$

D. $3\,ML^2$

20. A 20.0-kg steel cylinder has an 80-cm diameter. What is the cylinder's moment of inertia when it is rotated through an axis parallel to its length and 10 cm from its center?

A. $1.8\ \text{kg m}^2$

B. $6.6\ \text{kg m}^2$

C. $1.8 \times 10^4\ \text{kg m}^2$

D. $6.6 \times 10^4\ \text{kg m}^2$

21. A uniform thin rod of mass, M, and length, L, rotates around an axis perpendicular to its length and located at one of its ends. What is the moment of inertia for this arrangement?

A. $7\,ML^2/12$

B. $ML^2/3$

C. $ML^2/12$

D. $13\,ML^2/12$

22. Two identical weights are placed inside a long thin-walled tube. The diameter of each weight is slightly less than the inner diameter of the tube so the weights are free to move. The tube is suspended by a thin wire attached to what would be the center of mass of the empty tube. Four of the possible configurations for the system are shown below. In each case the tube is perfectly horizontal. List the configurations in order of increasing inertia about the suspending wire.

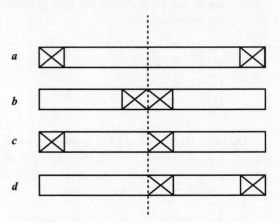

A. d b c a

B. b c d a

C. b d c a

D. a d c b

23. An artist makes a scale model of a kinetic sculpture. Two identical solid cylinders and a solid sphere with diameter equal to the cylinder length L are attached as shown. The sphere and each cylinder have the same mass, M. The sculpture is suspended by a small wire running vertically along the axis of rotation. The hole for the wire is negligible.

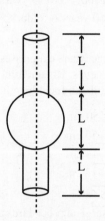

In the actual sculpture L is the only dimension altered. The new value of L is three times the value in the model. The materials are altered so that the new masses of the three components are still equal. How does the moment of inertia of the final sculpture compare to that of the model?

A. $I_{sculpture}$ will be the same as I_{model}

B. $I_{sculpture}$ will be three times greater I_{model}

C. $I_{sculpture}$ will be less than I_{model} by $4/5\ ML^2$

D. $I_{sculpture}$ will be greater than I_{model} by $4/5\ ML^2$

24. A hoop, a disk, and a solid sphere initially at rest are released simultaneously and allowed to roll down a ramp of length, L, inclined at an angle θ. What is the order in which they reach the bottom of the ramp?

A. Hoop is first, then disk, then sphere.

B. Sphere is first, then disk, then hoop.

C. Disk is first, then sphere, then hoop.

D. Since the only force acting is gravity, they all arrive at the same time.

25. A certain star collapses to $1/10^{th}$ its original radius. If the star is treated as a solid sphere, how does the new moment of inertia compare with the pre-collapsed value?

A. The moment of inertia increases by a factor of 10.

B. The moment of inertia decreases by a factor of 10.

C. The moment of inertia increases by a factor of 100.

D. The moment of inertia decreases by a factor of 100.

Passage V (Questions 26–32)

In the normal human eye, light from an object is refracted by the cornea-lens system at the front of the eye and produces a real image on the retina at the rear of the eye. For a given eye, its lens-to-retina distance is fixed at about 2.5 cm. Most of the focusing of an image is done by the cornea, which has a fixed curvature that is convex with respect to incoming light. The importance of the lens is that its radius of curvature can be changed, allowing the lens to fine-tune the focus.

The lens is surrounded by the ciliary muscle. Contraction of the muscle decreases tension on the lens. This allows the natural elasticity of the lens to produce an increase in the radius of curvature. When the muscle relaxes, the lens flattens out, decreasing its radius of curvature. Unfortunately, the lens loses elasticity with age and the ability to alter curvature decreases.

The range over which clear vision is possible is bounded by the *far point* and the *near point*. In normal vision the *far point* is infinity and the *near point* depends on the radius of curvature of the lens. For normal eyes the average near point for reading is 25 cm.

AGE, years	NEAR POINT, cm
10	7
20	10
30	14
40	22
50	40
60	200

In the myopic (nearsighted) eye, the lens-to-retina length is too long and/or the radius of curvature of the cornea is too great. This causes rays from an object at infinity to focus at a point in front of the retina. The far point is closer than normal. A corrective lens will put a virtual image of a distant object at the position of the actual far point of the eye.

In the hyperopic (farsighted) eye, the lens-to-retina length is too short and/or the radius of curvature of the cornea is not great enough. This causes rays from an object at infinity to focus at a point behind the retina. The near point is farther away than normal. A corrective lens will put a virtual image of the close object at the position of the actual near point.

The relation among the object (o) and image (i) distances from the eye and the focal length (f) of the lens is given by the lens-distance rule:

$1/o + 1/i = 1/f$

When using this equation, all distances are given in centimeters.

The power of corrective lenses is usually given in units called diopters. Power, in diopters, is the reciprocal of the focal length in meters: $P_{diopter} = 1/f_{meter}$

By convention:

I. Converging lenses have positive focal lengths, and diverging lenses have negative focal lengths.

II. Real images have positive distances from the lens, and virtual images have negative distances from the lens.

26. The lens system of the myopic eye is best described as:

   A. producing too much convergence.
   B. producing too little convergence.
   C. producing too much divergence.
   D. producing too little divergence.

27. An optometrist examined John's eyes. The farthest object he can clearly focus on with his right eye is 50 cm away. What is the power of the contact lens required to correct the vision in his right eye?

   A. −0.50 diopters
   B. −2.0 diopters
   C. +2.0 diopters
   D. +5.0 diopters

28. In a mildly hyperopic eye, the focal length of the eye's natural lens can be corrected by:

   A. contracting the ciliary muscle and increasing the radius of curvature.
   B. contracting the ciliary muscle and decreasing the radius of curvature.
   C. relaxing the ciliary muscle and increasing the radius of curvature.
   D. relaxing the ciliary muscle and decreasing the radius of curvature.

29. Jane must wear a contact lens with a power of +3.00 diopters in one eye to be able to clearly focus on an object 25 cm in front of the eye. Based on the vision in this eye, which of the following is the most likely age range for Jane?

   A. Less than 40 years old
   B. From 40 to 49 years old
   C. From 50 to 59 years old
   D. 60 years or older

30. George wears eyeglasses that sit 2.0 cm in front of his eyes. His uncorrected far point is 50 cm. What is the focal length of his eyeglasses?

   A. −50 cm
   B. +50 cm
   C. −48 cm
   D. +48 cm

31. In a surgical procedure called radial keratotomy, (RK), a laser is used to flatten the cornea by placing a series of hairline cuts around the perimeter of the cornea. Which statement is most accurate?

   A. RK corrects myopia by decreasing the focal length of the eye.
   B. RK corrects myopia by increasing the focal length of the eye.
   C. RK corrects hyperopia by decreasing the focal length of the eye.
   D. RK corrects hyperopia by increasing the focal length of the eye.

Questions 32–38 are independent of one another and not based on any passage.

---

32. A 100-kg space probe lands on Planet X. The planet's mass is three times that of Earth and its radius is also three times that of Earth. Approximately what is the weight of the probe on Planet X?

   A. 2.4×10^2 N
   B. 3.3×10^2 N
   C. 4.9×10^2 N
   D. 9.8×10^2 N

33. An object is moved along the principal axis of a converging lens from a position 5 focal lengths from the lens to a position that is 2 focal lengths from the lens. Which statement about the resulting image is most accurate?

A. The image increases in size and decreases in distance from the lens.

B. The image increases in size and increases in distance from the lens.

C. The image decreases in size and decreases in distance from the lens.

D. The image decreases in size and increases in distance from the lens.

34. A uniform bar of mass M and length L is horizontally suspended from the ceiling by two vertical light cables as shown. Cable A is connected ¼ the distance from the left end of the bar. Cable B is attached at the far right end of the bar. What is the tension in cable A?

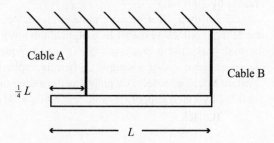

A. ¼ Mg

B. ⅓ Mg

C. ⅔ Mg

D. ¾ Mg

35. What is the magnitude of the intensity of an electric field E if a 4 μC charge placed in the field experiences a force of 0.08 N?

A. 5×10^{-3} kg m/s^{2}C

B. 2×10^{-4} kg m/s^2

C. 5×10^{3} kg m/s^2

D. 2×10^{4} kg m/s^2

36. Blocks A and B of masses 15 kg and 10 kg, respectively, are connected by a light cable passing over a frictionless pulley as shown below. Approximately what is the acceleration experienced by the system?

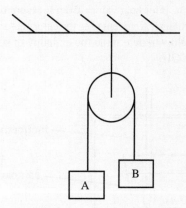

A. 2.0 m/s^2

B. 3.3 m/s^2

C. 4.9 m/s^2

D. 9.8 m/s^2

37. A 50-kg ice skater, initially at rest, throws a 0.15-kg snowball with a speed of 35 m/s. What is the approximate recoil speed of the skater?

A. 0.10 m/s

B. 0.20 m/s

C. 0.70 m/s

D. 1.4 m/s

38. The four wires from a larger circuit intersect at junction A as shown. What is the magnitude and direction of the current between points A and B?

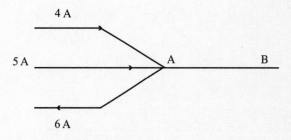

A. 2 A from A to B

B. 2 A from B to A

C. 3 A from A to B

D. 2 A from B to A

Passage VI (Questions 39–44)

Chemists' seemingly insatiable need to measure heat has led to a broad spectrum of measurement methods. Beginning students are familiar with simple "coffee-cup" style calorimeters that rely on the known specific heat of water to infer heat values from measurements of temperature change. A student uses the calorimeter shown in Figure 1 below to determine the enthalpy of solution, $\Delta H_{solution}$, of KOH:

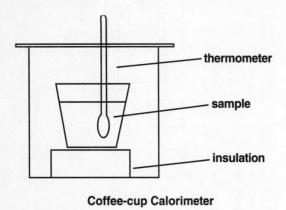

Coffee-cup Calorimeter

Figure 1

She finds that when a 4.56-g sample of solid KOH is added to 100 mL of water, the temperature in the solution rises from 24.0°C to 34.6°C.

Another traditional style of calorimeter is the ice calorimeter, in which the heat released in an exothermic reaction is trapped in an ice-water mixture, causing ice to melt (Figure 2). Each gram of ice that melts produces a gram of liquid having a somewhat greater density, with the result that the volume of the ice-water mixture contracts by 0.091 mL per gram of ice melted. Thus, a measurement of volume change, together with the knowledge that the specific heat of fusion of ice is 334 J/g, leads to a value for the heat liberated in a reaction.

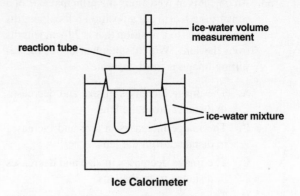

Ice Calorimeter

Figure 2

A student employs this method to determine the enthalpy of the combustion of methanol. He finds that when a sample of methanol weighing 0.300 g is burned in excess oxygen in an ice calorimeter, according to the reaction,

$$2CH_3OH(l) + 3O_2(g) \rightarrow 2CO_2(g) + 4H_2O(l)$$

the volume of ice and water surrounding the sample decreases by 1.86 mL.

Calorimetry has become quite sophisticated, and one of the methods available to analytical laboratories is thermal gravimetric analysis (TGA), a technique that measures the mass of a sample as heat is applied at a constant rate. The result is a graph, as illustrated in Figure 3 for hydrated copper (II) sulfate, $CuSO_4 \cdot 5H_2O$.

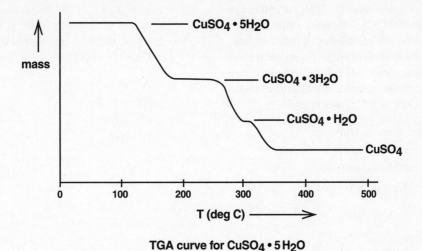

TGA curve for $CuSO_4 \cdot 5H_2O$

Figure 3

Figure 3 shows that as heat is added to the sample, mass is lost in distinct stages, each characterized by a loss of either one or two water molecules from an original molecule of hydrate.

39. If the specific heat of the solution of KOH in water is assumed to be 4.18 J/g°C, what is the approximate value of $\Delta H_{solution}$ for KOH? (Assume that the calorimeter is thermally insulated from its surroundings.)

    A. −57 kJ/mol
    B. −4.6 kJ/mol
    C. 57 kJ/mol
    D. 4.6 kJ/mol

40. Which of the following changes in the KOH solubility experiment would be the LEAST likely to change the measured value of ΔT?

    A. Doubling the amount of water used
    B. Doubling the amount of KOH used
    C. Doubling the amount of water and doubling the amount of KOH used
    D. Substituting an equal mass of NaOH for the KOH sample

41. Which of the following is the most serious *limitation* of ice calorimetry as a method of measuring enthalpies of the given reaction in the narrative?

    A. The method cannot be used to determine enthalpies of endothermic reactions.
    B. The method cannot be used directly to determine enthalpies of reactions that take place at 25°C.
    C. Because of the reliance on ice and water, the method cannot be used to determine enthalpies of reactions that involve water or ice as reactants or products.
    D. Although satisfactory for determining the heat of a reaction, this method cannot evaluate a reaction enthalpy.

42. What was the approximate value of the heat of the chemical reaction in the ice calorimetry determination described?

    A. 20 J
    B. 14 J
    C. −7 kJ
    D. 20 kJ

43. An experimenter wishes to substitute a mixture of solid and liquid benzene, C_6H_6 (which are in equilibrium at 5.5°C), for the ice-water mixture described above. The enthalpy of fusion of benzene is 10.59 kJ/mol. In which liquid-solid mixture will more grams of solid melt? (You may assume that the enthalpy of combustion of methane is the same at 5.5°C as it is at 0°C.)

A. The ice-water mixture
B. The liquid-solid benzene mixture
C. There will be no difference.
D. More information is needed.

44. Refer to the thermogravimetric analysis curve in Figure 3. If the initial mass of the fully hydrated sample was 0.100 g, what was its mass when it had been completely converted to $CuSO_4 \cdot 3H_2O$?

A. 0.007 g
B. 0.014 g
C. 0.085 g
D. 0.093 g

Passage VII (Questions 45–50)

Reduction potentials for elements and molecules are frequently presented in tables, but diagrams often convey their relationships more quickly. Figure 1, which is basically an ordered table, shows several half reactions and their relative reduction potentials.

	Half Reaction	Reduction Potential
_____	$MnO_4^-(aq) + 4H^+ + 3e^- \rightarrow MnO_2(2) + 2H_2O(\ell)$	1.700
_____	$Cu^{2+} + 2e^- \rightarrow Cu(s)$	0.340
_____	$Sn^{4+}(aq) + 2e^- \rightarrow Sn^{2+}(aq)$	0.154
_____	$2H^+(aq) + 2e^- \rightarrow H_2(g)$	0.000
_____	$Ni^{2+} + 2e^- \rightarrow Ni$	−0.236

Figure 1

When we want to focus attention on different oxidation states of the same element, we often use a *Latimer diagram*, such as the one illustrated in Figure 2 below, that describes several different states of chlorine in 1 M acid solution.

(7+)   (5+)   (4+)   (1+)

        1.20 V   1.18 V   1.70 V

$C\ell O_4^-$ ———> $\quad C\ell O_3^-$ ———> $\quad C\ell O_2$ ———> $\quad HC\ell O$

Figure 2

The diagram presents in condensed form a series of half reactions, together with the corresponding reduction potentials (above each arrow) and the oxidation state of each form of chlorine (above each species). For example, the middle segment of the diagram,

(+5)   (+4)

            1.18 V

$C\ell O_3^- \longrightarrow \quad C\ell O_2$

is a shorthand form of the half reaction

$ClO_3^-(aq) + 2H^+(aq) + e^- \rightarrow ClO_2^-(aq) + H_2O(\ell)$.

If we want to derive a new half reaction potential from the diagram, we cannot (except in special cases) simply add two potentials to get a new one. Rather, because of the relationship of free energy to potential,

$$\Delta G^\circ = -nFE^\circ$$

(where ΔG° is the standard free energy of a half reaction, E° is the potential, F is Faraday's constant, and n is the number of electrons transferred), we find the potential for a half reaction that is a combination of two other half reactions as follows:

If E°_1 is the potential for the first half reaction, which transfers n_1 electrons, and E°_2 is the potential for the second half reaction, which transfers n_2 electrons, then the overall potential E°_{total} is given by

$$E^\circ_{total} = (n_1 E^\circ_1 + n_2 E^\circ_2) / (n_1 + n_2).$$

For the overall reaction $ClO_4^- \rightarrow ClO_2$, the Latimer diagram shows that two electrons are transferred in the first half reaction, and one in the second, giving

$$E^\circ_{total} = [2(1.20) + (1)(1.18)] / (2 + 1)$$

$$= 1.19$$

The Latimer diagram can quickly predict whether a species is unstable with respect to disproportionation, i.e., a reaction of the form $2A \rightarrow B + C$.

We expect that disproportionation can occur if the potential to the right of a species is greater than the potential to the left.

Convenient as the Latimer diagram is, it can be usefully extended to the *Frost diagram*, as in Figure 3 for oxygen. In this depiction of reduction potentials, we *plot oxidation state on the x-axis* and *the quantity nE° on the vertical axis*, where n is the oxidation state and E° is the potential for the reduction from that oxidation state to the neutral element.

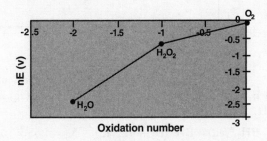

Oxidation number

Figure 3

Figure 3 gives us quick information about several key points about the various oxidation states of O:

- The most stable state comes at the lowest point on the chart (H_2O, where O is in the 2– state).
- The slope of the line drawn between any two points gives the value of the reduction potential for the corresponding half reaction. Qualitatively, we can say 5; e.g., E° for $H_2O_2 \rightarrow H_2O$ is greater than E° for $O_2 \rightarrow H_2O_2$.
- Disproportionation is expected in cases such as the point for H_2O_2 on the diagram, because the point lies above the line that can be drawn connecting the point to the left (H_2O) with the point to the right (O_2).

45. Which of the following will oxidize Sn^{2+} at standard conditions?

   A. MnO_4^-
   B. Cu
   C. H^+
   D. Sn^{4+}

46. Which of the following reactions is expected to react more completely at pH 1 than at pH 5? (Assume standard concentrations of all species except H+.)

   A. $Sn(NO_3)_2$ with $Cu(NO_3)_2$
   B. $NiCl_2$ with $Sn(NO_3)_2$
   C. $KMnO_4$ with Cu
   D. $NiCl_2$ with $Cu(NO_3)_2$

47. Find the balanced reaction for the section of the chlorine Latimer diagram that is written:

   $ClO_2 \rightarrow HClO$
   (Assume that $H^+ = 1$ M)

   A. $ClO_2 + H_2O + 3e^- \rightarrow HClO + 3OH^-$
   B. $ClO_2 + 3H^+ + 3e^- \rightarrow HClO + H_2O$
   C. $ClO_2 + 2H^+ + 3e^- \rightarrow HClO + H_2O$
   D. $ClO_2 + 5/2\ H^+ + 3e^- \rightarrow HClO + 2H_2O$

48. Consider the following Latimer diagram.

(3+)   (2+)   (0)

                0.77 V   −0.44 V

Fe^{3+} → Fe^{2+} →   Fe

Calculate E° for the half reaction $Fe^{3+} + 3e^- →$ Fe.

A. −0.04
B. 0.17
C. 0.37
D. 0.55

49. The Frost diagram for several Nb species in acidic solution is shown below. Using this diagram, plus any other relevant information from the passage, determine which of the following is/are true. (In the following, E° refers to reduction potential.)

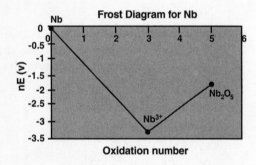

Frost Diagram for Nb

I. Nb^{3+} is stable with respect to disproportionation in acidic solution.
II. E° (Nb^{3+}/Nb) > E°(Nb_2O_5/ Nb^{3+})
III. Nb is the most stable of the 3 species on the diagram.

A. I only
B. II only
C. III only
D. I and II only

50. The Frost diagram below combines parts of the diagrams for Nb and for Hg. Which of the reactions below will proceed spontaneously?

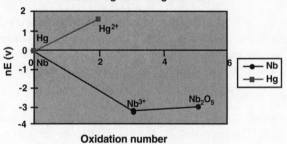

Frost Diagram for Hg and Nb

I. $Hg^{2+}(aq) + Nb(s) → Hg(s) + Nb^{3+} (aq)$
II. $Hg(s) + Nb^{3+} (aq) → Hg^{2+}(aq) + Nb(s)$
III. $Hg(s) + Nb(s) → Hg^{2+}(aq) + Nb^{3+} (aq)$

A. I only
B. II only
C. III only
D. I and III only

Passage VIII (Questions 51–56)

The titration curve for a 0.100 M solution of the weak base piperazine with 0.200 M HCl is given in the figure below.

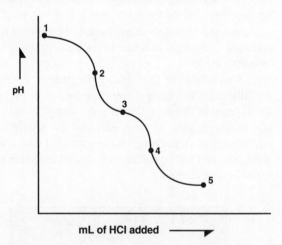

If the most basic form of piperazine is represented as B, then acid constants for the species $BH^+(aq)$ and $BH_2^{2+}(aq)$ are given as follows:

$$BH_2^{2+}(aq) = BH^+(aq) + H^+ (aq) \quad K_1 = 4.65 \times 10^{-6}$$
$$BH^+(aq) = B (aq) + H^+ (aq) \quad K_2 = 1.86 \times 10^{-10}$$

51. At which of the numbered points on the titration curve would the species $BH^+(aq)$ and $BH_2^{2+}(aq)$ both be found in appreciable quantities?

   A. Point 2

   B. Point 3

   C. Point 4

   D. Point 5

52. If the original volume of 0.100 M B solution was 20.00 mL, what is the approximate volume of acid that has been added at point 2?

   A. 5 mL

   B. 10 mL

   C. 15 mL

   D. 20 mL

53. What is the approximate pH at point 4 on the titration curve?

   A. 3

   B. 7

   C. 10

   D. 13

54. What is the predominant pH-determining reaction in the titration flask before any HCl is added?

   A. $BH_2^{2+}(aq) = BH^+(aq) + H^+(aq)$

   B. $BH^+(aq) = B(aq) + H^+(aq)$

   C. $B(aq) + H_2O(l) = BH^+(aq) + OH^-(aq)$

   D. $BH^+(aq) + OH^-(aq) = B(aq) + H_2O(l)$

55. Suppose that the indicator Phenol Red is used to monitor the titration. Phenol Red is a monoprotic acid with $pK_a = 7.81$; its acidic form, HInd is yellow in solution, and its basic form, Ind$^-$, is red. Which of the following correctly predicts the colors that Phenol Red will take on at two different pHs during the titration?

   A. pH 5: yellow; pH 10: yellow

   B. pH 5: yellow; pH 10: red

   C. pH 5: red; pH 10: yellow

   D. pH 5: red; pH 10: red

56. In an effort to discover combinations of piperazine species that will have buffering properties, a student decides to graph the rate of change of pH against volume of acid added. Which of the following best illustrates the graph that she would obtain?

A)

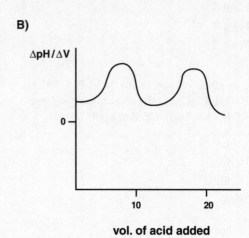

B)

C)

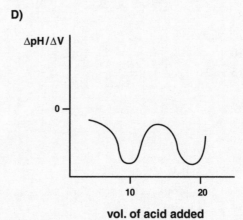

D)

Passage IX (Questions 57–61)

The concept of electronegativity is central to discussions of molecular bonding and structure. Linus Pauling compiled the values of electronegativity (EN) that are most widely used, and that are displayed for a few compounds in Table 1 below. To assign numerical values to individual atoms, Pauling used bond energy differences between atoms bonded to themselves (e.g., C–C) and to other atoms (e.g., C–Cl).

H 2.1						
Li 1.0	Be 1.5	B 2.0	C 2.5	N 3.0	O 3.5	F 4.0
Na 0.9	Mg 1.2	Al 1.5	Si 1.8	P 2.1	S 2.5	Cl 3.0
K 0.8	Ca 1.0	Ga 1.6	Ge 1.8	As 2.0	Se 2.4	Br 2.8

Table 1: Pauling electronegativities

Robert Millikan also defined a scale of electronegativities, using the formula

$EN_{Mill} = 1/2(IE + EA)$

where IE is the first ionization energy of the atom and EA is its first electron affinity. (Both quantities are measured in electron volts, eV.) Several values of IE and EA are given in Table 2.

atom	IE (eV)	EA (eV)
H	13.6	0.76
Li	5.32	0.622
C	11.25	1.27
N	14.52	-0.07
O	13.66	1.46
F	17.42	3.34
Cl	13.0	3.62
S	10.4	2.07
Br	11.8	3.40

Table 2: IE and EA for calculating Millikan electronegativities

Table 3 shows values of dipole moment and bond energy for several simple molecules.

molecule	dipole moment (Debye)?	bond energy (kJ/mol)
HF	6.37	565
H_2O	6.17	463
NH_3	4.90	388
NCl	3.60	431
HBr	2.67	366
HI	1.40	299

Table 3

Table 4 gives acid dissociation constants K_a for a number of acids.

Compound	Structure	K_a
Acetic Acid		1.8×10^{-5}
Bromoacetic acid		1.25×10^{-3}
Chloroacetic acid		1.36×10^{-3}

Table 4

57. Use the data provided to determine a criterion for classifying bonds as "ionic" versus "polar covalent" based on electronegativity difference.

A. "Ionic" if $\Delta EN < 1.2$; "polar covalent" if $\Delta EN > 1.2$

B. "Ionic" if $\Delta EN > 1.2$; "polar covalent" if $\Delta EN < 1.2$

C. "Ionic" if $\Delta EN < 2.0$; "polar covalent" if $\Delta EN > 2.0$

D. "Ionic" if $\Delta EN > 2.0$; "polar covalent" if $\Delta EN < 2.0$

58. Which of the following best explains the reason for Millikan's decision to define electronegativity as he did?

A. If the IE is high, an atom is more likely to lose it to another atom when a bond is formed. If the EA is high, an atom is more likely to attract the electron from another atom when a bond is formed.

B. If the IE is high, an atom is less likely to lose it to another atom when a bond is formed. If the EA is high, an atom is more likely to attract the electron from another atom when a bond is formed.

C. If the IE is high, an atom is less likely to lose it to another atom when a bond is formed. If the EA is high, an atom is less likely to attract the electron from another atom when a bond is formed.

D. If the IE is high, an atom is more likely to lose it to another atom when a bond is formed. If the EA is high, an atom is less likely to attract the electron from another atom when a bond is formed.

59. Which of the following is a difference in the order of electronegativities predicted by the Pauling method versus the Millikan method?

- **A.** Pauling: EN(F) > EN(Cl)
  Millikan: EN(F) < EN(Cl)
- **B.** Pauling: EN(C) > EN(H)
  Millikan: EN(C) < EN(H)
- **C.** Pauling: EN(N) > EN(C)
  Millikan: EN(N) < EN(C)
- **D.** Pauling: EN(O) > EN(N)
  Millikan: EN(O) < EN(N)

60. Which of the following best describes the relationship of electronegativity, bond enthalpy, and dipole moment?

- **A.** For a diatomic molecule (or a larger molecule with only one type of bond), as electronegativity increases, bond enthalpy *increases* because of the increasingly ionic character of the bond. Dipole moment *increases* because it depends on charge separation between atoms.
- **B.** For a diatomic molecule (or a larger molecule with only one type of bond), as electronegativity increases, bond enthalpy *decreases* because of the increasingly ionic character of the bond. Dipole moment *increases* because it depends on charge separation between atoms.
- **C.** For a diatomic molecule (or a larger molecule with only one type of bond), as electronegativity increases, bond enthalpy *increases* because of the increasingly ionic character of the bond. Dipole moment *decreases* because of the diminishing charge separation between atoms.
- **D.** For a diatomic molecule (or a larger molecule with only one type of bond), as electronegativity increases, bond enthalpy *decreases* because bonds are strongest between similar atoms. Dipole moment *decreases* because of the diminishing charge separation between atoms.

61. Use the trends illustrated in the given data to predict the order of acid dissociation constant of the acids HOCl, HOBr, and HOI.

- **A.** $K_a(HOCl) < K_a(HOI) < K_a(HOBr)$
- **B.** $K_a(HOCl) < K_a(HOBr) < K_a(HOI)$
- **C.** $K_a(HOI) < K_a(HOBr) < K_a(HOCl)$
- **D.** $K_a(HOBr) < K_a(HOI) < K_a(HOCl)$

Passage X (Questions 62–70)

Chemists have a variety of tools at their disposal to determine the carbon dioxide concentration in a gas mixture.

Method 1: A mixture containing CO_2 is introduced into a flask containing aqueous NaOH, after which the following reaction occurs:

$$CO_2(g) + H_2O(l) \rightarrow H_2CO_3(aq)$$
$$H_2CO_3(aq) + 2NaOH(aq) \rightarrow H_2O(l)\ Na_2CO_3(aq)$$

The pressure in the flask is monitored, and the pressure change allows us to compute the amount of CO_2 that has reacted.

Method 2: CO_2 can be trapped by an ion-exchange resin, where it is bound to resin cations in the form of carbonate ions. The resin is then rinsed with $NaNO_3$ and the resulting carbonate ions are titrated with sodium hydroxide.

Method 3: Because CO_2 absorbs efficiently in the infrared region of the spectrum, it can be detected and measured using infrared spectroscopy.

If infrared radiation enters a sample cell with intensity I_o and exits with intensity I, then the transmittance T is defined as

$$T = I/I_o$$
and the absorbance A is defined as
$$A = -\log T = -\log (I/I_o)$$

Beer's Law states that $A = abc$, where a is the molar absorptivity, a property of both the wavelength and the molecule itself; b is the path length of the cell in cm; and c is the concentration of the absorbing species in mol/L. Thus if A, a, and b are known, Beer's Law can then be used to determine the concentration of the gas.

The figure on page 125 shows the "normal modes" of CO_2, together with absorption frequencies that excite these modes.

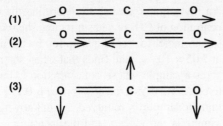

(1) symmetric stretch; $v1 = 4.16 \times 10$

(2) assymetric stretch; $v2 = 7.05 \times 10$

(3) bend; $v3 = 2.00 \times 10$

62. Using Method 1, a student attempts to determine the mass of CO_2 contained in a gaseous mixture of CO_2, O_2, and N_2 in a 250-mL flask. When 25.0 mL of 2.00 M NaOH is added and the flask is resealed, the pressure inside is observed to drop from 760 torr to 745 torr. Which of the following is closest to the original mass of CO_2?

   A. 0.004 g
   B. 0.009 g
   C. 0.020 g
   D. 0.050 g

63. For which of the following gas mixtures might this method fail to determine the mass of CO_2?

   A. CO_2, H_2, and N_2
   B. CO_2, H_2S, and O_2
   C. CO_2, Ar, F_2
   D. CO_2, N_2, Ne

64. Assume that the reaction to remove CO_2 is carried out at a constant temperature of 25.0°C. Which of the following best describes the process at a molecular level?

   I. The number of collisions per second of gas molecules with the wall of the flask is greater before the reaction than after.
   II. The average kinetic energy of gas molecules is greater before the reaction than after.
   III. The number of gas molecules per cm^3 is greater before the reaction than after.

   A. I only
   B. II only
   C. III only
   D. I and III only

65. A 10.0 mL gas sample, containing CO_2 as well as other gases, is collected at 760 torr and 25°C. The sample is passed through a moist ion-exchange resin, converting each CO_2 molecule to a CO_3^{2-} ion, and the resin is rinsed with $NaNO_3$. The rinse solution is titrated with 0.0200 M HNO_3, and a phenolphthalein end-point is reached at 20.40 mL. Which of the following best approximates the partial pressure of CO_2 in the original sample?

   A. 150 torr
   B. 380 torr
   C. 560 torr
   D. 760 torr

66. In a different analysis using the same method, a sample containing 8.00 mmol of CO_2 is passed through a resin column, then rinsed out as 10.00 mL of Na_2CO_3 solution. What is the approximate pH of this solution? (For H_2CO_3, $K_1 = 4.45$ 10^{-7} and $K_2 = 4.69$ 10^{-11}.)

   A. 2
   B. 6
   C. 9
   D. 12

67. The figure included in the passage shows the "normal modes" of CO_2, where a normal mode is defined as an independent mode of vibration. Each normal mode has a characteristic vibrational frequency given to the right of its illustration. Which of the following shows the correct order of wavelengths of absorption for each mode, in order from shortest to longest wavelength? (Assume, for this question, that all of the modes permit absorption.)

   A. $\lambda_1 < \lambda_2 < \lambda_3$
   B. $\lambda_2 < \lambda_1 < \lambda_3$
   C. $\lambda_3 < \lambda_1 < \lambda_2$
   D. $\lambda_1 < \lambda_3 < \lambda_2$

68. A molecule will absorb infrared light at a frequency that excites one of its normal modes, but only if that frequency produces a change in the dipole moment of the molecule. Which of the modes shown in the figure included in the passage would NOT lead to absorption of light?

A. The symmetric stretch

B. The asymmetric stretch

C. The bend

D. Both the symmetric and asymmetric stretches

69. An investigator wishes to determine the concentration of CO_2 in a gas mixture. She sets the spectrometer to record absorption by the mode at $7.05 \times 10^{13}\,s^{-1}$ and finds that when she measures a sample whose concentration is known to be $2.5 \times 10^{-4}\,M$, the absorbance is 0.195. The known sample is removed, an unknown CO_2 sample is introduced, and the measurement is repeated under identical conditions, producing an absorbance of 0.452. Which of the following best approximates the concentration of CO_2 in the unknown sample?

A. $1 \times 10^{-4}\,M$

B. $4 \times 10^{-4}\,M$

C. $6 \times 10^{-4}\,M$

D. $9 \times 10^{-4}\,M$

INDIVIDUAL PROBLEMS

70. A sample containing 1.00 mol of substance X was heated at a constant rate of 1.00 kJ/min, and the resulting temperature of the sample was recorded. The results of this process over several minutes are displayed in the figure below. What is the enthalpy of vaporization for substance X?

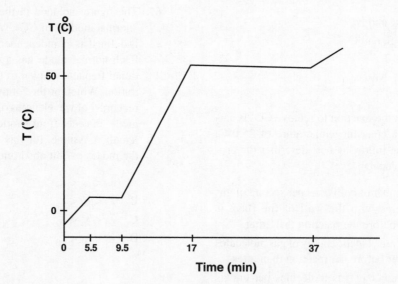

A. 4.0 kJ/mol

B. 7.5 kJ/mol

C. 20.0 kJ/mol

D. 37.0 kJ/mol

71. The figure below shows the energy change as the reaction A + B → C + D proceeds from reactants to products. ΔG for this reaction is –34 kJ/mol.

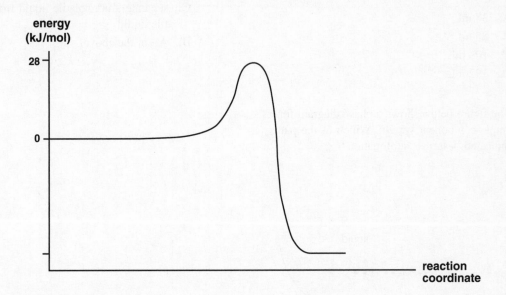

What is the activation energy, E_a, for the reaction C + D → A + B?

A. –6 kJ/mol

B. 6 kJ/mol

C. 34 kJ/mol

D. 62 kJ/mol

72. Which of the following will be expected to have the *lowest* vapor pressure at 25°C?

A. Pure H_2O

B. 1.0 M ethanol (boiling point = 78.0°C)

C. 1.0 M glucose

D. 1.0 M NaCl

73. Aluminum reacts with HCl according to the following reaction:

$$2Al(s) + 6HCl(aq) \rightarrow 2AlCl_3(aq) + 3H_2(g)$$

Find the volume of hydrogen gas that will be produced (at STP) when 2.70 mg of metallic aluminum reacts with 20.00 mL of 0.0100 M HCl.

A. 0.20 mL

B. 0.30 mL

C. 2.0 mL

D. 30 mL

74. In an effusion experiment, a 52.0-mL container holds argon gas at 1.00 atm pressure. A pinhole-sized valve is then opened, and the gas is allowed to escape into a large, evacuated container. After 24.0 minutes, the gas pressure in the original container has dropped effectively to zero.

The experiment is repeated with gas X, under otherwise identical conditions, and the time required for the pressure to drop to zero is found to be 20.0 min. What is the molar mass of gas X?

A. 28 g/mol

B. 35 g/mol

C. 48 g/mol

D. 57 g/mol

75. A sample of 0.25 M NaCl is diluted with 48.0 mL of water, with the result that the concentration drops to 0.20 M. What was the volume of the original sample?

    A. 38 mL

    B. 85 mL

    C. 106 mL

    D. 192 mL

76. The figure below shows a phase diagram for a single-component system. Which of the paths indicated describes sublimation?

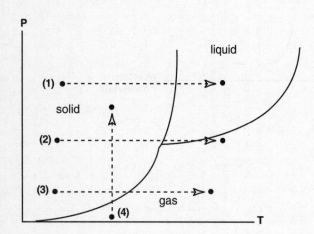

    A. 1

    B. 2

    C. 3

    D. 4

77. Chromatography can be used to:

    A. separate nonvolatile liquids.

    B. separate volatile liquids.

    C. separate a nonvolatile liquid from a volatile liquid.

    D. All of the above

END OF TEST 1.

**IF YOU FINISH BEFORE THE TIME IS UP, YOU MAY
CHECK YOUR WORK ON THIS TEST ONLY.**

VERBAL REASONING

Time: 85 Minutes
Questions 78–137

Directions: There are nine passages in this test. Each passage is followed by questions based on its content. After reading a passage, choose the one best answer to each question and indicate your selection by blackening the corresponding space on your answer sheet.

Passage I (Questions 78–84)

A hurricane is a cyclonic storm that forms in the tropics or subtropics over large bodies of warm water where the water temperature is at least 80 degrees Fahrenheit. This kind of storm must have a minimum sus-
(5) tained wind speed of at least 74 miles an hour and is one of the most powerful storms known to humanity.

For years, the development and paths of hurricanes and tropical storms (which are also cyclonic storms with sustained wind speeds of 39 to 74 miles
(10) an hour) were largely unpredictable. These storms intensify, change direction unpredictably, and make landfall where least expected, causing severe damage to people and property. But now that scientists have better knowledge of hurricanes and tropical storms,
(15) there is an increasing ability to predict the direction and intensity of such storms in advance of their landfall.

The ability to predict the paths of hurricanes has been greatly enhanced by the use of computers and sat-
(20) ellites. The existence of better knowledge of the storm tracks of previous hurricanes has helped predict storms, although spotter planes are still used to obtain exact readings. In addition, the increased knowledge of the role that steering winds play at high altitudes has be-
(25) come one of the most important factors in predicting storm paths. Such winds will steer a tropical system in clearly defined directions, allowing the forecaster to map a path for a tropical system days in advance of the storm hitting.
(30) Other reasons for the better understanding of storm tracks include a better understanding of the effects of wind shear (a situation where winds are blowing in different directions at different altitudes) on hurricanes and tropical storms. Strong wind shear is not
(35) conducive to the development of hurricanes, and strong cold fronts can often block the paths of approaching hurricanes, which act as a wall that redirects the hurricane. With this improved prediction of frontal passages,

the influence fronts will have on the paths of hurricanes
(40) and tropical storms can be better predicted.

Computers are also an enormous asset in predicting the possible paths of hurricanes, because a computer can generate likely models for the development and direction of hurricanes based on information on
(45) the histories of previous hurricanes. The models can be easily adjusted as new information comes in, allowing for increasing reliability of prediction as the hurricane comes closer to landfall. This data has also been useful in prediction of the direction and intensity of hurricanes
(50) and tropical storms.

Still, some traditional approaches to the prediction of tropical systems are used. Flying into the eye of a hurricane is still the best way to obtain accurate information about the tropical system, because other
(55) sources might be either unavailable or unable to confirm existing information. Only by using planes can a truly accurate reading on barometric pressure in the eye of the storm and exact wind speed be obtained. Though satellites give a good image of the eye of a hurricane
(60) and the expanse of the tropical system, the instruments on the planes can provide more accurate readings and therefore, a better understanding of how the storm is likely to develop. These exact readings become crucially important as the storm approaches landfall.
(65) There is still much to learn about tropical systems that develop into tropical storms and hurricanes. It would be arrogant to imagine that the progress of all such storms days in advance can be accurately predicted. However, the reliability of forecasts has greatly ad-
(70) vanced our ability to give advanced warning of systems that are among the most destructive known. As understanding grows, the reliability of forecasting will continue to improve, and the safety of the populations affected by tropical systems will increase. Yet hurri-
(75) canes are still very capable of the unpredictable and will remain that way for the foreseeable future.

78. A hurricane forms in which of the following conditions?

A. Only at water temperature over 80 degrees Fahrenheit

B. In the tropics or subtropics of water temperature over 80 degrees Fahrenheit

C. In the tropics or subtropics over large bodies of water with water temperature at 80 degrees Fahrenheit

D. In the tropics or subtropics over large bodies of water with a high water temperature

79. According to the passage, a hurricane can also be called a:

A. tropical storm.

B. maelstrom.

C. tornado.

D. cyclonic storm.

80. The prediction of the hurricane paths has been improved by the use of:

A. computers, satellites, and following storm tracks of previous hurricanes.

B. computers and satellites.

C. computers, satellites, and knowledge of previous hurricane storm tracks.

D. computers, satellites, and airplanes.

81. The author sees the use of computers in predicting possible hurricane paths as:

A. simply a useful tool.

B. an asset.

C. a machine to record information.

D. one of several tools to rely on.

82. The ability to better forecast tropical systems has been enhanced by a better understanding of:

A. the role of wind shear.

B. the role of steering winds at different altitudes.

C. the role of different storm fronts.

D. predicting frontal passages.

83. According to the author, what is still the best way to obtain accurate information about a tropical system?

A. Flying into the eye of the storm in a plane

B. Using radar

C. Using only previous information

D. Using only computers

84. The author points out that traditional methods of studying and tracking hurricanes, along with the use of modern technology, are beneficial but also believes that:

A. without both, the ability to predict the paths of tropical storms and hurricanes cannot be accomplished.

B. understanding advanced warning systems does not necessarily help predict future hurricanes.

C. forecasting future tropical storms will continue to advance, thereby increasing the chances of ensuring protection for people in areas prone to tropical storms.

D. forecasting can be reliable as long as we understand that it is possible to make mistakes in predicting the beginnings of hurricanes.

Passage II (Questions 85–91)

Of the 35 million Europeans who arrived in the United States between 1820 and 1920, one third were women. A larger wave of immigration that started in 1880 included approximately 20 million men, women,
(5) and children who emigrated mostly from southern and eastern Europe. These newer immigrants were Poles, Italians, Jews, Slovaks, Bohemians, Greeks, and Armenians. The majority were from the rural areas in their home countries. For the immigrant women, the transi-
(10) tion from the life and routine of the rural countryside to the slum conditions of the urban cities where most immigrant families settled was particularly difficult.

In many small European villages, a way of life was maintained for generations. For the peasant woman,
(15) life followed a simplistic order: she worked, married, raised children, and maintained customs and beliefs handed down from her mother, grandmother, and great-grandmother that she in turn would pass down to her own daughter. A woman was defined by her place in
(20) the family; a sense of individuality separate from one's family did not exist in Europe. Peasant society was based on a patriarchal system, so a woman's existence legally was dependent on her father or husband. Women

did not inherit property, which was passed from fathers
(25) to sons. Despite this restriction, a woman had considerable power within her family. She was respected as a mother and a worker, as she was responsible for her family's well-being. In many of these cultures, the mother was recognized as the moral and spiritual heart
(30) of the household, and many women carried these important bonds with them when they immigrated to America.

Immigrant women, however, found life during their early years in America arduous and challenging
(35) as they struggled to help their families survive in urban cities such as Chicago, Boston, and New York, where many immigrant families chose to live. Housing could be found, but only in densely populated immigrant enclaves. There was no longer open countryside to own
(40) land and garden vegetables, as the family had done in the old country. Instead, the immigrant woman lived in a tenement flat, usually on a slum street with no open space. Her small, but clean house built of logs was replaced in America by a cramped flat with three or four
(45) rooms in which one, and sometimes two, families lived. The average tenement flat in the early 1900s had a parlor, a kitchen, and one or two bedrooms in between, so small that at times there was space for only a bed. The rooms tended to be dark as most flats had one room
(50) with a window facing the street while other windows had back alleys to look out at. At night, no open-floor space could be found in a tenement, as every corner and inch of floor became sleeping space. Privacy in the cramped space was achieved by hanging sheets from
(55) ropes to divide rooms in half and quarter spaces.

The traditional jobs an immigrant woman was accustomed to doing in the old country had to give way as she adjusted to her new surroundings. In the old country, work such as gardening, milking cows, and har-
(60) vesting the crops were done outdoors. Forced to live in closed and uncomfortable spaces, it took much skill and ingenuity to keep some order in a room housing perhaps eight people, when there was hardly space enough for one to walk. Not only was she constantly working
(65) at finding space for family members in the cramped apartment, she also was trying to keep the flat clean. Resourcefulness was a necessity in juggling the space in the apartment to accommodate so many people. In addition, the kitchen had to be organized to be a work-
(70) room, a laundry room, a living room, and a bedroom. In the kitchen would be a coal stove, which was unfamiliar to the immigrant woman who used to cook on an open hearth in the old country. The oven in the kitchen could be broken, and when not properly ventilated,
(75) smoke would leak out of several joints. When she had garbage or "slops" in the old country, she would be able to sweep it into her garden or feed it to the livestock. In America, however, garbage could not be disposed in

the same way nor did it serve any purpose. It was quite
(80) common for a woman to toss it out the window, often in overflowing buckets, into the street. Doing so was easier because she would not have to walk down the stairs to throw the garbage out.

A trip to the market was an ordeal for the immi-
(85) grant woman. In the old country, an immigrant peasant woman fed her family with the produce from her garden and the family's farmyards. But in America she had to buy food instead and use cash. Market shopping was a daunting task that included pushing through
(90) crowds, fighting with other customers over produce that was often damaged or not fresh, and spending money on foods such as bread, which was normally homemade in the old country. In America, it became a practice to buy bread already baked. Money had to be stretched as
(95) far as possible, so the immigrant woman became an aggressive bargainer with merchants or peddlers.

Because immigrant men were paid too low a wage to support the family, other family members had to work as well. So, in addition to household duties, an immi-
(100) grant woman would often take on other jobs to earn wages to pay for food and rent. Immigrant mothers with small children earned money at home in different ways, such as doing piecework for one of the manufacturing trades that still employed home workers. Women in dif-
(105) ferent ethnic groups tended to work at different trades. For example, Jewish and Italian women sewed in their homes for the needle trades (the largest employers of immigrant women), which included manufacturers of coats, dresses, millinery, shirtwaists, and underwear.
(110) Married women stitched in their tenement flats, and unmarried women sewed in shops and factories.

While immigrants arriving in America adhered to traditional values and customs, the way of life they knew in the old country was not continued with their
(115) children, who were more readily absorbed into the American culture. This often created conflicts between parents and their children. The traditions handed down from mother to daughter in the old country, which had preserved a sense of continuity, were not possible to
(120) maintain in America. Perhaps one of the worst difficulties of the immigrant mother was the loss of a daughter's desire to observe the customs of the old country. The traditional way of life no longer could be handed down from mother to daughter, particularly if the daughter
(125) insisted on making her own choices and not having them made for her by her family.

85. One of the greatest difficulties an immigrant mother faced adjusting to life in America was:

A. the inability to find suitable factory work.

B. moving to a slum from the countryside.

C. not being able to have a daughter preserve the customs from the old country.

D. being forced to haggle with food vendors.

86. European peasant women were accustomed to observing specific customs and beliefs:

A. handed down by the women in their family.

B. that allowed them to adjust to American culture.

C. handed down by the women in their family that permitted women to be individualistic.

D. handed down that did not have to be followed should an individual choose not to.

87. The passage refers to housing for the poor at this time as a tenement flat, which means:

A. a private apartment with spacious rooms.

B. a run-down, low-rental apartment building whose facilities barely meet minimum standards.

C. a rental apartment with adequate facilities.

D. sharing a bath and toilet on the same floor with another family.

88. Although living in the city, an immigrant woman was able to substitute traditional chores done in the old country by:

A. selling baked items at the neighborhood market.

B. taking care of the children of women in the manufacturing trades.

C. spending time to care only of the apartment.

D. keeping the tenement flat clean, juggling space to allow people to fit, and turning the kitchen into several work areas.

89. The passage points out that in the old country the immigrant women were accustomed to:

A. gardening vegetables to feed the family.

B. gardening vegetables to feed the family. and often selling some in the marketplace.

C. using money to buy bread already baked.

D. using money to bargain at the market.

90. According to the passage, an immigrant woman in America often had to earn additional money because:

A. it was expected that she also work.

B. the immigrant man received such low wages that other family members had to work.

C. the immigrant women received higher wages then did immigrant men.

D. the family would starve and be evicted from their apartment.

91. One can infer from the passage's tone that the author is largely sympathetic about the:

A. unsanitary and poorly maintained apartments immigrant families were forced to live in.

B. immigrant woman's struggles to adapt to a different language.

C. many difficulties an immigrant woman faced in adapting to another culture.

D. poverty-stricken conditions the immigrant family lived in on a daily basis.

Passage III (Questions 92–98)

What were the results at the end of the Spanish-American War, which was fought in 1898 between the United States and Spain? The answer may seem obvious, but it is not. Why the war was fought is not com-
(5) pletely clear. There was growing desire among many Americans for a colonial empire but the feeling was hardly universal, and in fact, President William McKinley opposed a war with Spain. Four colonies owned by Spain were affected by the war: Cuba, Puerto
(10) Rico, Guam, and the Philippine Islands. By the 1890s, American citizens in Cuba owned about 50 million dollars' worth of Cuban property, primarily in the sugar, tobacco, and iron industries. The president was under tremendous pressure to defend U.S. interests on the is-
(15) land. By 1898, both Cuba and the Philippine Islands had revolted against Spain.

Jose Marti, who had lived in exile in the United States, led the revolution for Cuban independence. As the intensity of the revolution increased, with Cubans
(20) waging guerrilla warfare in trying to wear out the Spanish, the brutality of the Spanish response grew in retaliation. In the United States, sympathy for the Cuban revolution increased. Many Americans wanted the United States to intervene on the side of the Cuban
(25) rebels, because the Spanish were seen as unwanted foreigners to be driven out of the hemisphere. Two events crystallized American sentiment for going to war with Spain. One was a letter written by the Spanish minister in Washington, Enrique Dupuy de Lome, criticizing
(30) President McKinley as a "weakling and a bidder for admiration of the crowd." The second event was the sinking of the battleship *U.S.S. Maine* in Havana harbor, where 266 United States naval troops lost their lives. This event galvanized U.S. opinion and gave
(35) President McKinley little choice but to declare war on Spain, even though a Spanish inquiry claimed that the ship had an internal problem leading to its explosion. The American investigation of the *Maine*, ordered by McKinley, determined that the cause was a submarine
(40) mine, although no people or party was officially blamed for the ship's explosion. Spain broke diplomatic relations with the U.S. on April 23, 1898, and war was declared by Congress retroactively to April 21. From the beginning of hostilities, the United States made it clear
(45) that the sole motive at the beginning of the struggle was to win Cuban independence. Congress passed a resolution, the Teller Amendment, that made it clear that the U.S. had no intention of annexing Cuba. Although neither Spain nor the United States had desired
(50) war, both made preparations as the crisis deepened after the sinking of the *Maine*.

Once war broke out, the United States expanded the war to include the Philippine Islands, Puerto Rico, and Guam. In addition to a blockade of Cuba, the United
(55) States Navy, under the leadership of Commodore George Dewey, attacked the Spanish colony in the Philippine Islands by sea in Manila Bay. In addition, Dewey used Filipino troops under the leadership of Emilio Aguinaldo, who had become the leader of a revolution-
(60) ary outburst against Spain in 1896–1897 that ended in a truce. Although Aguinaldo attempted to re-energize his movement and capture Manila, seat of the Spanish colony, Dewey did not recognize the government. Aguinaldo was forced to form an uneasy alliance with
(65) American troops. The cooperation between the Filipino insurgents and the U.S. forces culminated in Spain surrendering in August. The U.S. did not want the Filipinos to gain control and was negotiating a separate surrender with the Spanish. Despite appreciation among
(70) the Filipinos for the U.S. helping evict Spanish rule, tensions increased as Filipinos realized that the inter-

est of the U.S. was not about protecting democracy but about territorial expansion. Before the peace treaty between the U.S. and Spain was formally signed, U.S.
(75) troops fired on a group of Filipinos, starting the Philippine-American War. The uprising of the Filipinos and the war in the Philippines continued until 1914, when the United States finally crushed the insurrection and annexed the Philippines. The estimated number of
(80) civilians killed ranged from 200,000 to 600,000.

By August, the Spanish realized they had no hope to win the Spanish-American War and signed a protocol ending all hostilities on August 12, 1898. The war officially ended December 10, 1898, with the signing
(85) of the Treaty of Paris. The treaty allowed the United States to annex Puerto Rico in lieu of indemnities, gave the United States the Philippines for the sum of $25,000,000, and also gave the United States control of Guam. Guam had surrendered without a fight. Puerto
(90) Rico was also annexed, mostly without resistance.

One of the results of the war was that Cuba received its independence, but with severe limitations through the Platt Amendment. The Platt Amendment gave the United States the right to intervene in Cuban
(95) internal affairs and determine Cuba's foreign affairs and granted the U.S. a naval base at Guantanamo Bay for perpetuity without rent. With this, the United States felt it had secured the Caribbean and felt secure in building the Panama Canal. In the case of Guam, the Philippine
(100) Islands, and Puerto Rico, the result of the war simply meant the replacement of one colonial ruler with another. At the end of the war, the United States had begun its own colonial empire.

92. According to the passage, the Spanish colonies involved in the Spanish-American War of 1898 were:

   A. Puerto Rico, the Dominican Republic, Cuba, and Guam.

   B. Puerto Rico, the Philippine Islands, Guam, and Haiti.

   C. Puerto Rico, Cuba, the Philippine Islands, and Guam.

   D. Puerto Rico, Cuba, the Philippine Islands, and Mexico.

93. Many Americans supported the idea of war because they:

- **A.** wanted to show the superiority of American troops in battle.
- **B.** believed that the colonies should be independent of Spanish rule.
- **C.** saw it as a means of preserving U.S. investments in all four colonies.
- **D.** envisioned having an American colonial empire by acquiring the four colonies.

94. An official American investigation of the explosion of the *U.S.S. Maine* was ordered by President McKinley with the findings that:

- **A.** Spanish insurgents were determined to gain independence by implicating Spain in the explosion.
- **B.** the cause was unofficially a Spanish submarine mine.
- **C.** the cause was an internal explosion, as a Spanish investigation determined.
- **D.** the cause was a submarine mine with no one officially blamed.

95. The Spanish-American War was fought primarily:

- **A.** on the terrains of all four colonies.
- **B.** on the seas, with a blockade of Cuba and an attack on the Spanish colony in the Philippine Islands.
- **C.** on the seas and finished with the surrender on land by the governor of Cuba.
- **D.** by the revolutionary insurgents of each colony.

96. The alliance between the Filipino insurrectionists and American troops ended at the end of the war:

- **A.** with an uprising by the Filipino population, lasting until 1914, when the United States destroyed the Filipino opposition.
- **B.** when Aguinaldo took over leadership of the Philippine Islands.
- **C.** with Filipino allegiance to the United States.
- **D.** immediately after the U.S. and Spain formally signed the peace treaty.

97. Actual fighting during the Spanish-American War occurred in the following Spanish colonies:

- **A.** Cuba, the Philippine Islands, and Puerto Rico.
- **B.** Cuba, the Philippine Islands, and Guam.
- **C.** Cuba and the Philippine Islands.
- **D.** the Philippine Islands and Guam.

98. The passage points out that although Cuba was given independence, the Philippine Islands, Puerto Rico, and Guam were:

- **A.** to remain under the protection of the United States as colonies.
- **B.** promised eventual freedom after a fifty-year period.
- **C.** thought to be incapable of self-determination after years of colonization.
- **D.** expected to pledge allegiance to the United States once freedom was granted to them by the U.S.

Passage IV (Questions 99–104)

Redwood trees once covered much of the world. Millions of years ago the climate was ideal for the development of many species of redwood trees throughout the northern hemisphere. They were particularly (5) common during the Jurassic period, or the age of dinosaurs. As the climate grew less moderate, the range of the redwood tree began to get smaller. The current range has existed for several million years. Many species of redwood trees disappeared and today only three varie- (10) ties remain and of the three, two have very limited ranges.

The rarest variety of all is the Dawn Redwood or *Metasequoia Gilyptostroboides*. This variety was thought to be extinct, but a small number of these trees (15) was found in a remote valley in China in the 1940s. As far as is known, these trees had survived in a single grove. This variety is the only non-evergreen variety still in existence and is also the smallest of the redwoods, reaching a height of 115 feet with a diameter of (20) less than 15 feet. The fact that they survived at all is quite surprising.

The second variety that has survived is the Sequoia Redwood, *Sequoia Giganteum,* which also has a very limited range. It is only found between 5,000 and (25) 8,000 feet on the west side of the Sierra Nevada Mountain Range. It is found from Yosemite National Park in the north to Sequoia National Park in the south, a range

of no more than 70 miles. Even in this region, the tree is only found in a few groves and some isolated indi-
(30) vidual specimens. The tree reaches a height of more than 300 feet and a diameter of up to 35 feet. Logging in the late 1800s and early 1900s would have destroyed the tree altogether except for a particular quality of this tree. When it falls to the ground, it breaks into splinters
(35) and is therefore not usable for lumber. Nonetheless, many of the few surviving groves where cut down.

The third variety of redwood is the California Coastal Redwood Tree, *Sequoia Sempervirens,* which is the redwood with the largest range. It is found from
(40) Big Sur, California, in the South to central Oregon in the north. It is found from right along the coast to as much as 20 to 30 miles inland and is not confined to groves but instead is found in significant forests. This tree is also the tallest tree known to humanity. Some
(45) trees reach a height of 360 feet or more, the height of a 36-story building and can have a diameter of 22 feet. This variety of redwood occupies a small micro-climate of mild winters and cool summers.

Though the redwood tree is very climate sensi-
(50) tive, in other ways it is remarkably well adapted for survival. The tree is almost completely fire resistant and can withstand major forest fires with minimal damage. It is also largely insect resistant due to unusually high levels of *tannin* in its bark. Insects that attack other
(55) evergreens are unable to attack redwood trees. Depending on the variety, these trees are also remarkably long lived. Many specimens live more than 2,000 years. Redwood trees are unusual in yet another way. They have no tap root like most other trees. This means that
(60) they are more likely subject to toppling. They reproduce in two ways: like many other trees they reproduce using sexual reproduction, which leads to the development of cones, but they can also produce asexually by producing genetic clones. This gives the species added
(65) ability to survive.

Redwood forests also create a micro-climate that is moist and ideal for the development of ferns. Coastal redwood forests are characterized by the moist ground in an otherwise dry summer climate. While coastal red-
(70) woods can survive long dry summers, though this survival is in large part made possible by the near daily penetration of coastal fog that keeps humidity levels very high for much of the night and morning, they need wet winters to flourish. Usually they need at least 30
(75) inches of rain a year. They are also rapid growers and can grow several feet in a year.

While redwood trees have a limited natural range, both Dawn Redwoods and Mountain Sequoias have been successfully planted in much of the northern hemi-
(80) sphere and have thrived. You can find these redwoods in Europe, Asia, and much of North America. Coastal Redwoods have also been planted in regions where they

do not grow naturally. As long as the climate is not too hot, not too cold, and not too dry, they too have been
(85) successful. As climate continues to moderate, the range of the redwood may grow.

99. The passage states that redwood trees existed as far back as:

   A. 50 million years ago.
   B. 100 million years ago.
   C. several million years ago.
   D. about one million years ago.

100. Of the varieties of redwood trees, the three that still exist have survived due to:

   A. immunity from fire and insects, and longevity.
   B. immunity from fire and insects and infrequent logging from the lumber industry.
   C. immunity from old age, no reliance on water, and asexual reproduction.
   D. immunity from old age, asexual reproduction, and the ability to create moist, humid climates for growth.

101. According to the passage, the Dawn Redwood was believed to be extinct but a small grove was discovered in:

   A. California in the 1940s.
   B. an enclosed canyon in California in the 1940s.
   C. China in a rural area in the 1940s.
   D. a remote valley in California in the 1940s.

102. An interesting fact about the Sequoia Redwood is that:

   A. its size of 300 feet was a major factor in its survival.
   B. it can be as tall as 300 feet with a diameter of up to 35 feet.
   C. despite its giant size, it can be found along the California and Oregon coastline.
   D. the logging industry was not interested in cutting down this variety of tree due to its indestructibility.

103. Redwood forests have the ability to foster an environment:

  A. where the climate is continuously damp.

  B. to perpetuate its growth.

  C. that allows for its tremendous growth and height.

  D. that hinders the development of ferns, plants that can choke the trees' roots.

104. The word *tannin* in paragraph 5 means:

  A. the type of chemicals found in redwood forests.

  B. the particular chemical that makes the trees insect resistant.

  C. material gathered from the base of the redwood trees.

  D. material derived from the bark and fruit of many plants.

Passage V (Questions 105–111)

More than 200 years ago, in his ground-breaking book on economics called *The Wealth of Nations,* Adam Smith said that capitalism functions best when left alone. He meant that the government should have little
(5) or no involvement in the economy, which is the concept of *laissez faire,* and the book became the bible of capitalism. To this day, capitalist and many other governments, particularly the United States, espouse the doctrine of *laissez faire*. But, in fact, governments in-
(10) volved themselves in the economy almost from the beginning of capitalism and often with the support of capitalism. This has been particularly true in the United States, in spite of the doctrine of *laissez faire*.

With the birth of the new nation, the United States
(15) began to regulate trade and protect American industry with tariffs that made imported goods more expensive than American goods, and the new government began to build and maintain roads to facilitate trade. In the early nineteenth century, one of the biggest public works
(20) projects ever undertaken began in New York State: the building of the Erie Canal, which linked Albany and Buffalo by a water channel. This channel was built at massive public expense to improve access to western markets. Other forms of government intervention in the
(25) economy continued throughout the nineteenth century. One of the most important of these interventions was the building of the transcontinental railroad, which would not have been built without government support. The government gave large land grants to the two com-
(30) panies that built the railroad, clearly a form of subsidy, and even picked the place that the two railroads were

to come together. Government also helped regulate wages during the nineteenth and early twentieth century by using federal troops to break strikes and federal
(35) courts to issue injunctions against unions. This involvement helped to make capitalism more profitable. All these forms of government intervention were welcomed by the capitalist class.

As the twentieth century approached, government
(40) intervention in the economy only increased. First, the Sherman Antitrust Act was passed, which regulated industries by giving the government power to break up monopolies and greater power to control unions. This act was followed by other antitrust acts. Though these
(45) acts were initially opposed by most industrial leaders, they were mainly used to benefit capitalism either by controlling unions or by breaking up companies such as Standard Oil, which had a virtual stranglehold on industry, making it difficult for other industries to buy
(50) oil at a reasonable price and expand.

Beginning with the progressives and continuing to the present, the government has increasingly regulated the conditions of work. First, child labor was outlawed and the exploitation of women was monitored.
(55) Also, beginning with the progressive movement, the quality of food and medications has been regulated by the government through the Pure Food and Drug Act. Then in the 1930s, by setting conditions of the work environment and setting labor standards that included
(60) the right of unions to negotiate in good faith, the government expanded its intervention into the workings of capitalism. During the 1930s, government continued to expand its role in regulating the economy. For the first time, the government began to regulate banks, the
(65) stock market, and brokers. This was done to create a reliable financial foundation so that capitalism could expand in a more rational way. Though many capitalists opposed these measures, it is clear that without them modern capitalism would not have survived and pros-
(70) pered in its present form. During the same period of time, the government began to regulate the money supply. The goal was to end deflation and create enough inflation so that it would be profitable for companies to expand. While initially the policy was only moderately
(75) successful, to this day—whether the president is a Republican or Democrat—monetary control of the economy has been a cornerstone of economic policy.

While critics continue to press the idea that government should have little or no involvement in the
(80) economy, new legislation that increases government regulation of capitalism is passed each year at the federal and state levels. Everything from how much control of the media can one company have to what rules brokers must follow when selling stocks to customers
(85) are regulated either at the federal or state level or both. The environmental movement has added another level

of regulation of capitalism by the government. Every car, every electric power plant, and every factory must meet environmental standards. Everything from how
(90) many miles per gallon a car must get to how much particulate matter factories can pump into the atmosphere is regulated by the federal government and in some cases by state governments as well. Which products can be sold and which cannot is regulated by the
(95) federal government. It is obvious that capitalism has flourished not because of little regulation, but because of extensive and continuous expanded regulation and that this trend is likely to continue for the foreseeable future. How often do industries ask for subsidies, loans,
(100) and the blockage of imports so that their company will be successful? Were Adam Smith alive today, he would be shocked by the way the capitalist system has developed and expanded into a highly regulated environment with government involvement often requested by the
(105) very capitalist that Adam Smith thought would not survive with such involvement. Obviously, while governments like the United States talk of *laissez faire*, they practice something much different.

105. The concept of *laissez faire* can best be understood by one of the following statements:

    A. For capitalism to survive, the government must be involved in the economy.

    B. Capitalism is most successful when the government has little or no involvement in the economy.

    C. There are times that government must protect the people from the excesses of capitalism.

    D. It is okay for the government to build roads, railroads, and canals, but otherwise the government should leave capitalism to develop on its own.

106. According to the passage, which of the following were the beginnings of involvement of the United States in the country's economy?

    I. Building of the Erie Canal and the transcontinental railroad

    II. Support of union strikes with the help of federal troops and federal courts

    III. Building and maintenance of transportation routes

    IV. Non-regulation of workers' wages

    A. I and III

    B. II and IV

    C. I and IV

    D. II and III

107. By the beginning of the twentieth century, the government's involvement in the economy expanded to passing antitrust acts in order to:

    A. work cooperatively with unions and regulate productivity.

    B. allow large corporations to continue monopolizing specific industries.

    C. allow private federal information gathered by the government to help private industries.

    D. break up major companies with monopolies and limit labor unions' ability to strike.

108. The implication in the passage is that the government:

    A. has gained so much control over its economy that it is a danger to the growth of capitalism.

    B. views its role as a balance of power between the *laissez-faire* policy and capitalism.

    C. does not practice *laissez faire* but rather has continuously been involved in regulating the economy since the beginning.

    D. has been successful in regulating numerous work conditions in various industries.

109. One can infer from the author's tone that the author believes:

    A. the government has the right to be involved with the country's economy.

    B. it is the government's role to take control of the country's economy.

    C. the government's actions contradict its actual practice of involvement in the economy with its declared policy of *laissez faire*.

    D. the government's regulation of the country's economy is necessary for the development of capitalism.

110. By regulating banks, the stock market, and brokers in the 1930s, the government:

    A. was planning to end inflation and develop deflation.

    B. would work with those capitalists willing to cooperate.

    C. would be able to determine policies to be used with the public.

    D. created a foundation for modern capitalism.

111. The author concludes with the premise that:

    A. the federal government realized its need to lessen its involvement in the country's economy.

    B. the federal government was forced to become involved in the country's economy.

    C. since the creation of the U.S. government, it has involved itself gradually with the economy and expanded its role and power.

    D. since the creation of the U.S. government, it has involved itself due to many economic situations that the state governments were unable to handle.

Passage VI (Questions 112–118)

Since the Constitutional Convention of 1787, the power of the presidency has grown in relationship to the legislative and judicial branches of the national government. While our forefathers saw three branches of
(5) government of equal power, the reality has been quite different.

Our forefathers were afraid of the development of tyranny and therefore tried to limit the power of the executive branch of the government. Laws origi-
(10) nated in the legislative branch, and even if the president refused to sign a bill passed by Congress, Congress could legitimately override a veto with a two-thirds vote. The president could negotiate treaties with foreign powers, but the Senate had to approve
(15) them. The president was commander and chief of the armed forces, but only Congress could declare war. The president had the ability to appoint people to the cabinet and also federal judges, but the Senate had to approve those choices. The president admin-
(20) istered the laws passed by Congress, but Congress could overview the administration. Finally, the Constitution gave Congress the power to impeach a president and federal appointees.

While the role of the judicial branch of the gov-
(25) ernment is not spelled out clearly in the Constitution, the role of judicial review was established from almost the very beginning of the federal government. This branch was yet another check and balance. The courts had the right to review federal and state laws
(30) to establish whether they were constitutional. Doing so meant that even if Congress passed and the president signed a law, the federal court system and ultimately the Supreme Court could rule that a law violated the Constitution and therefore could not be en-
(35) forced. The only way around this situation was to pass a constitutional amendment.

With these kinds of limitations on the presidency, how has the office become so powerful? Beginning with George Washington, the presidency came to represent
(40) the country in a way that Congress and the judiciary never could. Members of Congress represent their districts, senators represent their states, and the federal courts are thought to represent nobody, as they are appointed. But the president represents the whole nation.
(45) The development of a national media has become extremely important in increasing the power of the presidency. Newspapers became widespread in the 1830s and literacy gradually became more universal throughout the nineteenth century. In addition, technology, be-
(50) ginning with the telegraph, made the coverage of events national. The whole country could learn what the president was doing as he was doing it. While coverage was

and is given to congressional figures, that coverage is
(55) usually regional. Thus, increasingly, the president has
become the embodiment of the nation. Obviously, the
twentieth and twenty-first centuries have only enhanced
this process with the development of first radio in the
1920s, then television, which was not common in
(60) American households until the 1940s and, finally, the
Web, which became common in households in the early
1990s.

Franklin Delano Roosevelt was the first president
who recognized the power of the media radio, with his
(65) fireside chats to the people nationwide. The use of the
radio to communicate his policies was helpful because
it helped him gain support for the legislation that he
wanted passed through Congress. He could and did go
to the nation to encourage people to put pressure on
(70) Congress to pass his bills and to see that those members of Congress who did not support his programs
would not be re-elected. Today, no day goes by when
the president isn't featured in the media. If Congress
does not support his actions, he can focus negative at-
(75) tention on Congress. Congress has completely lost its
power to declare war. All wars since World War II have
only required a commitment from the executive branch.
Sometimes Congress has been asked for its approval,
but Congress was usually told even if the approval
(80) wasn't granted that the president would still continue
to conduct the war. Internationally, Congress has all
but abdicated its role. The president was always expected to conduct diplomacy, but it was assumed that
Congress, and particularly the Senate, would also play
(85) a role. With the exception of the approval of treaties
which the Senate must still perform, all other foreign
policy is conducted by the president. Congress's role is
still important on the domestic level, but even here the
power of the president has increased. It was assumed
(90) in the Constitution that legislation would originate in
Congress, but today virtually all major legislation origi-
nates in the executive branch of government. The legislation is formally introduced by a member of Congress, but written in the executive branch. In addition,
(95) broad powers have been granted to the president to
implement legislation and to use executive orders that
come directly from the president as legislation.

The most recent example of this expansion of
presidential powers is the Homeland Security Act. The
(100) act was passed by Congress, but it originated in the
executive office and was passed with significant pressure from that office. This act strengthens the presidency and weakens the role of the courts. The president, through the attorney general, has been given power
(105) for wiretaps and the issuing of certain warrants like arrest warrants. While the courts have maintained more
of their power than Congress, they also are influenced
by the presidency, as it is the president who appoints

federal judges. Recently, the president, through the at-
(110) torney general, has been monitoring decisions made by
federal judges with the implication that those judges
who make unfavorable rulings will be punished in some
unspecified way. The significance of this is a clear attempt to increase executive power in the judicial branch
(115) of government. With the Homeland Security Act, the
president now has clear power granted by Congress to
do what was formerly done by the court system.

What becomes clear is that the power of the presidency has grown far beyond what our forefathers envi-
(120) sioned and that this power continues to grow. It is also
likely that the power of the presidency will grow even
stronger as there is now no clear counterbalance.

112. According to the author of the passage, one
reason the power of the presidency has grown
over the last 200 years is because:

   A. of the need for a national leader.
   B. Congress has abdicated its legislative role.
   C. of the development of a national media.
   D. of the increased importance of foreign
      policy.

113. It would be reasonable, based on the passage,
to assume that the author:

   A. supports the growth of presidential power.
   B. opposes the growth of presidential power.
   C. has no opinion on the growth of presiden-
      tial power.
   D. There is not enough information in this
      passage to answer this question.

114. According to the passage, news became national with the:

   A. ability of newspapers to reach a wide au-
      dience.
   B. invention of the telegraph.
   C. invention of the radio.
   D. invention of television.

115. The following are powers the president currently has:

I. Sign warrants for unspecified reasons.
II. Appoint federal judges.
III. Approve wiretaps.
IV. Sign arrest warrants.

A. I, II, and III
B. II, III, and IV
C. I, III, and IV
D. II, III, and IV

116. The passage points out that one of the following reasons was responsible for increasing the president's image of power:

A. The president conducted all foreign policies.
B. It was difficult for the country to be aware of the president's actions as they were being carried out.
C. It was expected that the media did not focus news primarily on the president.
D. Legislation continued to be written by Congress.

117. Congress's power to declare war:

A. also includes giving the military monetary support.
B. does not need presidential approval today.
C. after World War II was not curtailed.
D. means the president is accountable for being supportive.

118. One can infer from the passage that:

A. the system of checks and balances for the government has worked well.
B. Congress has been more powerful than either the presidency or the judicial branch.
C. despite powers given to the three branches of government by the Constitution in 1787, the power of the presidency has overwhelmingly grown.
D. the judicial branch is free of retaliations from either the legislature or the president for decisions the Supreme Court gives.

Passage VII (Questions 119–125)

Whales, or Cetaceans, as they are scientifically known, are the largest animals to have ever lived. They are even bigger than any known dinosaur and belong to a family that actually includes whales, dolphins, and (5) porpoises. Cetaceans are mammals and are not closely related to fish. They breathe air, not water, have hair, give birth to live young, and nurse and raise those young.

During millions of years of evolution, Cetaceans went from being land mammals to being sea mammals. (10) It may be assumed that the sea provided more food and more buoyancy than the land for an already large animal. As they entered the oceans, their bodies adapted. Their hind limbs disappeared, their bodies became more tapered, and most body hair disappeared. They also de-(15) veloped the ability to breathe very infrequently. The lost body hair was replaced by the development of blubber as a form of protection from cold. Cetaceans' breathing apparatus moved to the top of the body, which allowed Cetaceans to breathe more efficiently in a water (20) environment. The external ears disappeared, as they were only effective for collecting sound waves in the air. Instead, Cetaceans developed a sonar system where they bounce sound off an object and in doing so, can tell both the size and the distance of that object. In fact, (25) this system is so effective that the armed forces have attempted to use dolphins to track undersea objects.

Of course, animals as large as Cetaceans need immense amounts of food to maintain their huge size. Generally, Cetaceans feed in one of two ways. The (30) Odontoceti use teeth to catch fish and other food, though they do not use their teeth to chew their food. Examples of Odontocetis are porpoises, dolphins, and whales such as the Sperm Whale. The second group, known as Mysticeti, do not have teeth, but instead have plates (35) made of keratin that act as filters to capture small sea creatures and is a substance similar to what our fingernails are made. They will eat plankton, krill fish, and other small sea life. Examples of this group are the Blue whale and the Orca. (40)

Cetaceans show a high level of intelligence, and many species seem to show communication skills. Dolphins are particularly vocal and may even have developed something that resembles a language. Like other members of the Cetacean family, they also use the (45) sounds they make to pinpoint objects both in terms of size and distance. There is evidence that they can warn each other of danger and also let other members of the group know where food is located. Cetaceans are also very social animals and will often travel in large groups. (50) They will use these groups to protect the young. Dolphins are unusually strong swimmers and often can keep up with speed boats.

One can only speculate why the evolutionary development of whales has led to such large size. Some
(55) whales can be 33 meters long and weigh 200 metric
tons. This size would absolutely not be sustainable by
the land, and in many ways it is remarkable that such a
large size is even sustainable in the ocean.

While these mammals have adjusted extremely
(60) well to their water environment, they do face a serious
threat to their survival. That threat comes from human
activity. Besides active hunting of whales that almost
drove some species to extinction, there are other threats
to their survival. Dolphins often die in the nets of tuna
(65) fishing boats. The increase in water pollution and the
decrease of the ozone layer are also a threat to the survival of Cetaceans. We do not yet know how much these
environmental changes affect the survival of Cetaceans,
but some have suggested that the beaching of large num-
(70) bers of whales may be related to environmental pollution. While some strong steps have been made to help
sustain the Cetacean population, it is not clear that what
has been done has been enough. While some populations have shown signs of recovery, others have con-
(75) tinued to decline.

A final serious threat particularly to whales is the
return of whaling. At least three nations have become
actively involved in whaling: Iceland, Japan, and Norway. These countries argue that the species which they
(80) whale are now abundant enough that there is no danger
to the species and further that the limits they have put
on their whaling fleet will guarantee this. However,
environmentalists remind us that it was previous whaling that brought so many species to the brink of extinc-
(85) tion and also ask, what might happen if other nations
also begin to hunt whales?

The future of Cetaceans is clearly in the hands of
humans; it will require a continued international effort
to protect Cetaceans and get a better understanding of
(90) these animals, if future generations are to see these mag-
nificent creatures.

119. According to the passage, the fate of Cetaceans
can be ensured:

A. by an international effort to protect them.
B. if countries cooperate by signing a bind-
ing agreement.
C. by an agreed international punishment of
countries that threaten the Cetaceans' ex-
istence.
D. if the three countries—Iceland, Japan, and
Norway—agree to stop hunting whales.

120. One of the following is NOT true about the
adaptation of Cetaceans to being sea mammals.

A. Blubber replaced body hair.
B. The breathing system moved to the top of
their bodies.
C. They lost four limbs.
D. Their body shape changed.

121. Whales, or using their scientific nomenclature,
Cetaceans, are considered to be the largest animals alive. Their family also includes:

A. sharks and salmon.
B. all mammals that breathe water.
C. dolphins and seals.
D. dolphins and porpoises.

122. According to the passage, the communication
skills of Cetaceans appear to be useful for them
in:

A. situations where they are forced to attack
aggressors.
B. warning one another of danger.
C. eating.
D. playful activities.

123. The Odontoceti's ability to consume tremendous amounts of food involves:

A. using their teeth to catch fish but not to
eat their food.
B. their sizes in catching fish.
C. their need to continuously feed themselves.
D. roaming wide regions of the oceans for
sufficient food.

124. The passage points out that humans are a threat
to Cetaceans by doing all the following activities EXCEPT:

A. polluting the oceans.
B. affecting the ozone layer.
C. actively advocating for their survival.
D. continuing to catch dolphins instead of
tuna.

125. Although the author discusses the positive attributes of Cetaceans, he points out that

    A. they are not enough to validate their existence.

    B. their extinction is inevitable.

    C. their continued existence depends on humankind.

    D. their existence is temporary.

Passage VIII (Questions 126–131)

    Slave narratives are autobiographical or semi-autobiographical accounts of emancipated slaves' lives under slavery written in the nineteenth century. Often, these narratives were written by the slaves themselves,
(5) but some narratives were written by white northerners based on accounts given by slaves. Though read by the public, at the time, the authenticity of many slave narratives as autobiographies was questioned, particularly when a second author was included. Many of these nar-
(10) ratives were written by male writers. The first autobiography of the life of a female slave, *Incidents in the Life of a Slave Girl, Written by Herself*, by Harriet Jacobs, was the first such book, released in 1861. *Incidents* recounts accurately and expressively Jacobs's
(15) experiences growing up as a house slave in the South before the Civil War. She tells how she was able to resist sexual attention from her master, and how she was able to escape from his attention by first going into hiding and later escaping to the North, where Harriet Jacobs
(20) became involved with the abolitionist movement and was determined to tell her life story. For the rest of her life, Jacobs also helped raise money for Southern Blacks with the profits from her writing.

    Incidents, however, is an example of those books
(25) not seen as authentic at the time because they were written by a ghost writer; in the case of *Incidents*, the ghost writer was a white author, Lydia Maria Child. Initially, Jacobs sought the assistance of a more influential voice, novelist Harriet Beecher Stowe. She persuaded Amy
(30) Post, an influential white abolitionist who was also involved in women's rights, to approach Harriet Beecher Stowe. Stowe had a novel ready for publication already, so she offered Jacobs the opportunity to include her story in the novel. Harriet Jacobs declined because she
(35) wanted to tell her own story. She began writing her narrative, but publishers were unwilling to print Jacobs's manuscript. One publisher finally agreed to print it but only if Lydia Maria Child would write an introduction to the autobiography and claim in this preface that her
(40) editorial work was limited.

    In *Incidents,* Harriet Jacobs decided to use the pseudonym Linda Brent and to disguise the names of people mentioned in her narrative in order to protect them from harm by their slave masters. At the time
(45) Jacobs was writing, authors who used pseudonymous names and published a book with no manuscript were suspect in the eyes of the public who believed the text was not authentic, whether the writer was an emancipated slave or not. In addition, critics of the time ques-
(50) tioned whether Jacobs had the necessary skills to write an autobiography by emphasizing her style of writing and dynamic use of language and literary conventions. Critics also felt Lydia Maria Child may have superimposed her own views as a white woman into the book.
(55) This critical speculation about Child's involvement eventually led to her being named the primary author of *Incidents,* even though Child wrote in the preface that she was not the author and had not made significant changes, emphasizing the small role she played as
(60) the editor. Child did help Harriet Jacobs to secure a contract that enabled Jacobs's work to get published and made widely available for public reading. In addition, Child recommended that the letters of correspondence from Amy Post to Harriet Jacobs be included as
(65) appendices, which was part of a tradition in verifying the authorship of African-American literature that first began with the 1773 publication of Phillis Wheatley's poetry. This practice in the publication of slave narratives had two advantages: It testified to the trustwor-
(70) thiness of the narrator and helped disperse Southern accusations that fictitious narratives were being used to fan antagonism against the South and slavery.

    Yet, the belief that *Incidents* was ghost-written was never dismissed. Although Jacobs's book received
(75) immediate publicity after its publication, it was largely ignored by modern scholars who doubted the authenticity and the authorship of the autobiography. It was believed that the narrative was dictated to Lydia Maria Child—despite her preface claiming the book's legiti-
(80) macy—or that, in fact, the text was an anti-slavery novel written by Child herself. The fact that Harriet Jacobs was a Black woman raised doubts that she wrote the book, a reflection of the racism and sexism of the time.

    Jean Fagan Yellin, professor of History at Pace
(85) University, extensively researched to validate Jacobs's authorship through painstaking archival work. She also searched for and located Jacobs's home and surroundings in the South and identified the people referred to in the autobiography. Yellin also found the papers of
(90) Amy and Isaac Post, abolitionists and advocates of temperance and women's rights, whose correspondence with Jacobs further served to confirm the validity of *Incidents.* Through this research, Yellin substantiated *Incidents* as an authentic autobiography. The conclusive proof of Jacobs's authorship and the authenticity

of the events she described in *Incidents,* included in
(95) Yellin's edition of Jacobs's work, published in 1981,
erased the doubts about the validity and authorship of
Incidents.

126. Harriet Jacobs's *Incidents in the Life of a Slave Girl* was:

    A. the first autobiography written by a female ex-slave.

    B. actually written by Lydia Maria Child.

    C. written by the owner of a former slave.

    D. written by a man.

127. When Harriet Beecher Stowe offered to include Jacobs's story in Stowe's forthcoming novel, Jacobs refused because:

    A. Stowe was unable to provide Jacobs assurance that the autobiography would be accepted by the public.

    B. Jacobs wanted to tell her own story.

    C. Stowe only wanted to include Jacobs's story in the novel since it was ready for publication.

    D. Jacobs decided that Stowe was not influential enough to help.

128. By using pseudonyms for the people she wrote about in her autobiography, Jacobs:

    A. wanted to keep their identities secret from each other.

    B. wanted to safeguard them from abuse by their masters.

    C. could not allow the public to search and identify these people.

    D. gave the public an opportunity to speculate further on the authenticity of her work.

129. Many people believed at the time that Lydia Maria Child had written or at least editorialized Jacobs's autobiography because:

    A. it was assumed that Jacobs could not write such a well-written book.

    B. Child's views on slavery were in the story.

    C. Child vehemently denied writing the autobiography.

    D. the public resented the involvement of Child, who was a well-known abolitionist.

130. Modern literary scholars would not accept Jacobs's autobiography as authentic due to:

    A. the fact that Jacobs was a woman.

    B. the belief that she dictated the story to Child.

    C. the belief that Lydia Maria Child, an abolitionist, wrote it as an anti-slavery novel.

    D. All of the above.

131. The main idea of the passage focuses on:

    A. the inability of sexist white Northerners to accept a slave narrative written by a woman.

    B. Jacobs's difficulties in having her autobiography published.

    C. the validation and authenticity of Jacobs's autobiography.

    D. the issue of slavery as an institution.

Practice Exam II

Passage IX (Questions 132–137)

The International Committee of the Red Cross (ICRC) was created through the efforts of Henri Dunant, a Swiss businessman from Geneva, and four other Genevan citizens in 1863. The reason for the founding
(5) can be found in events that began a few years earlier, in 1859, with the battle of Solferino in northern Italy, fought between Napoleon's French forces and the forces of the Austro-Hungarian Empire that occupied parts of Italy. Dunant, passing by the battlefield, was so over-
(10) whelmed with pity on hearing the tormented cries of the forty thousand soldiers helpless and unattended that he organized help from the nearest village, Solferino. He gathered volunteers who helped despite the chaos and horror of the battlefield, turning their homes and
(15) barns into makeshift hospitals, where soldiers from both sides were tended to. On his return to Geneva, Dunant wrote of his and the volunteers' experiences in a book titled *A Memory of Solferino*. In the book, Dunant expressed his idea to form volunteer relief societies to
(20) give care to the wounded in wartime.

Dunant's book became the incentive for him and four other Genevan citizens to establish an international organization dedicated to providing aid to victims of war. This aim was later widened to include assistance
(25) to all, not just war victims, regardless of nationality, religion, and politics. The Geneva Public Society set up the International Committee of the Red Cross. The first members were Guillaume Henri Dufour, a general of the Swiss army and a writer of military booklets,
(30) who became the committee's president for its first year and its honorary president thereafter; Gustave Moynier, a young lawyer and president of the sponsoring Public Welfare Society, who dedicated himself soon after to Red Cross work; Louis Appia and Theodore Maunoir,
(35) both medical doctors; and Henri Dunant.

In October of the same year the committee was founded, its members held an international conference, which was attended by sixteen nations, to adopt resolutions and principles along with an international em-
(40) blem. The committee also appealed to all nations to form voluntary units to help wartime sick and wounded. The aim of the 1863 Geneva Conference was to have its Red Cross principles become a part of international law. It was decided to hold an international convention,
(45) which was the historic Geneva Convention of 1864, to address specifically provisions to guarantee neutral status to military hospitals and medical personnel of the armies of the signing countries. To identify these non-combatants, the convention adopted a red cross on a
(50) white field, a reversal of the colors of the Swiss national flag. It was signed by the attending twelve European countries and Great Britain and Canada added their names a year later.

The Red Cross today is a strictly neutral and im-
(55) partial organization dedicated to humanitarian interests in general and to relieve human suffering in particular. There are three basic components of the organization. The first is the self-governing National Red Cross Societies, including the Red Crescent in Muslim coun-
(60) tries and the Red Lion and Sun in Iran, which work on the national level and can also participate in international work. Each society must be recognized by the International Committee and also have Junior Red Cross Societies. Secondly, there is the League of Red Cross
(65) Societies, which is the coordinating world federation of these societies, a result of proposals in 1919 by Henry P. Davison of the American Red Cross. The League performs multiple tasks: It continues contact between the societies, operates as a clearinghouse for information,
(70) facilitates the societies in setting up new programs and in improving or expanding old ones, and coordinates international disaster operations. The third component of the Red Cross is the International Committee of the Red Cross (ICRC) which acts today as a private, inde-
(75) pendent group of elected Swiss citizens, limited to 25 individuals. The ICRC acts during war or conflict whenever intervention by a neutral body is necessary, an action that emphasizes its special field of activity. The ICRC, as the protector of the Geneva Convention and
(80) Red Cross principles, is involved in numerous fields to encourage, for example, acceptance by governments, further development of international humanitarian law, and recognition of new Red Cross Societies.

The American Red Cross was created through the
(85) efforts of Clara Barton who, under doctor's orders to rest from her strenuous involvement in the Civil War, went to France. There, she discovered the existence of the Red Cross. The Franco-Prussian War of 1870 broke out while she was in Geneva. Miss Barton offered her
(90) services—even though the United States was not allied to the Red Cross—as she was familiar with the needs of war. She went to the war zone with volunteers of the International Red Cross. Miss Barton wore the internationally accepted symbol of the Red Cross by using a
(95) red ribbon she was wearing and making a cross to pin on her coat. She also helped to distribute relief supplies to the suffering people of Strasbourg and in other areas of France. Miss Barton corresponded with Red Cross officials in Switzerland after she returned home.
(100) The officials saw her as the natural leader for carrying the Red Cross movement to the United States and for pressuring it to sign the Geneva Treaty. In 1877, the head of the International Committee of the Red Cross sent her a letter addressed to the President of the United
(105) States, asking her to present it. Despite doing so, then President Hayes was reluctant to ally the United States with the Geneva Treaty. Clara Barton was persistent in her efforts and due to her determination, President

Arthur signed and the Senate ratified the treaty in 1882.
(110)   Today, the Red Cross is internationally known and respected with 114 National Red Cross Societies. The International Red Cross Movement is the largest disaster relief and community development organization in the world, carrying out emergency relief operations in
(115) more than 50 crises and war zones.

132. The origins of the foundation of the Red Cross was based on

A. Swiss citizens' concern for proper care of soldiers wounded and left behind on the battlefield during the conflict between the French and the Austro-Hungarian Empire.

B. the efforts of a Swiss businessman who had wounded soldiers from a battle temporarily taken care of by volunteering local townspeople.

C. the experiences of a Swiss businessman who wrote a book about his involvement in assembling volunteer local townspeople to take in wounded soldiers left behind from a nearby battlefield.

D. All of the above

133. Henri Dunant's novel describing his involvement with the local townspeople of Solferino in taking care of wounded soldiers from a nearby battle stressed the:

A. horrors of the battle so vividly that it became a best-selling book in Europe that captured the public's attention.

B. need to create agencies in times of peace that used qualified and dedicated volunteers to tend to the wounded during war.

C. need to create agencies whose skillful and dedicated volunteers were willing to die on the battlefield during war while nursing the wounded.

D. possibility of countries cooperating during peace times to create relief societies that relied on trained and efficient volunteers to take care of the wounded during war.

134. The Red Cross is internationally recognized for its neutral and impartial organization and dedication to humanitarian interests. Its organization is composed of several elements. The first element mentioned in the passage are:

A. National Red Cross Societies that are self-run, the Red Crescent in Muslim countries, and the Red Lion and Sun in Iran.

B. National Red Cross Societies run by a host country, the Red Crescent in Muslim countries, and the Red Lion and Sun in Iran.

C. National Red Cross Societies that are self-run and the Red Crescent and Lion and Sun in Muslim countries.

D. National Red Cross Societies that are run by Christian countries and two other separate divisions based on non-Christian religions.

135. The Geneva Convention of 1864 guaranteed that:

A. member countries of the Red Cross had the choice to grant neutral status to military hospitals and that medical personnel as non-combatants would wear the badge of a red cross on a white field.

B. member countries of the Red Cross would recognize any agency on the battlefield if members wore the badge of a red cross on a white field and cooperate with it.

C. member countries of the Red Cross would observe neutral status for military hospitals and medical personnel as non-combatants who would be recognized by the badge of a red cross on a white field.

D. countries, whether or not members of the Red Cross, would be offered neutral status for their hospitals and that medical personnel would be allowed to wear the badge of a red cross on a white field.

136. The passage refers to the American Red Cross, which was founded through the determined efforts of an American woman named:

A. Harriet Tubman.
B. Florence Nightingale.
C. Clara Barton.
D. Eleanor Roosevelt.

137. According to the passage, the Red Cross, from its inception in 1863 to today, is:

   A. considered to be a well-run, efficient organization dedicated to saving lives around the world during catastrophes.

   B. known as the largest worldwide disaster and relief organization.

   C. known for its development organizations throughout the world that train volunteers in responding professionally to disasters involving human lives.

   D. considered the only disaster relief organization in the world that can handle international emergencies.

END OF TEST 2.

**IF YOU FINISH BEFORE THE TIME IS UP, YOU MAY
CHECK YOUR WORK ON THIS TEST ONLY.**

WRITING SAMPLE

Time: 60 Minutes
2 Essays

Directions: This test consists of two parts. You will have 30 minutes to complete each part. During the first 30 minutes, you may work on Part 1 only. During the second 30 minutes, you may work on Part 2 only. You will have three pages for each essay answer (see pages 101–106), but you do not have to fill all three pages. Be sure to write legibly; illegible essays will not be scored.

Part 1

Consider this statement:

In war, truth is the first casualty.

Write a unified essay in which you perform the following tasks: Explain what you think the above statement means. Describe a specific situation in which truth is not the first casualty. Discuss what you think determines whether or not truth is a casualty of war.

Part 2

Consider this statement:

Practice yourself what you preach.

Write a unified essay in which you perform the following tasks: Explain what you think the above statement means. Describe a specific situation in which you do not follow what you advise. Discuss whether or not others accomplish what you tell them to follow.

BIOLOGICAL SCIENCES

Time: 100 Minutes
Questions 138–214

Directions: This test contains 77 questions. Most of the questions consist of a descriptive passage followed by a group of questions related to the passage. For these questions, study the passage carefully and then choose the best answer to each question in the group. Some questions in this test stand alone. These questions are independent of any passage and independent of each other. For these questions, too, you must select the one best answer. Indicate all of your answers by blackening the corresponding circles on your answer sheet.

A periodic table is provided at the beginning of the book. You may consult it whenever you feel it's necessary.

Passage I (Questions 138–144)

The fluid-mosaic model of the cell membrane put forward by Singer and Nicholson in the early 1970s presents a complex arrangement of diverse molecules that interact with each other and their surrounding environment in a number of ways. Membrane molecules can function as markers, as enzymes in signal-transduction, as attachment sites to maintain cell shape and tissue structure, and as transport channels or carriers involved with moving substances across the membrane. Transport proteins can be either ligand-gated or voltage-gated, depending on which type of stimulus causes them to open and close.

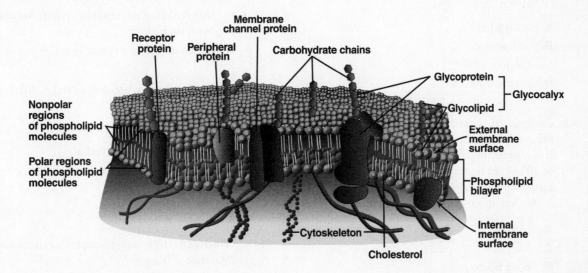

138. In the figure, the cytoskeletal structures just inside the plasma membrane are most likely:

A. cilia.

B. fibrous extensions of endoplasmic reticulum.

C. centrosomes and centrioles.

D. microtubules and microfilaments.

139. Which of the following can pass directly through the phospholipid bilayer?

A. Hydrophobic molecules and water

B. Hydrophobic molecules and glucose

C. Water and glucose

D. Hydrophobic molecules, water, and glucose

140. Certain carrier proteins in the membrane can undergo conformational changes after being phosphorylated by ATP so that two different substances can be transported in opposite directions. This type of carrier protein provides the cell with the capacity to:

  A. carry out phagocytosis.

  B. maintain its resting potential.

  C. respond to passing hormones.

  D. distinguish between "self" and "non-self" markers.

141. The molecules that are part of the glycocalyx are most likely involved in functions associated with:

  A. active transport.

  B. diffusion and facilitated transport.

  C. cell recognition.

  D. structural support.

142. Ligand-gated channels and voltage-gated channels are found on both neuron and muscle cell membranes. The ligand-gated channels that initiate depolarization in skeletal muscle cells respond to a signal from:

  A. acetylcholine.

  B. sodium ions.

  C. calcium ions.

  D. norepinephrine.

143. Cholesterol within the phospholipid bilayer helps maintain the fluidity of cell membranes. It is also a vital building block in the synthesis of all steroid hormones. Cholesterol is such an important molecule that if there is not enough in the diet, it will be synthesized in the:

  A. kidney.

  B. liver.

  C. bone marrow.

  D. spleen.

144. Intercalated discs in cardiac muscle cells allow ions to pass from cell to cell so that electrical activity is synchronized. This type of membrane junction is called a:

  A. tight junction.

  B. desmosome.

  C. gap junction.

  D. plasmodesmata.

Passage II (Questions 145–150)

Amines are derivatives of ammonia and are classified as primary, secondary, and tertiary. Except for tertiary amines, they form intermolecular hydrogen bonds and thus have higher than expected boiling points. Aliphatic amines, like ammonia, are basic, while aromatic amines are considerably less basic. Only the quarternary ammonium salts can show optical activity.

145. Which of the following statements about amines are correct?

  A. All classes of amines can form hydrogen bonds with water.

  B. Only primary and secondary amines form hydrogen bonds with water.

  C. All classes of amines form hydrogen bonds with each other.

  D. Some amines are optically active.

146. When nitrogen is bonded to three different groups:

  A. the molecule is optically active.

  B. the molecule is tetrahedral.

  C. the molecule is not superimposable on its mirror image.

  D. the amine is not basic.

147. Which of the following compounds exist as configurational isomers?

  A. $(CH_3)_4N^+I^-$

  B. methylallylphenylbenzylammonium bromide

  C. methylethylamine

  D. None of the above

148. Methylethylamine is not optically active because:

A. it is superimposable on its mirror image.

B. it is not tetrahedral.

C. the enantiomers are rapidly interconverted.

D. the hybridization around the nitrogen is sp^2.

149. Which is the best explanation for why aromatic amines are not as basic as aliphatic amines?

A. Aromatic amines are sterically hindered.

B. The compounds have different hybridization.

C. The aromatic ring donates charge to the nitrogen via resonance.

D. The aromatic ring removes charge from the nitrogen via resonance.

150. One would expect that the infrared spectra of primary and tertiary amines would differ by the appearance in the former of:

A. N-H stretching absorption peaks.

B. N-H bending absorption peaks.

C. N-H bending and stretching absorption peaks.

D. an exitation of the unshared electrons on nitrogen.

Passage III (Questions 151–156)

Agouti (y) is a grayish-brown coat color in mice. The yellow allele (Y) is dominant and produces a yellow coat but acts as a recessive lethal in utero when homozygous. In addition, coat color in mice is influenced by alleles at a separate locus for melanin production. Homozygous recessive individuals at this second locus are albinos (aa). A cross between heterozygous individuals at both loci does not produce the typical phenotypic ratio of 9:3:3:1.

151. What is the phenotype of the two mated individuals?

A. Agouti

B. Yellow

C. Albino

D. None of the above

152. What proportion of offspring is expected to die before birth?

A. 25%

B. 50%

C. 67%

D. 75%

153. What proportion of individuals born will be expected to have a pigmented coat?

A. 50%

B. 67%

C. 75%

D. 100%

154. What is the probability that the first offspring produced by two agouti mice heterozygous at the albino locus will be albino?

A. 0%

B. 25%

C. 50%

D. 75%

155. When alleles at one locus influence the expression of alleles at a separate locus, this phenomenon is called:

A. linkage.

B. pleiotropy.

C. polymorphism.

D. epistasis.

156. A monohybrid cross between two yellow mice is carried out. What is the expected phenotypic ratio of the offspring born to this pair?

A. 3 yellow : 1 agouti

B. 1 agouti : 3 yellow

C. 2 yellow : 1 agouti

D. 1 yellow : 2 agouti

Questions 157 through 161 are NOT based on a descriptive passage.

---

157. The human body is an ecosystem that supports 500 to 1000 species of microbes. In which part of the body would you expect to find the *fewest* number of microbial species?

    A. Skin
    B. Stomach
    C. Small intestine
    D. Large intestine

158. Which of the following conditions are maintained by the countercurrent multiplier effect at the loop of Henle in the human nephron?

    A. Hypertonicity in the renal medulla and hypotonicity in the urinary filtrate
    B. Hypotonicity in the renal medulla and hypertonicity in the urinary filtrate
    C. Hypertonicity in both the renal medulla and urinary filtrate
    D. Hypotonicity in both the renal medulla and urinary filtrate

159. Which of the following receptors do NOT always respond to changes in mechanical forces (mechanoreceptors)?

    A. Proprioceptors
    B. Hearing receptors
    C. Pain receptors
    D. Balance receptors

160. In addition to genetic sequences of DNA that encode mRNAs to be transcribed during protein synthesis, sequences of DNA have been identified that encode a cell's transfer RNAs (tRNAs), ribosomal RNAs (rRNAs), and the small nuclear RNAs (snRNAs) that are components of spliceosomes. Which of the following statements is correct?

    A. One of the four types of RNA is found in eukaryotes and prokaryotes.
    B. Two of the four types of RNA are found in eukaryotes and prokaryotes.
    C. Three of the four types of RNA are found in eukaryotes and prokaryotes.
    D. All four types of RNA are found in eukaryotes and prokaryotes.

161. Which of the following is correct?

    A. All amines react with acid chlorides to form amides.
    B. All peptides have amide linkages.
    C. Alkylation of a tertiary amine produces an amide.
    D. The alkylation of amines by alkyl halides is an electrophilic substitution reaction.

Passage IV (Questions 162–167)

The figure below shows some of the developmental differences between coelomate phyla that are categorized as either protostomes or deuterostomes. All coelomates have a fluid-filled body cavity completely lined with mesodermal tissues, whereas acoelomates lack this cavity between their digestive tract and body wall. Pseudocoelomates (Nematoda: roundworms) have such a cavity, but they are not completely lined with mesoderm. Phyla belonging to each coelomate category share characteristics associated with the planes of division that lead to the formation of cells in the early embryo, as well as the "fates" of these early cells.

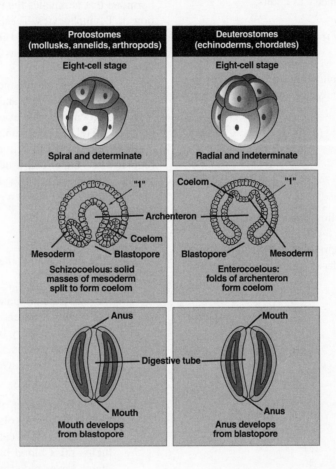

162. The region in the figure labeled "1" is the:

 A. trophoblast.

 B. blastocoel.

 C. pre-coelom.

 D. diploblast.

163. The coelom forms during the stage of development called:

 A. morulation.

 B. blastulation.

 C. gastrulation.

 D. neurulation.

164. Which of the following developmental patterns makes identical twins possible in humans?

 A. Spiral cleavage

 B. Radial cleavage

 C. Determinate cleavage

 D. Indeterminate cleavage

165. Which statement is true?

    A. Some organisms that undergo radial cleavage early in development exhibit radial symmetry as adults, while others exhibit bilateral symmetry as adults.

    B. Some organisms that undergo spiral cleavage early in development exhibit radial symmetry as adults, while others exhibit bilateral symmetry as adults.

    C. Both A and B

    D. Neither A nor B

166. In which of the following organisms does the blastopore eventually become the anus?

    A. Earthworm

    B. Grasshopper

    C. Snail

    D. Shark

167. In which of the following organisms will a cell removed from the 8-cell stage and grown separately in an appropriate medium form an inviable embryo that lacks important components?

    A. Fruit fly

    B. Frog

    C. Hagfish

    D. Sea star

Passage V (Questions 168–173)

The small intestine is one of many organs that has endocrine functions in addition to its more familiar roles in the body. By producing such hormones as intestinal gastrin, gastric inhibitory peptide (GIP), secretin, and cholecystokinin, the small intestine regulates the activities of neighboring digestive organs and their secretions.

The thymus gland secretes thymosin, a protein hormone that stimulates the maturation and differentiation of T-lymphocytes. These cells of the immune system provide cell-mediated immunity, which not only includes attacks on infectious agents, but on infected cells as well.

Other endocrine-producing structures include the pineal gland, the kidney, and the heart. In response to light stimuli entering the eye, the pineal gland (located in the brain) releases melatonin, which is believed to play a role in regulating daily circadian rhythms. The kidney regulates red blood cell production through the secretion of erythropoietin. The heart, by secreting atrial natriuretic factor (ANF), helps regulate blood pressure, salt, and water balance.

168. The factor(s) that these structures have in common is that:

    A. they are all glands.

    B. they release chemicals into the blood.

    C. their secretory function is regulated by the hypothalamus.

    D. All of the above

169. An indirect effect of erythropoietin is the increase in blood volume that accompanies increased red blood cell production. This, in turn, helps raise blood pressure. In contrast, ANF helps lower blood pressure by increasing the kidney's:

    A. reabsorption of sodium and excretion of water.

    B. reabsorption of water and excretion of sodium.

    C. reabsorption of sodium and water.

    D. excretion of sodium and water.

170. Secretin acts as a signal to the pancreas to release bicarbonate ions through the pancreatic duct. The release of secretin is itself stimulated because:

A. acidic chyme arrives in the small intestine.
B. digestive pancreatic enzymes require a slightly alkaline environment.
C. Both A and B
D. Neither A nor B

171. When cells from the pineal gland of various vertebrates are cultured in a dish under conditions of darkness, they release melatonin in a cyclic pattern. This suggests that:

A. the pineal cells themselves have an intrinsic rhythmic property.
B. melatonin production varies proportionately with light and dark cycles.
C. melatonin production is not cyclic during daylight.
D. pineal tissue probably has neural connections with the hypothalamus.

172. Thymosin can directly:

A. respond to specific foreign antigens and bind to receptors on invading organisms.
B. destroy infected host cells.
C. produce chemical (humoral) antibodies.
D. None of the above

173. Cholecystokinin stimulates the gallbladder to release bile when fats arrive in the small intestine. While in the gallbladder, bile can become overly concentrated and gallstones may form. If this necessitates removal of the gallbladder, which of the following statements is true?

A. Fats can no longer be emulsified before digestion in the small intestine.
B. Bile can still reach the small intestine from the liver.
C. Fats can no longer be digested.
D. None of the above

Passage VI (Questions 174–179)

The physical and chemical properties of carboxylic acids are determined by the carboxyl group, –COOH. Although the carboxyl group consists of C=O and –OH, it is the –OH that undergoes change—either loss of H^+ or replacement by another group. The carbonyl group, however, markedly influences the reactions of carboxylic acids. For example, their acidity is due to the resonance stabilization of its anion, which is possible due to the presence of the carbonyl group. The presence of the carbonyl group also is responsible for nucleophilic substitution reactions, which are characteristic of carboxylic acids and their derivatives.

174. Which statement best accounts for the acidity of carboxylic acids?

A. You can draw two inequivalent resonance structures for the acid.
B. You can draw two equivalent resonance structures for the anion.
C. Resonance stabilization is much greater for the anion than the acid.
D. Both acid and anions are resonance hybrids.

175. Chloroacetic acid is more acidic than acetic acid because:

A. electron-withdrawing groups increase the stability of the acid.
B. electron-donating groups destabilize the acid.
C. electron-withdrawing groups stabilize the carboxylate anion.
D. there is no resonance stabilization in the acetate anion.

176. The acidity of benzoic acid is also affected by the presence of substituents. Which statement is correct about acid-weakening groups?

A. Acid-weakening groups activate the ring toward nucleophilic substitution.
B. Acid-weakening groups activate the ring toward electrophilic substitution.
C. Acid-weakening groups deactivate the ring toward electrophilic substitution.
D. None of the above

Practice Exam II

177. The carbonyl group in carboxylic acids and their derivatives make acyl compounds more reactive than alkyl compounds toward nucleophilic attack because:

A. attack of a nucleophile on a flat acyl compound is less sterically hindered.
B. alkyl groups are electron donating.
C. the carbonyl group is an electron-donating substituent.
D. tetrahedral carbon atoms cannot have pentavalent transition states.

178. One would expect that the infrared spectrum of carboxylic acids would include:

A. O—H stretching band.
B. O—H and C=O stretching bands.
C. O—H , C=O, and C—O stretching bands.
D. C=O stretching band.

179. Aldehydes and ketones also undergo attack by nucleophiles, but they undergo nucleophilic addition because:

A. they are more acidic.
B. they are less acidic.
C. they are sterically hindered.
D. C-H and C-C bonds do not break easily.

Questions 180 through 184 are NOT based on a descriptive passage.

---

180. If the codon sequence for the dipeptide histidine-leucine is 5'CAU-CUA3', what is the sequence of nucleotides on the template strand of DNA from which it was transcribed?

A. 5'GTA-GAT3'
B. 5'GAT-GTA3'
C. 3'GAT-GTA5'
D. 3'GTA-GAT5'

181. In birds, females have the sex chromosomes Z and W, while males are homogametic (ZZ). Which statement is correct?

A. Offspring that receive a Z chromosome from the father will usually be males.
B. Offspring that receive a Z chromosome from the father will usually be females.
C. Offspring that receive a W chromosome from the mother will usually be males.
D. Offspring that receive a W chromosome from the mother will usually be females.

182. Toluene will show peaks in its:

A. IR spectrum only.
B. UV and IR spectrum only.
C. IR, UV, and NMR spectrum.
D. UV spectrum only.

183. The vitamins niacin and riboflavin are components of NAD and FAD, respectively. Based on this fact, which of the following processes would be affected *directly* by a lack of these vitamins?

A. Gas exchange between alveoli and pulmonary capillaries
B. Movement of water from hypotonic tissue cells to hypertonic capillaries
C. Maintenance of the normal resting membrane potential via the sodium/potassium ATP pump
D. Facilitated diffusion of glucose from capillaries to tissue cells

184. Which of the following is NOT a function of the liver?

A. Synthesis of coagulation proteins
B. Breakdown of fatty acids to ketones during beta oxidation
C. Synthesis of digestive enzymes
D. Destruction of old erythrocytes

Passage VII (Questions 185–190)

The analysis of mRNA molecules enables researchers to examine which genes (and their protein products) are active in a particular cell at a particular time, and to investigate differences in gene activity in different cells at the same time. Useful in such analyses is complementary DNA or cDNA, a double-stranded molecule made from mRNA.

In the first step of producing cDNA, a single-stranded DNA molecule is made using single-stranded mRNA as a template. Then, after the mRNA is degraded, a second step involves using the newly synthesized single-stranded DNA as a template for producing its complement. Since mRNA molecules transcribed during cellular activities are less stable than DNA, and techniques for purifying and amplifying these mRNAs are lacking, cDNAs derived from mRNA can be used to leisurely characterize mRNAs as well as their encoded products. This is especially important in eukaryotes, since considerable modification takes place between genomic activation and translation.

185. The first step in cDNA production involves the enzyme:

   A. reverse transcriptase.
   B. DNA polymerase.
   C. DNA helicase.
   D. Two of the above

186. The degradation of the template mRNA strand can be carried out by:

   A. deoxyribonuclease only.
   B. ribonuclease only.
   C. any nuclease.
   D. any protease.

187. The second step in cDNA production involves the enzyme:

   A. reverse transcriptase.
   B. DNA polymerase.
   C. DNA helicase.
   D. Two of the above

188. In eukaryotes, the final mRNA molecule does not reflect the precise DNA sequence of the gene from which it was transcribed because:

   A. introns have been added.
   B. exons have been added.
   C. introns have been removed.
   D. exons have been removed.

189. If cDNA molecules isolated from both a muscle cell and a brain cell are found to be identical, what conclusion can be drawn from this evidence?

   A. The two cells are genetically identical.
   B. The two cells are genetically identical but have different functions.
   C. The same gene has been activated in both cells.
   D. All of the above

190. Which gene product may be encoded by the cDNA in the previous question?

   A. Peptidyl transferase
   B. ATPase
   C. Acetylcholinesterase
   D. All of the above

Passage VIII (Questions 191–196)

All metabolic reactions that take place within cells in the interstitial fluid and in blood plasma are influenced by the pH of their immediate environment. As a result, acid-base balance is closely regulated. In the human body, normal blood pH is 7.35–7.45.

Although acidic substances that are sources of free hydrogen ions (H^+) can enter the body in foods, most are metabolic by-products. Carbon dioxide, which readily combines with water to form carbonic acid, is a constant and major source of acidity in cells and venous blood. Proper H^+ concentration is subsequently maintained through a combination of mechanisms including urinary adjustments, respiratory adjustments, and the activity of circulating chemical buffers that usually work in pairs. The alkaline member of the buffering pair binds to free H^+ whenever pH drops too low, while the acidic partner releases H^+ when pH rises too high. When one of the mechanisms fails to function adequately, one or both of the other mechanisms tries to compensate.

191. In healthy individuals, a rise in plasma H^+ concentration would be expected to:

    A. excite the respiratory center and produce deeper and more rapid breathing.

    B. excite the respiratory center and produce shallower and slower breathing.

    C. inhibit the respiratory center and produce deeper and more rapid breathing.

    D. inhibit the respiratory center and produce shallower and slower breathing.

192. Proteins present in blood plasma and in cells can act as buffers. Proteins can act as bases if they contain amino acids with exposed:

    A. carboxyl groups that dissociate to form R-COO$^-$ and H^+.

    B. amino groups that can bind to H^+ to form R-NH$_3^+$.

    C. carboxyl groups that can bind to H^+ to form R-COOH$_2$.

    D. amino groups that can dissociate to form R-NH$^-$ and H^+.

193. The pair of molecules in the bicarbonate buffering system are sodium bicarbonate and carbonic acid. In an acidic solution, most carbonic acid molecules do not dissociate. When H^+ concentration greatly increases and threatens homeostasis, the sodium bicarbonate dissociates into Na^+ and HCO_3^-, and the bicarbonate ions tie up excess H^+ to form carbonic acid. This is an example of forming a weak:

    A. base to substitute for a strong base.

    B. acid to substitute for a strong base.

    C. base to substitute for a strong acid.

    D. acid to substitute for a strong acid.

194. Which of the following would NOT be an appropriate urinary adjustment in response to temporary metabolic acidosis?

    A. Increase H^+ secretion.

    B. Combine H^+ with ammonia and then increase secretion of NH_4^+.

    C. Decrease bicarbonate ion reabsorption.

    D. All are appropriate.

195. Extended periods of fasting can lead to metabolic:

    A. alkalosis as fats are broken down and blood ketones increase.

    B. acidosis as fats are broken down and blood ketones increase.

    C. alkalosis as fats are stored and blood ketones decrease.

    D. acidosis as fats are stored and blood ketones decrease.

196. If blood pH is measured to be 7.25 and blood carbon dioxide levels are lower than normal, this suggests a condition of:

    A. acidosis, with the respiratory system as the cause.

    B. acidosis, with the respiratory system compensating.

    C. alkalosis, with the respiratory system as the cause.

    D. alkalosis, with the respiratory system compensating.

Passage IX (Questions 197–202)

Reactions of an alcohol involve either breaking of the C—OH bond or the O—H bond. Both of these reactions can involve substitution or elimination with the formation of a double bond. Cleavage of the C—OH bond must always involve converting the OH group into a good cleaving group.

197. Which statement is always true about the reaction of hydrogen halides with alcohols?

A. Elimination occurs.
B. Substitution occurs.
C. The alcohol is protonated.
D. The reaction occurs in one step.

198. Rearrangement of alkyl groups occur when hydrogen halides react with alcohols except with most primary alcohols. The best explanation is the:

A. reaction is catalyzed by acids.
B. formation of a carbanion intermediate.
C. O—H bond is broken.
D. formation of a carbocation intermediate.

199. Neopentyl alcohol, although primary, reacts with HX according to an S_N1 mechanism. This is due most likely to:

A. steric hindrance.
B. a polar effect.
C. a bimolecular reaction.
D. an elimination reaction.

200. Both alkyl halides and alcohols react by S_N1 and S_N2 reactions. Alcohols lean more towards the latter because:

A. –OH is a better cleaving group than –X.
B. the –OH group must be protonated so strong nucleophiles cannot be present.
C. alcohols are sterically hindered.
D. alcohols are acidic.

201. It can be said that dehydrohalogenation is base promoted while dehydration is acid catalyzed. The difference is that:

A. base is consumed in dehydrohalogenation while it is regenerated in dehydration.
B. dehydration can only occur in an acidic medium, while dehydrohalogenation can only occur in a basic medium.
C. dehydration occurs in basic solution as well.
D. acid can be in trace amounts for both dehydration and dehalogenation to occur.

202. Tertiary alcohols readily undergo dehydration in the presence of an acid because:

A. they form the most stable carbocations.
B. a base can readily abstract a proton from the protonated alcohol.
C. they form the less substituted alkenes.
D. the protonation of the –OH group is rate determining.

Passage X (Questions 203–209)

The formed elements of the blood—erythrocytes (RBCs), leukocytes (WBCs), and thrombocytes (platelets)—all develop in red bone marrow from a common stem cell, the hemocytoblast. In newborns, the medullary cavity in the diaphysis, or shaft of a long bone, as well as both epiphyses at the ends, contain hemopoietic tissues. In adults, however, the medullary cavity contains fat, and hemopoiesis occurs only in the proximal epiphyses of the femur and humerus, and in some flat bones of the axial skeleton and appendicular girdles.

Erythrocytes are numerous (5–6 million/mm^3 blood) and go through many stages before entering the circulation. Late normoblasts lose their nuclei and reticulocytes must first lose their ribosomes and rough endoplasmic reticulum before becoming mature erythrocytes. Only about 2 percent of circulating RBCs are reticulocytes.

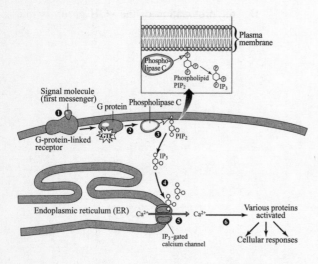

Leukocytes are categorized as granular or agranular, depending on the presence or absence of cytoplasmic granules with unique staining properties. They all carry out one or more protective functions, but are far less numerous than RBCs (5,000–10,000/mm^3 blood). All leukocytes except T-lymphocytes or T-cells, a type of agranulocyte, complete their maturation before leaving the bone marrow.

Thrombocytes are not complete cells. They are tiny fragments of enormous cells called megakaryocytes (approximately 600 platelets form from one such cell). Thrombocytes (150,000–400,000/mm^3 blood) are major contributors in the steps leading to coagulation during the hemostatic process.

203. In which of the following locations would new blood cells be LEAST likely to form in adults?

A. Heads of the femur and humerus

B. Sternum

C. Ilium

D. Vertebrae

204. Which statement is *false* about the various stages of erythrocyte development?

A. Transcription of hemoglobin can occur in the early erythroblast.

B. Transcription and translation of hemoglobin can occur in the late erythroblast.

C. Neither transcription nor translation of hemoglobin can occur in the reticulocyte.

D. None of the above

205. The hormone erythropoietin (EPO) stimulates erythropoiesis. Which of the following factors is most likely to stimulate an increase in EPO production *directly*?

A. Lower than normal oxygen levels in the kidney

B. Decreased numbers of RBCs circulating in the spleen

C. High blood viscosity detected in the medulla oblongata

D. Higher than normal oxygen levels in the blood

206. The final maturation of T-lymphocytes after they enter the bloodstream is influenced by the hormone:

A. thyroxine.

B. triiodothyronine.

C. thymosin.

D. thyroid stimulating hormone (TSH).

207. Which of the following is probably true concerning complete blood count (CBC) procedures during clinical evaluations?

A. Leukocytes are included in the sample when erythrocytes are counted.

B. Erythrocytes are destroyed in the sample before leukocytes are counted.

C. Both A and B

D. Neither A nor B

208. Thromboxanes, which are derived from certain prostaglandins, help in the activation of platelets. Aspirin, by inhibiting prostaglandin synthesis, has the indirect effect of:

A. increasing antibody production.

B. slowing normal hemostasis.

C. stimulating excess inflammation.

D. causing unnecessary blood clots.

209. Vitamin B_{12} and folic acid are required for normal DNA synthesis. Which cells produced in the bone marrow would be most affected by deficiencies in these vitamins?

A. Thrombocytes

B. Granular leukocytes

C. Agranular leukocytes

D. Erythrocytes

Questions 210 through 214 are NOT based on a descriptive passage.

210. To which taxonomic group do microbes such as methanogens, thermophiles, and halophiles most likely belong?

A. Archaea

B. Bacteria

C. Protista

D. Fungi

211. Phenols have a characteristic acidity in that they are stronger acids than water but weaker than carbonic acid. Therefore they are:

A. soluble in aqueous NaOH and $NaHCO_3$.

B. insoluble in aqueous NaOH but soluble in $NaHCO_3$.

C. insoluble in both bases.

D. soluble in NaOH but insoluble in $NaCO_3$.

212. Which hormone is *least* affected by the direct influence of the anterior pituitary gland?

A. Estrogen

B. Progesterone

C. Parathyroid hormone

D. Thyroxine

213. In skeletal muscle tissue, the troponin-tropomyosin complex has a strong affinity for actin. To what does the troponin-tropomyosin complex have an even greater affinity?

A. Sodium

B. Potassium

C. Calcium

D. Acetylcholine

214. Telomeres contain repetitive noncoding sequences at the ends of eukaryotic chromosomes. Parts of these sequences are lost each time a cell replicates its DNA during the cell cycle. The shortening of these telomeres with each cell division limits the number of divisions cells can undergo because important coding sequences of DNA will eventually be lost once the telomeres are gone. The enzyme telomerase seems to "reset the clock" of a cell's life span by replacing the repetitive noncoding DNA sequences of the telomeres. In which type of cells would telomerase be expected to be active?

A. Oogonia

B. Skeletal muscle cells

C. Cancer cells

D. Yeast cells

END OF TEST 3.

IF YOU FINISH BEFORE THE TIME IS UP, YOU MAY CHECK YOUR WORK ON THIS TEST ONLY.

PRACTICE EXAM II ANSWER KEY

PHYSICAL SCIENCES		VERBAL REASONING		BIOLOGICAL SCIENCES	
1. D	41. B	78. A	111. C	138. D	177. A
2. B	42. C	79. D	112. D	139. A	178. C
3. B	43. B	80. A	113. D	140. B	179. D
4. C	44. C	81. B	114. B	141. C	180. D
5. B	45. A	82. B	115. B	142. A	181. D
6. A	46. C	83. A	116. A	143. B	182. C
7. C	47. B	84. C	117. D	144. C	183. C
8. B	48. A	85. B	118. C	145. A	184. C
9. C	49. A	86. B	119. A	146. C	185. A
10. B	50. D	87. B	120. C	147. B	186. B
11. C	51. C	88. D	121. D	148. C	187. B
12. D	52. B	89. A	122. B	149. D	188. C
13. B	53. C	90. B	123. A	150. C	189. C
14. D	54. C	91. C	124. C	151. B	190. D
15. C	55. B	92. C	125. C	152. A	191. A
16. B	56. D	93. B	126. A	153. C	192. B
17. B	57. D	94. D	127. B	154. B	193. D
18. A	58. B	95. B	128. B	155. D	194. C
19. A	59. B	96. A	129. A	156. C	195. B
20. A	60. A	97. C	130. D	157. B	196. B
21. B	61. C	98. A	131. C	158. A	197. C
22. C	62. B	99. C	132. D	159. C	198. D
23. D	63. B	100. D	133. B	160. C	199. A
24. B	64. D	101. C	134. A	161. B	200. B
25. D	65. B	102. B	135. C	162. B	201. A
26. A	66. D	103. A	136. C	163. C	202. A
27. B	67. B	104. B	137. B	164. D	203. D
28. C	68. A	105. B		165. A	204. C
29. C	69. C	106. A		166. D	205. A
30. C	70. C	107. D		167. A	206. C
31. B	71. D	108. B		168. B	207. C
32. B	72. D	109. C		169. D	208. B
33. B	73. C	110. D		170. C	209. D
34. C	74. A			171. A	210. A
35. D	75. D			172. D	211. D
36. A	76. C			173. B	212. C
37. A	77. D			174. C	213. C
38. C				175. C	214. C
39. A				176. B	
40. C					

PRACTICE EXAM II EXPLANATORY ANSWERS

PHYSICAL SCIENCES

1. **The correct answer is (D).** Area = side^2, therefore if the length of the side is tripled the area increases by a factor of 9.

   From the capacitance C = 8.85×10^{-15} KA/d, the area and separation are directly proportional. As the area increases, the separation must increase. This eliminates choices (A) and (B). The calculated value for the new separation between the plates is 9(0.012 mm) = 0.108 mm.

2. **The correct answer is (B).** Once the capacitor is isolated by removing the power source, no net current flows:
   q = CV = $(5 \times 10^{-6}$ F)(10V) = 50×10^{-6} C = 50 μC.

   Changing the dielectric material will change the strength of the electric field between the plates but not the charge on each plate.

3. **The correct answer is (B).** Be careful, C_1 and C_2 are connected in parallel, therefore the potential difference across each capacitor is the same but the charge q on each is different.

   $C_1V_{original}$ = $C_1V_{final} + C_2V_{final}$ = $(C_1 + C_2)V_{final}$

   V_{final} = $C_1V_{original}/(C_1 + C_2)$ = 6000 V(10 mC/ 15 mC) = 4000 V

4. **The correct answer is (C).** In pattern I the capacitors are connected in series: $1/C_{equivalent}$ = $\Sigma 1/ C_{individual}$ = 3/C, therefore $C_{equivalent}$ = C/3

   In pattern II the capacitors are connected in parallel: $C_{equivalent}$ = $\Sigma C_{individual}$ = 3C

   In pattern III two capacitors are connected in parallel giving $C_{//equivalent}$ = 2C. This is in series with the third capacitor giving $1/C_{equivalent}$ = 1/C + 1/2C = 3/2C.

   Therefore $C_{equivalent}$ = 2C/3.

   The order of increasing capacitance is C/3 < 2C/3 < 3C or I < III < II.

5. **The correct answer is (B).** Remember, the dielectric constant K is unitless. In terms of units:

   C = KA/(4πk)d. = m^2/(Nm^2/C^2)m = C^2/Nm = C^2/J = C/(J/C) = C/V = F

   The unit of work and energy is the joule, J = Nm for force × distance.

   Actually you didn't have to do the derivation to find the answer. Choices (A) and (D) are the units for 1/k and k, respectively, and they don't include units for area and distance. From the definition of the farad given in the passage, choice (C) is the reciprocal of the farad.

6. **The correct answer is (A).** Rearranging C = q/V and q = KC_oV gives C_o = C/K. For comparing two conditions of the same capacitor:

   C_1/K_1 = C_2/K_2 = C_o = constant

   Let case 1 be for glass and case 2 for rubber:

   K_2= C_2K_1/C_1 = (6.0 μF)(8)/19.2 μF

   K_2 = K_{rubber} = 2.5

7. **The correct answer is (C).** From $C = 8.85 \times 10^{-15}$ KA/d. C and d are inversely proportional:

    Cd = constant

    d increases as the plates are pulled apart, therefore the capacitance, C, decreases. This eliminates choices (A) and (B).

    From $C = q/V$ q and C are directly proportional. As C decreases, q increases. Be careful, V is constant because the capacitor remained connected to the battery so the potential difference between the plates remains fixed.

8. **The correct answer is (B).** For a circular orbit $F_{centripetal} = F_{gravity}$: $mv^2/r = GMm/r^2$ which reduces to

    $v^2 = GM_{planet}/r$.

    Rearranging gives: $[v^2 r]_{SeekerI} = [v^2 r]_{SeekerII} = GM_{planet}$ = constant. The square of the velocity and the distance are inversely proportional. If r doubles in value, v^2 must be reduced to half its value:

    $v^2 R_{SeekerI} = (v^2/2)(2R_{SeekerII})$,

    therefore, $v_{SeekerII} = (v^2/2)^{1/2} = v/2^{1/2}$

9. **The correct answer is (C).** From the law of universal gravitation: $(F_g/m_1 m_2)_{initial} = (F_g/m_1 m_2)_{final}$ = constant $= G/r^2$.

    We don't need to know the actual mass of a ball bearing, just that all of them have the same mass. We can then use any arbitrary value for the mass of one ball bearing. So, let each mass = 1.

    Initially: $m_1 m_2 = 15 \times 15 = 225$ mass units

    Finally: $m_1 m_2 = 25 \times 5 = 125$ mass units

    Since F_g and $m_1 m_2$ are directly proportional, the final F_g is less than the initial F_g.

    In fact the gravitational attractive force has decreased by a factor of 5/9.

    F_g(final) = (125/225)F_g(initial) = (5/9)F_g

10. **The correct answer is (B).** From Newton's second law, $F_{gravity}$ = ma. Therefore, the acceleration due to gravity at the surface of a body is:

     $a = GM_i/R_i^2 = g$.

     From density, D = M/V = M/[(4/3)πR^3] = constant.

     If the radius doubles we get: $(2R)^3 = 8R^3$. Since M and R are directly proportional, the planet's mass, M, must increase by a factor of 8 if the density is to remain the same.

     $g = GM/R^2$ becomes $G(8M)/(2R)^2 = (8/4)(GM/R^2) = 2GM/R^2 = 2g$. The value is twice the original value.

11. **The correct answer is (C).** Since kinetic energy is $mv^2/2$ we're looking for an expression that contains mv^2. From $F_c = F_g$ we get: $mv^2/r = GMm/r^2$ or $mv^2 = GMm/r$. Therefore, (1/2) mv^2 = (1/2)GMm/r = GMm/2r = E_K

12. **The correct answer is (D).** Solving this problem quickly relies on knowing that the kinetic energy can be expressed by E_K = GMm/2r. (See Question 4 above).

     $E_{total} = E_K + E_P$ = GMm/2r + (–GMm/r) = –GMm/2r. The total mechanical energy is equal to the negative of the kinetic energy.

13. **The correct answer is (B).** From point a-g of the paragraph, for a projectile to escape gravity:

     $E_{total} = 0 = E_K + E_P = mv^2/2 + (–GMm/R)$.

     This rearranges to:

     $v^2 = 2GM/R$ or $v = (2GM/R)^{1/2}$

14. **The correct answer is (D).** Results for the test transformer show that the number of turns/coil and the voltage are directly proportional. In Transformer 1 the number of turns in the secondary coil is twice that of the primary coil and the secondary voltage is twice that of the primary. Similarly in Transformer 2 the secondary coil has half as many turns as the primary and the secondary voltage is half of the primary voltage:

$$N_{1\circ}/V_{1\circ} = N_{2\circ}/V_{2\circ}$$

$$N_{2\circ} = (N_{1\circ}V_{2\circ})/V_{1\circ} = (100 \times 2400V)/120V = 2000 \text{ turns}$$

15. **The correct answer is (C).** Again looking at the test transformers we see that the number of turns/coil and the current are inversely proportional. Transformer 1 doubles the turns in going from the primary to the secondary coil but the current in the secondary coil is half that of the primary coil:

$$N_{1\circ}I_{1\circ} = N_{2\circ}I_{2\circ}$$

$$I_{1\circ} = I_{2\circ}(N_{2\circ}/N_{1\circ}) = (3.0mA)(3N_{1\circ}/N_{1\circ}) = 3.0mA \times 3 = 9.0mA$$

16. **The correct answer is (B).** This requires that you remember the definition for electric power, $P = IV$. A transformer changes the ratio of the voltage and current. Comparing the primary and secondary coil values for any of the three test transformers, we see that if the voltage increases the current decrease (and vice versa) but that their produce, IV, is constant for the given transformer. Transformers transform voltage and current but not power.

17. **The correct answer is (B).** From Ohm's Law, $R = V_{2\circ}/I_{2\circ}$ but all of the choices involve $(V_{1\circ}/I_{1\circ})$. Therefore use the relation between voltage and number of turns/coil to eliminate $V_{2\circ}$.

$$N_{1\circ}/V_{1\circ} = N_{2\circ}/V_{2\circ} \rightarrow V_{2\circ} = (N_{2\circ}V_{1\circ})/N_{1\circ}$$

Similarly, use the relation between current and turns/coil to eliminate $I_{2\circ}$.

$$N_{1\circ}I_{1\circ} = N_{2\circ}I_{2\circ} \rightarrow I_{2\circ} = (N_{2\circ}I_{2\circ})/N_{1\circ}$$

Then, $R = V_{2\circ}/I_{2\circ}$ becomes:

$$R = ((N_{2\circ}V_{1\circ})/N_{1\circ})/((N_{2\circ}I_{2\circ})/N_{1\circ}) = (V_{1\circ}/I_{1\circ})(N_{2\circ}/N_{1\circ})^2$$

18. **The correct answer is (A).** A battery is a DC source, not an AC source. While it produces a direct current in the primary coil, it can't produce an oscillating magnetic field required to induce current in the secondary coil.

19. **The correct answer is (A).** The center mass is on the axis of rotation so its radius is zero and it does not contribute to the moment of inertia. The two end masses are a distance L/2 from the axis of rotation. Therefore:

$$I = \Sigma m_i r_i = m(L/2)^2 + m(L/2)^2 = mL^2/4 + mL^2/4 = mL^2/2$$

20. **The correct answer is (A).** Use the Parallel Axis Theorem: $I = I_{cm} + Md^2 = MR^2/2 + Md^2$

I_{cm} for a cylinder is given in the passage. Since the units in the answer are kg m^2, convert cm to m. Also note that 80 cm is the diameter.

$$I = 20.0 \text{ kg } (0.40m)^2/2 + 20.0 \text{ kg } (0.10m)^2 = 1.6 \text{ kg m}^2 = 0.2 \text{ kg m}^2 = 1.8 \text{ kg m}^2$$

21. **The correct answer is (B).**

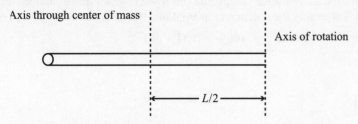

Use the Parallel Axis Theorem:

$$I = I_{cm} + Md^2 = ML^2/12 + M(L/2)^2 = ML^2/12 + ML^2/4 = 4ML^2/12 = ML^2/3$$

22. **The correct answer is (C).** The moment of inertia depends on the distance of a rotating mass from the axis of rotation. The greater the distance, the larger its contribution to the total inertia of the system.

Arrangement **a** has the greatest I_a because the center of each weight is the maximum distance from the axis of rotation, r = L/2.

In **b** the centers of both weights are very close to the axis of rotation and I_b should be quite small This should be the minimum moment of inertia arrangement.

In **c** one weight is at the maximum distance from the axis of rotation and the other is very close.

In **d** the weight at the center of rotation doesn't contribute to I because r = 0. I_d is ½ I_a and less than I_c.

23. **The correct answer is (D).** The moment of inertia of the sculpture is the sum of the moments of inertia of its three components.

For the model:

$$I_{model} = 2I_{cmCylinder} + I_{cmSphere} = 2(MR^2/2) + 2/5\ MR^2$$
$$= MR^2 + 2/5\ M(L/2)^2 = MR^2 + 1/10\ ML^2$$

For the sculpture:

$I_{cmCylinder}$ depends on the radius of the cylinder, NOT on its length, so the contributions of the two cylinders are unaltered.

However, for the enlarged sphere, $I_{cmSphere} = 2/5\ M(3L/2)^2 = 9/10\ ML^2$

$$I_{sculpture} = MR^2 + 9/10\ ML^2$$

The best answer is choice (D).

24. **The correct answer is (B).** The smaller the percentage of rotational kinetic energy, the greater the percentage of translational energy. The greater the translational energy, the faster the object's linear motion. From the relation $I_{cm} = \beta MR^2$ it's clear that β is simply the coefficient in front of MR^2. For the three objects, we get:

Object	Moment of Inertia	$100\% \times \beta/(1 + \beta)$
Hoop	MR^2	50%
Disk	$\frac{1}{2}MR^2$	33%
Sphere	$2/5\ MR^2$	29%

The sphere has the smallest fraction of its kinetic energy in the form of rotational energy. Therefore, it has the greatest translational motion. It will cover the length of the ramp more quickly.

25. **The correct answer is (D).** $I_{sphere} = 2/5\ MR^2$, therefore $I/R^2 = $ constant., I and R are directly proportional.

$$I/R^2 = I_{NEW}/(R/10)^2 = I_{NEW}/(R^2/100) = (I/100)/(R^2/100) = (I/100)(100/R^3) = I/R^2$$

Therefore, I decreases by a factor of 100 when R decreases by a factor of 10.

26. **The correct answer is (A).** In myopia (nearsightedness) the curvature of the cornea-lens system shows too much convergence. This eliminates choices (B) and (C). While choices (A) and (D) are acceptable, based on the definition of the passage, choice (A) is the better choice.

27. **The correct answer is (B).** The far point is closer to the eye than normal. John is, therefore, nearsighted and requires a diverging lens that creates a virtual image of the object at the far point for his eye. Since a diverging lens is required, this eliminates choices (C) and (D).

$$P = 1/f = 1/o + 1/i = 1/\infty - 1/0.50m = -2.0 \text{ diopters}$$

28. **The correct answer is (C).** In farsightedness, the image of a distant object appears to focus behind the retina. The lens must increase its convergence power to move the image forward onto the retina. Relaxing the ciliary muscle increases the radius of curvature which decreases the focal length.

29. **The correct answer is (C).** Power is the reciprocal of the focal length measured in meters. Since the power is +, Jane is farsighted.

Since $P = 3.00$ diopters, the focal length of the corrective lens is $f = 0.33$ m = 33 cm. A corrective lens creates a virtual image, therefore, $1/i$ is negative.

The object distance is 25 cm.

The lens distance equation rearranges to:

$$1/i = 1/o - 1/f = 1/25 \text{ cm} - 1/33 \text{ cm} \sim 1/100 \text{ cm}$$

$$i \sim 100 \text{ cm}$$

In order to see the image of the object 25 cm in front of the eye, the contact lens must form a virtual image of the object 100 cm in front of the eye. 25 cm is where the near point should be, 100 cm is where the near point actually is.

According to the table in the passage, her near point of 100 cm is greater than the near point for a 50-year-old but less than that of a 60-year-old.

30. The correct answer is (C). George is myopic and requires a converging lens. This eliminates choices (B) and (D). The lens creates a virtual image at his natural far point which is 50 cm from his eyes but 48 cm from his eyeglass lenses. It is the focal length of the eyeglasses we need to calculate:

$$1/f = 1/o + 1/i = 1/\infty - 1/48 \text{ cm} = -1/48 \text{ cm} \text{ and } f = -48 \text{ cm}$$

31. The correct answer is (B). Flattening the cornea reduces its radius of curvature which increases its focal length. This is needed to correct nearsightedness (myopia).

32. The correct answer is (B). $F_{Gravity} = G\,Mm/r^2 = mg$, therefore, $g = G\,M/r^2$

where M is the mass of the planet and for objects on the surface, r is the radius of the planet.

$$g_{\text{Planet X}} = G(3M_{Earth})/(3r_{Earth})^2 = 3GM_{Earth}/9r^2_{Earth} = (3/9)g_{Earth}$$
$$= (1/3)(9.8 \times 10^6 \text{ m/s}^2) \sim 3.3 \times 10^6 \text{ m/s}^2$$

Therefore, weight of probe is approximately:

$$mg = (100 \text{ kg})(3.3 \times 10^6 \text{ m/s}^2) = 3.3 \times 10^2 \text{ N}$$

33. The correct answer is (B). The easiest way to answer this question is with a fast sketch. For a given object's position, draw two rays from the top of the object. One ray is parallel to the principal axis and passes through the focal point on the opposite side of the lens. The other ray passes through the center of the lens. The top of the image appears where these two rays intersect.

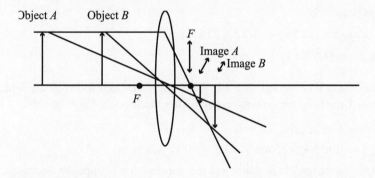

Change the object's position and repeat the process. You will observe that as the object approaches the lens while remaining beyond the focal length, the image produced on the opposite side of the lens moves away from the lens and increases in size. As an aside, the image is real and inverted.

34. The correct answer is (C). This is a torque problem. While the fulcrum can be placed anywhere, placing it at the far right end of the bar eliminated cable B from the calculation. There are now only two forces acting on the bar: the weight that produces a counterclockwise rotation and the tension in cable A that produces a clockwise rotation. Since the bar is in equilibrium, these two torques must sum to zero.

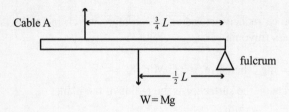

$$\Sigma\tau = T_A(3/4\ L) - Mg(1/2\ L) = 0$$

Therefore, $T_A = (MgL/2)/(3L/4) = (MgL/2)(4/3L) = 2Mg/3$

35. The correct answer is (D). By definition $E = F/q = 8 \times 10^{-2}\ N/4 \times 10^{-6}\ C = 2 \times 10^4\ N/C = 2 \times 10^4\ kg\ m/s^2C$

36. The correct answer is (A). Two external forces, F_A and F_B, act on the system and move in opposite directions. Let's arbitrarily assume that the downward direction is positive and that F_A provides downward motion while F_B provides upward motion.

$F_A = (+15kg)(9.8\ m/s^2) = 147\ N$ and $F_B = (-10kg)(9.8\ m/s^2) = -98\ N$

$F_{total} = F_A + F_B = 147\ N + (-98\ N) = 49\ N$

The total mass that must be set in motion is 15 kg + 10 kg = 25 kg.

Since $F_{total} = m_{total}a$, $a = F_{total}/m_{total} = 49\ N/25\ kg \sim 2\ m/s^2$

37. The correct answer is (A). Momentum is always conserved. Since the skater and snowball are initially at rest, the initial momentum is zero. Therefore, the final momentum after the toss must also be zero.

$P_{skater} + P_{snowball} = 0$ or $m_{skater}\ v_{skater} + m_{snowball}v_{snowball} = 0$

$v_{skater} = -m_{snowball}v_{snowball}/\ m_{skater} = -(0.15\ kg)(35\ m/s)/50\ kg = -0.10\ m/s$

The negative sign indicates that the momenta of the skater and the snowball are in opposite directions.

38. The correct answer is (C). Kirchhoff's junction rule states that the algebraic sum of all currents into and out of any branch point is zero: $\Sigma I = 0$. By convention, the sign of current entering a junction is positive and current leaving a junction is negative.

$4A + 5A - 6A + I_{AB} = 0$, therefore, $I_{AB} = -3A$. The wire between points A and B carries a current of 3A away from the junction.

39. The correct answer is (A). We can use the following relationship:

$q_{solution} = m(sh) \Delta T = (100 \text{ g} + 4.56 \text{ g})(4.18 \text{ J/g°C})(34.6°C - 24.0 °C) = 4630 \text{ J}$

But since the calorimeter is thermally insulated,

$q_{reaction} + q_{solution} = 0$

$q_{reaction} = -q_{solution} = -4630 \text{ J}$

To convert this heat value to enthalpy of solution, we need to calculate the moles of KOH:

moles KOH = (4.56 g) / (56.11 g/mol) = 0.08127 mol

$\Delta H_{solution} = -4630 \text{ J} / 0.08127 \text{ mol} = -5.70 \times 10^5 \text{ J/mol}$

$= -57.0 \text{ kJ/mol}$

[Note: We expect ΔH to be negative since the temperature rose. Thus, we could have eliminated choices (C) and (D) at the outset.]

40. The correct answer is (C). Doubling the mass of water will "dilute" the temperature change due to the heat evolved by a factor of two; doubling the mass of KOH as well will produce twice as much heat and will restore the temperature change to that of the original experiment. Choice (D) is unlikely to be true for two reasons: equal masses of KOH and NaOH contain different numbers of moles, and without further data we have no way of knowing how the enthalpies of solution of these two solids are related.

41. The correct answer is (B). Since the method requires a constant temperature of 0°C, heat measured in this way would have to be modified based on additional information to give information about other temperatures. Choice (A) is incorrect, since a reaction that absorbed heat would be expected to cause more ice to form quantitatively, resulting in a measurable increase in the ice-water volume. Choice (C) is incorrect, since the ice-water mixture does not come in contact with the reacting chemicals. As for choice (D), any measured-reaction heat can be converted to an enthalpy by adjusting for the number of moles of limiting reactant and for the coefficient in the balanced reaction.

42. The correct answer is (C). We need to use the change in volume to determine the mass of ice that melted and the specific heat of fusion to find the heat needed to melt that mass of ice. Since the ice absorbed positive heat when it melted, $q_{reaction}$ must be negative:

$m_{ice} = (-1.86 \text{ mL})(1.00 \text{ g ice} / -0.091 \text{ mL})$

$= 20.4 \text{ g}$

$q_{ice} = (20.4 \text{ g})(334 \text{ J/g}) = 6810 \text{ J}$

$q_{reaction} = -q_{ice} = -6810 \text{ J} \approx -7 \text{ kJ}$

43. The correct answer is (B). We need to calculate the specific heat of fusion of benzene in order to make the necessary comparison:

(10.59 kJ/mol) / (78.1 g/mol) = 0.136 kJ/g = 136 J/g

Since the corresponding value for water-ice is higher, 334 J/g, the heat produced by identical samples of methanol will melt a greater mass of solid benzene. Specifically, the mass of benzene melted will be

(6810 J)(1.00 g benzene/136 J) = 50.1 g benzene.

This is considerably larger than the value of 20.4 g of ice that was calculated to have melted from the same amount of heat.

44. **The correct answer is (C).** One way to approach this problem is to compute the molar mass of $CuSO_4 \cdot 5H_2O$ (249.7 g/mol), then find the number of moles present in 0.100 g. After the conversion to $CuSO_4 \cdot 3H_2O$, we can use the same number of moles to find the new mass, using the molar mass of the lighter hydrate (213.7 g/mol).

$$\text{moles } CuSO_4 \cdot 5H_2O = (0.100 \text{ g}) / (249.7 \text{ g/mol})$$
$$= 4.00 \times 10^{-4} \text{ mol}$$
$$\text{mass } CuSO_4 \cdot 3 \text{ } H_2O = (4.00 \times 10^{-4} \text{ mol})(213.7 \text{g/mol})$$
$$= 0.085 \text{ g}$$

45. **The correct answer is (A).** A good oxidizing agent for Sn^{2+} must be capable of being reduced itself [ruling out choice (B)] and must have a reduction potential that is greater than 0.154. Only MnO_4^- meets these criteria.

46. **The correct answer is (C).** The question could be rephrased as asking for a reaction that is driven to the right by increased H^+ concentration. Of the species mentioned, only MnO_4^- has H^+ in its half reaction, and since H^+ will be on the left-hand side of the overall reaction with Cu, LeChatelier's Principle predicts that increasing the amount of H^+ will drive the reaction farther to the right.

47. **The correct answer is (B).** Choice (A) would be correct if the reaction took place in basic solution.

48. **The correct answer is (A).** Use the formula from the passage:
$$E^\circ_{total} = (n_1E^\circ_1 + n_2E^\circ_2) / (n_1 + n_2)$$
$$= [(1)(0.77) + (2)(-0.44)] / (2 + 1)$$
$$= -0.04$$

49. **The correct answer is (A).** Response I is correct, since Nb^{3+} lies below the midpoint of the line between Nb and Nb_2O_5. Response II is false, since the Nb_2O_5 / Nb^{3+} couple has the more positive slope. Response III is false—since Nb^{3+} is the lowest point on the diagram, it is the most stable.

50. **The correct answer is (D).** In reaction I, both the mercury and niobium species change in the "downhill" direction on the graph, toward more stable products. In reaction III, Hg must change "uphill" to Hg^{2+}, but Nb changes in a "downhill" direction to Nb^{3+}, and the steeper slope of the Nb^{3+}/Nb couple makes the overall process favorable. In contrast, reaction II requires that Hg be oxidized "uphill" to Hg^{2+}, while Nb^{3+} must be reduced "uphill" to Nb; this reaction is not spontaneous.

51. **The correct answer is (B).** Point 3 is a buffer region that is approximately halfway between the first equivalence point (at which all of the original B was converted to BH^+) and second equivalence point (at which all of the original B will be converted to BH_2^{2+}). Thus, it contains both BH^+ and BH_2^{2+}.

52. **The correct answer is (B).** Point 2 represents the first equivalence point, at which the moles of acid added are equal to the original moles of B. Since the HCl is twice as concentrated as the B, this equivalence point comes at half the value of the original base volume, or 10.00 mL.

Alternatively, the original 0.100 M sample of base contains

$$(20.00 \text{ mL})(0.100 \text{ mmol}) = 2.00 \text{ mmol}$$

To obtain an equal number of mmol acid, we need

$$V_{acid} = (2.00 \text{ mmol}) / (0.200 \text{ mmol/mL}) = 10.00 \text{ mmol}$$

53. **The correct answer is (A).** Point 4 represents the second equivalence point, at which all of the original base B has been converted to BH_2^{2+}. Since 20.00 mL of HCl was required to reach this point, the total volume is 40.00 mL. Therefore the concentration of BH_2^{2+} equals one-half the concentration of the original B, or 0.0500 M.

   We now have the problem of finding the pH of a weak acid solution; for K_a, we use K_2 for BH_2^{2+}. (Note that we might guess an answer at this point, since only one of the choices is less than 7!)

   $$BH_2^{2+}(aq) \quad \rightarrow \quad BH^+(aq) \quad + \quad H^+(aq)$$
   $$(0.0500 - x) \qquad x \qquad\qquad x$$
   $$x^2/(0.0500 - x) \quad = \quad 4.65 \times 10^{-6}$$

   Using the approximation that $0.0500 \gg x$, we have

   $$x^2/0.0500 = 4.65 \times 10^{-6}$$
   $$x = [H^+] = 4.82 \times 10^{-4}\ M$$
   $$pH = -\log(4.82 \times 10^{-4}\ M)$$
   $$= 3.3$$

54. **The correct answer is (C).** A pure solution of a weak base undergoes hydrolysis, leading to small amounts of hydroxide ion, which causes the pH to rise above 7.

55. **The correct answer is (B).** The color change from yellow (for low pH values) to red (for high pH values) occurs when [HInd] = [Ind$^-$], which corresponds to a pH determined as follows:

   $$[H^+] = K_a([HInd]/[Ind^-]) = (10^{-7.81})(1)$$
   $$= 1.5 \times 10^{-8}\ M$$

   At pH 5, where $[H^+] = 1.0 \times 10^{-5}$ M, the solution is more acidic than the value calculated, so the yellow color will predominate; at pH 10, where $[H^+] = 1.0 \times 10^{-10}$ M, the solution is less acidic than the value calculated, so the red color will predominate.

56. **The correct answer is (D).** This graph shows sharply negative values for the rate of change at the places in the original graph that correspond to steep drops in pH, and less negative values at the places in the original graph that correspond to buffer regions.

57. **The correct answer is (D).** Here we need to use Table 1 to test compounds that we consider to be strongly ionic, such as NaF and $CaCl_2$, against the Pauling electronegativity differences. (For NaF, $\Delta EN = 3.1$; for $CaCl_2$, $\Delta EN = 2.0$.)

58. **The correct answer is (B).** The Millikan definition ranks a bond high on the electronegativity scale if it holds on tightly to its own valence electron and successfully competes for a valence electron of other atoms.

59. **The correct answer is (B).** The large value of IE shown in Table 2 for H puts the Millikan EN for H above that for carbon, in contrast to the order given in the Pauling system.

60. **The correct answer is (A).** Table 3 (used together with Table 1 for EN values) shows a general trend of increased bond enthalpy and dipole moment as EN increases.

61. **The correct answer is (C).** The data in Table 4 show consistently that the strength of an acid increases as the electronegativity of a neighboring atom is increased by substitution. In this case, the highly electronegative chlorine is better than bromine at pulling negative charge toward itself and away from the hydrogen atom, leaving it freer to leave as H$^+$. Bromine, in turn, is more effective than iodine.

62. **The correct answer is (B).** We can use the ideal gas law, using "ΔP" = 760 torr – 745 torr = 15 torr to determine Δn, the decrease in moles of gas. Note that (15 torr)(1 atm/760 torr) = 0.0197 atm

$\Delta n = \Delta P V / RT$ = (0.0197 atm)(0.250 L) / (0.08206 L atm/K mol) (298 K)

= 2.02×10^{-4} mol CO_2

mass of CO_2 = (2.02×10^{-4} mol)(44.0 g/mol)

= 8.89×10^{-3} g

63. **The correct answer is (B).** Since the method relies on the reaction of carbon dioxide with sodium hydroxide, we need to be aware of any other species that would react similarly. H_2S dissolves in water to form a weak acid, which would also react with NaOH.

$H_2S(aq) + 2\ NaOH(aq) \rightarrow 2H_2O(l) + Na_2S(aq)$

64. **The correct answer is (D).** Since gas molecules are removed by the reaction with NaOH, both the total pressure in the flask—interpreted as the number of wall collisions per second—and the total number of molecules per unit volume—will decrease.

65. **The correct answer is (B).** Use the titration data to determine the number of moles of carbonate, equate this value to moles of original CO_2, then use the ideal gas law to determine the partial pressure of CO_2 in the original sample.

The titration reaction is

$CO_3^{2-}(aq) + 2H^+(aq) \rightarrow H_2O + CO_2(g)$

mmol CO_3^{2-} = (1/2) mmol H^+ = (1/2)(0.0200 mmol/mL)(20.40 mL)

= 0.204 mmol = 2.04×10^{-4} mol = moles original CO_2

$P_{CO2} = n_{CO2} RT / V$

= (2.04×10^{-4} mol)(0.08206 Latm/Kmol)(298 K) / (0.0100 L)

= 0.499 atm

0.499 atm (760 torr/1 atm) = 379 torr

66. **The correct answer is (D).** Since carbonate is a weak base, the pH of a carbonate solution is determined primarily by the hydrolysis reaction.

$CO_3^{2-} + H_2O = HCO_3^-(aq) + OH^-(aq)$ K_h

where $K_h = K_w/K_2 = (1.00 \times 10^{-14}) / (4.69 \times 10^{-11})$

= 2.13×10^{-4}

The concentration of CO_3^{2-} before dissociation is 8 mmol/10 ml, or 0.80 M. Setting x equal to $[OH^-(aq)]$ and to $[HCO_3^-]$ produced, we have

$2.13 \times 10^{-4} = x^2 / (0.80 - x)$

For an approximate answer, we may neglect x in the denominator, so

$x^2 \approx (2.13 \times 10^{-4})(0.80)$

$x \approx [OH^-] = 0.013$ M

pOH = –log (0.013) = 1.9

pH = 14.0 – 1.0 = 12.1

67. **The correct answer is (B).** Since $\lambda = c/\nu$, we can list the modes in order of increasing wavelength by going in order of decreasing frequency.

68. **The correct answer is (A).** The dipole moment of the molecule remains at zero during all phases of this mode. Both of the other modes produce a varying dipole moment.

69. The correct answer is (C). We cannot use Beer's Law directly, since we haven't been given *a* (a property of the molecule) or *b* (the optical path length). But the "identical conditions" mentioned ensure that these are fixed for both measurements. Therefore

$$C_2 / C_1 = A_2 / A_1 = (0.452 / 0.195) = 2.32$$
$$C_2 = 2.32\, C_1 = 2.32\, (2.5 \times 10^{-4}\ M)$$
$$= 5.8 \times 10^{-4}\ M$$

70. The correct answer is (C). The first horizontal region of the curve represents melting, while the second horizontal region represents evaporation. Since the rate of heating was 1.00 kJ/mol, the 20-min. interval represents 20.0 kJ/mol as the enthalpy of vaporization.

71. The correct answer is (D). E_a for the reverse reaction is the barrier faced going from right to left. From the diagram, the products must climb first by +34 kJ/mol (since ΔG is –34 kJ/mol) and then by an additional 28 kJ/mol, for a total of 62 kJ/mol.

72. The correct answer is (D). Ethanol has the highest vapor pressure of the four choices because it is much closer to its boiling point at 25.0°C than are water or aqueous solutions. Choices (C) and (D) both have lower vapor pressure than pure water, since a nonvolatile solute lowers the vapor pressure in proportion to its mole fraction. Since NaCl has more solute particles than glucose, it will have the lowest vapor pressure.

73. The correct answer is (C). First find the limiting reactant, using mg and mmol as time savers:

2.70 mg Al (1 mmol Al / 27.0 mg) = 0.100 mmol

20.00 mL HCl (0.0100 mmol/mL) = 0.200 mmol

We have twice as much HCl as Al, but we would need three times as much for all of the reactants to be used up; therefore HCl is the limiting reactant, and there will be some excess Al.

$(2.00 \times 10^{-4}\ \text{mol HCl})(3\ \text{mol } H_2/6\ \text{mol HCl})(22.4\ \text{L/mol } H_2)$

$= 2.24 \times 10^{-3}\ L \approx 2\ mL$

74. The correct answer is (A).

$$(\text{rate for X} / \text{rate for Ar}) = (\text{time for Ar} / \text{rate for X}) = (M_{Ar} / M_X)^{1/2}$$
$$(M_{Ar} / M_X) = (t_{Ar}/t_X)^2$$
$$M_X = M_{Ar}\, (t_X/t_{Ar})^2 = (39.9\ \text{g/mol})\, (20.0\ \text{min} / 24.0\ \text{min})^2$$

= 27.7 g/mol [Note that the shorter time for gas *x* leads us to predict at once that *x* has a lower molar mass than Ar, thus, narrowing the choices to (A) or (B).]

75. The correct answer is (D). If V is the original volume of the sample, then

$$M_1V_1 = M_2V_2$$
$$V(0.25) = (V + 48)(0.20)$$
$$V = 192\ \text{mL}$$

76. The correct answer is (C). The diagram can be interpreted with the following labels for the phases:

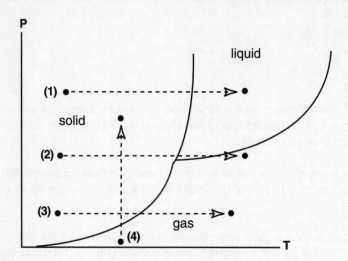

We see that path 3, which leads from solid directly to gas, represents sublimation, which by definition is to go directly from a solid to a gas.

77. The correct answer is (D).

VERBAL REASONING

78. **The correct answer is (A).** This is stated in the first sentence of the paragraph.

79. **The correct answer is (D).** This answer can be found in the parenthetical reference in the first sentence of the second paragraph.

80. **The correct answer is (A).** The author states in the third paragraph that "The ability to predict the paths of hurricanes has been greatly enhanced by the use of computers and satellites. The existence of better knowledge of the storm tracks…"

81. **The correct answer is (B).** In the fifth paragraph, the author says computers are an "enormous asset."

82. **The correct answer is (B).** Steering winds are discussed in the third paragraph.

83. **The correct answer is (A).** The author states that flying into the eye of a storm in an airplane is the best way to obtain information not provided by computers and previous predictions.

84. **The correct answer is (C).** The author makes this point in the last paragraph.

85. **The correct answer is (B).** This is stated in the last sentence of the first paragraph.

86. **The correct answer is (A).** The second paragraph discusses the way of life and customs of peasant women and how they were passed down through the generations.

87. **The correct answer is (B).** Tenements are described in the third paragraph. Many immigrants at this time lived in tenement buildings in large cities.

88. **The correct answer is (D).** Immigrant mothers were often consumed with responsibility, which included keeping the flat as livable as possible. This can be found in the fourth paragraph.

89. **The correct answer is (A).** The article mentions women gardening vegetables but does not mention selling them in a marketplace.

90. **The correct answer is (B).** Immigrant wages were often so low that the man alone could not support the family, causing others in the family to work. This can be found in the first sentence of paragraph 6.

91. **The correct answer is (C).** Although the author mentions the conditions of the whole immigrant family, it is clear that his focus is on the hardships of immigrant women, and that the author is sympathetic.

92. **The correct answer is (C).** The third paragraph explicitly states this.

93. **The correct answer is (B).** Although the other choices are true of some, the article states in paragraph 2 that "Many Americans wanted the United States to intervene on the side of the Cuban rebels, because the Spanish were seen as unwanted foreigners to be driven out of the hemisphere."

94. **The correct answer is (D).** This is stated in the second paragraph. Although the American investigation found that a land mine caused the explosion, no one was ever officially blamed.

95. **The correct answer is (B).**

96. **The correct answer is (A).** This answer can be found near the end of the third paragraph.

97. **The correct answer is (C).**

98. **The correct answer is (A).** The last paragraph talks about the results of the war and mentions that these three islands simply had one colonial ruler replaced by another.

99. **The correct answer is (C).** The second sentence in the first paragraph states, "Millions of years ago…" Thus, choice (C) makes the most sense. Choice (D) can be eliminated as millions is plural, so it's not less than a million, and (A) and (B) are too large.

100. **The correct answer is (D).** These things are all mentioned in the fifth paragraph.

101. **The correct answer is (C).** This is explicitly stated in the second paragraph.

102. **The correct answer is (B).** This is explicitly stated in the third paragraph.

103. **The correct answer is (A).** This can be found in the fifth paragraph.

104. **The correct answer is (B).** This is explicitly stated.

105. **The correct answer is (B).** This is the traditional definition of *laissez faire*.

106. **The correct answer is (A).** The passage mentions both the Erie Canal and transportation routes.

107. **The correct answer is (D).** This can be found in the third paragraph.

108. **The correct answer is (B).**

109. **The correct answer is (C).** See the last paragraph.

110. **The correct answer is (D).**

111. **The correct answer is (C).**

112. **The correct answer is (D).** This can be inferred from the first paragraph.

113. **The correct answer is (D).** Although it seems the author is uncomfortable with the growth of presidential power, it is not explicitly stated, and therefore more information is necessary.

114. **The correct answer is (B).** This can be found in the second paragraph.

115. **The correct answer is (B).** This is all stated in the passage.

116. **The correct answer is (A).**

117. **The correct answer is (D).**

118. **The correct answer is (C).**

119. **The correct answer is (A).** This is stated in the first sentence of the last paragraph.

120. **The correct answer is (C).** The passage mentions the loss of hind limbs, not all four limbs.

121. **The correct answer is (D).** This can be found in the first paragraph of the passage.

122. **The correct answer is (B).** The passage states that there is some evidence that communication skills are used to warn others of danger.

123. **The correct answer is (A).** The third paragraph explains that Odontoceti use their teeth to catch fish.

124. **The correct answer is (C).** A person actively advocating for the survival of Cetaceans would not be a threat.

125. **The correct answer is (C).** The author states that human intervention is essential to their survival.

126. **The correct answer is (A).** This is stated in the first paragraph.

127. **The correct answer is (B).** Jacobs did not want her story to be included in another novel. She wanted to tell her own story.

128. **The correct answer is (B).** Jacobs did not want the people she wrote about to suffer reprisals from their masters.

129. **The correct answer is (A).** Many believed at the time that an African-American woman could not write a work of such quality. This is mentioned in the third paragraph.

130. **The correct answer is (D).** Support for each of these claims can be found in the passage.

131. **The correct answer is (C).** Although the passage mentions choices (A) and (B), the focus of the passage is the eventual validation of the narrative.

132. **The correct answer is (D).**

133. **The correct answer is (B).** Dunant wanted to create a society of volunteers to help the wounded in battle.

134. **The correct answer is (A).**

135. **The correct answer is (C).** The passage states that the privileges were for signing members only.

136. **The correct answer is (C).**

137. **The correct answer is (B).** This is explicitly stated in the last paragraph.

BIOLOGICAL SCIENCES

138. The correct answer is (D). Microtubules and microfilaments help maintain cell shape, provide structural support, and influence cell motility. They are considered the cell's cytoskeleton.

139. The correct answer is (A). The lipid bilayer allows other lipids (hydrophobic molecules) to cross the membrane freely. Small polar molecules such as water can pass *between* the membrane phospholipids. Glucose molecules, however, require channel proteins to assist in facilitated diffusion.

140. The correct answer is (B). The described carrier proteins are involved with the sodium/potassium ATP pump. The active transport of these ions is vital in repolarization and in the maintenance of the cell's resting potential.

141. The correct answer is (C). The glycocalyx includes glycoproteins, glycolipids, and other carbohydrate components of the membrane. These molecules are important as markers in the embryonic arrangement of cells into tissues and organs, as well as in the ability to distinguish between "self" and "non-self" by the body's immune system.

142. The correct answer is (A). Acetylcholine, released from motor neuron vesicles, is the ligand that binds to ligand-gated channels. This event leads to the inflow of sodium ions at the onset of depolarization of the sarcolemma.

143. The correct answer is (B). Cholesterol can be synthesized by the liver.

144. The correct answer is (C). Although plasmodesmata are membrane connections that allow material through, they are only found in plant cells.

145. The correct answer is (A). All amines have a lone-pair of electrons on the nitrogen which enables a hydrogen bond to form. Tertiary amines cannot form hydrogen bonds because the N is not bonded to a hydrogen atom. Amines are not optically active because of their rapid rate of inversion which convert between enantiomers.

146. The correct answer is (C). This molecule is not superimposable on its mirror image. However, it is not optically active because of rapid inversion of its configuration; the energy barrier between the two arrangements of groups is exceedingly low so that enantiomers have not been isolated.

147. The correct answer is (B). Quarternary ammonium salts containing four different groups has a tetrahedral arrangement and therefore exist as configurational enantiomers.

148. The correct answer is (C). Rapid inversion about the pyramidal N precludes the isolation of enantiomers.

149. The correct answer is (D). The nonbonding electrons on aromatic amines are delocalized according to

They therefore are less available for attack by a H^+.

150. The correct answer is (C). A free N-H group stretches at 3050–3550 cm^{-1} while the N-H bending occurs at 1600–1640 cm^{-1}.

151. The correct answer is (B). Heterozygous individuals at both loci (YyAa) produce pigment (A_) and have a yellow coat (Yy).

152. The correct answer is (A). If a Punnett square is completed for this cross, four out of sixteen possible offspring will have the lethal YY combination as part of their genotype.

153. The correct answer is (C). Further examination of this same Punnett square reveals that out of the twelve possible offspring that will live to birth, nine will have a pigmented coat (6 yellow, 3 agouti) and three will be albinos.

154. The correct answer is (B). The cross described (yyAa x yyAa) has a 25% chance of producing an albino individual (yyaa) and a 75% chance of producing an agouti individual (yyAA or yyAa).

155. The correct answer is (D). A common incorrect choice is pleiotropy, which refers to an allele at one locus affecting many different traits or aspects of the individual's phenotype.

156. The correct answer is (C). This monohybrid cross disregards alleles at the albino locus. Two yellow mice (Yy) can produce two yellow offspring (Yy) and one agouti offspring (yy). YY individuals die prior to birth.

157. The correct answer is (B). A highly acidic pH limits the number of *any* cells that can survive in the environment of the stomach.

158. The correct answer is (A). By maintaining a hypertonic renal medulla between the ascending loop of Henle and the collecting duct and a hypotonic urinary filtrate in the distal convoluted tubule and collecting duct, water can be reabsorbed with extreme efficiency when ADH is present.

159. The correct answer is (C). Proprioceptors respond to mechanical stretch in the muscles, tendons, and joints. Hearing receptors respond to mechanical vibrations caused by sound waves and (subsequently) fluids in the cochlea. Balance receptors respond to mechanical forces caused by otoconia (saccule and utricle) and fluid movements (semicircular canals). Pain receptors *may* respond to intense mechanical forces. However, they also respond to chemicals and thermal changes as well.

160. The correct answer is (C). mRNAs, tRNAs, and rRNAs are needed for protein synthesis in both eukaryotes and prokaryotes. However, snRNAs are components of spliceosomes, which help in post-transcriptional modification by removing introns from pre-mRNA in eukaryotes.

161. The correct answer is (B). Tertiary amines do not react with acid chlorides to form amides because tertiary amines cannot lose a proton after attacking the carbon. The alkylation of amines by alkyl halides is a nucleophilic substitution reaction in which the organic halide is attacked by the nucleophilic amine. Peptides are formed by the reaction between the carboxyl group of an amino acid and the amino terminal of another amino acid to form an amide linkage.

162. The correct answer is (B). The region shows the blastocoel of the former blastula decreasing in size as the archenteron of the gastrula forms.

163. The correct answer is (C). The coelom forms as the three primary germ layers proceed through gastrulation.

164. The correct answer is (D). Each cell produced by indeterminate cleavage in the early embryo maintains its capacity to develop into a complete embryo.

165. The correct answer is (A). Radial and spiral cleavage are terms that refer to particular planes of division with respect to the vertical axis in the early embryo (parallel or perpendicular vs. diagonal, respectively). Organisms with radial cleavage include the sea star (an echinoderm with radial symmetry) and the elephant (a chordate with bilateral symmetry). Choice (B) is not considered correct because the phyla that exhibit spiral cleavage (mollusks, annelids, and arthropods) are all bilaterally symmetrical. Although the octopus (a cephalopod mollusk) appears to be radially symmetrical, the distinct head and tail regions confirm bilateral symmetry.

166. The correct answer is (D). In deuterostomes (echinoderms and chordates), the anus develops from the blastopore. The shark (a chordate) is the only correct answer.

167. The correct answer is (A). The question describes an organism with determinate cleavage (a protostome). The only protostome among the choices is the fruit fly, an arthropod. The hagfish is a chordate (a jawless vertebrate like the lamprey, belonging to the class Agnatha).

168. The correct answer is (B). If each of these structures has endocrine functions, the secretions must enter the blood. The hypothalamus only regulates the activity of the pituitary gland.

169. The correct answer is (D). The question states that an increase in blood volume will increase blood pressure. When reabsorption of sodium occurs, reabsorption of water usually follows (increasing blood volume). Therefore, without knowing anything about ANF, choice (D) is the only possible answer.

170. The correct answer is (C). Knowledge about the role of bicarbonate ion (here, in the form of sodium bicarbonate) as an alkaline secretion that helps neutralize acidity is helpful. The arrival of acidic chyme signals the small intestine to release secretin ("proximate" reason). The fact that pancreatic enzymes are most active in the slightly alkaline pH of the small intestine (they require a slightly alkaline environment to function properly) is the "ultimate" reason.

171. The correct answer is (A). When cells in a noncyclic environment (darkness) display a cyclic pattern of response, an "internal" cyclic rhythm is suggested. Choices (B) and (C) do not apply to the conditions described in the question. There is no relevant basis for selecting choice (D).

172. The correct answer is (D). The passage states that thymosin only influences the differentiation of T-lymphocytes. Choices (A), (B), and (C) are each specific roles of lymphocytes (either T- or B-lymphocytes).

173. The correct answer is (B). Knowledge of the source and function of bile is important. The liver produces bile, while the gallbladder stores and concentrates bile. The role of bile is to emulsify fats so that they can be efficiently digested by pancreatic lipase. Without the gallbladder, bile can still be sent to the small intestine via the liver directly.

174. The correct answer is (C). Resonance structures can be drawn for both the acid and its anion, but those for the acid are inequivalent. Thus, resonance stabilization is greater for the anion.

175. The correct answer is (C). Acidity increases as electron-withdrawing groups are added to the acid. Electron-withdrawing groups attached to the α-carbon are particularly effective in raising the acidity of the acid.

176. The correct answer is (B). Acid-weakening groups donate charge so that they activate the ring toward attack by an electron-deficient species.

177. The correct answer is (A). The carbonyl carbon is sp^2 hybridized so it is planar near the site of attack and therefore less sterically hindered.

178. The correct answer is (C). The carboxyl group is made of these three groups and therefore they will appear in the infrared spectrum.

179. The correct answer is (D). For substitution to occur, C-C or C-H bonds would need to break.

180. The correct answer is (D). A DNA sequence is complementary and antiparallel to its mRNA transcript.

181. The correct answer is (D). In birds, sex determination works in the opposite way from humans, where the male is heterogametic (XY). The female bird is heterogametic (ZW) and will produce a male offspring if her egg carries the Z chromosome (ZZ), and a female offspring if her egg carries the W chromosome (ZW).

182. The correct answer is (C). Aromatic systems show strong absorptions in the UV region of the system. C—C and C—H bonds will absorb in the IR region. The NMR will show the inequivalent hydrogens.

183. The correct answer is (C). NAD and FAD are hydrogen acceptors in cellular respiration during which time most of a cell's ATP is produced. Among the answers, only active transport via the sodium/potassium pump requires ATP.

184. The correct answer is (C). The liver produces bile, which emulsifies fats prior to digestion by pancreatic lipase. However, the liver makes no enzymes that digest food directly.

185. The correct answer is (A). To make DNA from an RNA template requires the enzyme reverse transcriptase (originally identified in retroviruses).

186. The correct answer is (B). Ribonuclease is specifically needed to break down RNA. Deoxyribonuclease can degrade DNA, while proteases can initiate the breakdown of proteins.

187. **The correct answer is (B).** The complementary strand of DNA is synthesized using DNA polymerase. DNA helicase is not needed to separate the DNA double helix because there is no DNA double helix.

188. **The correct answer is (C).** In eukaryotes, as a result of post-transcriptional modification, the final mRNA transcript has had introns (intervening sequences) removed. Only the exons (expressed sequences) remain.

189. **The correct answer is (C).** Although all answers are true statements, only choice (C) is a statement that one can conclude from the evidence presented.

190. **The correct answer is (D).** All three protein gene products are utilized by both brain cells and muscle cells. Peptidyl transferase is used during translation, ATPase is used during cellular respiration, and acetylcholinesterase is used after depolarization.

191. **The correct answer is (A).** Since increased carbon dioxide levels contribute to increased acidity (too many H^+), the appropriate response to a rise in plasma H^+ concentration would be to breathe more deeply and more rapidly. This will decrease blood carbon dioxide levels.

192. **The correct answer is (B).** Bases remove free H^+ from solution. An exposed $R\text{-}NH_2$ can bind to H^+ to form $R\text{-}NH_3^+$. An exposed $R\text{-}COOH$ has no available site for binding to an additional H^+.

193. **The correct answer is (D).** Buffers either substitute weak acids for strong acids or weak bases for strong bases. Carbonic acid is a weak acid that does not dissociate as much as a strong acid such as hydrochloric acid.

194. **The correct answer is (C).** Acidosis is a condition in which H^+ concentration is too high. The kidney will *increase* reabsorption of bicarbonate ions under these conditions so that this basic ion can tie up many of the excess H^+.

195. **The correct answer is (B).** Without adequate intake of glucose, fats will be mobilized to form glycerol and fatty acids to be used as substitutes in cellular respiration. The utilization of fatty acids for energy produces acidic ketone bodies.

196. **The correct answer is (B).** A pH lower than 7.35 indicates acidosis. If the respiratory system was the cause, carbon dioxide levels would be higher than normal. Since carbon dioxide levels in this example are lower than normal, the respiratory system seems to be eliminating carbon dioxide faster than usual in order to compensate for the acidity caused elsewhere.

197. **The correct answer is (C).** The –OH group when protonated becomes the good leaving group, H_2O.

198. **The correct answer is (D).** Alkyl groups rearrange to form the most stable carbocation. Most primary alcohols do not react with a carbocation intermediate.

199. **The correct answer is (A).** The neopentyl group is bulky, thus making a bimolecular reaction less favorable.

200. **The correct answer is (B).** Strong nucleophiles are generally strong bases so they will become protonated in acidic solution.

201. **The correct answer is (A).** In dehydration the proton is used to generate H_2O but is then produced when a neighboring hydrogen is removed by the conjugate base.

202. **The correct answer is (A).** In acid solution the –OH group is protonated, which then undergoes heterolysis to release the weakly basic H_2O and form the carbocation. The most stable carbocation contains the most alkyl groups around the site of positive charge.

203. **The correct answer is (D).** The heads of the femur and humerus are the proximal ends. The sternum is a flat bone of the axial skeleton, while the ilia are flat bones of the pelvic girdle. Although vertebrae are part of the axial skeleton, they are not flat bones.

204. **The correct answer is (C).** Since reticulocytes still contain ribosomes and rough ER, translation of previously transcribed mRNA can still take place.

205. The correct answer is (A). Erythropoietin is made by the kidney in direct response to hypoxia. A drop in RBCs in the spleen will cause the spleen to release stored RBCs into the circulation, but will not *directly* affect kidney production of EPO. High blood viscosity can have an inhibitory effect on EPO, since increased RBCs can further increase viscosity.

206. The correct answer is (C). T-cells derive their name from the influence of the thymus gland and its hormone, thymosin, on their maturation.

207. The correct answer is (C). Since the number of WBCs is insignificant compared to the number of RBCs in a sample, they are counted and ignored. In contrast, RBCs in a sample are destroyed with a hemolyzing agent before WBCs can be counted accurately.

208. The correct answer is (B). The inhibition of prostaglandin synthesis by aspirin will reduce thromboxane activation of platelets and thereby slow down the various stages of hemostasis, including coagulation. Since prostaglandins can stimulate inflammation, choice (C) cannot be correct.

209. The correct answer is (D). DNA synthesis occurs during interphase in all cells undergoing mitosis and meiosis. Since there are so many RBCs, and the rate of turnover is so high, anything that would interfere with mitosis would affect them the most.

210. The correct answer is (A). Methanogens, thermophiles, and halophiles are organisms belonging to the prokaryotic domain Archaea.

211. The correct answer is (D). Phenols distinguish themselves by being a water-soluble compound that dissolves in NaOH but not in $NaHCO_3$. They can form the weaker acid water but not the stronger carbonic acid.

212. The correct answer is (C). Parathyroid hormone is influenced directly by calcium levels in the blood. Anterior pituitary hormones affect the other three hormones (FSH/estrogen, LH/progesterone, TSH/thyroxine).

213. The correct answer is (C). During resting conditions in skeletal muscle tissue, the troponin-tropomyosin complex binds to actin. Depolarization results in the outflow of calcium from the sarcoplasmic reticulum and the release of actin by the protein complex in order to bind with calcium.

214. The correct answer is (C). Telomerase activity has been detected in cancer cells. This helps explain their seemingly limitless ability to divide.

PRACTICE EXAM III

	Time
Physical Sciences Questions 1–77	100 minutes
Verbal Reasoning Questions 78–137	85 minutes
Writing Sample 2 Essays	60 minutes
Biological Sciences Questions 138–214	100 minutes

ANSWER SHEET
PRACTICE EXAM III

Physical Sciences	Verbal Reasoning	Biological Sciences

Physical Sciences

1. Ⓐ Ⓑ Ⓒ Ⓓ   40. Ⓐ Ⓑ Ⓒ Ⓓ
2. Ⓐ Ⓑ Ⓒ Ⓓ   41. Ⓐ Ⓑ Ⓒ Ⓓ
3. Ⓐ Ⓑ Ⓒ Ⓓ   42. Ⓐ Ⓑ Ⓒ Ⓓ
4. Ⓐ Ⓑ Ⓒ Ⓓ   43. Ⓐ Ⓑ Ⓒ Ⓓ
5. Ⓐ Ⓑ Ⓒ Ⓓ   44. Ⓐ Ⓑ Ⓒ Ⓓ
6. Ⓐ Ⓑ Ⓒ Ⓓ   45. Ⓐ Ⓑ Ⓒ Ⓓ
7. Ⓐ Ⓑ Ⓒ Ⓓ   46. Ⓐ Ⓑ Ⓒ Ⓓ
8. Ⓐ Ⓑ Ⓒ Ⓓ   47. Ⓐ Ⓑ Ⓒ Ⓓ
9. Ⓐ Ⓑ Ⓒ Ⓓ   48. Ⓐ Ⓑ Ⓒ Ⓓ
10. Ⓐ Ⓑ Ⓒ Ⓓ   49. Ⓐ Ⓑ Ⓒ Ⓓ
11. Ⓐ Ⓑ Ⓒ Ⓓ   50. Ⓐ Ⓑ Ⓒ Ⓓ
12. Ⓐ Ⓑ Ⓒ Ⓓ   51. Ⓐ Ⓑ Ⓒ Ⓓ
13. Ⓐ Ⓑ Ⓒ Ⓓ   52. Ⓐ Ⓑ Ⓒ Ⓓ
14. Ⓐ Ⓑ Ⓒ Ⓓ   53. Ⓐ Ⓑ Ⓒ Ⓓ
15. Ⓐ Ⓑ Ⓒ Ⓓ   54. Ⓐ Ⓑ Ⓒ Ⓓ
16. Ⓐ Ⓑ Ⓒ Ⓓ   55. Ⓐ Ⓑ Ⓒ Ⓓ
17. Ⓐ Ⓑ Ⓒ Ⓓ   56. Ⓐ Ⓑ Ⓒ Ⓓ
18. Ⓐ Ⓑ Ⓒ Ⓓ   57. Ⓐ Ⓑ Ⓒ Ⓓ
19. Ⓐ Ⓑ Ⓒ Ⓓ   58. Ⓐ Ⓑ Ⓒ Ⓓ
20. Ⓐ Ⓑ Ⓒ Ⓓ   59. Ⓐ Ⓑ Ⓒ Ⓓ
21. Ⓐ Ⓑ Ⓒ Ⓓ   60. Ⓐ Ⓑ Ⓒ Ⓓ
22. Ⓐ Ⓑ Ⓒ Ⓓ   61. Ⓐ Ⓑ Ⓒ Ⓓ
23. Ⓐ Ⓑ Ⓒ Ⓓ   62. Ⓐ Ⓑ Ⓒ Ⓓ
24. Ⓐ Ⓑ Ⓒ Ⓓ   63. Ⓐ Ⓑ Ⓒ Ⓓ
25. Ⓐ Ⓑ Ⓒ Ⓓ   64. Ⓐ Ⓑ Ⓒ Ⓓ
26. Ⓐ Ⓑ Ⓒ Ⓓ   65. Ⓐ Ⓑ Ⓒ Ⓓ
27. Ⓐ Ⓑ Ⓒ Ⓓ   66. Ⓐ Ⓑ Ⓒ Ⓓ
28. Ⓐ Ⓑ Ⓒ Ⓓ   67. Ⓐ Ⓑ Ⓒ Ⓓ
29. Ⓐ Ⓑ Ⓒ Ⓓ   68. Ⓐ Ⓑ Ⓒ Ⓓ
30. Ⓐ Ⓑ Ⓒ Ⓓ   69. Ⓐ Ⓑ Ⓒ Ⓓ
31. Ⓐ Ⓑ Ⓒ Ⓓ   70. Ⓐ Ⓑ Ⓒ Ⓓ
32. Ⓐ Ⓑ Ⓒ Ⓓ   71. Ⓐ Ⓑ Ⓒ Ⓓ
33. Ⓐ Ⓑ Ⓒ Ⓓ   72. Ⓐ Ⓑ Ⓒ Ⓓ
34. Ⓐ Ⓑ Ⓒ Ⓓ   73. Ⓐ Ⓑ Ⓒ Ⓓ
35. Ⓐ Ⓑ Ⓒ Ⓓ   74. Ⓐ Ⓑ Ⓒ Ⓓ
36. Ⓐ Ⓑ Ⓒ Ⓓ   75. Ⓐ Ⓑ Ⓒ Ⓓ
37. Ⓐ Ⓑ Ⓒ Ⓓ   76. Ⓐ Ⓑ Ⓒ Ⓓ
38. Ⓐ Ⓑ Ⓒ Ⓓ   77. Ⓐ Ⓑ Ⓒ Ⓓ
39. Ⓐ Ⓑ Ⓒ Ⓓ

Verbal Reasoning

78. Ⓐ Ⓑ Ⓒ Ⓓ   108. Ⓐ Ⓑ Ⓒ Ⓓ
79. Ⓐ Ⓑ Ⓒ Ⓓ   109. Ⓐ Ⓑ Ⓒ Ⓓ
80. Ⓐ Ⓑ Ⓒ Ⓓ   110. Ⓐ Ⓑ Ⓒ Ⓓ
81. Ⓐ Ⓑ Ⓒ Ⓓ   111. Ⓐ Ⓑ Ⓒ Ⓓ
82. Ⓐ Ⓑ Ⓒ Ⓓ   112. Ⓐ Ⓑ Ⓒ Ⓓ
83. Ⓐ Ⓑ Ⓒ Ⓓ   113. Ⓐ Ⓑ Ⓒ Ⓓ
84. Ⓐ Ⓑ Ⓒ Ⓓ   114. Ⓐ Ⓑ Ⓒ Ⓓ
85. Ⓐ Ⓑ Ⓒ Ⓓ   115. Ⓐ Ⓑ Ⓒ Ⓓ
86. Ⓐ Ⓑ Ⓒ Ⓓ   116. Ⓐ Ⓑ Ⓒ Ⓓ
87. Ⓐ Ⓑ Ⓒ Ⓓ   117. Ⓐ Ⓑ Ⓒ Ⓓ
88. Ⓐ Ⓑ Ⓒ Ⓓ   118. Ⓐ Ⓑ Ⓒ Ⓓ
89. Ⓐ Ⓑ Ⓒ Ⓓ   119. Ⓐ Ⓑ Ⓒ Ⓓ
90. Ⓐ Ⓑ Ⓒ Ⓓ   120. Ⓐ Ⓑ Ⓒ Ⓓ
91. Ⓐ Ⓑ Ⓒ Ⓓ   121. Ⓐ Ⓑ Ⓒ Ⓓ
92. Ⓐ Ⓑ Ⓒ Ⓓ   122. Ⓐ Ⓑ Ⓒ Ⓓ
93. Ⓐ Ⓑ Ⓒ Ⓓ   123. Ⓐ Ⓑ Ⓒ Ⓓ
94. Ⓐ Ⓑ Ⓒ Ⓓ   124. Ⓐ Ⓑ Ⓒ Ⓓ
95. Ⓐ Ⓑ Ⓒ Ⓓ   125. Ⓐ Ⓑ Ⓒ Ⓓ
96. Ⓐ Ⓑ Ⓒ Ⓓ   126. Ⓐ Ⓑ Ⓒ Ⓓ
97. Ⓐ Ⓑ Ⓒ Ⓓ   127. Ⓐ Ⓑ Ⓒ Ⓓ
98. Ⓐ Ⓑ Ⓒ Ⓓ   128. Ⓐ Ⓑ Ⓒ Ⓓ
99. Ⓐ Ⓑ Ⓒ Ⓓ   129. Ⓐ Ⓑ Ⓒ Ⓓ
100. Ⓐ Ⓑ Ⓒ Ⓓ   130. Ⓐ Ⓑ Ⓒ Ⓓ
101. Ⓐ Ⓑ Ⓒ Ⓓ   131. Ⓐ Ⓑ Ⓒ Ⓓ
102. Ⓐ Ⓑ Ⓒ Ⓓ   132. Ⓐ Ⓑ Ⓒ Ⓓ
103. Ⓐ Ⓑ Ⓒ Ⓓ   133. Ⓐ Ⓑ Ⓒ Ⓓ
104. Ⓐ Ⓑ Ⓒ Ⓓ   134. Ⓐ Ⓑ Ⓒ Ⓓ
105. Ⓐ Ⓑ Ⓒ Ⓓ   135. Ⓐ Ⓑ Ⓒ Ⓓ
106. Ⓐ Ⓑ Ⓒ Ⓓ   136. Ⓐ Ⓑ Ⓒ Ⓓ
107. Ⓐ Ⓑ Ⓒ Ⓓ   137. Ⓐ Ⓑ Ⓒ Ⓓ

Biological Sciences

138. Ⓐ Ⓑ Ⓒ Ⓓ   177. Ⓐ Ⓑ Ⓒ Ⓓ
139. Ⓐ Ⓑ Ⓒ Ⓓ   178. Ⓐ Ⓑ Ⓒ Ⓓ
140. Ⓐ Ⓑ Ⓒ Ⓓ   179. Ⓐ Ⓑ Ⓒ Ⓓ
141. Ⓐ Ⓑ Ⓒ Ⓓ   180. Ⓐ Ⓑ Ⓒ Ⓓ
142. Ⓐ Ⓑ Ⓒ Ⓓ   181. Ⓐ Ⓑ Ⓒ Ⓓ
143. Ⓐ Ⓑ Ⓒ Ⓓ   182. Ⓐ Ⓑ Ⓒ Ⓓ
144. Ⓐ Ⓑ Ⓒ Ⓓ   183. Ⓐ Ⓑ Ⓒ Ⓓ
145. Ⓐ Ⓑ Ⓒ Ⓓ   184. Ⓐ Ⓑ Ⓒ Ⓓ
146. Ⓐ Ⓑ Ⓒ Ⓓ   185. Ⓐ Ⓑ Ⓒ Ⓓ
147. Ⓐ Ⓑ Ⓒ Ⓓ   186. Ⓐ Ⓑ Ⓒ Ⓓ
148. Ⓐ Ⓑ Ⓒ Ⓓ   187. Ⓐ Ⓑ Ⓒ Ⓓ
149. Ⓐ Ⓑ Ⓒ Ⓓ   188. Ⓐ Ⓑ Ⓒ Ⓓ
150. Ⓐ Ⓑ Ⓒ Ⓓ   189. Ⓐ Ⓑ Ⓒ Ⓓ
151. Ⓐ Ⓑ Ⓒ Ⓓ   190. Ⓐ Ⓑ Ⓒ Ⓓ
152. Ⓐ Ⓑ Ⓒ Ⓓ   191. Ⓐ Ⓑ Ⓒ Ⓓ
153. Ⓐ Ⓑ Ⓒ Ⓓ   192. Ⓐ Ⓑ Ⓒ Ⓓ
154. Ⓐ Ⓑ Ⓒ Ⓓ   193. Ⓐ Ⓑ Ⓒ Ⓓ
155. Ⓐ Ⓑ Ⓒ Ⓓ   194. Ⓐ Ⓑ Ⓒ Ⓓ
156. Ⓐ Ⓑ Ⓒ Ⓓ   195. Ⓐ Ⓑ Ⓒ Ⓓ
157. Ⓐ Ⓑ Ⓒ Ⓓ   196. Ⓐ Ⓑ Ⓒ Ⓓ
158. Ⓐ Ⓑ Ⓒ Ⓓ   197. Ⓐ Ⓑ Ⓒ Ⓓ
159. Ⓐ Ⓑ Ⓒ Ⓓ   198. Ⓐ Ⓑ Ⓒ Ⓓ
160. Ⓐ Ⓑ Ⓒ Ⓓ   199. Ⓐ Ⓑ Ⓒ Ⓓ
161. Ⓐ Ⓑ Ⓒ Ⓓ   200. Ⓐ Ⓑ Ⓒ Ⓓ
162. Ⓐ Ⓑ Ⓒ Ⓓ   201. Ⓐ Ⓑ Ⓒ Ⓓ
163. Ⓐ Ⓑ Ⓒ Ⓓ   202. Ⓐ Ⓑ Ⓒ Ⓓ
164. Ⓐ Ⓑ Ⓒ Ⓓ   203. Ⓐ Ⓑ Ⓒ Ⓓ
165. Ⓐ Ⓑ Ⓒ Ⓓ   204. Ⓐ Ⓑ Ⓒ Ⓓ
166. Ⓐ Ⓑ Ⓒ Ⓓ   205. Ⓐ Ⓑ Ⓒ Ⓓ
167. Ⓐ Ⓑ Ⓒ Ⓓ   206. Ⓐ Ⓑ Ⓒ Ⓓ
168. Ⓐ Ⓑ Ⓒ Ⓓ   207. Ⓐ Ⓑ Ⓒ Ⓓ
169. Ⓐ Ⓑ Ⓒ Ⓓ   208. Ⓐ Ⓑ Ⓒ Ⓓ
170. Ⓐ Ⓑ Ⓒ Ⓓ   209. Ⓐ Ⓑ Ⓒ Ⓓ
171. Ⓐ Ⓑ Ⓒ Ⓓ   210. Ⓐ Ⓑ Ⓒ Ⓓ
172. Ⓐ Ⓑ Ⓒ Ⓓ   211. Ⓐ Ⓑ Ⓒ Ⓓ
173. Ⓐ Ⓑ Ⓒ Ⓓ   212. Ⓐ Ⓑ Ⓒ Ⓓ
174. Ⓐ Ⓑ Ⓒ Ⓓ   213. Ⓐ Ⓑ Ⓒ Ⓓ
175. Ⓐ Ⓑ Ⓒ Ⓓ   214. Ⓐ Ⓑ Ⓒ Ⓓ
176. Ⓐ Ⓑ Ⓒ Ⓓ

Writing Sample 1

_____

_____

_____

_____

_____

_____

_____

_____

_____

_____

_____

_____

_____

_____

_____

_____

_____

_____

_____

_____

_____

_____

_____

END OF PART 1

Writing Sample 2

_____

_____

_____

_____

_____

_____

_____

_____

_____

_____

_____

_____

_____

_____

_____

_____

_____

_____

_____

_____

_____

_____

END OF PART 2

PHYSICAL SCIENCES

Time: 100 Minutes
Questions 1–77

Directions: This test contains 77 questions. Most of the questions consist of a descriptive passage followed by a group of questions related to the passage. For these questions, study the passage carefully and then choose the best answer to each question in the group. Some questions in this test stand alone. These questions are independent of any passage and independent of each other. For these questions, too, you must select the one best answer. Indicate all your answers by blackening the corresponding circles on your answer sheet.

A periodic table is provided at the beginning of this book. You may consult it whenever you feel it's necessary.

Passage I (Questions 1–7)

Jane is attending a seminar on the application of high speed, or ultrasonic, sound waves in medicine. For example, ultrasound is used in a noninvasive method that can determine the rate of blood flow. An instrument placed on a patient's arm or neck directs the waves into an artery where they are reflected by the red blood cells back to a receiver. The frequency detected, f_r, relative to the frequency originally emitted, f, indicates the speed of the cell and thereby, of the blood, v_b. The relationship is:

$$f_r = f\,(v + v_b)/(v - v_b) \qquad \text{eqn. 1}$$

The speed of sound, v, in human body tissue including blood, at normal body temperature is approximately 1500 m/s.

Ultrasound is also commonly used to monitor a fetus in the womb. In fetal cardiology the waves are reflected from the wall of the fetal heart, which is moving towards the ultrasonic receiver as the heart beats.

Jane realizes these techniques make use of the Doppler effect. The general form of the Doppler equation is:

$$f_o = f_s(v \pm v_o)/(v \pm v_s) \qquad \text{eqn. 2}$$

The subscripts s and o stand for source and observer (detector), respectively. Unfortunately, Jane can't remember when to use the plus signs and when to use the minus signs.

She tries to logically determine when to use the operations of addition and/or subtraction in the numerator and denominator of equation 2. Jane recalls that the apparent frequency of a sound, such as a police siren, seems to increase as the source approaches her. In order for the observed frequency to become greater than the source frequency, the ratio $(v \pm v_o)/(v \pm v_s)$ must be greater than one. This can occur if the numerator increases and/or the denominator decreases suggesting the form $(v + v_o)/(v - v_s)$. If Jane is standing still, her speed, v_o, becomes zero.

1. Which expression best describes the Doppler shifted frequency for a moving source following a moving observer?

    A. $f_o = f_s(v + v_o)/(v - v_s)$
    B. $f_o = f_s(v - v_o)/(v + v_s)$
    C. $f_o = f_s(v + v_o)/(v + v_s)$
    D. $f_o = f_s(v - v_o)/(v - v_s)$

2. Which expression best describes the Doppler shifted frequency for a source and an observer moving in opposite directions?

    A. $f_o = f_s(v + v_o)/(v - v_s)$
    B. $f_o = f_s(v - v_o)/(v + v_s)$
    C. $f_o = f_s(v + v_o)/(v + v_s)$
    D. $f_o = f_s(v - v_o)/(v - v_s)$

3. Which expression best describes the Doppler shifted frequency for an observer moving away from a fixed sound source?

    A. $f_o = f_s(v)/(v - v_s)$
    B. $f_o = f_s(v)/(v + v_s)$
    C. $f_o = f_s(v + v_o)/v$
    D. $f_o = f_s(v - v_o)/v$

4. Which expression best describes the Doppler shifted frequency for $v_s = 0$?

A. $f_o = f_s(v)/(v - v_s)$

B. $f_o = f_s(v)/(v + v_s)$

C. $f_o = f_s(v + v_o)/v$

D. $f_o = f_s(v - v_o)/v$

5. On a day when the speed of sound in air is v, a police car with its siren going drives with speed S toward a stationary wall. What frequency of reflected sound is heard by the officer in the car?

A. f

B. $f(v)/(v + S)$

C. $f(v + S)/(v)$

D. $f(v + S)/(v - S)$

6. What is the observed frequency when 2.0000 MHz waves reflect off blood cells moving towards the source at 0.4 m/s?

A. 1.9989 MHz

B. 1.9996 MHz

C. 2.0011 MHz

D. 2.0024 MHz

7. A 6.0000-MHz ultrasonic beam is used to determine the speed of the heart of a particular high-risk fetus. What is the speed of the fetal heart if the observed frequency is shifted by 12 kHz?

A. 3.0 m/s

B. 2.0 m/s

C. 1.5 m/s

D. 1.2 m/s

Passage II (Questions 8–14)

A simple circuit consists of an emf source such as a battery, V, connected by perfectly conducting, resistance-less wires to a resistor, R.

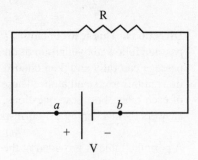

Figure 1

An electromotive force (emf), such as a battery, creates a potential difference (voltage, V) between points *a* and *b* by separating positive and negative charges. A current of positive charge (I) flows through the circuit from the positive (+) terminal to the negative (–) terminal of the emf. The electric potential energy of the moving charges is converted to heat energy in the resistor (R).

Circuit theory has three fundamental equations:

I. Kirchhoff's loop law: The algebraic sum of the changes in potential around any closed circuit loop must equal zero.

   i. Follow the current from the negative terminal of the emf, across the emf source, around the circuit, and back to the negative terminal of the emf.

   ii. The path through the emf (from the – terminal to the + terminal) is a voltage rise. A rise in voltage is assigned a positive (+) algebraic value while a voltage drop is assigned a negative (–) algebraic value.

   iii. If there's more than one emf, select one as the starting point. If the resulting current direction is correct, the value of the other emf source will be positive.

II. Kirchhoff's junction law: The sum of the currents entering a junction must equal the sum of the currents leaving the junction. A junction is any point in a circuit where the current can be split.

III. Ohm's law: The voltage across a resistor and the current through a resistor are related to the resistance of the resistor by: $R = V/I$

   i. Resistors connected in series can be replaced by an equivalent resistor:

$$R_{equiv} = \Sigma R_{individual}$$

   ii. Resistors connected in parallel can be replaced by an equivalent resistor:

$$1/R_{equiv} = \Sigma 1/R_{individual}$$

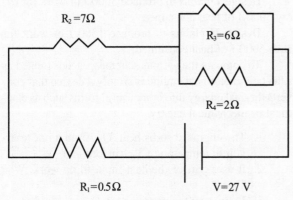

Figure 2

8. Based on Figure 2, which statement is most accurate?

  A. The current through R_4 is less than the current through R_2 but is equal to the current through R_3.

  B. The current through R_4 is less than the current through R_2 but is three times the current through R_3.

  C. The current through R_4 is less than the current through R_2 but one third of the current through R_3.

  D. The current through R_4 is equal to the current through R_2.

9. Based on Figure 2, which statement is most accurate?

  A. The current through R_1 is 14 times the current through R_2.

  B. The current through R_1 is $1/14^{th}$ the current through R_2.

  C. The current through R_1 is equal to the current through R_2.

  D. The current through R_1 is slightly less than the current through R_2.

10. Based on Figure 2, which statement is most accurate?

  A. The voltage across R_1 is 14 times the voltage across R_2.

  B. The voltage across R_1 is $1/14^{th}$ the voltage across R_2.

  C. The voltage across R_1 is equal to the voltage across R_2.

  D. The voltage across R_1 is slightly less than the voltage across R_2.

11. Based on Figure 2, what is the voltage drop across R_2?

  A. 2.3 V

  B. 12.2 V

  C. 16.4 V

  D. 21.0 V

12. In the circuit below, the emf provides a current of 30 A in split in the directions shown. What is the value of I_5?

  A. 4 A

  B. 8 A

  C. 14 A

  D. 20 A

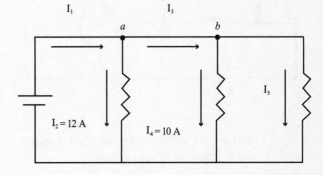

13. In the circuit below, each resistor has the voltage shown. What is the voltage across emf source V_X?

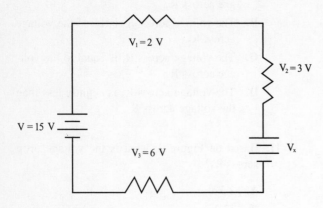

V = 15 V
V₁ = 2 V
V₂ = 3 V
V₃ = 6 V
Vₓ

A. 4 A

B. 8 A

C. 14 A

D. 20 A

14. Current through a resistor is measured by an ammeter, A, and voltage across a resistor is measured by a voltmeter, V, as shown below.

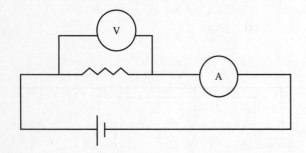

For an ideal voltmeter and an ideal ammeter, which statement is most accurate?

A. The resistance of the voltmeter and the ammeter should both be zero.

B. The resistance of the voltmeter and the ammeter should both be infinite.

C. The resistance of the voltmeter should be infinite and the resistance of the ammeter should be zero.

D. The resistance of the voltmeter should be zero and the resistance of the ammeter should be infinite.

Passage III (Questions 15–21)

Smallville is growing and needs to build a municipal power plant to provide electricity. The main debate is between supporters of a nuclear power plant and those in favor of a conventional coal-burning plant. Major concerns are the energy costs of producing the electricity and the thermal pollution the plant will create.

Several entrepreneurs have also submitted designs that transfer energy between a 427°C hot reservoir and a 27°C cold reservoir.

Design I claims to produce 3000 J of work for every 5000 J of heat consumed.

Design II claims to produce 1500 J of work for each 5000 J of heat consumed.

To compare the various schemes, each is treated as a heat engine. A heat engine is simply a device that converts thermal energy into more useful forms such as electrical or mechanical energy.

1. The engine absorbs heat, Q_H, from a hot reservoir at temperature T_H. (in kelvins)
2. It uses part of the heat input to do work, $W = T_H - T_C$.
3. It gives up the unused heat, Q_C, to a cold reservoir at temperature T_C. (in kelvins)
4. No real device can convert all of the energy absorbed into work.

A theoretical engine that has maximum efficiency, e_{max}, is called a Carnot engine. For the Carnot engine:
$$e_{max} = W/Q_H = (T_H - T_C)/T_H = 1 - T_C/T_H$$
No real device operating between T_H and T_C can be more efficient than the Carnot engine running between the same two temperatures.

The maximum power for the Carnot engine is:
$$P_{max} = W/t = (e_{max}Q_H)$$

15. What is the maximum efficiency of the coal-burning plant? Coal burns at 627°C and the unused heat is dumped into a nearby river with an average temperature of 27°C.

A. 0.04

B. 0.33

C. 0.67

D. 0.95

16. How much heat, Q, in joules per second must be put into the coal-burning plant for it to produce 1000 MW of electrical power?

  A. 1.5×10^9 J/s
  B. 2.5×10^9 J/s
  C. 3.0×10^9 J/s
  D. 3.5×10^9 J/s

17. The neighboring town of Midville has an old power plant that releases 7.8×10^8 J/s of waste heat into a nearby river with a flow rate of 2.0×10^6 kg/s. By how much will this thermal pollution change the river's temperature?

  A. 0.026°C
  B. 0.047°C
  C. 0.093°C
  D. 0.14°C

18. A pilot nuclear plant is designed to have a maximum efficiency of 0.88. If the unused heat is vented to a 500-K heat sink, what is the temperature of the nuclear reaction?

  A. 1000 K
  B. 1500 K
  C. 2500 K
  D. 4000

19. Engineers reviewing the two alternative designs submitted by the entrepreneurs concluded that:

  A. both Design I and Design II are feasible.
  B. neither Design I nor Design II is feasible.
  C. only Design I is feasible.
  D. only Design II is feasible.

20. Another heat engine is designed with a maximum efficiency of 0.20 when receiving heat from a 400-K reservoir. To what temperature must this reservoir be changed if the maximum efficiency is to double?

  A. 320 K
  B. 458 K
  C. 600 K
  D. 714 K

21. An ideal heat engine takes energy from the high temperature reservoir, converts part of the energy to work, and exhausts the rest to the low temperature reservoir. What is the efficiency of the engine if the amount of energy exhausted is three times ($3x$) the amount of work done by the engine?

  A. 0.25
  B. 0.33
  C. 0.67
  D. 0.75

Passage IV (Questions 22–26)

Mass spectrometers can be used to identify and separate ions. Typically a mass spectrometer has three main components.

1. A source produces ionized atoms and/or molecules in a gaseous state.

2. A potential difference accelerates the ions followed by a filter system that only allows ions with a particular velocity to pass into a magnetic field.

3. These ions, all traveling with the same velocity, are then deflected into a circular path by a uniform magnetic field oriented perpendicular to the trajectory of the ions.

   i. Since the magnetic force is perpendicular to the ion's velocity, it can't change the magnitude of the velocity, only its direction.

   ii. The magnetic force, $F_{magnetic} = qvB$, supplies the centripetal force, $F_{centripetal} = mv^2/R$, that causes the circular path.

   iii. The radius R of the circular path depends on the charge to mass ratio, q/m. It is determined by observing where the ion strikes a detector after moving halfway around the circle (180°).

   iv. The time required for an ion to complete one full circle is called its period, T and equals the ratio of the circumference of the path to the speed of the ion. The ion's frequency is the reciprocal of its period.

   v. Information about the ions in a sample is contained not only in the position of the signals detected but also in the number of signals detected. For example, carbon has two isotopes, ^{12}C and ^{13}C, while fluorine has only one, ^{19}F. Therefore, a sample of carbon tetrafluoride ions, CF^+, will produce a maximum of two signals. One is for $^{12}C^{19}F^+$ and the second is for $^{13}C^{19}F^+$.

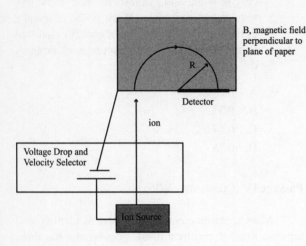

B, magnetic field perpendicular to plane of paper

R

Detector

ion

Voltage Drop and Velocity Selector

Ion Source

22. Ion X with charge q, mass m, and speed v, enters a uniform magnetic field, of strength B, that is perpendicular to the ion's trajectory. Ion X is deflected into a circular path of radius R. Ion Y has the same charge but twice the mass and twice the velocity of Ion X. If it enters the same magnetic field as Ion X, what will be the radius of its path?

A. R/4
B. R/2
C. 2R
D. 4R

23. In a particular mass spectrometer, an ion with charge q and mass m enters a perpendicular magnetic field and moves in a circular path of radius R with a frequency f. Which of the following best describes the magnitude of the magnetic field?

A. mf/q
B. 2πfm/q
C. m/2πfq
D. mqf/2πR

24. Which expression is equivalent to the kinetic energy of an ion in the magnetic field of a mass spectrometer?

A. $q^3R^3B^3/3m$
B. $q^6R^4B^2/2m$
C. $q^2R^2B^2/2m$
D. $q^5R^3B^2/3m$

25. Hydrogen, $_1H$, has two stable isotopes, ^1H and ^2H. Sulfur, $_{16}S$, has four, ^{32}S, ^{33}S, ^{34}S, and ^{36}S. What is the maximum number of signals possible in the mass spectrograph of a sample of hydrogen sulfide ions, H_2S^+?

A. 4
B. 7
C. 8
D. 12

26. Each of the following four ions with charge 1.6 $\times 10^{-19}$C and speed 3.0 $\times 10^5$m/s moves into and perpendicular to the 0.50T magnetic field of a mass spectrometer. Which ion produces a circular path with the smallest radius?

A. FH^+
B. H_2O^+
C. NH_3^+
D. CH_4^+

Passage V (Questions 27–31)

Plant growth is limited in part to the ability of the plant's vascular system, the xylem, to transport H_2O and dissolved nutrient by capillary action from the roots to the top of the plant where most growth occurs.

Capillary action is easily modeled by placing a small diameter tube (capillary) vertically into a container of liquid and measuring how high the liquid in the capillary rises above the level of the liquid in the container. The surface of the liquid in the capillary is called the meniscus.

The height of the column of liquid and the shape of the meniscus depend on the interplay of cohesive and adhesive forces among the molecules involved.

I. Cohesion is the force of attraction between similar type molecules. The solvent and solute molecules of the liquid are similar in type.

II. Adhesion is the force of attraction between dissimilar molecules. The molecules of the capillary wall are dissimilar from those of the liquid.

III. Adhesion tends to make the meniscus concave while cohesion tends to flatten it out

This rise is due partly on the ability of the liquid to creep up, or "wet," the capillary wall and partly on the ability of the surface tension of the liquid to support the weight of the liquid lifted. Surface tension is created by forces pulling surface molecules towards the interior of the liquid, reducing the surface area, and causing it to assume a spherical shape.

To a good approximation, the height to which a liquid rises is a function of four variables and one constant. The variables are the liquid's density, ρ, and surface tension, γ; the radius, r, of the capillary; and the acceleration due to gravity ($g = 9.8 m/s^2$ on Earth).

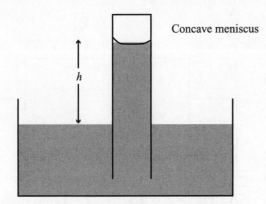

Concave meniscus

h

Liquid "wets" capillary wall

An agricultural research laboratory collected data comparing the capillary action of pure water and two solutions, A and B, of different plant food mixtures. The two solutions have the same molar concentration. In each experiment, capillary tubes are placed in containers of the appropriate liquid and the following data were acquired:

Exp't#	Liquid	r mm	ρ kg/m^3	γ N/m	h m
1	H_2O	0.5	1.0×10^3	0.08	0.0327
2	H_2O	1.0	1.0×10^3	0.08	0.0163
3	Nutrient A Solution	1.0	1.0×10^3	0.02	0.00408
4	Nutrient B Solution	1.0	2.0×10^3	0.08	0.00816
5*	H_2O	1.0	1.0×10^3	0.08	0.0327

Experiment 5 was run on a space station where the acceleration due to gravity is half that at the Earth's surface.

27. The height to which a liquid rises is a function of four variables and a proportionality constant c. What is the value of the constant?

    A. ¼
    B. ½
    C. 2
    D. 4

28. In a second experiment, xylem functionality is modeled by two cylindrical capillary tubes of different radii placed in a container of H_2O. The water rises to a height of 15 cm in the first tube and 45 cm in the second. What is the ratio of the cross-sectional area of tube 1 to tube 2?

    A. 1:3
    B. 3:1
    C. 1:9
    D. 9:1

29. In a given capillary tube, the Nutrient A solution rises 50 cm. Under identical conditions how high will the Nutrient B solution rise?

    A. 25 cm
    B. 50 cm
    C. 100 cm
    D. 200 cm

30. Which liquid or liquids exhibit the strongest cohesive forces?

    A. Water only
    B. Solution A only
    C. Solution B only
    D. Water and Solution B

31. Capillary action can be improved by:

    A. increasing adhesive forces and increasing cohesive forces.
    B. increasing adhesive forces and decreasing cohesive forces.
    C. decreasing adhesive forces and increasing cohesive forces.
    D. decreasing adhesive forces and decreasing cohesive forces.

32. The surface area of each of diver Dan's eardrums is $0.140\,\text{cm}^2$. How much force is exerted on each eardrum when Dan is scuba diving 4.0 m below the surface of a lake? The air pressure is 1.01×10^5 Pa and the density of the lake water is $10^3\,\text{kg/m}^3$.

   A. 1.0 N
   B. 1.4 N
   C. 2.0 N
   D. 2.8 N

33. A thin diverging lens has a focal length of –10 cm. Which of the values below best describes the position of the image produced when an object is placed 20 cm to the left of this lens?

   A. 0.45 cm
   B. 2.2 cm
   C. –0.15 cm
   D. –6.7 cm

34. On an upper floor of an apartment building, a cat is sunning itself on the ledge of an open window next to a flowerpot. The cat knocks the pot off the ledge just as a man, strolling with constant speed, passes beneath the window. How far has the man traveled when the pot hits the ground? Assume air resistance is negligible.

   A. $(2gh^2/v^2)^{1/2}$
   B. $(gh^2/2v^2)^{1/2}$
   C. $(2hv^2/g)^{1/2}$
   D. $(hv^2/2g)^{1/2}$

35. A 50-kg cross-country skier starts at an altitude of 500 m, goes up a 20-m hill and down the other side returning to an altitude of 500 m. The skier cover a total distance of 100 m in 40 seconds. The average frictional force between the snow and the skies is 80 N. What was the average power output of the skier?

   A. 200 W
   B. 245 W
   C. 445 W
   D. 690 W

36. What is the current through the 6Ω resistor in the circuit below?

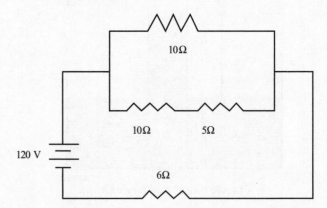

   A. 2 A
   B. 6 A
   C. 10 A
   D. 12 A

37. Two waves traveling in the same direction have the same frequency, wavelength, and amplitude but are 90° out of phase. Compared to the two original waves, the resultant interference wave will have the same:

   A. amplitude and frequency but different velocity.
   B. frequency and velocity but different wavelength.
   C. amplitude and wavelength but different velocity.
   D. wavelength and velocity but different amplitude.

38. A particle undergoes simple harmonic motion with amplitude A. What is the magnitude of the displacement when the kinetic energy is twice the potential energy?

A. $(kA^2/2)^{1/2}$

B. $(mv^2/A)^{1/2}$

C. $(A^2/3)^{1/2}$

D. $(v^2/2k)^{1/2}$

39. Two charges, q_A and q_B, are separated by a distance, r. The charge on q_A remains the same but the distance to q_B is tripled. If the electric force between the two charges is to remain the same, the new value of q_B must change by a factor of:

A. 1/3

B. 1/9

C. 3

D. 9

Passage VI (Questions 40–47)

Determination of molecular mass is a classic problem for chemists. Experiments using two traditional methods are discussed below.

Experiment 1: In the Dumas bulb experiment, the molecular mass of benzene is to be determined using a round flask with a narrow, open neck, which has a volume of 342.0 mL. A sample of 3.00 mL of liquid benzene is introduced into the preweighed flask, which is then immersed in a continuously stirred boiling water bath for 15 minutes. (Barometric pressure is 756.0 torr.) During the heating, all of the benzene evaporates, sweeping out all of the air and filling the flask with benzene vapor, while excess benzene leaves the flask. After 15 minutes, the flask is removed from the water bath and allowed to cool to room temperature at 25.0°C. The flask is then weighed and the mass of benzene is determined.

Results of four trials are shown in Table 1 below.

Trial	mass of benzene (g)	Temp. of water bath (°C)
1	0.931	99.3
2	0.928	99.6
3	0.923	100.4
4	0.958	99.8

Table 1

Experiment 2: Molar mass can be determined by a freezing-point depression experiment, which utilizes the fact that when a solute such as benzene is dissolved in a solvent such as cyclohexane, the freezing point of the solution is lowered by an amount ΔT, where

$$\Delta T = mK_f$$

where m is the molality of the solution and K_f is a property of the solvent. (For cyclohexane, $T_f = 6.47°C$ and $K_f = 20.0$ kg mol^{-1} L^{-1}.)

The following data were recorded using benzene as a solute and cyclohexane as a solvent. T_f is the freezing point of the solution.

mass solute (g)	mass solvent (g)	T_f (g)
0.421	100.1	5.47
0.461	99.8	5.38
0.451	99.9	5.40
0.462	100.3	5.69

Table 2

The chart below (Figure 1) helps to explain the phenomenon of freezing-point depression:

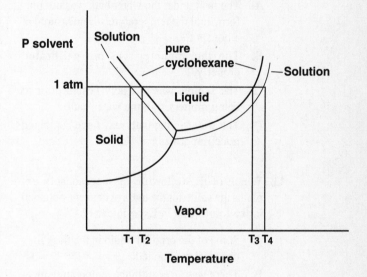

Figure 1

40. Referring to Trial 1 from Experiment 1, which of the following is closest to the calculated molar mass of benzene?

A. 82.6 g/mol

B. 83.1 g/mol

C. 83.8 g/mol

D. 84.4 g/mol

41. Which of the following assumptions need to be made when determining the molar mass using this method?

   I. The pressure of the benzene vapor is equal to that of the atmosphere.

   II. The temperature of the benzene vapor is equal to the temperature of the water bath.

   III. In the gas phase, benzene exists as single molecules.

A. I only

B. II only

C. III only

D. I, II, and III

42. Which of the following most reasonably explains values obtained in the third trial in Experiment 1?

A. The heat under the water bath was not uniform, and the temperature was measured at a hot spot.

B. The thermometer was not calibrated properly.

C. The sample was probably heated prior to being immersed in the water bath.

D. The water in the bath may have contained trace impurities.

43. Which of the following most reasonably explains the value for the mass of benzene obtained in the fourth trial in Experiment 1?

A. Some of the original liquid in the flask may not have evaporated.

B. There was an error in the temperature measurement: the value was too high.

C. There was an error in the pressure measurement: the value was too high.

D. There was an error in the measurement of the volume of the flask: the value was too low.

44. Which of the following properties of the benzene sample does NOT change as it cools from 100°C to room temperature, prior to being weighed?

A. The average kinetic energy of the molecules

B. The average distance between the molecules

C. The total bond energy of each molecule

D. The fraction of molecules having speeds of less than 500 m/s

45. Use Trial 1 from Table 2 to select the best estimate of the molar mass of the solute.

A. 8 g/mol

B. 16 g/mol

C. 84 g/mol

D. 160 g/mol

46. Which of the following could best explain the data obtained in the fourth trial in Table 2?

A. K_f for cyclohexane is less than 20.0 for this trial.

B. The mass of the solute was measured incorrectly; it was actually less than the value recorded.

C. The mass of the solvent was measured incorrectly; it was actually less than the value recorded.

D. Pentane was substituted for benzene as the solute.

47. Refer to Figure 1, which plots vapor pressure against temperature for both the pure solvent and the solution, to choose the best explanation for the phenomenon of freezing point lowering.

A. For pure solid cyclohexane to coexist with pure liquid cyclohexane, they must have the same vapor pressure; therefore, if the pure liquid changes to solid at T_1, the solution must do so at T_2.

B. For pure solid cyclohexane to coexist with pure liquid cyclohexane, they must have the same vapor pressure; therefore, if the pure liquid changes to solid at T_2, the solution must do so at T_1.

C. For pure solid cyclohexane to coexist with pure liquid cyclohexane, they must have the same vapor pressure; therefore, if the pure liquid changes to solid at T_3, the solution must do so at T_4.

D. For pure solid cyclohexane to coexist with pure liquid cyclohexane, they must have the same vapor pressure; therefore, if the pure liquid changes to solid at T_4, the solution must do so at T_3.

Passage VII (Questions 48–53)

The decomposition of hydrogen peroxide, H_2O_2, evolves oxygen according to the reaction

$$H_2O_2(aq) \rightarrow H_2O(l) + O_2(g).$$

A number of catalysts increase the speed of the reaction, including H^+ and I^-. The table below shows the initial rate of the reaction for varying initial concentrations of H_2O_2 and I^- ($[H^+]$ has been controlled using a pH 9 buffer).

H_2O_2	$[I^-]$	mL O_2/min
0.100 M	0.0200 M	0.85
0.300 M	0.0200 M	2.55
0.100 M	0.0300 M	1.03

48. Which of the following expressions give the rate of the decomposition reaction?

   I. $-\Delta [H_2O_2] / \Delta t$
  II. $-\Delta [H_2O] / \Delta t$
 III. $\Delta [O_2] / \Delta t$

A. I only
B. II only
C. III only
D. I and III

49. What can be concluded from the table?

A. The reaction is first-order in H_2O_2 and first-order in I^-.

B. The reaction is first-order in H_2O_2 and second-order in I^-.

C. The reaction is second-order in H_2O_2 and first-order in I^-.

D. The reaction is third-order in H_2O_2 and second-order in I^-.

50. If the decomposition reaction is assumed to be second-order in H_2O_2, which of the following graphs would correctly describe the dependence of the *initial rate of production of O_2* on the *initial concentration H_2O_2*?

A.

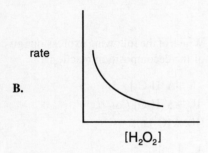

B.

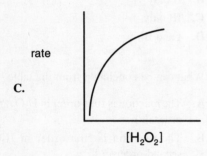

C.

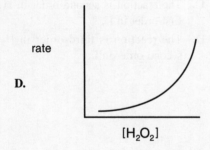

D.

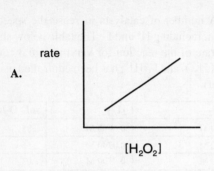

51. Which of the following curves best predicts the total volume of O_2 produced over time? (Assume that the reaction is first-order in H_2O_2.)

A.

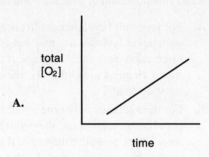

B.

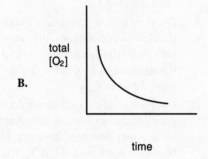

C.

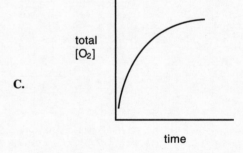

D.

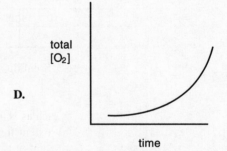

52. Which of the following mechanisms is consistent with the assumption that the reaction is first-order in both H_2O_2 and I^-?

    A. $2H_2O_2 \rightarrow + 2H_2O + O_2$

    B. (1) $H_2O_2 + I^- \rightarrow + H_2O + IO^-$ (slow)
       (2) $H_2O_2 + IO^- \rightarrow H_2O + O_2 + I^-$ (fast)

    C. (1) $H_2O_2 + I^- \rightarrow + H_2O + IO^-$ (fast)
       (2) $H_2O_2 + IO^- \rightarrow H_2O + O_2 + I^-$ (slow)

    D. (1) $H_2O_2 + I^- \rightarrow H_2O + IO^-$ (slow)
       (2) $H_2O_2 + I^- + IO^- \rightarrow H_2O + IO_2^+$ (fast)

53. The reaction below describes a different first-order decomposition process that also produces oxygen.

$$N_2O_5(g) \rightarrow 2NO(g) + 1/2O_2(g)$$

The value of $t_{1/2}$ for the reaction is 23 minutes. Bulb 1 has an initial concentration of N_2O_5 equal to 0.0750 M, while bulb 2 has an initial concentration of N_2O_5 equal to 0.150 M. If the reactions are initiated in each bulb at the same time, what will be the value of the following ratio after 92 minutes?

$$[N_2O_5]_{flask\ 2} / [N_2O_5]_{flask\ 1}$$

    A. 0.250
    B. 2.00
    C. 4.00
    D. 16.0

Passage VIII (Questions 54–59)

The solubility of ionic compounds in water is strongly affected by other soluble species that are present.

Common ion effect: The tables below show that reasonably high concentrations of either an anion or cation that is also found in the sparingly soluble salt—in this case AgI or CaC_2O_4—have a large impact on the solubility of the latter.

Other species present	pure H_2O only	0.100 M KI	1.00×10^{-3} M KI	0.100 M $AgNO_3$
Solubility of AgI	9.1×10^{-9} M	8.3×10^{-16} M	8.3×10^{-14} M	8.3×10^{-16} M

Table 1. Solubility of AgI under various conditions

Other species present	pure H_2O	0.100 M $K_2C_2O_4$	1.00×10^{-3} M $K_2C_2O_4$	0.100 M $Ca(NO_3)_2$
Solubility of CaC_2O_4	1.1×10^{-4} M	1.3×10^{-3} M	1.3×10^{-5} M	1.3×10^{-7} M

Table 2. Solubility of CaC_2O_4 under various conditions

The role of activity: When a salt such as $NaNO_3$ is added to a solution of a sparingly soluble salt, e.g., PbF_2, the salt dissolves to a significantly greater extent than in pure water. This surprising result can be explained using the concept of "activity," which may be thought of as a "corrected" value of the concentration of an ion or other aqueous species. When equilibrium expressions are written with activities substituted for the usual concentrations, the results are generally closer to experimental results.

As an example, we write

$$A_{Pb2+} = [Pb^{2+}]\gamma_{Pb2+}$$

where A_{Pb2+} is the activity of Pb^{2+} and γ_{Pb2+}, the activity coefficient, has a value less than 1.00. The value of this or any other activity coefficient decreases as the concentration of total ions—K^+ and NO_3^- in this example—in the solution rises. This is true because each Pb^{2+} is surrounded in solution by an "ionic atmosphere" of NO_3^- anions that are attracted to its positive charge and that tend to prevent F^- ions from approaching close enough to form a PbF_2 precipitate.

54. Which of the following trends is illustrated by the data in Tables 1 and 2?

   I. Excess cation concentration causes the solubility to decrease from its value in pure water.

   II. Excess anion concentration causes the solubility to decrease from its value in pure water.

   III. Excess cation concentration causes the solubility product to decrease from its value in pure water.

   A. I only

   B. II only

   C. III only

   D. I and II

55. Which of the following calculations correctly predicts K_{sp} for AgI?

   I. $K_{sp} = (9.1 \times 10^{-9})^2$

   II. $(8.3 \times 10^{-16})^2$

   III. $(0.100)(8.3 \times 10^{-16})$

   A. I only

   B. II only

   C. III only

   D. I and III

56. Suppose that a new column were added to Tables 1 and 2, in which the solubilities of each salt were to be given in 0.0010 M HNO_3. Which of the following best predicts the values that would be found? (You may neglect the effect of "activity.")

   A. Compared to the solubilities in pure water, the solubility of both AgI and CaC_2O_4 would be *unchanged* in 0.0010 M HNO_3.

   B. Compared to the solubilities in pure water, the solubility of both AgI and CaC_2O_4 would be *greater* in 0.0010 M HNO_3.

   C. Compared to the solubilities in pure water, the solubility of AgI would be unchanged and CaC_2O_4 would be greater in 0.0010 M HNO_3.

   D. Compared to the solubilities in pure water, the solubility of AgI would be greater and CaC_2O_4 would be unchanged in 0.0010 M HNO_3.

57. The solubility of $CaSO_4$ in pure water is found to 7.8 × 10^{-3} M. Which of the following is expected to occur when 10.0 mL of 0.100 M $Ca(NO_3)_2$ is mixed with 10.0 mL of 0.200 M K_2SO_4 and 10.0 mL of 0.200 M $K_2C_2O_4$?

   A. No solid will form.

   B. The first solid to form will be $CaSO_4$.

   C. The first solid to form will be CaC_2O_4.

   D. Both solids will form in equal amounts.

58. According to the paragraph in the passage on *activity*, which is the most likely error in the following problem solution?

Problem: Find $[Ag^+]$ when excess AgBr is dissolved in 0.0100 M NaBr. ($Ksp = 5.0 \times 10^{-13}$)

Solution: $[Ag^+][Br^-] = 5.0 \times 10^{-13}$
Assume $[Br^-] = 0.0100$ M
$[Ag^+] = 5.0 \times 10^{-13} / (0.0100)$
$= 5.0 \times 10^{-8}$

   A. The value computed for $[Ag^+]$ is too large. In the calculation, we should have replaced $[Ag^+]$ with $[Ag^+]\gamma_{Ag+}$.

   B. The value computed for $[Ag^+]$ is too small. In the calculation, we should have replaced $[Ag^+]$ with $[Ag^+]\gamma_{Ag+}$.

   C. The value computed for $[Ag^+]$ is too large. In the calculation, we should have replaced $[Ag^+]$ with $[Ag^+]\gamma_{Ag+}$, and we should have replaced $[Br^-]$ with $[Br^-]\gamma_{Br-}$.

   D. The value computed for $[Ag^+]$ is too small. In the calculation, we should have replaced $[Ag^+]$ with $[Ag^+]\gamma_{Ag+}$, and we should have replaced $[Br^-]$ with $[Br^-]\gamma_{Br-}$.

59. Using the concepts in the passage, identify the solution in which the solubility of MgF_2 would be greatest.

   A. Pure water

   B. 0.10 M KNO_3

   C. 0.10 M NaF

   D. 0.10 M $Mg(NO_3)_2$

Passage IX (Questions 60–64)

Chemists have succeeded in describing covalent bonding using a combination of "localized" descriptions that focus on individual bonds between atoms, and "delocalized" descriptions that emphasize molecule-wide electron distribution. A familiar example of the latter is the molecular orbital description of a diatomic molecule, such as the following set of levels, which can be used to describe homonuclear molecules of the form A_2, where A is boron, carbon, or nitrogen. (A modified diagram can be used for oxygen and fluorine.) This diagram shows the C_2 molecule.

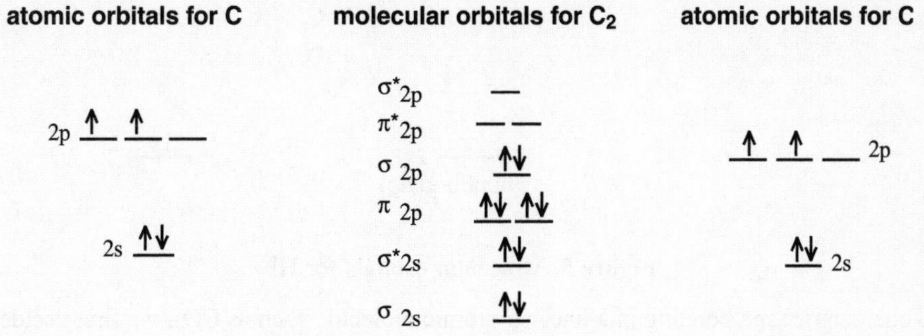

atomic orbitals for C   **molecular orbitals for C$_2$**   **atomic orbitals for C**

Figure 1. Molecular orbitals for C_2

When a diatomic molecule contains two different atoms, the diagram must be altered. If the two atoms do not differ greatly in electronegativity, the diagram will resemble the one below for BN. Note that the atomic levels for N, the most electronegative atom, are lower than those for B.

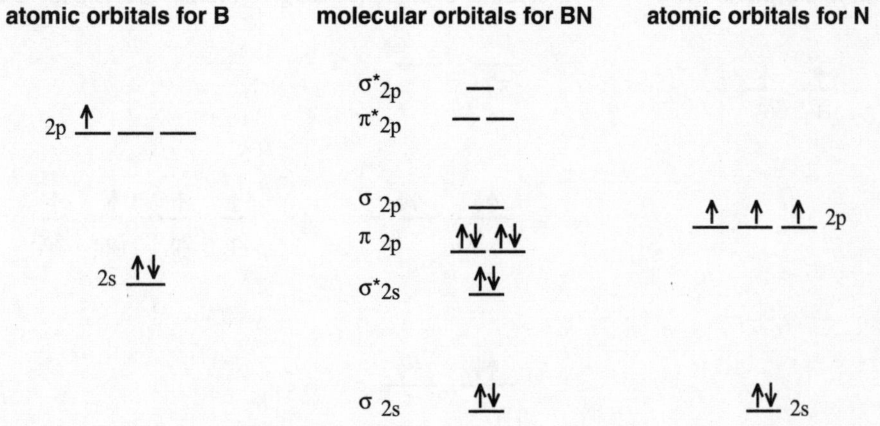

atomic orbitals for B   **molecular orbitals for BN**   **atomic orbitals for N**

Figure 2. Molecular orbitals for CN

For a high degree of difference in electronegativity, such as that found in HF, the diagram differs considerably from the original homonuclear one. Here the high-energy, antibonding orbital is much closer in energy to the original hydrogen 1s atomic orbital than to any of the original fluorine atomic levels, and thus is not greatly changed from the hydrogen 1s orbital. Similarly, the bonding orbital closely resembles the original fluorine atomic p orbital that points along the bond axis. Figure 3 contains nonbonding orbitals whose levels are essentially unchanged from the original atomic fluorine p_x and p_y levels.

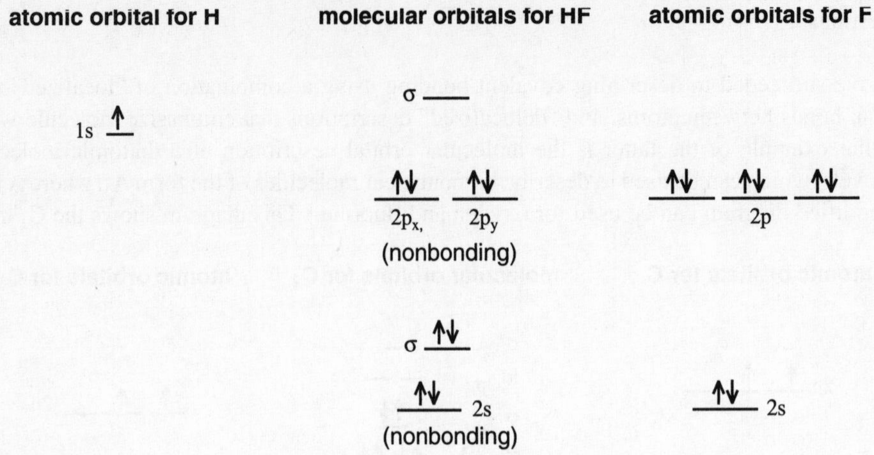

atomic orbital for H   **molecular orbitals for HF**   **atomic orbitals for F**

σ —

1s ↑

↑↓   ↑↓   ↑↓   ↑↓   ↑↓
$2p_x$, $2p_y$ 2p
(nonbonding)

σ ↑↓

↑↓ 2s   ↑↓ 2s
(nonbonding)

Figure 3. Molecular orbitals for HF

In order to characterize the bonding in a linear triatomic molecule such as CO_2, we first decide which electrons to consider in the bonding scheme. Together, the three atoms contain 16 valence electrons. One pair of electrons on each of the outer oxygen atoms is assigned to a nonbonding oxygen 2s orbital. The carbon 2s orbital and one of the carbon 2p orbitals are hybridized to create two sp hybrids, which overlap with one 2p orbital from each oxygen to form the s single-bond framework for the molecule. Four electrons are assigned to these hybrid orbitals.

The eight remaining electrons are assigned to the p orbitals whose energies are shown in Figure 4. The first four electrons enter bonding p orbitals, but the remaining four are placed in the nonbonding orbitals labeled p_x^{nb} and p_y^{nb}.

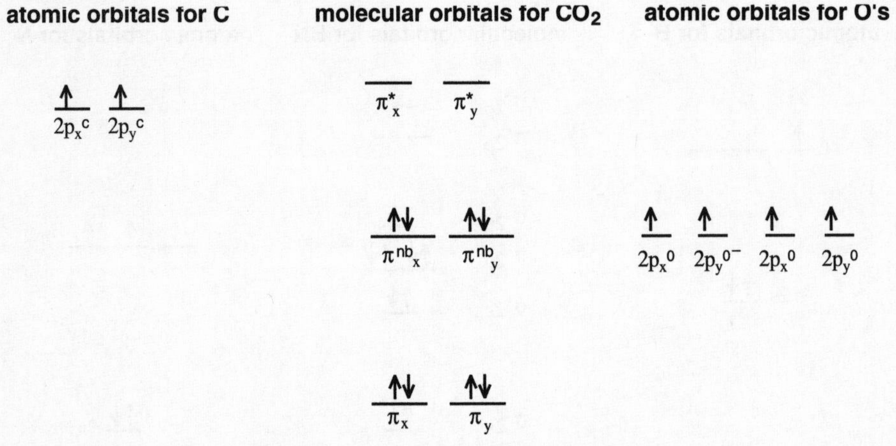

atomic orbitals for C   **molecular orbitals for CO₂**   **atomic orbitals for O's**

↑   ↑ π_x^* π_y^*
$2p_x^c$ $2p_y^c$

↑↓   ↑↓   ↑   ↑   ↑   ↑
π_x^{nb} π_y^{nb} $2p_x^0$ $2p_y^{0-}$ $2p_x^0$ $2p_y^0$

↑↓   ↑↓
π_x π_y

Figure 4. Molecular orbitals for CO_2

60. Which of the following species is correctly described by the configuration $(\sigma_{2s})^2 (\sigma^*_{2s})^2 (\pi_{2px})^2 (\pi_{py})^2 (\sigma_{2pz})^1$?

   I. C_2^-

   II. N_2

   III. CN

   A. I only

   B. II only

   C. III only

   D. I and III

61. Which of the following choices lists the species given in order of increasing bond length?

   A. C_2^+, C_2, C_2^-

   B. C_2^-, C_2, C_2^+

   C. C_2^+, C_2^-, C_2

   D. C_2^-, C_2^+, C_2

62. According to Figure 3, what is the bond order in HF?

  A. 1
  B. 1.5
  C. 2
  D. 2.5

63. Assume that an electron in HF were to be promoted to the σ* orbital by absorption of light. Which of the following would best explain the location of the promoted electron?

  A. Since HF is a covalently bonded molecule, the electron will, on average, be equally shared in the region between the H and the F atoms.
  B. Since HF has a polar bond, the electron will, on average, be found closer to the more electronegative fluorine atom.
  C. Since HF has a polar bond, the negatively charged electron will, on average, be found closer to the more electropositive hydrogen atom.
  D. Since the electron will be promoted to the σ* orbital, which lies closer to the original 1s orbital of hydrogen than to any of the original fluorine p orbitals, the electron will be found closer to the hydrogen atom than to the fluorine atom.

64. According to Figure 4, which of the following partial Lewis structures is most consistent with the predicted bonding in the linear molecule NNO?

  I. $[:\ddot{O} - N \equiv O:]^+$

  II. $[:O \equiv N - \ddot{O}:]^+$

  III. $[:\ddot{O} = N = \ddot{O}:]^+$

  A. I only
  B. II only
  C. III only
  D. All three structures are correct.

Passage X (Questions 65–71)

Why do any molecular compounds show a liquid or solid state, rather than remaining in the gas phase at all temperatures? The answer is that the forces between molecules, while not so strong as covalent bonds, are pervasive and lead to the existence of liquid and solid phases at appropriate temperatures.

The following tables show various series of molecules and atoms, together with properties such as melting and freezing points that are indicative of the strength of intermolecular forces. All atoms and molecules have *London dispersion forces*, which arise from instantaneous dipole moments created by fluctuations in electron density. Molecules with permanent dipole moments *exhibit dipole-dipole* forces. A particularly strong version of a dipole force, the *hydrogen bond*, is found when a molecule containing a hydrogen covalently bonded to oxygen, nitrogen, or fluorine forms a bond through the hydrogen to an oxygen, nitrogen, or fluorine atom on an adjacent molecule.

Atom	m.p. (°C)
He	–270
Ne	–249
Ar	–189
Kr	–157
Xe	–112

Table 1

Compound	m.p. (°C)
CH_4	–183
CF_4	–150
CCl_4	–23
CBr_4	90
CI_4	141

Table 2

molecule	b.p. (°C)
CH_3F	–78.4
CCl_4	76.5

Table 3

molecule	ΔH vaporization (kJ/mol)
CH_4	9.2
CH_3-O-CH_3	26.0
CH_3CH_2OH	39.3
H_2O	40.8

Table 4

molecule	Viscosity (Kg/ms)
C_6H_6	6.25×10^{-4}
H_2O	1.0×10^{-3}
glycerol $CH_2(OH)CH(OH)CH_2(OH)$	1.49×10^2

Table 5

Acid	K_a in water
HF	6.6×10^{-4}
HCl	$>10^6$
HBr	$>10^6$
HI	$>10^6$

Table 6

65. From the trends indicated in the tables, which of the following lists the hydrocarbons CH_4, C_2H_5, and C_3H_8 in order of *increasing boiling point*?

    A. CH_4, C_2H_5, C_3H_8
    B. C_3H_8, C_2H_5, CH_4
    C. C_2H_5, C_3H_8, CH_4
    D. C_2H_5, CH_4, C_3H_8

66. What general conclusion is most compatible with the boiling point data on CH_3F and CCl_4?

    A. Strength of dipole moment of a molecule correlates highly with strong intermolecular forces.
    B. Dipole-dipole forces are stronger than London dispersion forces.
    C. London dispersion forces are stronger than dipole-dipole forces.
    D. Highly symmetrical molecules tend to have strong intermolecular forces.

67. Which of the tables presents data that could be used to determine trends in hydrogen bond strength?

    A. Tables 2 and 4
    B. Table 4 only
    C. Table 5 only
    D. Tables 4, 5, and 6

68. Tables 1–6 show several measurable properties of atoms or molecules that can be correlated with weak intermolecular forces. Which of the following properties of a molecular compound would be *least* likely to provide information about these weak forces?

    A. Enthalpy of fusion
    B. Surface tension
    C. Enthalpy of formation
    D. Vapor pressure

69. Which of the following would best explain why acetic acid, C_2H_3OOH, might be soluble (at least to some extent) in hexane?

    A. Hydrogen bonding between –OH groups in acetic acid and hydrogens in cyclohexane
    B. Dipole-dipole interactions between the two molecules
    C. London forces between CH-containing parts of both molecules, plus hydrogen bonding between pairs of acetic acid molecules
    D. Covalent interactions between acetic acid and hexane

70. What is a likely value for the melting point for the compound CAt_4?

    A. $-195°C$
    B. $-15°C$
    C. $149°C$
    D. $200°C$

71. Which of the following shows the indicated molecules in the expected order of increasing vapor pressure at 25°C?

    A. $P_{vap}(CH_3\text{-}O\text{-}CH_3) < P_{vap}(CH_3CH_2OH) < P_{vap}(H_2O)$

    B. $P_{vap}(CH_3CH_2OH) < P_{vap}(CH_3\text{-}O\text{-}CH_3) < P_{vap}(H_2O)$

    C. $P_{vap}(H_2O) < P_{vap}(CH_3\text{-}O\text{-}CH_3) < P_{vap}(CH_3CH_2OH)$

    D. $P_{vap}(H_2O) < P_{vap}(CH_3CH_2OH) < P_{vap}(CH_3\text{-}O\text{-}CH_3)$

INDIVIDUAL PROBLEMS

72. 60.00 mL of 1.00 M HCl is mixed with 60.00 mL of 2.00 M NaOH in a constant-pressure calorimeter. The temperature of the solution increases by 6.7°C. What is ΔH for the reaction? (Assume that the specific heat of the solution is equal to that of pure water, which is 4.18 J/g°C.)

    A. −3340 J

    B. 3340 J

    C. −56 kJ

    D. 56 kJ/mol

73. In the reaction $CaCO_3(s) \rightarrow CaO(s) + CO_2(g)$ carried out in an open container at STP, how much work is done by the reaction of 40.0 g of $CaCO_3$?

    A. −22.4 L atm

    B. −9.0 L atm

    C. 9.0 L atm

    D. 22.4 L atm

74. Which of the following would be expected to shift the equilibrium of the following reaction to the right?

    $2NaHCO_3(s) = Na_2CO_3(s) + CO_2(g) + H_2O(g)$
    $\Delta H = 135$ kJ at 100°C

    I. Add more Na_2CO_3.
    II. Raise the temperature to 150°C.
    III. Remove H_2O.

    A. I only

    B. II only

    C. III only

    D. II and III

75. Use the chart below to choose the best indicator for a titration of approximately 0.20M NH_3 with 0.20M HCl. (K_b for NH_3 is 1.8×10^{-5}.)

    A. Erithrosin B

    B. Methyl red

    C. Phenol red

    D. Phenolphthalein

pH Ranges for Indicators	
Erythrosin B	2.2–3.6
Methyl Red	4.2–6.3
Phenol Red	6.8–8.2
Phenolphthalein	8.1–10.0

76. Use the data provided for the reactions

    (1) $H_2(g) + F_2(g) \rightarrow 2HF(g)$ $\Delta H_1 = -537$ kJ

    (2) $C(s) + 2 F_2(g) \rightarrow CF_4(g)$ $\Delta H_2 = -680$ kJ

    to compute the value of ΔH for the following reaction:

    $$C(s) + 4HF(g) \rightarrow CF_4(g) + 4H_2(g)$$

    A. −1217 kJ

    B. −1754 kJ

    C. 143 kJ

    D. 394 kJ

77. Which of the following statements best describes the processes that occur in the following reaction?

    $6ClO^-(aq) + 2Cr(OH)_3(s) \rightarrow 2CrO_4^{2-}(aq) + 3Cl_2(g) + 2OH^-(aq) + 2H_2O(l)$

    A. Oxidation/reduction: Cl is reduced; Cr is oxidized

    B. Oxidation/reduction: Cr is reduced; Cl is oxidized

    C. Acid/base: $Cr(OH)_3$ is the base; ClO^- is the acid

    D. Acid/base: OH^- is the base; ClO^- is the acid

END OF TEST 1.

IF YOU FINISH BEFORE THE TIME IS UP, YOU MAY CHECK YOUR WORK ON THIS TEST ONLY.

VERBAL REASONING

Time: 85 Minutes
Questions 78–137

Directions: There are nine passages in this test. Each passage is followed by questions based on its content. After reading a passage, choose the one best answer to each question and indicate your selection by blackening the corresponding space on your answer sheet.

Passage I (Questions 78–84)

"Life in the Coal Patch" is the first of a six-part lecture/discussion series on the history and culture of these towns. Organized by the Center in the Woods, a senior organization in California, Pennsylvania, the
(5) series begins August 22 and runs through September 12. For many participants, the series will tap into their own memories of what life was like growing up in these tight-knit communities.

"I remember my father and brother leaving at 5:30
(10) in the morning for the mines," recalls Dr. Stephen Pavlak, a historian and one of the discussion leaders. "That song, you know, 'You haul sixteen tons and what do you get?' Well, that song means something even today for those who worked and lived in a coal town. The
(15) usual price was 50 cents per ton of coal, and 5 tons was a good day."

Pavlak says the steel companies built the Coal Patches to attract workers, control labor, and retrieve some of their costs by owning the only store in town.
(20) (It was often the infirmary and the morgue as well.) Everything had to be bought at the store: dynamite for the mines, insurance, and food. Items were deducted from the worker's paycheck.

The company owned everything, including the
(25) police. The Coal and Iron Police, as they were called, were hired by the steel companies and patrolled the Patches on horseback, breaking up gatherings of men and boys. According to Pavlak, unionization was a great fear of the steel companies during the 1920s and 1930s;
(30) the unions finally took hold in the 1940s after much discord and bloodshed.

Workers were recruited from Czechoslovakia, Hungary, Lithuania, Italy, and other European countries. This influx of immigrants produced ethnic pock-
(35) ets that maintained their old-country customs and closeness of community. Pavlak says that the idea of the family in the Coal Patch extended beyond the immediate family and the cousins who came over for work to all

members of the ethnic group. Religious beliefs, tradi-
(40) tional foods, and a sense of family still remain strong.

It was a hard life: The day began at 5:30 a.m. for the miners and at 4:30 a.m. for their wives. The series explores what life was like for these families—knowing little English, having few amenities such as run-
(45) ning water, raising a family in a tight space, and wresting a wage from the darkness of the mines. The sessions include "Family Life Then and Now: A Comparison of Work and Lifestyles," "Where Did They Come From: Family Origins," "Artifacts and Illustrations: The
(50) Coal Patch Way of Life," "Pennsylvania's Coal and Iron Police, 1866–1935," and "Cinema Images of the Coal Miner's Struggle."

Daisytown, named after the fields of daisies on the hillsides next to the coal mine, still exists. Today
(55) the residents who stayed own their homes. Many bought and remodeled them once the mines closed, and the inexpensive quiet communities have lured new people to continue the story of life in the Coal Patch.

78. The passage indicates that the author would NOT agree with which of the following statements?

   A. Life in a coal community was difficult for many families because control and power over the industry and living conditions were determined by the coal companies.

   B. Strong community ties among the ethnic population was common in the coal towns.

   C. Workers earned a decent living in the coal mines, earning at least a minimum wage during that time.

   D. Although some coal towns no longer remain, others have continued despite the shutdown of the industry.

217

79. The passage implies that company towns such as Daisytown were created by steel companies:

A. to improve the life of the workers.

B. to provide housing close to the coal mines.

C. so that the company could exert greater control over the workers.

D. to give the workers a sense of community.

80. Company stores were created to:

A. maximize the profits of the steel companies.

B. provide a place for coal miners to shop.

C. create credit for the community.

D. keep workers from having to travel long distances.

81. Steel companies feared that workers would:

A. find better jobs somewhere else.

B. form unions.

C. organize gangs.

D. None of the above

82. You could say that one focus of the passage was that company coal towns were developed to:

A. create a better life for coal miners.

B. provide housing in rural areas where coal mines were often located.

C. give the work force a better sense of community.

D. give the steel companies greater control over their work force and to increase the profits of the steel companies.

83. Daisytown survived after the coal mines closed because:

A. it provided a small, quiet community.

B. the residents had nowhere else to go.

C. other industries moved into town after the coal mines left.

D. it became a suburb of a large city.

84. Which of the following would the author most likely describe as NOT reflecting the major points of the passage?

A. The power of the steel companies in the lives of its coal miners was unlimited.

B. Daily life in the coal towns was arduous and demanding.

C. To keep workers happy, the steel companies allowed free enterprise to flourish in the coal towns.

D. The family unit and the importance of the kinship structure were important components in the various ethnic cultures.

Passage II (Questions 85–91)

How to solve airport congestion continues to plague the airline industry. Even before more stringent security procedures were put into place in response to the terror attacks of September 11, 2001, wait time for
(5) airplanes were extensive. Often passengers boarded late and then sat on runways and tarmacs—sometimes for hours—as aircraft waited in snaking lines to be cleared for takeoff. Both terminal space and landing space was and still is at a premium, which causes significant flight
(10) delays. And now, because of increased airport security and a constant array of ever-changing rules, the snaking lines on the tarmac have infested the baggage check-in stations and security screening areas.

There may be a partial solution to relieving such
(15) congestion in a much older form of transportation: the train. Europe and Japan have improved their rail systems not only by ensuring that trains arrive and depart on time, but also by introducing high-speed trains, many of which travel in excess of 200 miles an hour. It is
(20) likely that even faster trains will be developed in the near future, which would expand the distances trains could cover efficiently, thereby giving travelers an option of whether to travel long distances by train or by air. Currently, however, long-distance train travel would
(25) provide a reasonable alternative to air travel for distances up to 600 miles due to speed issues.

Unlike Europe and Japan, however, the United States has not invested in the technology to improve rail service. Many experts question spending the large
(30) sums of capital it would take to upgrade railroads and argue that consumers would still prefer flying over high-speed rail. What many Americans don't realize is that train travel has numerous advantages over air travel, including the ability to hold more passengers, greater
(35) passenger comfort, and the convenient locations of train stations. Thousands of informed Americans living along the Eastern seaboard already know this, and use

Amtrak's efficient high-speed rail service that runs from Boston to Washington, D.C.

(40) The U.S. Department of Transportation believes that similar service across the United States would help improve travel options for Americans, and has submitted to Congress the Passenger Rail Investment Reform Act to build on such successful service models to pro-
(45) vide states and localities greater flexibility to plan and invest in rail service operations to create a truly national system. The proposal would replace subsidy payments to the national rail service Amtrak after a transition period, with direct federal matches for capital in-
(50) vestment to be paid directly to the states. States and multi-state compacts would submit proposals for passenger rail capital investment and train operations to the Department of Transportation. States would then have the option to choose which rail carrier they would
(55) prefer to use.

This proposal, if accepted and passed by Congress, would allow high-speed train service to compete favorably with air service because states would have the means to put the services in place. Additionally,
(60) passengers would be more apt to use the improved train service—particularly if one takes into account that most train stations are located in the centers of cities, whereas most airports are situated far from downtown locations. As for the cost, while funds appropriated by the gov-
(65) ernment would help foot the bill, they certainly would not cover the entire cost of overhauling our nation's rail system. Estimating the cost is a large task; however, many approximate that it might well be no larger than the investment that is made to maintain current
(70) airports and to build new ones. Like airlines, train operators and states could require ticket-buyers to pay a small surcharge to help pay for improved service.

While the greater use of trains might not solve all the difficulties of airport congestion, it would at least
(75) provide some relief and give passengers an effective alternative for many trips. Though there are many obstacles to this kind of expenditure, not the least of which is the airline industry that is afraid of losing passengers to trains, overcoming this opposition might help create
(80) a significantly more efficient transportation system in the United States and reduce the long delays at airports.

85. The main point of the passage is:

A. to discuss primarily the problems of congestion at airports and long waits in line for passengers before boarding.

B. the efficiency of railway transportation over air travel.

C. that the best solution to traveling in the country is only railway transportation.

D. that the use of the railway system could help alleviate many of the problems with airport congestion.

86. According to the passage, which statement is most likely to be true about future train travel in the United States?

A. The legislation that has passed through Congress will help the U.S. Department of Transportation increase spending on rail travel, thereby making train travel more attractive to American citizens.

B. With the right technology in place, train travel has the potential to be an admirable competitor to the airline industry.

C. Train travel is a ghost of the past and doesn't have a chance to redeem itself in the eyes of American travelers.

D. Soon Americans will be able to travel distances of 600 miles or more by train in the same amount of time it takes to travel the same distance by air.

87. In determining the author's viewpoint in the passage, you can say that he:

A. supports the use of railway systems completely over passenger commute by airplane.

B. offers what he considers a possible alternative, although it may not solve all of the problems raised about the airport problems.

C. sees increased usage of airports once the congestion and security problems are resolved.

D. fears that the usage of the railway system is completely inadequate in addressing the problems that airports face.

88. Among the advantages of train travel presented in the passage are all of the following EXCEPT:

    A. trains are less threatened by terrorism than airplanes.

    B. passenger space on trains is roomier and more comfortable than airplanes.

    C. train stations are more conveniently located than airports.

    D. trains have the ability to hold more passengers than airplanes.

89. The passage says that the United States has failed to maintain the rail system with the result that

    A. train schedules for passenger routes have diminished.

    B. there is currently no high-speed rail service anywhere in the U.S. that potential passengers could use.

    C. this country's railway service is behind in the latest technology.

    D. Europe and Japan have improved their own rail systems.

90. Which of the following claims is made to support the improvement of the U.S. rail system?

    I. The wait time at U.S. airports has increased to such a degree that an alternative needs to be offered to American travelers for more efficient service.

    II. The cost of improving the U.S. rail system would be minimal, and therefore should be undertaken immediately by the U.S. Department of Transportation.

    III. Many Americans are already using high-speed rail service instead of airplanes on the East Coast, and if such rail service were offered elsewhere in the United States, passengers would use it.

    A. I only

    B. I and II only

    C. I and III

    D. I, II, and III

91. What is the most probable outcome of the following statement from paragraph 4?

"States would then have the option to choose which rail carrier they would prefer to use."

    A. More than one rail company to choose from would create competition among rail carriers, forcing them to improve their services more quickly.

    B. Amtrak would become a railroad company of the past.

    C. European and Japanese railroad companies would export their services to the United States.

    D. Improved train service would be delayed because of the bureaucratic decision-making process involved in choosing a railroad company.

Passage III (Questions 92–97)

    Bipolar disorder, commonly known as manic depressive behavior, affects millions of Americans. This brain disorder is a disease characterized by wide mood swings from the manic state to a depressive state. The
(5) condition poses a serious health threat due to the common nature of the disease and the fact that the depressive state that affects so many patients causes significant numbers of suicidal thoughts and attempts. In fact, people with bipolar disorder are 14 times more likely
(10) to commit suicide than the population as a whole.

    The manic episode, which can last for a week or more, is a distinct period during which a person exhibits symptoms of extreme elation, aggression, irritability, distractibility, and poor judgment. During this time,
(15) the patient often has unusual amounts of energy and is unable to relax. The manic stage is often followed by an episode of serious depression, which can last for more than two weeks and include such symptoms as feelings of hopelessness or pessimism, decreased energy, in-
(20) creased sleep needs, change in appetite, and suicidal thoughts and/or attempts. Some patients will experience a mixed episode during which they experience a combination of manic-state and depressive-state symptoms.

(25)   Individuals who suffer from bipolar disorder usually require psychiatric monitoring and care, which involves individual and group therapy along with medication. While medication needs will vary from patient to patient, the following drugs are commonly used in
(30) treating people with the disorder. Lithium, the first mood stabilizer used to treat bipolar disorder, is still a common treatment for patients suffering from the disease. Some anticonvulsants, such as valproate and

carbamazepine, also help stabilize the mood swings that
(35) are common in manic-depressive disorder. High-potency benzodiazepine medications such as clonazepam or lorazepam are sometimes prescribed to help patients with bouts of insomnia, though these drugs have been found to be addictive and therefore are prescribed only
(40) in short-term doses. Several antidepressants are also commonly prescribed to help treat the depressive state of bipolar disorder. These drugs may be used in combination with other drugs or independently, depending on the individual case. Drug therapy should be under
(45) the constant supervision of a psychiatrist.

Can patients live a normal life and is this condition likely to be permanent? Most patients will respond favorably to some combination of the medications listed above; however, the success of such treatment will vary.
(50) While patients cannot be "cured" of bipolar disorder, prognosis is generally good if the patient is taking the proper drug treatments and remains actively involved in psychotherapy with a psychiatrist. However, it is important to stress the critical need for continuous reevalu-
(55) ation of drug therapy; often, the effect of the medication on the patient may diminish with time. In these instances, drug regimens will need to change in order to maintain a patient's mood balance. Additionally, patients suffering from this disorder commonly experi-
(60) ence a feeling of being "cured" by the medication, and thus stop taking the medication as prescribed.

It is likely in the future that a better understanding of the disease and more effective diagnosis and treatments will be developed, giving physicians greater flex-
(65) ibility to help patients live more emotionally stable lives. It is also likely that with more effective and earlier diagnosis, we will discover that bipolar disorder is more common in the population than previously thought.

92. Bipolar disorder can best be defined as a:

   A. state of depression that can last for many weeks.
   B. condition that produces wide mood swings in individuals.
   C. curable state of constant elation.
   D. brain disorder that usually results in suicide.

93. According to information provided in the passage, a person with bipolar disorder may:

   I. attempt suicide.
   II. be hospitalized unnecessarily.
   III. experience manic episodes more often than depressive episodes.

   A. I only
   B. II only
   C. I and II
   D. I and III

94. According to the passage, all of the following are mentioned as important for successful treatment of bipolar disorder EXCEPT:

   A. support of the family.
   B. maintaining the effectiveness of the medications.
   C. a regimen of psychotherapy.
   D. using support groups.

95. The information presented in this passage would likely be of most use to a:

   A. psychiatrist treating a patient with bipolar disorder.
   B. friend or a family member of an individual diagnosed with bipolar disorder.
   C. third-year medical school student doing a rotation in a psychiatric hospital.
   D. pharmacy student learning about the various drugs that treat bipolar disorder.

96. Which of the following statements does the author support with an example?

   A. Bipolar disorder affects millions of people.
   B. Most patients respond favorably to medication.
   C. More effective diagnosis and treatments will be developed in the future.
   D. It is important to continuously reevaluate drug therapy.

97. According to the passage, a person experiencing a manic episode might possibly:

    A. go on a spending spree.

    B. enroll in group therapy.

    C. attempt suicide.

    D. sleep for extended periods of time.

Passage IV (Questions 98–103)

The immediate cause, so far as apparent to us, of the Great War was the murder, on June 29, 1914, of the Austrian Crown Prince Francis Ferdinand and his wife, while on a visit to Sarajevo, the capital of Bosnia, the
(5) assassin being a Serbian student, supposed to have come for that purpose from Belgrade, the Serbian capital. The inspiring cause of this dastardly act was the feeling of hostility towards Austria which was widely entertained in Serbia. Bosnia was a part of the ancient kingdom of
(10) Serbia. The bulk of its people are of Slavic origin and speaks the Serbian language. Serbia was eager to regain Bosnia as a possible outlet for a border on the Mediterranean Sea. Therefore, when Austria in 1908 annexed Bosnia and Herzegovina, which had been under its mili-
(15) tary control since 1878, the indignation in Serbia was great. While it had died down in a measure in the subsequent years, the feeling of injury survived in many hearts, and there is little reason to doubt that the assassination of Archduke Ferdinand was a result of this
(20) pervading sentiment.

In fact, the Austrian government was satisfied that the murder plot was hatched in Belgrade and held that Serbian officials were in some way concerned in it. The Serbian press gave some warrant for this, being openly
(25) boastful and defiant in its comments. When the Austrian consul-general at Belgrade dropped dead in the consulate, the papers showed their satisfaction and hinted that he had been poisoned. This attitude of the press evidently was one of the reasons for the stringent
(30) demand made by Austria on July 23, requiring apology and change of attitude from Serbia and asking for a reply by the hour of 6 p.m. on the 25th. The demands were in part as follows:

1. An apology by the Serbian government in its of-
(35) ficial journal for all Pan-Serbian propaganda and for the participation of Serbian army officers in it, and warning all Serbians in the future to desist from anti-Austrian demonstrations.
2. That orders to this effect should be issued to the
(40) Serbian army.
3. That Serbia should dissolve all societies capable of conducting intrigues against Austria.
4. That Serbia should curb the activities of the Serbian press in regard to Austria.

(45) 5. That Austrian officials should be permitted to conduct an inquiry in Serbia independent of the Serbian government into the Sarajevo plot.

An answer to these demands was sent out at ten minutes before 6 o'clock on the 25th, in which Serbia
(50) accepted all demands except the last, which it did not deem "in accordance with international law and good neighborly relations." It asked that this demand should be submitted to The Hague Tribunal. The Austrian Minister at Belgrade, Baron Giesl von Gieslingen, refused
(55) to accept this reply and at once left the capital with the entire staff of the legation. The die was cast, as Austria probably intended that it should be.

Adapted from *The World War; A History of the Nations and Empires Involved and a Study of the Events Culminating in the Great Conflict,* Chapter 2, by Logan Marshall, 1915. (Work is in the public domain.)

98. In the context of the passage, the word *intrigues* (line 42) most nearly means:

    A. tricks.

    B. schemes.

    C. arousals.

    D. battles.

99. Given the information provided in the passage, you can infer that the author probably feels:

    A. that the Serbians should not have been held accountable for the start of World War I.

    B. that Austria did nothing to provoke the anti-Austrian sentiments felt by the Serbian population.

    C. that the Serbian press helped to aggravate the situation by publishing anti-Austrian propaganda.

    D. neutral toward both the Serbian and Austrian positions in the war.

100. According to the passage, which of the following events led to the assassination of Archduke Ferdinand and his wife?

  I. The poisoning of the Austrian consul-general at Belgrade

  II. The Austrian minister's refusal to accept Serbia's reply to Austrian demands

  III. Austria's annexation of Bosnia and Herzegovina

  A. I only

  B. I and II

  C. II and III

  D. III only

101. According to the passage, which of the following was NOT demanded of the Serbian government by the Austrian government?

  A. An official apology by Serbia to Austria

  B. The disbanding of anti-Austrian organizations

  C. The censoring of the Serbian press

  D. The right to prosecute under Austrian law the student who assassinated Archbishop Ferdinand

102. According to the passage, what is the most likely reason the Austrian government believed that the assassinations were incited by the Serbian government?

  A. Austrian intelligence uncovered clandestine documents in the Serbian capital that authorized the assassinations.

  B. Serbia did not accept Austria's request to conduct an inquiry independent of the Serbian government.

  C. The Austrian consul-general overheard a conversation in a diplomatic meeting that confirmed the Austrian government's suspicion.

  D. The Serbian government claimed responsibility for the assassinations in its newspapers.

103. The statement "The immediate cause, so far as apparent to us, of the Great War was the murder, on June 29, 1914, of the Austrian Crown Prince Francis Ferdinand and his wife, while on a visit to Sarajevo, the capital of Bosnia, the assassin being a Serbian student, supposed to have come for that purpose from Belgrade, the Serbian capital" suggests that:

  A. Serbian students were highly political during the time and were willing to make great sacrifices for their country.

  B. there are most likely additional causes of World War I than the assassinations that took place in Sarajevo.

  C. Archduke Ferdinand and his wife were not welcome in the town of Sarajevo.

  D. the undercurrents that continue in the Balkans today stem from the events that took place in Sarajevo in 1914.

Passage V (Questions 104–110)

The use of the death penalty has been an extensively debated subject. While many countries in the world abolished the death penalty long ago, it still flourishes in the United States. Those who support the death *(5)* penalty say that it deters crime. Those who oppose the death penalty argue, in part, that it is cruel and unusual punishment.

Since the late 1970s, following a decision by the United States Supreme Court which ruled that current *(10)* capital punishment laws at the time were unconstitutional and violated the constitutional ban on cruel and unusual punishment, thirty-eight states have rewritten their death penalty laws to meet Supreme Court guidelines, and since 1976, over 900 executions have taken *(15)* place nationwide. While the death penalty has been reintroduced in many states, the actual use of the death penalty varies widely. Two states, Texas and Virginia, account for more than 400 of the executions, whereas states like New York and New Jersey have yet to ex- *(20)* ecute anyone, even though it is permitted in certain cases. On the other hand, some states, like Rhode Island and Wisconsin, have not even reinstituted the death penalty.

A big reason for the debate over the death pen- *(25)* alty involves the ability to prove an individual's guilt beyond a reasonable doubt when recommending a death penalty sentence. Opponents of the death penalty argue that district attorneys can be overeager to obtain a conviction and ignore evidence that suggests the ac- *(30)* cused is innocent. In fact, probes into death penalty convictions in Illinois uncovered so many cases of questionable legal tactics by district attorneys that the death sentence has been suspended in that state until each death penalty case can be properly investigated. So far, (35) these probes have led to the release of several death-row inmates. It is clear that many of the issues raised in Illinois could also be raised in other death penalty states. Those who support the death penalty argue that mistakes are rare and, because of the long appeals process, (40) these errors are usually discovered before the execution takes place.

While polls show that the majority of Americans approve of the death penalty, support for it varies widely based on the region of the country. The death penalty is (45) most popular in the South and Midwest and least popular in the West and Northeast. One possible explanation for regional differences in attitude toward the death penalty may be the political nature of the regions. The South and Midwest tend toward the conservative side, (50) which generally supports the death penalty, whereas the West and Northeast are more liberal as a group and hence are more hesitant to impose the death penalty.

The debate over the death penalty is likely to continue for a long time without resolution. The only way (55) it could ever be resolved is if the Supreme Court reengages itself in the issue by ruling that capital punishment in any form is cruel and unusual punishment. For this to happen, we would have to see a change in the makeup of the Supreme Court to a more liberal body. (60) Currently, the Supreme Court contains seven justices appointed by Republican presidents, and two appointed by a Democratic president. With the current members of the Supreme Court being overwhelmingly conservative (and the fact that Supreme Court Justices are (65) appointed for life terms), a change in the political nature of the Supreme Court will likely not occur in the near future. Therefore, one can expect that not much will change at the federal level with regard to any constitutional amendments targeting the nationwide repeal (70) of the death penalty.

104. According to the passage, it can be assumed that the death penalty has been accepted most widely in which states?

    A. New York and New Jersey
    B. Wisconsin and Rhode Island
    C. California and Illinois
    D. Texas and Virginia

105. According to the passage, which of the following explains why there is a regional difference surrounding the use of the death penalty?

    I. The general political beliefs of a region greatly affect the number of death penalty sentences that are enforced in that region.

    II. The conservative nature of the current Supreme Court justices influences the use of the death penalty in certain regions of the United States.

    III. The recent issues surrounding the release of death-row inmates in Illinois has spurred regional debate surrounding the necessity of the death penalty.

    A. I only
    B. I and II
    C. II and III
    D. I, II, and III

106. The author's attitude toward the issue of the death penalty is:

    A. biased.
    B. compassionate.
    C. objective.
    D. disinterested.

107. The passage provides support to which of the following points of contention surrounding the death penalty?

    A. The death penalty is a form of cruel and unusual punishment.
    B. Determining the absolute nature of a defendant's guilt can be next to impossible.
    C. Religious doctrine challenges the morality of imposing the death penalty on a convicted criminal.
    D. Death penalty laws are regulated by individual states, thereby offering no federal control over this type of sentencing.

108. Why does the author believe that only a change in the Supreme Court Justice panel could resolve the issue of the death penalty once and for all?

   A. Federal intervention is required to effect a national change in the regulation of capital punishment because states don't have the power to control the use of the death penalty on a nationwide basis.

   B. Because the debate on the death penalty is so controversial, the Supreme Court is the only establishment that could rule for or against such a topic.

   C. Given the fact that the majority of Supreme Court Justices are conservative, the likelihood of reopening a case for or against capital punishment is low because right-wing lawmakers tend to favor capital punishment.

   D. The majority of the Supreme Court Justices are over the age of 65; hence, the Court most likely will not reopen the case for or against capital punishment until a younger, more liberal group of Justices are appointed.

109. What effect might the issues in Illinois have on capital punishment in other states?

   A. States that currently do not impose the death penalty may reconsider their laws.

   B. States that currently impose the death penalty in certain cases may temporarily halt the use of capital punishment for certain crimes.

   C. States may permanently repeal the use of capital punishment because of the untrustworthiness of district attorneys.

   D. States may seek guidance from the U.S. Supreme Court before sentencing a convicted criminal to death.

110. You can conclude from the author's view on the death penalty that he believes:

   A. progress on resolving the issue will not likely be made in the near future.

   B. the United States should outlaw it.

   C. the decision to use it or not should be ultimately decided by the Supreme Court.

   D. its continued use reflects the barbarity of the Untied States in its treatment toward defendants accused of murder.

Passage VI (Questions 111–117)

In 1792, Mary Wollstonecraft's book-length essay, *A Vindication of the Rights of Woman,* caused an immediate public uproar in reaction to the radical ideas she expressed on allowing more civil rights for women.
(5) The ideas were radical because in 18th-century England, middle class women were educated to essentially learn skills to attract and keep a husband, since it was believed that a woman must have a man to take care of and could expect this man to adequately support her.
(10) Wollstonecraft argued that through equal and quality education, women would become emancipated and would be able to have a stable marriage as a partnership between husband and wife. In defending the right for better education for women, Wollstonecraft accepted
(15) what her time considered a woman's sphere, the home, but she did not isolate the home from public life, as she saw them as connected. She felt the home created a solid foundation for both the social life and the public life. She believed that the "state," the public life, en-
(20) hanced and served man and woman and the family, so that men had duties in the family and women had duties to the state. Better education for women would offer them knowledge and sense to maintain this partnership, which in turn would provide for the proper edu-
(25) cation of children.

Wollstonecraft also emphasized that if female chastity and fidelity were expected of women, then to maintain a stable marriage, men must also practice chastity and fidelity. In addition, both the man and the
(30) woman would agree on the size of their family and control it accordingly. The result of this control would serve the public interest by the nurturing of well-advised and intelligent citizens. Lastly in her essay, Wollstonecraft expressed an ethical goal to bring feeling and thought
(35) into harmony. In combining feeling and thought, rather than the traditional division of women being capable of feeling only and men of thought only, women would be equal to men in also being capable of thought and reason.

(40) One must look at Wollstonecraft's early life to understand how her family's living conditions affected her views on the education of women. Born in 1759, she was the oldest daughter of a large family whose livelihood depended on her father's earnings as a hand-
(45) kerchief weaver. Wollstonecraft assumed responsibility for her four younger siblings, since her mother's sickly condition made it impossible for her to take care of them. Her father's failure to make sufficient money for the family forced them to move often. Through these
(50) experiences, Wollstonecraft realized that having a man did not necessarily provide security. Women depended on men because they were taught to do so, and thus were incapable of learning how to support themselves.

Despite the family's poverty and constant moving,
(55) Wollstonecraft was able to rudimentarily educate herself.

Her early adult life was spent in finding suitable
working positions. In 1784, she opened a school with
her sister Eliza and a friend, Fanny Blood. Working as
(60) the schoolteacher and the headmistress of the school,
Wollstonecraft and Eliza realized that the young women
they tried to teach had already accepted their social status as inferior to men. Disappointed, Wollstonecraft then
left the administration of the school to her sisters to
(65) visit her friend Fanny Blood, who by then was married
and living in Lisbon to improve her health. Unfortunately, Blood died in childbirth in Wollstonecraft's arms.
When Wollstonecraft returned to England, she discovered her school had failed under her sisters' care. She
(70) then became a governess to Lord Kingsborough in Ireland, where she had the opportunity to observe the daily
lives of an affluent and aristocratic family whose values she did not approve of. Although her service as a
governess was brief, her observations of the aristocratic
(75) family affected her political thinking in seeing how
powerful, yet empty, these privileged lives were.

When she had returned to England, Wollstonecraft
became friends with a group of men who were considered radical thinkers, among them Richard Price and
(80) Joseph Priestly, who argued that individual conscience
and reason should be used when making moral choices.
Price introduced Wollstonecraft to other leading radicals including the publisher Joseph Johnson.
Wollstonecraft's ideas on the education of women im-
(85) pressed him sufficiently that he commissioned her to
write about the subject. In 1786, Wollstonecraft's
Thoughts on the Education of Girls was published and
focused on criticizing traditional teaching methods and
offered new topics that young girls should study.
(90) Wollstonecraft went further with her revolutionary ideas
when her essay *A Vindication of the Rights of Woman*
was published and attacked the educational restrictions
that perpetuated for women a lack of enlightenment of
their social status as subordination to men.
(95) Wollstonecraft's ideas on the state of women were
revolutionary at the time, so one can view her as a remarkable individual, certainly ahead of her time.
Wollstonecraft's ideas created such controversy that she
was vilified by many conservative politicians. Even the
(100) group of radical thinkers with whom she associated were
surprised by her ideas that challenged what was considered acceptable for women. Today, Wollstonecraft
is generally viewed as a liberal feminist, since she was
mainly concerned with individual women and their
(105) rights. Because of her emphasis on quality education
for women and not measuring them by men's standards,
she is considered today the "first feminist" or "mother
of feminism."

111. You can infer from the passage's tone that the
author

A. disagrees with Wollstonecraft's goals.
B. considers Wollstonecraft a remarkable
woman.
C. emphasizes the importance of 18th-cen-
tury education for English women.
D. focuses on Wollstonecraft's association
with English radicals.

112. According to the passage:

A. Wollstonecraft's ideas about educating
women were in agreement with the status
quo.
B. education for women was essential in
learning how to read and write.
C. Wollstonecraft believed that women, if
better educated, were equal and not inferior to men.
D. Wollstonecraft's early life proved that
with education expected of women, there
was no fear of living in poverty with a
husband and family.

113. Wollstonecraft firmly believed that:

A. women's place was solely in the home.
B. women, just as men, were capable of
reason.
C. English society supported education for
women as a means to find suitable work.
D. women who were not better educated were
incapable of taking care of a family.

114. In 18th-century English society, moral standards in reference to marriage meant:

A. men and women were faithful to one
another.
B. a double standard existed where women
were expected to be faithful and men
could be philanderers.
C. women were expected to share equally the
responsibilities of taking care of the
family.
D. only the aristocracy could indulge in
extra-marital affairs.

115. Early in life, Wollstonecraft discovered:

- **A.** that being a part of a family living in poverty made it impossible for a young woman to attain social status.
- **B.** the falsehood that even if a mother was in poor health, she was still forced to rely on older children to manage a large family.
- **C.** the falsehood that her father's difficulties in providing for the family were temporary and the family could still hope that eventually he would succeed.
- **D.** the falsehood that women were educated to believe they had to be supported by a man who would also ensure her sufficient security.

116. Wollstonecraft's school, set up to provide the better education she believed in for women, failed:

- **A.** because she was unable to gather a qualified staff who shared her point of view.
- **B.** due to financial problems and poor administration.
- **C.** because her pupils, the young women attending the school, accepted the standards of their time on the relationships between men and women.
- **D.** because attendance was insufficient to provide the money to maintain the school.

117. The passage's tone can be inferred as:

- **A.** admiring.
- **B.** shocked.
- **C.** dismissive.
- **D.** disapproving.

Passage VII (Questions 118–123)

Mad Cow disease was first detected in 1984 in Great Britain and rapidly became an epidemic. In 1994, the first human case was diagnosed and since then, just over 140 cases have been diagnosed in humans, mostly
(5) in Great Britain. Though the numbers are comparatively small, the disease still causes widespread fear, because so far, the disease has proven to be fatal. The idea of the disease also causes panic because the incubation period is unknown, though it is assumed to be several
(10) years, and there is fear that many people are infected with the disease and are not yet aware of it. The final cause of fear of the disease is due to the fact that it seems it is as likely to attack the young as the old.

The discovery of Mad Cow has led to another
(15) very important discovery. It is thought that the disease is not caused by a bacteria or a virus but by a newly discovered infectious agent known as a prion. A prion is a protein usually found in a brain that is folded incorrectly. The normal version of the protein is common
(20) in the brain, but it is hypothesized that the incorrectly folded protein causes other proteins in the brain to fold themselves incorrectly. At some point, a critical mass occurs and the proteins begin to damage the brain by basically turning it into sponge. This results in the vic-
(25) tim losing his or her mental and physical abilities and ultimately dying. Diseases thought to be caused by prions are known as spongiform encephalopathies. These related diseases are able to spread from one mammal species to another. One of these diseases, scrapies,
(30) is thought to have spread to cows some time during the early 1980s. From cows it spread to house cats and some zoo animals and then to humans. The mechanism of contagion is thought to be the ingestion of organ parts of infected animals, particularly brains, though the evi-
(35) dence is not yet conclusive. It used to be common practice in many countries to feed livestock food that contained organ parts from other animals. Often, the parts came from different species of animals, which may support the contagion theory.

(40) Now, Mad Cow disease has spread to the United States. Again, the source of contagion is suspected to be the ingestion of dead animal parts by living cattle. It is surprising that the United States has continued the practice of using animal parts in cattle feed, even after
(45) the experience of other countries. A second factor in the development of Mad Cow disease in the United States may be that 150,000 sick cattle a year are slaughtered and sold as meat that is both used for animal feed and human consumption. While the outbreak in the
(50) United States is so far very limited, the potential for the outbreak to spread to other cows and to humans is large. It is likely that the United States will follow the lead of other countries and create much tighter restric-

tions on how cows are fed and which cows can be slaughtered for meat. Without new stringent laws for
(55) beef from the United States, an increasing number of countries will ban its importation, and even in the United States, many may choose not to eat beef.

The key to the future in terms of Mad Cow disease is probably prevention. As with sheep and goats,
(60) it is likely that some cows have a higher resistance to prion than others, and it will be important to identify the genetic characteristics of these cows. This step is already being done with sheep and goats where the disease scrapie is hopefully being eradicated by using ge-
(65) netic information to breed more resistant goats and sheep. This process is more difficult with Mad Cow disease, because the incubation period is much longer and there are fewer cases of the disease. If it is possible to do it at all, it will take years to identify those strains
(70) of cattle that are resistant to the disease and those that are likely to get Mad Cow disease. Even then, it would take extensive breeding and possibly genetic engineering to ensure that the American herd would be safe from Mad Cow disease. Control of the disease will be fur-
(75) ther enhanced as we get a more complete understanding of how the disease spreads within a species and between species. This knowledge will come with a better understanding of how prions affect healthy proteins and cause them to become diseased. The research of
(80) these related diseases may also improve our understanding of other diseases and how they spread.

For now, our methods of control are primitive and basically call for the extermination of infected cows and cows they have been in contact with. The second
(85) part of our control program is to better supervise the raising and slaughtering of cattle. As our knowledge base grows, so will a better understanding of what methods work best for the prevention of Mad Cow disease. It is even possible that we will discover that prions do
(90) not cause the disease after all, as some scientists already argue, and that the cause is either a bacteria or virus or some combination of bacteria, virus, and prion.

118. According to the passage, the discovery of Mad Cow disease has led to another very important discovery, which is that:

A. diseases can spread from one species of animals to another.

B. certain kinds of infections can be spread from cows to humans.

C. prions act as a new infectious agent causing Mad Cow disease.

D. Mad Cow disease is caused by a misfolded virus.

119. The following results occur to a victim of Mad Cow disease:

A. impaired ability to move and a slow death.

B. brain damage and death.

C. numerous tumors developing inside the brain causing death.

D. eventual paralysis and death.

120. The author of the passage believes that one reason Mad Cow disease has appeared in the United States is the government's failure to:

A. limit the importation of infected cattle into the country.

B. warn the public about buying infected beef.

C. develop better methods of detecting infected cattle.

D. learn from other countries' experiences and not implementing strong limits.

121. The implication of this sentence in paragraph 3, "It is surprising that the United States has continued the practice of using animal parts in cattle feed, even after the experience of other countries," is that the author:

A. finds it amazing that the United States has not reviewed its practice to prevent further outbreaks.

B. realizes that eventually the United States will improve its practice to prevent further outbreaks.

C. believes that the United States should still continue to feed animals this way.

D. is rationalizing the continued practice of this type of feeding.

122. The passage points out that Mad Cow disease is more difficult to eliminate because:

A. of its ability to mutate despite genetic engineering.

B. of our need to better understand how the disease exists.

C. of the need for continuous breeding and genetic engineering.

D. finding the genetic characteristics is almost impossible.

123. The author acknowledges that the methods of control of Mad Cow disease:

A. should rely on a program separating infected cows from healthy cows, with better supervision.

B. should focus on destroying infected cows and cows they have been exposed to and improving the standards of raising and slaughtering cattle.

C. will be effective with better monitoring and slaughtering all infected cattle.

D. should be based on better supervision of cattle and how they are slaughtered.

Passage VIII (Questions 124–130)

Not long ago, the Atlantic salmon supply came from fishing. The fishing fleet went out and returned with a boat-load of salmon if fishing went well. This traditional custom has changed over the last few years.
(5) Most Atlantic salmon are now farmed, and the fishing fleet has been severely reduced both because the Atlantic salmon population has declined and environmentalists have been paying fishermen to go out of business. The decline of the population of wild Atlantic
(10) salmon has been particularly significant and there are serious questions as to whether the salmon population can recover.

One factor that led to the development of salmon farms was the rapid decline of the Atlantic salmon popu-
(15) lation. This decline took place because of overfishing, ocean water pollution, and the pollution and damming of many of the rivers and streams that salmon had previously used to spawn, making it impossible for the salmon to lay their eggs. To understand the significance
(20) of this consequence and how it led to the rapid decline of the wild Atlantic salmon population, one must have some knowledge of the life cycle of the Atlantic salmon. While Atlantic salmon spend most of their life in the ocean, they must breed in fresh water. Generally, spawn-
(25) ing requires a long journey against the current of rivers and streams. With the ever-growing need for electricity and the desire for flood control, many of these rivers and streams were dammed, making it impossible for the salmon to spawn. Other rivers became so pol-
(30) luted with industrial waste that the Atlantic salmon could not survive. These two factors, plus the overfishing of Atlantic salmon, were and are the main causes of the dramatic drop in the Atlantic salmon population. While there has been a major effort by environmental-
(35) ists to try to restore the population of Atlantic salmon, this effort has been only partially successful, and it is unlikely that the salmon population will ever meet people's demand.

Salmon farms seemed to provide the answer to
(40) the shortage of Atlantic salmon. The salmon could be raised in a controlled environment and could be bred to produce larger salmon in a shorter time. These salmon would then be rushed to the market to meet the consumer demand. Though these farms have produced large
(45) numbers of salmon, they also produce a large number of environmental hazards. The density of the salmon on salmon farms produces large-scale water pollution to the areas that are farmed, thus reducing other sea life in the area. The domesticated salmon are less resistant
(50) to disease. When they are infected because of the density of the population, they are more prone to epidemic than wild salmon. Unfortunately, the diseases that the domestic salmon become infected with can spread to the wild salmon population and also to other fish, do-
(55) ing serious damage to the groups that the diseases spread to. It is also possible that domestic salmon will escape and spawn with wild salmon. This occurrence would most likely weaken the species and put the wild salmon at further risk. Finally, the domestic salmon are fed very
(60) differently from wild salmon. The diet is different and, of course, domestic salmon do not hunt. This different diet poses a hazard to humans as it is likely that higher levels of certain chemicals deemed unhealthy occur in domestic salmon than in wild salmon. In the first test
(65) of domestic salmon for polychlorinatbiphenyls (PCPs), it was found that domestic salmon had 16 times the dioxin levels of wild salmon. This level makes domestic salmon the most contaminated meat that is sold in a grocery store. There is cause for concern because PCPs
(70) have been linked to a number of forms of cancer and possibly to birth defects. Though the nutritional value has not yet been fully studied, it is possible that domestic Atlantic salmon does not have the nutritional value of wild salmon. Given that the priority on raising them
(75) is to create the largest salmon in the fastest time, the result might well produce a fat fish without much health value.

While it is reasonable to assume that salmon fish farming is here to stay, it is clear that the way salmon
(80) are farmed needs to be better monitored. Methods to reduce the water pollution caused by the farming must be developed and implemented on a worldwide scale. The content of harmful chemicals in domestic salmon must be more closely monitored to protect the public.
(85) The public should not be exposed to high-risk fish. Greater care must be taken to make sure that the domestic fish do not escape and pollute the genetic pool of the wild Atlantic salmon. Current spawning grounds for the Atlantic salmon must be protected and a greater
(90) effort must be made to clean rivers and remove dams where possible so that more spawning grounds become available for the Atlantic salmon. If these procedures are not implemented, then salmon farming will seri-

ously endanger the environment of the oceans and, in (95) addition, the farmed fish will threaten the health of the human population that consumes them.

124. All but one of the following is listed as a reason for the decline in the wild Atlantic salmon population.

    A. Overfishing

    B. Ocean water pollution

    C. Many rivers and streams that the Atlantic salmon used for spawning were dammed and polluted beyond the point where they could support a salmon population.

    D. Warming of the ocean made the environment less suitable for Atlantic salmon.

125. The author is concerned that the public realizes that farmed salmon:

    A. will be less expensive to buy and therefore in more demand than wild salmon.

    B. will produce fat fish with exceptional nutritional value.

    C. is contaminated with chemicals since it is fed on a different diet than wild salmon.

    D. is contaminated with chemicals that may seriously affect people with respiratory illnesses.

126. According to the passage, the presence of salmon farms:

    A. provides sufficient salmon for public consumption.

    B. is a result of environmental problems such as polluted ocean water.

    C. was far more profitable for fishermen.

    D. indicates the enormous demand for salmon to supplement traditional fishing.

127. The passage points out that farmed salmon:

    A. are healthier to eat than wild salmon.

    B. are less prone to disease than wild salmon.

    C. are profitable for owners who raised the domestic fish.

    D. can spread diseases to other fish and wild salmon, should they escape.

128. In stating that PCP levels of farmed salmon are 16 times that of wild salmon, it can be interpreted that the author is expressing his:

    A. disbelief that such a fact is possible as his contention is that farmed salmon is better to eat than wild salmon.

    B. useful knowledge of recent scientific data that can be shared with the public.

    C. sense of responsibility that the public be aware of the health dangers of consuming farmed salmon.

    D. confidence that such figures are accurate and therefore trustworthy.

129. Although it is stated in the passage that salmon fish farming is developing as a substitute industry for the traditional salmon fishing, the author contends that such farms:

    A. should be required to follow standards to prevent environmental water pollution.

    B. should be allowed sufficient leeway to develop methods on producing quantities of fish to meet customer demand.

    C. can prevent environmental water pollution.

    D. are necessary due to the diminishing spawning grounds for wild salmon.

130. You can interpret the author's tone concerning the consequences of the public eating domestic salmon as:

    A. confident.

    B. dismissive.

    C. apologetic.

    D. apprehensive.

Passage IX (Questions 131–137)

    Esmeralda Santiago's autobiography, *When I Was Puerto Rican*, is a coming-of-age memoir set in the 1950s and early 1960s, written from the author's point of view as a child. Recollecting episodes of her life (5) growing up on the island of Puerto Rico, Santiago also talks of the roles of men and women in Puerto Rican society. Descriptions of the social behavior expected of men and women are often presented through personal experiences and observations. Although Santiago (10) narrates events in her family's life as well as her own, she also weaves into the novel the observations of how men and women should behave. What today would be

regarded as sexism and classism, was considered ac-
(15) ceptable behavior when Santiago was young. There are
clear gender differences between men and women in
regards to the unequal distribution of work, sexual standards, and acceptable social behavior. These differences
favor men, while women are penalized, overburdened,
(20) and limited to the confines of the home and family.
Though the men work hard, 1950s and 1960s Puerto
Rican society allows them time for recreation, while
women work far harder with no time off at all. However, women who serve the men also scorn them.
(25) Santiago describes the concept of *dignidad*, a social
code that allows men to look at women in whatever
manner they can. Men can speak suggestively to women
strolling by on the street, but women can not reply and
are expected to simply ignore verbal disrespect.
(30) *dignidad* also includes specific rules for children in the
presence of adults. Signs of respect, for example, require children to never look directly into an adult's eye,
not to speak until given permission to do so, and not to
question adults, particularly the elderly, as adults are
(35) always correct.

    Santiago chooses to share with readers the per-
sonal lives of her family. Her mother, Ramona, is a beautiful, strong-willed, and spirited individual who is also
a good mother and eventually becomes the breadwin-
(40) ner in Santiago's family after they move to New York
City. Ramona is in a common law relationship with
Santiago's father, Pablo, a gentle father who can give
answers to Santiago's questions of curiosities. However, he prefers not to face confrontations with Ramona
(45) over his repeated failure to provide economically for
his family and affairs he had with other women. Their
turbulent relationship ends when Ramona decides to
take her eight children to New York City, to start over,
and also give her children opportunities to hopefully
(50) succeed in their new country.

    In telling her story from a child's point of view
about her family's history, her pride in being Puerto
Rican, and her memories of the beauty of the island,
Santiago captures a period of time that she once said in
(55) an interview no longer existed. She talks of her family
being poor and at a time when the poor had, for example, no access to electricity and running water.

    Santiago learns early that double standards for
the sexes are acceptable. "Men's natures" are the rea-
(60) sons that men's infidelities are permitted and not considered shameful. Respectable women are expected to
tolerate their men's indiscretions. Santiago uses the
word *sinverguenza,* applying it to men who behave in
ways that cause "good women" to suffer because such
(65) behavior is explained to the reader as "men's nature."
The concept of *dignidad*, when men can look at women
in whatever way they choose and in whatever manner
they want, reinforces such behavior. Yet, on the other

hand, women are expected to tolerate this even when
(70) men are unfaithful womanizers who treat them and children inconsiderately. Santiago discovers her father's
continued unfaithfulness to her mother when he takes
her to visit his mother for a week promising he would
return to pick her up at the end of that time. However,
(75) when weeks pass, Santiago realizes her father is not
coming back for her. She feels betrayed by Pablo because he has simply left her at her grandmother's home.
When Ramona comes to bring Santiago home, Santiago
overhears bits of conversation between her mother and
(80) grandmother about Pablo's behavior. Returning to the
room, Santiago realizes her mother has been crying although Ramona puts up a brave front. Santiago ends
that episode with the wish to remain *jamona*, single,
since even her beautiful mother is forced to suffer by
(85) her father. Eventually, Santiago's father, having lived
with Ramona for 14 years and fathered seven children
with her, refuses to marry Ramona. Two months after
Ramona and Santiago have left for New York, Pablo
abandons four of his children Ramona has left with him
(90) to marry someone else.

    Santiago also relates how she is expected to be-
have once she becomes a *senorita*, a young woman.
Her former tomboyish behavior and playing with boys
is to be replaced with demure behavior among grown-
(95) ups and acting lady-like. She has to always sit with her
legs together, learn the responsibilities of housework
and cooking, and avoid acting improperly in public.

    When Ramona has to go to New York again for
Raymond's treatment of his ankle, Santiago and her sib-
(100) lings are being taken care of by a family relative who
believes everything they tell her. Whatever restrictions
on behavior Ramona had placed on her children—not
being allowed out to wander around the neighborhood,
not bathing daily, no chores to perform, and wearing
(105) whatever they wanted—are completely disregarded by
the children. Being free to move about without com-
panionship is allowed to boys only. However, Santiago
takes advantage of this freedom by walking alone, not
realizing that it is inappropriate behavior. Another epi-
(110) sode involves Santiago taking piano lessons with the
school principal as her instructor. Her father arranges
lessons for Santiago to take with the music instructor
who is also the school principal. Santiago sees that her
taking lessons is beyond being a senorita. She can wear
(115) her scoop-neck dress with its wide skirt, which enables
her to sit cross-legged without her panties showing.
During what becomes her last lesson, she realizes the
music instructor is standing over her at the piano looking down at her chest since her dress's neckline has
(120) puffed out. Santiago feels violated and calls the principal a name, forgetting the rule that adults are to be
treated with respect. Needless to say, the music lessons
stop.

131. According to the passage, one of the gender differences between men and women noted by Santiago is that men:

A. are expected to help with household chores.

B. are expected to be continuously financially responsible to their families.

C. can have time for enjoyment.

D. are faithful to their wives.

132. In Santiago's explanation of the concept of *dignidad*, she is talking about:

A. men behaving as gentlemen by treating women respectfully.

B. the behavior of men who are expected to be devoted to their families.

C. men interacting with women in any way they want.

D. the behavior of men as considerate fathers.

133. According to Santiago, one possible explanation about Puerto Rican women tolerating men's unfaithfulness is that:

A. they cannot stop such behavior since their society permits men to commit adultery.

B. men do not care that they are committing adultery.

C. men cannot avoid being philanderers.

D. the women know the men will not desert them.

134. Santiago uses the word *sinverguenza* to clarify what is:

A. meant by the importance of behaving with good manners.

B. meant by the acceptable rules for dating between young men and women.

C. considered appropriate behavior for single women.

D. meant by men's insensitive and unprincipled behavior toward women that is tolerated.

135. Being a *senorita*, Santiago learns that she:

A. is responsible for the behavior of her brothers and sisters.

B. must conduct herself as a young lady.

C. is considered to be of marriageable age.

D. is allowed to be outside her home without supervision.

136. Santiago uses her father as an example of a(n):

A. faithful husband and caring father.

B. faithful husband unable to financially support his family.

C. unfaithful husband and inconsistently caring father.

D. unfaithful husband but caring father.

137. You can infer from Santiago's tone that during the period of time she talks about, she:

A. accepts as normal the double standards that exist for Puerto Rican men and women.

B. is baffled by the double standards that exist for Puerto Rican men and women.

C. is surprised that double standards exist for Puerto Rican men and women.

D. sees nothing wrong with the double standards that exist for Puerto Rican men and women.

END OF TEST 2

IF YOU FINISH BEFORE THE TIME IS UP, YOU MAY CHECK YOUR WORK ON THIS TEST ONLY.

WRITING SAMPLE

Time: 60 Minutes
2 Essays

Directions: This test consists of two parts. You will have 30 minutes to complete each part. During the first 30 minutes, you may work on Part 1 only. During the second 30 minutes, you may work on Part 2 only. You will have three pages for each essay answer (see pages 191–196), but you do not have to fill all three pages. Be sure to write legibly; illegible essays will not be scored.

Part 1

Consider this statement:

There is a point beyond which even justice becomes unjust.

Write a unified essay in which you perform the following tasks: Explain what you think the above statement means. Describe a specific situation in which there is no point that justice can become unjust. Discuss what you think determines whether or not justice can be unjust.

Part 2

Consider this statement:

Trust is something that must be learned.

Write a unified essay in which you perform the following tasks: Explain what you think the above statement means. Describe a specific situation in which trust does not have to be learned. Discuss what you think determines whether or not trust should be learned.

BIOLOGICAL SCIENCES

Time: 100 Minutes
Questions 138–214

Directions: This test contains 77 questions. Most of the questions consist of a descriptive passage followed by a group of questions related to the passage. For these questions, study the passage carefully and then choose the best answer to each question in the group. Some questions in this test stand alone. These questions are independent of any passage and independent of each other. For these questions, too, you must select the one best answer. Indicate all of your answers by blackening the corresponding circles on your answer sheet.

A periodic table is provided at the beginning of the book. You may consult it whenever you feel it's necessary.

Passage I (Questions 138–143)

Phenylketonuria (PKU) is an autosomal recessive disease caused by a mutation in the gene coding for the enzyme phenylalanine hydroxylase (PAH). In the absence of PAH, the amino acid phenylalanine is not broken down, accumulates, and is converted to phenylpyruvic acid. When transported to the brain, high levels of phenylpyruvic acid and other metabolites can interfere with myelination, causing mental retardation. In normal individuals, PAH and a cofactor, tetrahydrobiopterin (THB), help convert phenylalanine to its normal metabolic product, the amino acid tyrosine.

Heterozygotes express normal phenotypes even though they produce only half the typical amount of PAH, and have slightly elevated levels of phenylalanine in their blood. This is because one copy of the normal allele produces enough PAH for adequate enzyme activity (haplosufficiency). Although homozygous recessive individuals die early in life without treatment, the PKU allele has persisted over time. Heterozygotes, with their slightly elevated phenylalanine levels, have historically been found to exhibit a lower incidence of miscarriage. An elevated phenylalanine level is thought to inactivate a fungal poison, ochratoxin A, which causes spontaneous miscarriage. Evidence supporting this idea relates to the fact that PKU is most common in populations from Ireland and Scotland, where people ate large amounts of moldy grain during periods of famine. It is speculated that PKU carriers appear to have been protected from the fungus and were more likely to have successful, full-term pregnancies.

138. In which organ is phenylalanine hydroxylase (PAH) most likely to be found?

- **A.** Kidney
- **B.** Liver
- **C.** Brain
- **D.** Muscle

139. If tyrosine is part of the normal biochemical pathway leading to the production of melanin, what other symptoms are often found in PKU individuals?

- **A.** Lighter skin and hair
- **B.** Darker skin and hair
- **C.** Highly regulated 24-hour circadian rhythms
- **D.** Disruption of 24-hour circadian rhythms

140. The persistence of the PKU allele as a result of heterozygote advantage is an example of:

- **A.** codominance.
- **B.** incomplete dominance.
- **C.** coevolution.
- **D.** balanced polymorphism.

141. Some individuals exhibit all the symptoms of PKU even though they are homozygous for the normal PAH allele and produce normal levels of PAH. Disease symptoms may be due to:

    A. haplo insufficiency.
    B. excessive tyrosine in the diet.
    C. a defect in the THB gene.
    D. susceptibility to ochratoxin A.

142. If detected early enough, nervous system damage can be minimized in PKU individuals by:

    A. restricting dietary intake of tyrosine.
    B. restricting dietary intake of phenylalanine.
    C. increasing intake of PAH inhibitors.
    D. increasing dietary intake of foods containing phenylpyruvic acid.

143. Mental retardation most likely occurs in untreated PKU individuals because of:

    A. abnormal dendrite development.
    B. abnormal axonal development.
    C. abnormal synaptic development.
    D. All of the above

Passage II (Questions 144–149)

Nitrogen, a basic constituent of amino acids and nucleotides, is one of the most common elements found in cells. Although nitrogen makes up nearly 80 percent of the Earth's atmosphere, its availability to living systems is primarily dependent on microorganisms. Gaseous nitrogen (N_2) in the air can be converted by bacteria and blue-green algae (cyanobacteria) to ammonia. Then additional biochemical pathways lead to the formation of ammonium ions, nitrites, and nitrates, all of which are forms that can be assimilated by plants. After nitrogen has been converted into forms that can be utilized by living organisms, it is incorporated into their proteins, nucleic acids, a variety of salts, and other biologically important substances. Then when organisms die, nitrogenous molecules are recycled into the environment, again with the help of microorganisms.

144. The conversion of nitrogen gas into ammonia is called:

    A. nitrification.
    B. denitrification.
    C. ammonification.
    D. nitrogen fixation.

145. After plants absorb ammonium, nitrite, and nitrate into their roots, these and other newly formed nitrogenous molecules are sent upward throughout the shoot system in:

    A. phloem tissue.
    B. xylem tissue.
    C. parenchyma tissue.
    D. sclerenchyma tissue.

146. In humans, the normal metabolism of amino acids includes their deamination by the liver during both the absorptive state and post-absorptive state. For what purposes are amino acids deaminated during these two states?

    A. Absorptive state: conversion to fat; post-absorptive state: utilization in cellular respiration
    B. Absorptive state and post-absorptive state: conversion to fat
    C. Absorptive state and post-absorptive state: utilization in cellular respiration
    D. Absorptive state: utilization in cellular respiration; post-absorptive state: conversion to fat

147. The deamination of amino acids leads to the formation of ammonia and urea, while the deamination of nucleotide bases leads to the formation of uric acid. In humans, all three are nitrogenous waste products removed by the kidney. In which organisms would ammonia be expected to be the primary nitrogenous waste product?

    A. Terrestrial mammals and reptiles
    B. Desert mammals and reptiles
    C. Fish
    D. Birds

148. The decomposition of organic nitrogen compounds into ammonia and ammonium ions by bacteria and fungi is called:

A. nitrification.

B. denitrification.

C. ammonification.

D. nitrogen fixation.

149. Nitrites, intermediates in the metabolic pathways of nitrogenous molecules, recently have been associated with the production of nitric oxide in human tissues. Therefore, nitrites may be useful therapeutically for certain forms of heart and circulatory disorders because nitric oxide is a powerful:

A. immunosuppressor.

B. vasodilator.

C. buffer.

D. coagulation factor.

Passage III (Questions 150–155)

Carbonyl groups strengthen the acidity of the hydrogens bonded to the α-carbon. Ionization of an α-hydrogen produces a carbanion that can act as a nucleophile and thus attack carbon atoms forming new carbon-carbon bonds. The aldol condensation reaction is an example of such a reaction: a carbanion of one aldehyde or ketone adds to the carbonyl group of another aldehyde or ketone. The carbanion can be formed from the reaction between a base and an α-hydrogen. The Claisen condensation reaction involves esters.

150. α-hydrogens are acidic because the:

A. carbanion is resonance stabilized.

B. carbonyl group is a strong nucleophile.

C. carbonyl group releases a negative charge.

D. carbonyl group is a good leaving group.

151. Given two resonance structures for the carbanion formed from ionization of an α-hydrogen, determine which of the following statements is correct.

A. Structure I contributes more to the carbanion.

B. Structure II contributes more to the carbanion.

C. The resonance structures are equivalent.

D. Neither structure contributes to the carbanion.

152. The aldol condensation product formed from the reaction between two molecules of acetaldehyde is:

A. 2-hydroxybutanal

B. 3-hydroxybutanol

C. 2-hydroxybutanal

D. 3-hydroxybutanal

153. Which molecule cannot participate in an aldo condensation reaction?

A. Benzaldehyde

B. Acetone

C. Propionaldehyde

D. Phenylacetaldehyde

154. The Claisen condensation reaction involving ethylacetate forms:

A. α-ketobutyrate.

B. β-ketobutyrate.

C. γ-ketobutyrate.

D. β-hydroxybutyrate.

155. The aldol condensation and the Claisen condensation give different products because:

A. nucleophilic attack of acyl compounds leads to substitution reactions.

B. nucleophilic attack of ketones and aldehydes leads to addition reactions.

C. nucleophilic attack of acyl compounds and aldehydes and ketones leads to elimination reactions.

D. Both A and B are correct.

Passage IV (Questions 156–161)

Cells require a particular range of temperature to function properly. Animals can maintain their body temperatures within this range through thermoregulation. Thermoregulatory mechanisms are numerous and can vary considerably between ectothermic organisms that derive heat mostly from their surrounding environment and endotherms that derive most of their heat from their own metabolism. Often the proper classification of organisms as ectotherm or endotherm is not clear-cut, and a combination of adaptations is seen as part of a species' thermoregulatory repertoire. Mechanisms can include changes in heat production, physiological changes affecting the rate of heat exchange between the organism and its environment, and behavioral responses that influence heat loss and heat gain.

156. In humans, when body temperature drops below the "set-point" in the hypothalamus, homeostasis is maintained by a combination of nervous system and endocrine system responses. These include:

A. constriction of superficial blood vessels and a decrease in thyroxine.

B. dilation of superficial blood vessels and a decrease in thyroxine.

C. constriction of superficial blood vessels and an increase in thyroxine.

D. dilation of superficial blood vessels and an increase in thyroxine.

157. Countercurrent heat exchangers help reduce heat loss by establishing a thermal gradient between blood vessels carrying blood in opposite directions. Which of the following is an efficient example of this type of system?

A. Arteries bringing blood back to centrally located core organs give up heat to veins carrying blood from the core to the periphery.

B. Arteries bringing blood back to centrally located core organs pick up heat from veins carrying blood from the core to the periphery.

C. Veins bringing blood back to centrally located core organs give up heat to arteries carrying blood from the core to the periphery.

D. Veins bringing blood back to centrally located core organs pick up heat from arteries carrying blood from the core to the periphery.

158. One of the "costs" of endothermy is to maintain a constant high rate of metabolic activity. Some small birds and mammals reduce this constant demand for energy consumption and expenditure by exhibiting daily periods of torpor during which time body temperature drops and energy is conserved. Many such 24-hour biological rhythms are influenced by:

A. melatonin from the pineal gland.

B. serotonin from the pineal gland.

C. melatonin from the anterior pituitary gland.

D. serotonin from the anterior pituitary gland.

159. After a cold night, ectothermic organisms like snakes and lizards bask in the sun in order to raise their body temperature high enough to hunt and otherwise go about their daily business. If they remained on their basking rock on a hot day, what would eventually happen?

A. Their body temperature would rise continuously until it reached ambient temperature and they would die.

B. Their body temperature would rise beyond homeostatic range and then drop within normal limits.

C. Their body temperature would rise to the upper limit of homeostatic range and then be maintained at that level or below by physiological mechanisms such as sweating and vasomotor changes.

D. Their body temperature would rise to the upper limit of homeostatic range and then be maintained at that level or below by physical mechanisms such as radiation, convection, and evaporation.

160. Fever is a nonspecific weapon in the human body's arsenal of defenses. Pyrogens, the molecules released by immune cells to alter the thermostat in the hypothalamus, have which of the following effects?

- **A.** They lower the set-point so that the individual feels cold even though body temperature is higher than normal.
- **B.** They raise the set-point so that the individual feels cold even though body temperature is higher than normal.
- **C.** They lower the set-point so that the individual feels warm even though body temperature is lower than normal.
- **D.** They raise the set-point so that the individual feels warm even though body temperature is lower than normal.

161. Heat exhaustion refers to the heat-associated collapse of an individual, usually after vigorous physical activity. Elevated body temperature, mental confusion, and loss of consciousness can result from this condition even though the body's heat-loss mechanisms may still be functional. The most likely causes of heat exhaustion are:

- **A.** dehydration, decreased blood volume, and increased blood pressure.
- **B.** overhydration, increased blood volume, and increased blood pressure.
- **C.** dehydration, decreased blood volume, and decreased blood pressure.
- **D.** overhydration, increased blood volume, and decreased blood pressure.

> **Questions 162 through 166 are NOT based on a descriptive passage.**

162. In *E. coli*, the genetic control of the eight-step arginine biosynthetic pathway involves nine genes encoding eight enzymes. This contradicts the one gene–one enzyme hypothesis put forward by Beadle and Tatum in their classical experiments with *Neurospora*. What is the best explanation for this contradiction?

- **A.** One of the steps in the pathway involves more than one enzyme.
- **B.** One of the enzymes has more than one polypeptide component.

- **C.** An additional gene is needed to initiate transcription of the first enzyme.
- **D.** An additional gene is needed to terminate translation of the last enzyme.

163. Which of the following processes is NOT dependent upon the presence of calcium?

- **A.** Muscle contraction
- **B.** Erythrocyte development
- **C.** Coagulation
- **D.** Transmission of nerve impulses

164. In *Drosophila* mating experiment, the frequency of progeny that are recombinants from a crossover between genes A and B is 0.20, and the frequency of progeny that are recombinants from a crossover between genes B and C is 0.10. Assuming no chromosomal interference, what will be the frequency of progeny resulting from a double crossover?

- **A.** 0.30
- **B.** 0.15
- **C.** 0.02
- **D.** 0.015

165. When the cyanide ion reacts with an alkyl halide, it can form both substitution and elimination products because:

- **A.** HCN is a weak acid, so the conjugate base is strong.
- **B.** HCN is a strong acid, so the conjugate base is weak.
- **C.** the cyanide ion is unstable.
- **D.** nitriles are unstable compounds.

166. Which of the following structures is derived from the same germ layer as the heart?

- **A.** Skeletal muscle
- **B.** Brain
- **C.** Adrenal medulla
- **D.** Pancreas

Passage V (Questions 167–173)

The production and release of hormones is controlled in a variety of ways. Some endocrine glands are regulated by hormones from other glands (hormonal control); some are regulated by stimuli from the nervous system (neural control); and others are controlled by certain ions, nutrients, or enzyme-activated components of the blood (humoral control). In each regulatory category, some form of negative feedback system is involved, whereby an increase in a specific hormone produces an effect within target cells that then contributes to the subsequent inhibition of further hormone release. Many glands are regulated by a combination of these control mechanisms. Additionally, when target cells are examined, their response may be the result of more than one hormone working synergistically or hormones working antagonistically.

167. Which of the following hormones is NOT paired with the blood component it helps regulate via a negative feedback system?

A. Aldosterone : sodium

B. ADH : water

C. Parathormone : potassium

D. Insulin : glucose

168. Which of the following hormones is regulated by blood levels of more than one ion as well as by changes in blood volume and blood pressure?

A. Aldosterone

B. Cortisol

C. Thyroxine

D. Epinephrine

169. Which of the following glands does NOT contribute to the synergistic regulation of glucose?

A. Adrenal cortex

B. Adrenal medulla

C. Anterior pituitary

D. Posterior pituitary

170. Which substance is regulated in part by the antagonistic actions of two different hormones released from the same gland?

A. Sodium

B. Glucose

C. Calcium

D. Estrogen

171. Which of the following is NOT the result of interacting hormones released by at least three different sources?

A. Development of the endometrial lining during the menstrual cycle

B. Metabolic rate

C. Potassium levels in the blood

D. Blood pressure

172. Which hormone is NOT released into the blood as a direct result of neuron stimulation?

A. Thyroxine

B. Epinephrine

C. Oxytocin

D. ADH

173. Which of the following hormones is maintained at *low* levels due to the continuous inhibitory effects of another hormone?

A. Thyroxine

B. Estrogen

C. Prolactin

D. Testosterone

Passage VI (Questions 174–179)

The kidneys help remove metabolic waste products from the blood. They further contribute to the maintenance of homeostasis by regulating the volume, composition, and pH of the blood. The nephrons of the kidney carry out these various roles through the processes of filtration, reabsorption, and secretion. Filtration takes place from glomerular capillaries into Bowman's capsule. Materials forced out of the blood this way make up the resulting fluid, the filtrate. Substances in the filtrate include waste products, water,

nutrients, and electrolytes. Vital substances needed by the body are reabsorbed from filtrate to peritubular capillaries, while wastes and materials not needed continue in the filtrate and are excreted in the urine. Additional changes can be made by transporting materials from peritubular capillaries to filtrate (secretion).

The following table shows some of the chemical constituents of the plasma, as well as how much of each chemical is filtered and reabsorbed in the nephron in one day (all values, except for water, are expressed in grams).

Chemical Constituents in Plasma; Filtered and Reabsorbed in 24 hours

CHEMICAL	PLASMA	FILTRATE IMMEDIATELY AFTER GLOMERULAR CAPSULE	REABSORBED FROM FILTRATE
Water	180,000 mL	180,000 mL	178,000–179,000 mL
Proteins	7,000–9,000	10–20	10–20
Chloride (Cl−)	630	630	625
Sodium (Na+)	540	540	537
Bicarbonate (HCO3−)	300	300	299.7
Glucose	180	180	180
Urea	53	53	28
Potassium (K−)	28	28	24
Uric acid	8.5	8.5	7.7
Creatinine	1.5	1.5	0

174. In a single day, approximately what percentage of water filtered from the plasma leaves the body as urine?

A. 0.05 percent–0.1 percent
B. 0.5 percent–1 percent
C. 1.5 percent–2 percent
D. 5 percent–10 percent

175. According to information in the table, all plasma constituents are filtered completely EXCEPT:

A. chloride ions.
B. sodium ions.
C. urea.
D. proteins.

176. The afferent arteriole leading into the glomerulus has a wider diameter than the efferent arteriole, which carries blood away to the peritubular capillaries. This arrangement:

A. increases the efficiency of reabsorption.
B. represents a countercurrent mechanism.
C. increases pressure in the glomerulus.
D. allows red blood cells to pass into the filtrate.

177. Normally, glucose from the plasma is filtered into Bowman's capsule and then completely reabsorbed by active transport in the proximal convoluted tubules. Which of the following is a probable reason that diabetics have high glucose levels in the urine?

   A. The level of glucose that is filtered is higher than normal.
   B. The number of glucose carrier molecules is limited.
   C. Both A and B
   D. Neither A nor B

178. The kidney helps maintain pH balance with a variety of urinary adjustments. If an individual's blood pH is too high, which of the following would be an appropriate urinary system response?

   A. Secrete bicarbonate ions.
   B. Reabsorb additional bicarbonate ions in the distal convoluted tubules.
   C. Filter additional acidic proteins.
   D. Allow the larger alkaline proteins through the glomerulus.

179. The kidney can increase red blood cell production by releasing the hormone erythropoietin. It can also cause additional reabsorption of sodium ions through the renin-angiotensin system's stimulatory effects on aldosterone production. Why do both of these actions help raise blood pressure?

   A. Both lead to a decrease in plasma water content.
   B. Both lead to vasodilation of blood vessels.
   C. Both lead to an increase in blood volume.
   D. Both lead to an increase in secretion at the collecting tubules.

Passage VII (Questions 180–185)

Most dicarboxylic acids show the same chemical behavior as monocarboxylic acids and are also prepared in similar ways. Certain reactions, however, yield different products because there are two carboxyl groups in each molecule.

180. Malonic acid, $CH_2(COOH)_2$, can be prepared from:

   A. hydrolysis of sodium cyanoacetate.
   B. hydrolysis of sodium chloroacetate.
   C. oxidation of ethane.
   D. oxidation of ethanol.

181. You would predict that the first ionization constant of oxalic acid, HOOC-COOH, would be:

   A. less than for malonic acid.
   B. the same as for malonic acid.
   C. greater than for malonic acid.
   D. It is impossible to make a prediction from the information provided.

182. When dicarboxylic acids combine with alcohols, they form:

   A. esters.
   B. anhydrides.
   C. aldehydes.
   D. polyesters.

183. Dicarboxylic acids react with diamines to produce:

   A. amides.
   B. polyamides.
   C. nitrosoamines.
   D. imines.

184. The second ionization constant for dicarboxylic acids is always less than the first because:

   A. more energy is needed to release H^+ from a dianion.
   B. more energy is needed to separate H^+ from a singly charged anion.
   C. second ionization constants depend on the alkyl groups present.
   D. the carboxylate anion is resonance stabilized.

185. The esterification of malonic acid with ethanol yields:

A. diethyl malonate.

B. ethyl oxalate.

C. ethyl malonate.

D. ethyl propionate.

Questions 186 through 190 are NOT based on a descriptive passage.

---

186. The tobacco mosaic virus contains a single-stranded RNA molecule as its genetic material. If the TMV genetic material is extracted and found to contain 20% guanine, what percentage of nucleotide bases will contain adenine?

A. 20%

B. 30%

C. 60%

D. The answer cannot be determined.

187. *Plasmodium falciparum*, the protozoan parasite that causes malaria, produces protein knobs on the surface of the red blood cells it infects. These protein knobs cling to the inner lining of the host's blood vessels so that infected cells are not swept away for destruction. This allows the parasite to persist. Where would infected blood cells ordinarily be removed from the circulation and destroyed?

A. Kidney and spleen

B. Kidney and liver

C. Spleen and liver

D. Kidney, spleen, and liver

188. When an individual burns his hand on a hot frying pan, which of the following events is NOT associated with brain activity?

A. Withdrawal of the hand

B. Pain

C. Sudden inhalation of air

D. Shaking of the hand

189. The wings of bats, birds, and moths provide similar functions for their respective species. Which of the following relationships are described correctly?

A. The wings of bats and moths are homologous.

B. The wings of bats and birds represent convergence.

C. The wings of birds and moths are analogous.

D. The wings of bats and birds are analogous.

190. Although they are ethers, epoxides are a very reactive class of compounds because of:

A. their acidity.

B. their electrophilic character.

C. their tendency to open their ring.

D. the presence of the –C-O-C- linkage.

Passage VIII (Questions 191–196)

A variety of blood cell antigens encoded at different gene loci can be detected by simple blood tests. Four phenotypes (blood types) described below were tested in each listed individual.

Blood Types	Description of Possible Alleles
ABO	autosomal: A (I^A) and B (I^B) are codominant, O (i) is recessive to both
Rh	autosomal: Rh^+ is dominant to Rh^-
MN	autosomal: M and N are codominant
$Xg^{(a)}$	X-linked: $Xg^{(a+)}$ is dominant to $Xg^{(a-)}$

Tested Individuals	ABO	Rh	MN	$Xg^{(a)}$
Mother	AB	Rh^-	MN	$Xg^{(a+)}$
Daughter	A	Rh^+	MN	$Xg^{(a-)}$
Son	AB	Rh^-	MN	$Xg^{(a+)}$
Alleged Father 1	AB	Rh^+	M	$Xg^{(a+)}$
Alleged Father 2	A	Rh^-	N	$Xg^{(a-)}$
Alleged Father 3	B	Rh^+	N	$Xg^{(a-)}$
Alleged Father 4	O	Rh^-	MN	$Xg^{(a-)}$

191. What is the mother's genotype at the $Xg^{(a)}$ locus?

   A. $Xg^{(a+)} Xg^{(a+)}$
   B. $Xg^{(a+)} Xg^{(a-)}$
   C. $Xg^{(a-)} Xg^{(a-)}$
   D. $Xg^{(a+)} Y$

192. Which of the alleged fathers is the real father of the two children?

   A. Father 1
   B. Father 2
   C. Father 3
   D. Father 4

193. Which one locus does not allow you to rule out any of the alleged fathers?

   A. ABO
   B. Rh
   C. MN
   D. $Xg^{(a)}$

194. At how many loci is the real father definitely heterozygous?

   A. One
   B. Two
   C. Three
   D. Four

195. At how many loci can you definitely rule out only one of the alleged fathers?

   A. One
   B. Two
   C. Three
   D. Four

196. Which of the following are correct genotypes of the daughter?

   A. $I^A I^A$, $Rh^+ Rh^+$
   B. $I^A i$, $Rh^+ Rh^+$
   C. $I^A I^A$, $Rh^+ Rh^-$
   D. $I^A i$, $Rh^+ Rh^-$

Passage IX (Questions 197–203)

Movement involves interactions between the nervous, muscular, and skeletal systems. Variation in muscle response can be dependent, in part, on the number of muscle fibers stimulated, the frequency of stimulation, and the load muscles are asked to bear. Forces exerted by muscle on skeletal elements then influence long-term changes in bones as they are remodeled in response to load, gravity, and mechanical stresses.

Figure 1 shows the generalized response of a *single muscle fiber* to a single, threshold-level stimulus. Figure 2 represents the changing response of a typical *whole muscle* to different loads when appropriate stimuli are applied.

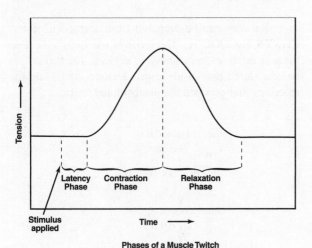

Figure 1

(a)

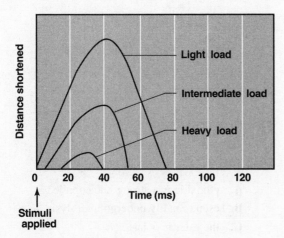

(b)

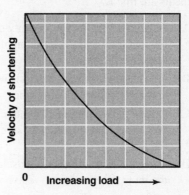

Figure 2. Influence of load on contraction velocity and duration.

197. Individual muscle fibers do not normally "twitch." Instead, they usually produce smooth, strong, sustained contractions in response to multiple stimuli given consecutively with no time for relaxation. This phenomenon is called:

A. treppe.

B. myogradation.

C. complete tetanus.

D. wave summation.

198. Which statement is true concerning muscle physiology and the "all-or-none" principle?

A. It only applies to single muscle fibers receiving single stimuli with adequate time to relax completely.

B. It applies to single muscle fibers receiving single or multiple stimuli.

C. It applies to single muscle fibers and whole muscles receiving single stimuli with adequate time to relax completely.

D. It applies to single muscle fibers and whole muscles receiving single or multiple stimuli.

199. According to Figure 2, which of the following variables in muscle response increases as load increases?

A. Contraction phase

B. Relaxation phase

C. Latency phase

D. None of the above

200. According to Figure 2, all of the following statements are true EXCEPT:

A. As load decreases, the velocity of shortening increases and the duration of the entire response increases.

B. As a load gets heavier, a muscle will shorten less and contract for less time.

C. Once a muscle begins to contract, contraction and relaxation times are approximately the same.

D. The greater the distance a muscle shortens, the more time it takes to relax.

201. In response to hormones and changing physical stresses on the skeleton, osteoclasts and osteoblasts work to remodel bones throughout life. Which of the following statements makes sense?

A. The loss of bone density in bedridden patients is due to general increases in osteoblast activity and decreases in osteoclast activity.

B. The thickening of muscle attachment sites in weight lifters is due to local decreases in osteoblast activity and increases in osteoclast activity.

C. Both statements make sense.

D. Neither statement makes sense.

202. The "light" and "dark" meat associated with poultry is directly related to myoglobin content of fibers in different skeletal muscles. Myoglobin is a pigment molecule that can bind to and store extra oxygen. Which list of characteristics is correctly matched with its "color"?

A. Light (white): slow speed of contraction, low myoglobin content, slow rate of fatigue, good for short-term intense activity

B. Dark (red): slow speed of contraction, high myoglobin content, slow rate of fatigue, good for endurance activities

C. Light (white): fast speed of contraction, low myoglobin content, high rate of fatigue, good for endurance activities

D. Dark (red): fast speed of contraction, high myoglobin content, high rate of fatigue, good for short-term intense activities

203. Which statement is correct concerning interactions between the central nervous system (CNS) and muscles?

A. Interactions involve both motor output from the CNS to muscles as well as sensory input from muscles to CNS.

B. Interactions only involve motor output from the CNS to muscles.

C. Interactions involve only sensory output from the CNS to muscles.

D. Interactions involve both sensory and motor output from the CNS to muscles.

Passage X (Questions 204–209)

Ketones can be prepared from acetoacetic ester: $CH_3COCH_2COOC_2H_5$. The series of reactions are called the acetoacetic ester synthesis of ketones. The ketone can be considered as a disubstituted acetone. Below are the reactions that produce the disubstituted acetone.

204. Steps (1) and (3) occur because:

A. ethoxide is a strong nucleophile.

B. esters readily undergo hydrolysis.

C. the ester is polar.

D. α-hydrogens are acidic.

205. Steps (2) and (4) involve the attack of a(n):

- **A.** electrophile.
- **B.** nucleophile.
- **C.** alkane.
- **D.** carbocation.

206. If the alkyl halides were methyl bromide and ethyl bromide, the product would be:

- **A.** 3-methyl-2-hexanone.
- **B.** 3-methyl-2-pentanone.
- **C.** 3-ethyl-2-butanone.
- **D.** 2-methyl-3-pentanone.

207. Which two alkyl halides would be used to synthesize 3-methyl-2-hexanone?

- **A.** Methyl bromide, isopropyl bromide
- **B.** Ethyl bromide, n-propyl bromide
- **C.** Methyl bromide, n-propyl bromide
- **D.** Methyl bromide, n-butyl bromide

208. Step (7) occurs because:

- **A.** β-keto acids readily undergo decarboxylation.
- **B.** carboxylic acids readily undergo decarboxylation.
- **C.** ketones readily undergo decarboxylation.
- **D.** disubstituted acetones are unstable.

209. Step (5) involves:

- **A.** ionization of an ester.
- **B.** a condensation reaction.
- **C.** an elimination reaction.
- **D.** a hydrolysis reaction.

Questions 210 through 214 are NOT based on a descriptive passage.

210. Vaccines stimulate antibody production in vaccinated individuals. The main ingredient of the vaccine that stimulates this immune response is usually:

- **A.** DNA of the infectious agent.
- **B.** surface molecules of the infectious agent.
- **C.** DNA and surface molecules of the infectious agent.
- **D.** recombinant DNA of the infectious agent and the vaccinated individual.

211. The bile pigments bilirubin and biliverdin are waste products resulting from the metabolism of:

- **A.** steroid hormones.
- **B.** hemoglobin.
- **C.** cholesterol.
- **D.** alcohol.

212. In humans, which of the following conditions occurs inside the lungs just prior to inspiration?

- **A.** A decrease in volume and an increase in pressure
- **B.** An increase in volume and a decrease in pressure
- **C.** An increase in volume and an increase in pressure
- **D.** A decrease in volume and a decrease in pressure

213. Post-transcriptional processing of RNA in eukaryotes usually includes:

- **A.** splicing of introns.
- **B.** formation of a 5' cap.
- **C.** formation of a poly (A) tail.
- **D.** All of the above

214. The NMR spectra of alcohols generally exhibits the absorption of the hydroxyl proton –O-H shifted downfield due to:

    A. the temperature.

    B. concentration.

    C. hydrogen bonding.

    D. the nature of the solvent.

END OF TEST 3

**IF YOU FINISH BEFORE THE TIME IS UP,
YOU MAY CHECK YOUR WORK
ON THIS TEST ONLY.**

PRACTICE EXAM III ANSWER KEY

PHYSICAL SCIENCES		VERBAL REASONING		BIOLOGICAL SCIENCES	
1. D	40. C	78. C	109. B	138. B	177. C
2. B	41. D	79. C	110. A	139. A	178. A
3. B	42. B	80. A	111. B	140. D	179. C
4. D	43. A	81. B	112. C	141. C	180. A
5. D	44. C	82. D	113. B	142. B	181. C
6. C	45. C	83. A	114. B	143. B	182. D
7. A	46. B	84. C	115. D	144. D	183. B
8. B	47. B	85. D	116. C	145. B	184. A
9. C	48. D	86. B	117. A	146. A	185. C
10. A	49. A	87. B	118. C	147. C	186. D
11. D	50. D	88. A	119. B	148. C	187. C
12. B	51. C	89. C	120. D	149. B	188. A
13. A	52. B	90. C	121. A	150. A	189. C
14. C	53. B	91. A	122. C	151. B	190. C
15. C	54. D	92. B	123. B	152. D	191. B
16. A	55. D	93. A	124. D	153. A	192. C
17. C	56. C	94. A	125. C	154. B	193. C
18. C	57. C	95. B	126. B	155. D	194. B
19. D	58. D	96. D	127. D	156. C	195. B
20. B	59. B	97. A	128. C	157. D	196. D
21. A	60. D	98. B	129. A	158. A	197. C
22. D	61. B	99. C	130. D	159. A	198. A
23. B	62. A	100. D	131. C	160. B	199. C
24. C	63. D	101. D	132. C	161. C	200. C
25. B	64. D	102. B	133. A	162. B	201. D
26. C	65. A	103. B	134. D	163. B	202. B
27. D	66. C	104. D	135. B	164. C	203. A
28. D	67. D	105. A	136. C	165. A	204. D
29. C	68. C	106. C	137. A	166. A	205. A
30. D	69. C	107. B		167. C	206. B
31. B	70. D	108. C		168. A	207. C
32. C	71. D			169. D	208. A
33. D	72. C			170. B	209. D
34. C	73. B			171. C	210. B
35. A	74. D			172. A	211. B
36. C	75. B			173. C	212. B
37. D	76. D			174. B	213. D
38. C	77. A			175. D	214. C
39. D				176. C	

PRACTICE EXAM III EXPLANATORY ANSWERS

PHYSICAL SCIENCES

1. **The correct answer is (D).** Since the source is following the observer, they are moving in the same direction. The Doppler shift depends on the change in the distance between them. If the source is overtaking the observer, the frequency will increase. This means $(v \pm v_o)/(v \pm v_s) > 1$. If the observer is pulling away from the source, the frequency will drop. This means the ratio $(v \pm v_o)/(v \pm v_s) < 1$. Using the ratio form $(v - v_o)/(v - v_s)$ guarantees that when $v_s > v_o$ the denominator is less than the numerator and the ratio is less than one. Similarly, when $v_o > v_s$ the numerator is less than the denominator and the ratio is greater than one.

2. **The correct answer is (B).** Since the source and the observer are moving apart, the observed frequency will decrease. The ratio $(v - v_o)/(v + v_s)$ is always less than one. This is the reverse of the problem Jane worked out for the approaching siren. There the ratio $(v + v_o)/(v - v_s)$ is always less than one.

3. **The correct answer is (B).** The observer is stationary, $v_o = 0$, so $(v \pm v_o)/(v \pm v_s)$ immediately reduces to $(v)/(v \pm v_s)$. Since the source is moving away from the observer, we expect the observed frequency to decrease. The form $(v)/(v + v_s)$ is always less than one.

4. **The correct answer is (D).** The source is stationary, $v_s = 0$, so $(v \pm v_o)/(v \pm v_s)$ immediately reduces to $(v \pm v_o)/v$. Since the observer is moving away from the source, we expect the observed frequency to decrease. The form $(v + v_o)/v$ is always greater than one.

5. **The correct answer is (D).** The observer is the officer who is moving toward the wall. The source is the reflected wave that is moving back towards the officer. The observed frequency is expected to increase so the source frequency must be multiplied by a ratio that is greater than one. Choice (D) satisfies the requirements. Be careful. You may be tempted to select (A) because the observer (the officer) and the source (siren) are traveling together. But the question asks about the *reflected* wave. You may also be tempted to select (C) because the wall is sta-

tionary, but again, the question asks about the *reflected* wave, which is moving.

6. **The correct answer is (C).** Use equation 1:

   $f_r = f(v + v_b)/(v - v_b)$

   $\quad = 2.0000 \text{ MHz}(1500\text{m/s} + 0.4 \text{ m/s})/$
   $(1500\text{m/s} + 0.4 \text{ m/s})$

   $= 2.0000 \text{ MHz}(1.0005) = 2.0011 \text{ MHz}$

   Be careful not to round off too early because the ratio $(v + v_b)/(v - v_b)$ is very close to 1.

7. **The correct answer is (A).** From the passage we know the wall of the heart is moving towards the stationary source. The appropriate equation to use is:

   $f_o = f_s(v + v_o)/v$

   Rearranging gives:

   $v_o = (f_o/f_s)v - v = (6.012/6.000)1500 \text{ m/s} -$
   $1500 \text{ m/s} = (1.002)1500 - 1500$

   $= 1503 \text{ m/s} - 1500 \text{ m/s} = 3 \text{ m/s}$

8. **The correct answer is (B).** According to Kirchhoff's junction law, the current is split between R_3 and R_4. Therefore $I_3 < I_2$. This eliminates choice (D). The voltage drop is the same for both R_3 and R_4. From Ohm's law, current and resistance are inversely proportional, $V = IR$. Therefore, since $R_3 > R_4$ it follows that $I_3 < I_4$. This eliminates choices (A) and (C).

9. **The correct answer is (C).** Recall Kirchhoff's junction law. There is only one path the current can take through R_1 and R_2, therefore the current must be the same through both of them.

10. **The correct answer is (A).** From Kirchhoff's junction law, the current is the same in both resistors. From Ohm's law, the voltage and the resistance are directly proportional $(I = V/R)$. The resistance of R_2 is 14 times the resistance of R_1: $R_2/R_1 = 7\Omega/0.5\Omega = 14$.

    Therefore the voltage drop across R_2 must be 14 times the voltage drop across R_1.

11. **The correct answer is (D).** To find V_2 across R_2 we need to find the current, I_2, through it. Since there is only one path the current can take from the emf source through R_2, it follows that $I_2 = I_{total}$. Therefore we must replace the four re-

sistors with a single equivalent resistor, R_{total}.

Start with the parallel resistors R_3 and R_4:

$$1/R_{//eqiv} = 1/R_3 + 1/R_4 = 1/6 + \frac{1}{2} = 4/6$$

$$R_{//eqiv} = 6/4 = 1.5\ \Omega$$

Now R_1, R_2, and $R_{//eqiv}$ are in series. They can be replaced by the single resistor:

$$R_{total} = R_1 + R_2 + R_{//eqiv} = 0.5\ \Omega + 7.0\ \Omega + 1.5\ \Omega = 9.0\ \Omega$$

Applying Ohm's law to the equivalent circuit gives:

$$I_{total} = V_{total}/R_{total} = 27\ V/9\ \Omega = 3\ A$$
$$I_{total} = I_2$$

Now apply Ohm's law to the individual resistor R_2:

$$V_2 = I_2R_2 = (3\ A)(7.0\ \Omega) = 21.0\ V$$

12. The correct answer is (B). I_1 is the current provided by the emf. Next determine the value of I_3 by applying Kirchhoff's junction law to junction *a*.

$$I_1 - I_2 - I_3 = 0 = 30\ A - 12\ A - I_2$$
$$I_3 = 18\ A$$

Finally use the law at junction *b* to solve for I_5.

$$I_3 - I_4 - I_5 = 0 = 18\ A - 10\ A - I_5$$
$$I_5 = 8\ A$$

13. The correct answer is (A). There are two emf sources in this circuit, V_0 and V_X. It doesn't matter which one you start with, the magnitude of the voltage drop across the emf source in question will be the same. The sign will be reversed. Arbitrarily starting at the emf, V_o, the current, I, is moving clockwise around the circuit and the polarity at each element is as marked. This means there is a voltage rise for V_o and voltage drops for each resistor and for V_X. Kirchhoff's loop law gives:

$$\Sigma V = V_0 - V_1 - V_2 - V_X - V_3 = 0$$

$$V_X = V_0 - V_1 - V_2 - V_3 = 15\ V - 2\ V - 3\ V - 6\ V = 4\ V$$

If we had started at V_X the direction of the current and each polarity would have been reversed:

$$\Sigma V = V_X - V_2 - V_1 + V_0 - V_3 = 0$$

$$V_X = V_2 + V_1 - V_0 + V_3 = 3\ V + 2\ V - 15\ V + 6\ V = -4\ V$$

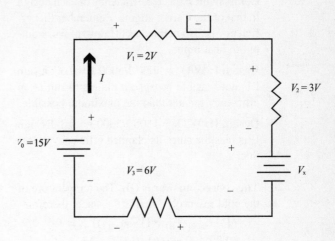

14. The correct answer is (C). Ideally the voltmeter resistance should be infinite so it doesn't draw any current. That way all of the current passes through the resistor R and is read by the ammeter.

Ideally the ammeter resistance should be zero so it doesn't develop a voltage drop. That way the voltage drop measured by the voltmeter is due solely to the drop across the resistor R.

15. The correct answer is (C). Remember to convert the temperature from centigrade to kelvin.

i. $e_{max} = 1 - T_C/T_H = 1 - 300\ K/900\ K = 0.67$

16. The correct answer is (A). Power is work per unit time and work is efficiency times the heat input, Q_H.

ii. $P_{max} = W/t = (e_{max}Q_H)/t$

iii. $(Q_H/t) = P_{max}/e_{max} = 10^9\ W/0.67 = 1.5 \times 10^9\ W = 1.5 \times 10^9\ J/s$

17. The correct answer is (C). Use the heat capacity relation: $q = mc\Delta T$

i. $\Delta T = q/mc = (7.8 \times 10^8\ J/s)/(2.0 \times 10^6\ klg/s)(4180\ J/kg°C) = 0.093°C$

18. The correct answer is (C). Rearranging $e_{max} = 1 - T_C/T_H$ gives:

i. $T_H = T_C/(1 - e_{max}) = 500\ K/0.20 = 2500\ K$

19. The correct answer is (D). For a Carnot engine operating between 427°C and 27°C, the maximum efficiency is: $e_{max} = 1 - T_C/T_H = 1 - 300\ K/600\ K = 1 - 0.5 = 0.5$

Compare the expected efficiency of each design to that of the Carnot engine. Remember that efficiency is also defined as the ratio of work output to heat input.

Design I: $W/Q_H = 3000 \text{ J}/5000 \text{ J} = 0.6$. Design I is not feasible because it claims to run at an efficiency greater than the maximum possible.

Design II: $W/Q_H = 1500 \text{ J}/5000 \text{ J} = 0.3$. Design II is feasible since its claimed efficiency is less than e_{max}.

20. **The correct answer is (B).** The temperature of the cold reservoir remains the same, therefore:
    i. $(1 - e_{max\,1})T_{H\,1} = (1 - e_{max\,1})T_{H\,1} = T_C$
    ii. $(0.80)400 \text{ K} = (0.70)T_{H\,1}$
    iii. $T_{H\,1} = 458 \text{ K}$

21. **The correct answer is (A).** From the conservation of energy, the total energy input equals the energy converted to work plus the energy exhausted:
    i. $Q_H = W + Q_{exhausted} = x + 3x = 4x$
    Efficiency is : $e = W/Q_H = x/4x = 0.25$

22. **The correct answer is (D).** By definition, $F_{magnetic} = F_{centripetal}$, $qvB = mv2/R$, which rearranges to $R = mv/qB$.
    For Ion X, $R_X = m_X v_X/q_X B$.
    For Ion Y: $m_Y = 2m_X$, $q_Y = q_X$, $v_Y = 2v_X$.
    Therefore, $R_y = 2m_X 2v_X/q_X B = 4Rx$

23. **The correct answer is (B).** The choices all involve the frequency, f, of the ion in its circular path through the magnetic field. Frequency can be determined from the definition of period, T.
    $T = 1/f = 2\pi R/v = (2\pi/v)(mv/qB) = 2\pi m/qB$
    This gives: $f = qB/2\pi m$
    And: $B = 2\pi mf/q$

24. **The correct answer is (C).** From $F_{magnetic} = F_{centripetal}$ we have $qvB = mv^2/R$. This rearranges to:
    $mv = qRB$ and $v = qRB/m$
    Kinetic energy:
    $E_K = (1/2)mv^2 = (1/2)(mv)(v) =$
    $(1/2)(qRB)(qRB/m) = q^2R^2B^2/2m$

25. **The correct answer is (B).** Ions with the same charge-to-mass ratio will have paths with the same radius, R. Since all of the hydrogen sul-

fide ions in this sample have the same charge, those with the same mass will produce signals at the same position.

For $^1H^1H^xS$:

Mass Sulfur	32	33	34	36
Mass Hydrogen	2	2	2	2
Total Mass of Ion	34	35	36	38

For $^1H^2H^xS$:

Mass Sulfur	32	33	34	36
Mass Hydrogen	3	3	3	3
Total Mass of Ion	35	36	37	39

For $^2H^2H^xS$:

Mass Sulfur	32	33	34	36
Mass Hydrogen	4	4	4	4
Total Mass of Ion	36	37	38	40

$^1H^1H^{33}S$ and $^1H^2H^{32}S$ have the same mass, 35, and together provide one signal.

$^1H^1H^{34}S$, $^1H^2H^{33}S$, and $^2H^2H^{32}S$ have the same mass, 36, and together produce one signal.

$^1H^2H^{34}S$ and $^2H^2H^{33}S$ have the same mass, 37, and together produce one signal.

$^1H^1H^{36}S$ and $^2H^2H^{34}S$ have the same mass, 38.

$^1H^1H^{32}S$, $^1H^2H^{36}S$, and $^2H^2H^{36}S$ each produce one signal.

Therefore 7 signals will be detected with masses of 34, 35, 36, 37, 38, 39, and 40.

26. **The correct answer is (C)** The mass, m, and the radius, R, are directly proportional.
    $mv^2/R = qvB \rightarrow m/R = qB/v = \text{constant}$
    Therefore the lighter the ion, the smaller the radius of the path it follows in the magnetic field.
    $FH^+ = 20 \qquad H_2O^+ = 18 \qquad NH_3^+ = 10$
    $CH_4^+ = 16$

27. **The correct answer is (D).** First determine the relation between h and the 4 variables, r, γ, ρ, and g. Then use any single experiment to solve for the constant.

    i. Experiments 1 and show r and h are inversely proportional. Double r decreases h by half.

    ii. Experiments 2 and 3 show g and h are directly proportional. Decrease the surface tension to ¼ and height decreases to ¼.

    iii. Experiments 2 and 4 show ρ and h are inversely proportional.

    iv. Experiments 2 and 5 show g and h are also inversely proportional. Cut gravity in half and the height is cut in half.

    This gives the general equation: $h = c\gamma/r\rho g$. Therefore $c = hr\rho g/\gamma$.

    Arbitrarily selecting Experiment 1, this gives:

    $c = (0.0327m)(0.5 \times 10^{-3}m)(1.0 \times 10^3 kg/m^3)(9.8m/s^2)/0.08N/m = 2.00 = 2$

    The individual units cancel so the constant is unit-less.

    The final working equation is:

    $h = 2\gamma/r\rho g$

28. **The correct answer is (D).** Height and radius are inversely related: $h_1 r_1 = h_2 r_2 = $ constant. Radius and area are related by: $A = \pi r^2 \rightarrow r = (A/\pi)^{1/2}$

    Therefore, $r_1/r_2 = (A_1/A_2)^{1/2} = h_2/h_1 = 45cm/15cm = 3$

    $(A_1/A_2) = (h_2/h_1)^2 = (45cm/15cm)^2 = 3^2 = 9$

29. **The correct answer is (C).** In going from solution A to solution B, the surface tension is quadrupled. This factor quadruples the height. On the other hand, in going from A to B, the density is doubled. This factor reduces the height by half. The height changes by the factor 4/2 = 2. Solution B rises to 2(50cm) = 100cm.

30. **The correct answer is (D).** The greater the strength of the cohesive forces of attraction, the greater the surface tension.

31. **The correct answer is (B).** Capillary action is improved by increasing the ability of the liquid to wet the capillary walls. This occurs if the adhesive forces between the molecules of the walls and those of the liquid increase. This elimi-

nates choices (C) and (D). Cohesive forces are strongest between solvent and solute molecules and, therefore, oppose interaction between the liquid and the walls.

32. **The correct answer is (C).** The pressure at a given depth due to the pressure of the air and the water above that depth. $P = P_{air} + P_{water}$

    $= P_{air} + \rho gh = 1.01 \times 10\ Pa + (10^3\ kg/m^3)(9.8\ m/s^2)(4.0\ m)$

    $= 1.4 \times 10^5\ Pa$

    Remember to convert the surface area of ear from cm^2 to m^2:

    $0.140\ cm^2\ (m^2/10^4\ cm^2) = 1.40 \times 10^{-5}\ m^2$

    Force = pressure × area = $(1.4 \times 10^5\ Pa)(1.40 \times 10^{-5}\ m^2) = \sim 2.0\ N$

33. **The correct answer is (D).** Apply the thin lens equation: $1/f = 1/s + 1/s'$

    where f is the focal length of the lens, s is the distance of the object from the lens, and s' is the distance of the image from the lens.

    Be careful with the signs. By convention, the negative focal length is used for diverging lenses and must be included when using the thin lens equation.

    $1/s' = 1/f - 1/s = -1/10\ cm - 1/20\ cm = -0.10\ cm^{-1} - 0.05\ cm^{-1} = -0.15\ cm^{-1}$

    $s' = -1/.15\ cm^{-1} \sim -6.7\ cm.$

34. **The correct answer is (C).** First find the time it takes for the flower pot to reach the ground. Taking the downward direction as positive we get:

    $h = v_0 t + gt^2/2 = 0$ and therefore $t = (2h/g)^{1/2}$

    The man travels a distance $d = vt = v(2h/g)^{1/2} = (2hv^2/g)^{1/2}$

35. **The correct answer is (A).** In going over the hill the skier returns to her initial altitude. Since there is no net change in potential energy, there is no work associated with this aspect of the trip. All the work comes from overcoming the frictional force.

    $W = f_{friction}d = (80\ N)(100\ m) = 8000\ J$

    The resulting power is $P = W/\Delta t = 8000\ J/40\ s = 200\ W$

36. The correct answer is (C). Simplify the circuit and determine the single resistor that would be equivalent to the set of resistors shown.

Starting with the parallel loop:

1. The 10Ω and a 5Ω resistor connected in series can be replaced by a single 15Ω resistor. $R_{equiv} = \Sigma R_{individual}$

2. This equivalent 15Ω resistor is connected in parallel with the second 10Ω resistor. Here $1/R_{equiv} = \Sigma R_{individual} = 1/15\Omega + 1/10\Omega = 5/30\Omega = 1/6\Omega$. And $R_{equiv} = 6\Omega$.

3. Finally the two 6Ω resistors connected in series can be replaced by a single 12Ω resistor.

From Ohm's law, $I = V/R = 120V/12\Omega = 10A$ is the total current in the circuit.

Since the 6Ω resistor is in series with the voltage source, the entire 10 A passes through it.

37. The correct answer is (D). Since the medium is unchanged, the velocity of the wave is unchanged. This eliminated choices (A) and (B). Since frequency and wavelength are inversely related, you can't change one without changing the other. This eliminates choice (C).

38. The correct answer is (C). $E_{total} = E_k + E_p = mv^2/2 + kx^2/2$

Since $E_k = 2E_p, = kx^2$ $E_{total} = 3\,kx^2/2$

But the total mechanical energy of an oscillator is also equal to its maximum potential energy, $E_{pMAX} = kA^2/2$.

Therefore $3\,kx^2/2 = kA^2/2$.

Solving for the displacement x gives: $x^2 = A^2/3 \rightarrow x = (A^2/3)$

39. The correct answer is (D). $F = k\,q_A q_B/r^2$. Since q_B and r^2 are directly proportional $q_B/r^2 = q_{Bnew}/(3r)^2$

$q_{Bnew} = 9r^2 q_B/r^2 = 9q_B$

40. The correct answer is (C). Find the number of moles of benzene, then use the sample mass to determine the molar mass.

$n = PV\ /\ RT = (756\ \text{torr}/760\ \text{torr/atm})(0.342\ \text{L})/(0.08206\ \text{Latm/Kmol})(373.15\ \text{K})$

$= 0.0111\ \text{mol}$

molar mass $= 0.931\ \text{g}/0.0111\ \text{mol} = 83.8\ \text{g/mol}$

41. The correct answer is (D). In order to use the ideal gas law for this problem, we must assume that the temperature and pressure of the gas *within* the flask is equal to quantities that we can easily measure, namely the bath temperature and the external pressure. We must also assume that the value of n that we calculate refers to moles of single benzene molecules and not, for example, "dimers" produced when two benzenes form a weak bond with each other.

42. The correct answer is (B). The third trial has a surprising value of 100.4°C as the boiling temperature of the water in the bath; miscalibration of the thermometer is the most likely explanation. Since the bath is said to have been continuously stirred, hot spots are unlikely to explain the high reading. It is true that the presence of a nonvolatile solute would have increased the boiling point of the water, but since it requires 1.86 mol solute particles per kg of water to raise the temperature by 1.00°C, a "trace" impurity would not have produced an increase of 0.4°C.

43. The correct answer is (A). The value for the mass of benzene obtained in the fourth trial was considerably higher than those of the other trials. This could have been caused by incomplete evaporation of the liquid sample. All of the other possible errors listed would lead to a smaller, not larger, value for the final mass of benzene.

44. The correct answer is (C). The individual bond energies of the molecules, and therefore their total bond energy, is unaffected by molecular speed. On the other hand, kinetic energy drops as temperature drops [choice (A)], average intermolecular distance drops as the gas condenses to a liquid [choice (B)], and the fraction of molecules below a given speed increases as temperature drops [choice (D)].

45. The correct answer is (C). From Trial 1:

$$m = \Delta T / K_f = (6.47°C - 5.47 °C) / (20.0 \text{ kg/mol°C}) = 0.0500 \text{ mol/kg}$$

Now we can find the total moles of solute in the sample, which contains 100 g (or 0.100 kg) of solvent:

$$(0.0500 \text{ mol solute/kg solvent})$$
$$(0.100 \text{ kg solvent}) = .00500 \text{ mol solute}$$

Finally we can solve for molar mass, using the mass of solute as 0.421g:

$$MM = 0.421g/0.00500 \text{ mol} = 84.2 \text{ g}$$

46. The correct answer is (B). Since $\Delta T = m K_f$, a smaller amount for the mass (and therefore the molality) of the solute would explain the anomalously small value for ΔT_f in Trial 4. K_f for this solvent cannot have a different value [choice (A)]. Choice (C) predicts an even smaller value for ΔT_f. If pentane (with its smaller MM) were used in place of benzene [choice (D)], then the molality and (therefore ΔT_f) would increase rather than decrease.

47. The correct answer is (B). This choice is the only one that shows that the freezing point [and not the boiling point, which is actually addressed by choices (C) and (D)] decreases when the pure solvent is diluted with solute. Note that T_2, which corresponds to the freezing point of the pure solvent, is greater than T_1, the freezing point of the pure solution.

48. The correct answer is (D). Reaction rates are always positive or zero. Response I puts a minus sign in front of a negative rate of change, giving a positive quantity; Response III is positive as well. Response II, however, is a negative quantity.

49. The correct answer is (A). Rows 1 and 2 show that as $[H_2O_2]$ increases by a factor of 3 (with $[I^-]$ held constant), the rate of production of O_2 increases by the same factor. Rows 1 and 3 show a similar linear dependence on $[I^-]$.

50. The correct answer is (D). A reaction that is second-order in $[H_2O_2]$ has a quadratic dependence of initial rate on $[H_2O_2]$. Note this is not to say that the *time* behavior of the reaction surges upward; see the next question for clarification.

51. The correct answer is (C). The reaction continues to produce oxygen until all of the initial H_2O_2 is depleted. But since the reaction rate is proportional to $[H_2O_2]$ (i.e., first-order in $[H_2O_2]$), as the reaction continues and $[H_2O_2]$ is depleted, the rate slows as the reaction approaches completion.

52. The correct answer is (B). When the left and right sides of this reaction are added, the overall reaction is obtained. Further, the slow step, which will determine the overall reaction rate, is first-order in both $[H_2O_2]$ and $[I^-]$, as the question specifies. Choice (C) looks similar, but the "fast" and "slow" designations are reversed. Choice (A), a one-step reaction, will be second-order in $[H_2O_2]$, not first-order as required. The two steps in choice (D) add to a different reaction than the one required.

53. The correct answer is (B). The period of 92 minutes represents 4.0 half lives for this reaction. Since the concentration of a first-order reaction drops by one-half over each half life, the concentration of reactant in each flask will be reduced by the factor $(1/2)^4 = 1/16$. The result is that the flasks maintain their 2:1 ratio throughout the process.

After 4 half-lives,

$$[N_2O_5]_{\text{flask 2}} / [N_2O_5]_{\text{flask 1}} = (1/16)(0.150 \text{ M}) / (1/16)(0.0750 \text{ M})$$

$$= 2.00$$

54. The correct answer is (D). According to the tables, increasing either the cation concentration (Ag^+ or Ca^{2+}) or the anion concentration (I^- or C_2O_4) causes the solubility to decrease from its value in pure water, as expected from the solubility expressions

$$K_{sp} (AgI) = [Ag^+][I^-]$$

$$\text{and } K_{sp}(CaC_2O_4) = [Ca^{2+}][C_2O_4^{2-}]$$

Response III is incorrect, since the solubility product, K_{sp}, is a constant (at constant temperature) that is independent of particular species concentration.

55. The correct answer is (D). Both I and III correctly evaluate K_{sp} using the data in Table 1 and the general expression $K_{sp} = [Ag^+][I^-]$. Response I uses the solubility in pure water, in which $[Ag^+] = [I^-] = 9.1 \times 10^{-9}$. Response III uses the solubility in 0.100 M $AgNO_3$, in which $[Ag^+] = 0.100$ M and $[I^-] = 8.3 \times 10^{-16}$ M.

56. The correct answer is (C). To determine the answer to this question, write down the solubility reaction for each salt.

$$AgI(s) = Ag^+(aq) + I^-(aq)$$

$$CaC_2O_4(s) = Ca^{2+}(aq) + C_2O_4^{2-}(aq)$$

Look to LeChatelier's Principle for insight into the effect of added hydrogen ion in the 0.0010 M HNO_3 solution. Neither reaction has H^+ as a species, but since $C_2O_4^{2-}$ is a weak base, it will react with H^+ to form either $HC_2O_4^-$ or $H_2C_2O_4$.

$$C_2O_4^{2-}(aq) + 2\ H^+(aq) \rightarrow H_2C_2O_4(aq)$$

Since this reaction depletes the concentration of oxalate ion, which is a product in the solubility reaction, the solubility of this salt increases. There is no comparable reaction between solid AgI and H^+. Since HI is a strong acid, its conjugate base, I^-, is extremely weak and will not react with H^+.

57. The correct answer is (C). You should lean toward choice (C) on intuitive grounds: since the pure-water solubility of CaC_2O_4 is less than that for $CaSO_4$, then CaC_2O_4 is more likely to precipitate. However, a straightforward calculation must be done to rule out choice (A), that both calcium salts are sufficiently soluble that neither precipitates; and choice (D), that enough calcium exists in the solution that it will precipitate as both the oxalate and the sulfate.

First, calculate the value of K_{sp} for each sparingly soluble calcium salt.

$$K_{sp}(CaSO_4) = (7.8 \times 10^{-3})^2 = 6.1 \times 10^{-5}$$

$$K_{sp}(CaC_2O_4) = (1.1 \times 10^{-4})^2 = 1.2 \times 10^{-8}$$

Now let's see if the solution is dilute enough that the least soluble salt, which is CaC_2O_4, might remain in solution. If no solid forms, the concentrations of calcium ion and oxalate ion are given by one-third of their original values, since each is diluted from 10 mL to 30 mL.

$$[Ca^{2+}] = 0.0033\ M;\ [C_2O_4^{2-}] = 0.0067\ M$$

$$[Ca^{2+}][C_2O_4^{2-}] = (0.0033)(0.067) = 2.2 \times 10^{-5} > K_{sp}(CaC_2O_4)$$

Our assumption that calcium oxalate remains in solution leads to a contradiction since the ion product exceeds K_{sp}. Therefore calcium oxalate will precipitate.

Might calcium sulfate precipitate as well? No, since the ion product we calculated is less than K_{sp} for $CaSO_4$.

58. The correct answer is (D). In order to solve the problem correctly using activity coefficients, you should have first multiplied each concentration by its activity coefficient.

$$(A_{Ag+})(A_{Br-}) = K_{sp}$$

$$[Ag^+]\gamma_{Ag+}[Br^-]\gamma_{Br-} = 5.0 \times 10^{-13}$$

Assume $[Br^-] = 0.0100\ M$

$$[Ag^+] = 5.0 \times 10^{-13} / \gamma_{Ag+}\ \gamma_{Br-}\ (0.0100)$$

The passage explains that each activity coefficient g is less than one. As a result, the actual value of $[Ag^+]$ will be greater than predicted without the use of the activity concept.

59. The correct answer is (B). Choices (C) and (D) are ruled out because they each contain a common ion that will drive down the solubility of MgF_2. Choices (A) and (B) both provide a higher solubility of MgF_2. Choice (B) is better than Choice (A) because choice (B) provides NO_3^-, an anion that will enter the ionic atmosphere of the Mg^{2+} ions, preventing F^- ions from approaching them and thus inhibiting the formation of solid. Choices (A) and (B) also can be compared algebraically, including activity coefficients. For choice (A):

$$K_{sp} = (A_{Mg2+})(A_{F-})^2$$
$$= [Ag^+]\gamma_{Ag}[F^-]^2\gamma^2_{F-}$$
$$= [Ag^+][F^-]^2\gamma_{Ag}\ \gamma^2_{F-}$$

Let $[Ag^+] = x$, then $[F^-] = 2x$ and

$$K_{sp} = x(2x)^2\gamma_{Ag}\ \gamma^2_{F-}$$
$$4x^3 = K_{sp} / \gamma_{Ag}\ \gamma^2_{F-}$$

If the activity coefficients γ_{Ag} and γ_{F-} were each equal to 1.00, then we would have the usual textbook expression that can be solved for x to give the pure-water solubility of AgF_2. But since we have seen that the actual values of these coefficients are less than 1.00, the value of x will be greater.

60. The correct answer is (D). The configuration shows nine electrons in the same order as indicated in Figures 1 and 2. All of the molecules in the choices given can be correctly described by these energy levels, since they contain either C or N. Since there are nine electrons, both I and III are correct choices.

61. The correct answer is (B). The species shown in choice (B) vary from left to right by subtracting one electron at a time to bonding orbitals, thus decreasing the bond order from left to right and therefore lengthening the bond.

62. The correct answer is (A). Although there are six electrons in the HF orbital diagram, only two of them are in a bonding orbital, while the other four are in nonbonding orbitals. Thus, the bond order is $1/2(2) = 1$.

63. The correct answer is (D). The passage explains that in this highly polar molecule, some of the molecular orbitals more greatly resemble the original hydrogen orbitals, and some more greatly resemble the original fluorine orbitals. The high-lying σ^* s orbital resembles the hydrogen 1s orbital, so an electron promoted to it will be found closer to the H than to the F.

64. The correct answer is (D). Since NNO has 16 valence electrons, we can employ the argument given for CO_2 to predict the same configuration as in Figure 4. The diagram predicts a total π-bond order of 2, added to a σ-framework of 2 single bonds. All three of the Lewis structure choices given are consistent with this result.

65. The correct answer is (A). Since we cannot find these compounds listed in any of the tables, we need to find an analogous series. These hydrocarbons can have only London dispersion forces holding them together in the liquid phase; the most similar series are found in Tables 1 and 2, where we see that as noble gas atoms or nonpolar halocarbons increase in atomic/molecular mass, their melting point increases. If we assume that the same trend holds for boiling point, then we arrive at choice (A).

66. The correct answer is (C). The surprise in the data of Table 5 is that London forces simply overwhelm dipole-dipole forces in these molecules, as seen by the strikingly higher boiling point for CCl_4, which has zero dipole moment but whose large Cl atoms make it considerably more polarizable than the smaller but strongly polar CH_3F molecule.

67. The correct answer is (D). Tables 4 and 5 feature oxygen-containing compounds, several of which (e.g., CH_3CH_2OH, H_2O, glycerol) form hydrogen bonds that contribute to high enthalpy of vaporization or to high viscosity. Table 6 illustrates the anomalously low acidity of HF compared to HCl and HBr. The strong hydrogen bonds that form between hydrogen atoms and the highly electronegative fluorines preclude the extensive dissociation that is found in HCl and HBr.

68. The correct answer is (C). Enthalpy of formation gives information about stability of a compound but does not directly predict strength of inter-molecular bonding. Conversely, we may take water as an example to confirm that its high enthalpy of fusion and surface tension, as well as its low vapor pressure, all are indicators of strong intermolecular forces.

69. The correct answer is (C). The nonpolar regions of each molecule will attract each other with London dispersion forces, while pairs of acetic acid molecules can fit closely together at their polar ends. Choice (A) is ruled out because hydrogen bonds cannot form when the hydrogen atom in question is attached to carbon; only N, O, and F are sufficiently electronegative. Choice (B) is ruled out because hexane has no dipole moment. Choice (D) is wrong because covalent bond formation would imply a chemical reaction between hexane and acetic acid, which is not suggested by simple solution formation.

70. The correct answer is (D). The relevant table is evidently Table 2, which lists fully halogenated methane derivatives. Since At is below I in the Periodic Table, and since the previous increases in the table have been by at least 50°C increases in melting point for each successive halogen, choice (D) is the most reasonable.

71. The correct answer is (D). Table 4 shows that the value of $\Delta H_{vaporization}$ for these molecules rises from the ether to the alcohol to water—a trend that lets us conclude that the intermolecular forces also rise in that order. But vapor pressure falls off as $\Delta H_{vaporization}$ rises, leading to the trend of choice (D).

72. The correct answer is (C).

$$q_{rxn} = -q_{calorimeter}$$
$$= -(120 \text{ g})(4.18 \text{ J/g°C})(6.7°C)$$
$$= -3.36 \times 10^3 \text{ J}$$

We have 0.0600 mol of HCl, which is the limiting reactant.

$$\Delta H = -3.34 \times 10^3 \text{ J} / 0.0600 \text{ mol}$$
$$-56.0 \text{ kJ}$$

73. The correct answer is (B).

(40.0 g $CaCO_3$)(1 mol $CaCO_3$ / 100 g $CaCO_3$) (1 mol CO_2 /1 mol $CaCO_3$) (22.4 L CO_2 / mol CO_2) = 8.96 L CO_2

work = $-P_{ext}\Delta V$ = $-(1.00 \text{ atm})(8.96 \text{ L})$ = -8.96 L atm

74. The correct answer is (D). Since the reaction is endothermic, we can think of heat as a reactant; by adding heat by raising the temperature and by removing water (a product), we push the equilibrium to the right.

75. The correct answer is (B). The titration reaction is:

$$NH_3(aq) + HCl(aq) \rightarrow NH_4^+(aq) + Cl^-(aq)$$

The result is a solution of approximately 0.10 M ammonium ion, which is expected to be acidic.

$$K_a = (1.00 \times 10^{-14} / 1.8 \times 10^{-5}) = 5.6 \times 10^{-10}$$

Let $x = [H^+]$; then

$$x^2 / (0.10 - x) = 5.6 \times 10^{-10}$$
$$x \approx 7.5 \times 10^{-6} \text{ M, so pH} = 5.12$$

76. The correct answer is (D). Combine reactions 1 and 2 as follows:

1 x Rxn. (2): $H_2(g) + F_2(g) \rightarrow 2HF(g)$
$\Delta H = -680$ kJ

-2 x Rxn. (1): $4HF(g) \rightarrow 2H_2(g) + 2 F_2(g)$
$\Delta H = -2(-537 \text{ kJ})$

$C(s) + 4HF(g) \rightarrow CF_4(g) + 4H_2(g)$

$\Delta H = (-680 \text{ kJ}) + (-2)(-537\text{kJ}) = 394$ kJ

77. The correct answer is (A). Cl is reduced from the +1 state to 0; Cr is oxidized from +3 to +6. There is no source of H^+ to react with OH^- to provide an acid/base reaction.

VERBAL REASONING

78. The correct answer is (C). The answer is based on lines 14–16, which point out that "the usual price was 50 cents per ton of coal, and 5 tons was a good day."

79. The correct answer is (C). The answer is found in lines 17–19: ". . . the steel companies built the Coal Patches to attract workers, control labor, and retrieve some of their costs by owning the only store in town."

80. The correct answer is (A). The answer is found in lines 17–21: ". . . the steel companies built the Coal Patches to attract workers, control labor, and retrieve some of their costs by owning the only store in town. . . . Everything had to be bought at the store. . . ."

81. The correct answer is (B). The answer can be found in lines 28–29 in the statement, ". . . unionization was a great fear of the steel companies during the 1920s and 1930s. . . ."

82. The correct answer is (D). This answer is the only answer possible because it is in support of the passage's emphasis that the steel companies controlled the workers and owned everything in the Coal Patch towns.

83. The correct answer is (A). The answer is based on lines 56–58, which state: ". . . and the inexpensive quiet communities have lured new people to continue the story of life in the Coal Patch."

84. The correct answer is (C). This answer is based on one of the passage's major points that the steel companies owned the only store in town and, by being in complete control of that business, did not allow workers to be involved in either running it or earning money from it.

85. The correct answer is (D). The main idea of the passage is found in the first sentence of paragraph 2: "There may be a partial solution to relieving such congestion in a much older form of transportation: the train."

86. The correct answer is (B). Paragraph 3 states that "Unlike Europe and Japan . . . the United States has not invested in the technology to improve rail service." This implies that with the right technology, trains in the United States could travel as quickly as those in Europe, thereby making train travel a competitor to the airline industry.

87. **The correct answer is (B).** The author's viewpoint is best stated in the main idea, presented in paragraph 2: "There may be a partial solution to relieving such congestion in a much older form of transportation: the train." Choice (A) is incorrect because in paragraph 2, the author clearly states that train travel would only be an equal choice to air travel for distances of 600 miles or less.

88. **The correct answer is (A).** The passage doesn't mention anything about the vulnerability of trains to terrorism.

89. **The correct answer is (C).** While choices (A) and (D) are all true statements, choice (C) is the only choice that correctly answers the question. Paragraph 2 states that the U.S. "has not invested in the technology to improve rail service." Choice (B) is an incorrect statement.

90. **The correct answer is (C).** Response I is stated in paragraphs 1 and 2. Paragraph 1 discusses the long waits that passengers have been subjected to at airports, and paragraph 2 offers train travel as a partial solution. Response III is supported in paragraphs 3 and 4, which state: "Thousands of informed Americans living along the Eastern seaboard already know this, and use Amtrak's efficient high-speed rail service that runs from Boston to Washington, D.C." (paragraph 3) and "The U.S. Department of Transportation believes that similar service across the United States would help improve travel options for Americans . . ." (paragraph 4).

91. **The correct answer is (A).** It is most reasonable to conclude from the information provided in the passage that with greater competition among railroad companies, races to get contracts from states would provide incentives for the railroad companies to provide the best service options possible.

92. **The correct answer is (B).** Choice (B) provides the most accurate definition of bipolar disorder, which is described clearly in paragraph 1: "This brain disorder is a disease characterized by wide mood swings from the manic state to a depressive state."

93. **The correct answer is (A).** The passage states that a person with bipolar disorder may have suicidal thoughts or tendencies (paragraph 1). The author does not mention whether or not an individual suffering from the disorder may be hospitalized unnecessarily or that a manic state is more common than a depressive state.

94. **The correct answer is (A).** While family support may indeed be a necessary component to the treatment success of an individual with bipolar disorder, this factor is not mentioned in the passage. Medication [choice (B)], psychotherapy [choice (C)], and support groups [choice (D)] are all mentioned in paragraph 3.

95. **The correct answer is (B).** The passage provides a very general overview of bipolar disorder. Therefore the information would probably be most suitable for a friend or a family member of someone diagnosed with the disease. Medical students and psychiatrists would need more in-depth information for this passage to be useful to them. If this passage were intended for pharmacy students, more details on the drugs would have been provided.

96. **The correct answer is (D).** Paragraph 4 states: "However, it is important to stress the critical need for continuous reevaluation of drug therapy; often, the effect of the medication on the patient may diminish with time. In these instances, drug regimens will need to change in order to maintain a patient's mood balance. Additionally, patients suffering from this disorder commonly experience a feeling of being 'cured' by the medication, and thus stop taking the medication as prescribed." The fact that the effect of medication will diminish over time and that patients may stop taking the drug because of a false sense of security are two examples that back up the statement that drug therapy needs constant reevaluation.

97. **The correct answer is (A).** Consider the characteristics of a manic state provided in paragraph 2: "The manic episode, which can last for a week or more, is a distinct period during which a person exhibits symptoms of extreme elation, aggression, irritability, distractibility, and poor judgment." The only answer choice that makes sense given this information is choice (A). A spending spree would fall under the area of poor judgment.

98. The correct answer is (B). While an intrigue may also be a trick, the answer choice closest in meaning to *intrigues* is *schemes*.

99. The correct answer is (C). Paragraph 2 supports the author's belief that the Serbian papers helped to aggravate the situation by publishing anti-Austrian propaganda. "The Serbian press [was] openly boastful and defiant in its comments. When the Austrian consul-general at Belgrade dropped dead in the consulate, the papers showed their satisfaction and hinted that he had been poisoned. This attitude of the press evidently was one of the reasons for the stringent demand made by Austria … requiring apology and change of attitude from Serbia. . . ."

100. The correct answer is (D). Responses I and II occurred after the assassination of Archduke Ferdinand and his wife.

101. The correct answer is (D). Choices (A), (B), and (C) are listed clearly in the list of demands following paragraph 2. The passage does not mention what happened to the student who assassinated the Archduke.

102. The correct answer is (B). The final paragraph of the passage states that Serbia agreed to all of the demands except for the request that the Austrian government would be permitted to investigate the incident without interference from the Serbian government. This implies that the Serbian government had something to hide.

103. The correct answer is (B). The key words in the statement provided that give a clue to the answer are: "The immediate cause, so far as apparent to us, of the Great War...." This statement suggests that while the assassination provided the instantaneous response of war between Austria and Serbia, additional factors probably led to consequence of World War I. The passage doesn't mention the political involvement of Serbian students [choice (A)], the Bosnian sentiment toward Francis Ferdinand and his wife [choice (C)], or the current issues in the Balkan Peninsula [choice (D)].

104. The correct answer is (D). Paragraph 2 states that the majority of all executions have taken place in Texas and Virginia. It is reasonable based on this statement to assume that the death penalty has had its greatest acceptance in these two states.

105. The correct answer is (A). Paragraph 4 addresses the reason for regional differences in opinion surrounding the death penalty. "One possible explanation for regional differences in attitude toward the death penalty may be the political nature of the regions. The South and Midwest tend toward the conservative side, which generally supports the death penalty, whereas the West and Northeast are more liberal as a group and hence are more hesitant to impose the death penalty."

106. The correct answer is (C). The author provides reasons that support and oppose the death penalty. Therefore, the author is presenting an objective attitude toward the issue.

107. The correct answer is (B). While all of these answers may be reasonable arguments for or against the death penalty, only choice (B) is backed with support in the passage. Paragraph 3 states: "A big reason for the debate over the death penalty involves the ability to prove an individual's guilt beyond a reasonable doubt when recommending a death penalty sentence." None of the other choices are mentioned in the passage.

108. The correct answer is (C). The final paragraph in the passage addresses the changes required in the Supreme Court panel to affect change in the constitutionality of capital punishment. "For this to happen, we would have to see a change in the makeup of the Supreme Court to a more liberal body. Currently, the Supreme Court contains seven justices appointed by Republican presidents, and two appointed by a Democratic president. With the current members of the Supreme Court being overwhelmingly conservative...." Information on the conservative viewpoint on capital punishment is discussed in paragraph 4.

109. The correct answer is (B). Paragraph 3 addresses the death penalty issues that have arisen in Illinois. Because Illinois has found errors in cases involving capital punishment, it has put a halt to sentencing convicted criminals to death until each death penalty case has been investigated. The paragraph goes on to state: "It is clear that many of the issues raised in Illinois could also be raised in other death penalty states."

110. The correct answer is (A). Consider the last sentence in paragraph 5: "Therefore, one can expect that not much will change at the federal level with regard to any constitutional amendments surrounding the nationwide repeal of the death penalty."

111. The correct answer is (B). The answer is based on the sentences in the last paragraph: "Wollstonecraft's ideas on the state of women were revolutionary at the time, so one can view her as a remarkable individual, certainly ahead of her time." Wollstonecraft was convinced that equal and quality education for women was essential as it would foster a woman's duty to educate her own children, be an equal partner with her husband, and would recognize that a woman, just as a man, had thought, feeling, and the ability to reason. "Today Wollstonecraft is generally viewed as a liberal feminist, since she was mainly concerned with individual women and their rights."

112. The correct answer is (C). Wollstonecraft argued that through equal and quality education, women would become emancipated and able to have a stable marriage as a partnership between husband and wife. The implication is that without better education for women, they would be subordinate and inferior to men.

113. The correct answer is (B). Wollstonecraft believed women were capable of thought and reason, not just feeling.

114. The correct answer is (B). The answer is based on the process of elimination. Choices (A) and (C) are contradicted by Wollstonecraft's emphasis in her essay that to maintain a stable marriage meant that men practice chastity and fidelity also, clearly implying that infidelity among men in eighteenth-century English society was acceptable. There is no reference to the moral standards for the aristocracy, choice (D) in this passage.

115. The correct answer is (D). The passage explains that Wollstonecraft's father was not able to sufficiently provide for his family or provide a stable life.

116. The correct answer is (C). The answer is based on this sentence in paragraph 4: "Working as the schoolteacher and the headmistress of the school, Wollstonecraft and Eliza realized that the young women they tried to teach had already accepted their social status as inferior to men."

117. The correct answer is (A). Nowhere in the passage is the author shocked, dismissive, or disapproving.

118. The correct answer is (C). In the second paragraph it states that Mad Cow disease is thought to be caused by a newly discovered infectious agent, known as a prion.

119. The correct answer is (B). According to the following sentence in paragraph 2: "At some point, a critical mass occurs and the proteins begin to damage the brain by basically turning it into sponge. This results in the victim losing his or her mental and physical abilities and ultimately dying."

120. The correct answer is (D). The answer is found in paragraph 3 according to the following sentence: "It is likely that the United States will follow the lead of other countries and create much tighter restrictions on how cows are fed and which cows can be slaughtered for meat. Without new stringent laws for beef from the United States, an increasing number of countries will ban its importation, and even in the United States, many may choose not to eat beef." Choices (A), (B), and (C) are inaccurate statements.

121. The correct answer is (A). The key word in choice (A) is "surprising" and a synonym for surprising *is amazing*. Choices (B), (C), and (D) are inaccurate statements as they are not in the passage.

122. The correct answer is (C). "Even then, it would take extensive breeding and possibly genetic engineering to ensure that the American herd would be safe from Mad Cow disease." (paragraph 4)

123. The correct answer is (B). The answer is based on the following sentences in paragraph 5: "For now, our methods of control are primitive and basically call for the extermination of infected cows and cows they have been in contact with. The second part of our control program is to better supervise the raising and slaughtering of cattle."

124. The correct answer is (D). In paragraph 2, the following quote lists the first three reasons, but does not list the fourth, therefore, (D) is the correct answer. "This decline took place because of overfishing, ocean water pollution, the pollution and damming of many of the rivers and streams that salmon had previously used to spawn . . ."

125. The correct answer is (C). This answer is based on these sentences in paragraph 3: "Finally, the domestic salmon are fed very differently from wild salmon. . . . This different diet poses a hazard to humans as it is likely that higher levels of certain chemicals deemed unhealthy occur in domestic salmon than in wild salmon. In the first test of domestic salmon for polychlorinat-biphenyls (PCPs), it was found that domestic salmon had 16 times the dioxin levels of wild salmon. This level makes domestic salmon the most contaminated meat that is sold in a grocery store."

126. The correct answer is (B). The correct answer is based on this sentence in paragraph 2: "This decline took place because of overfishing, ocean water pollution, and the pollution and damming of many of the rivers and streams that salmon had previously used to spawn . . ."

127. The correct answer is (D). The answer can be found in paragraph 3: "Unfortunately, the diseases that the domestic salmon become infected with can spread to the wild salmon population and also to other fish, doing serious damage to the groups that the diseases spread to. It is also possible that domestic salmon will escape and spawn with wild salmon. This occurrence would most likely weaken the species and put the wild salmon at further risk."

128. The correct answer is (C). In paragraph 3, it states "This level makes domestic salmon the most contaminated meat that is sold in a grocery store. There is cause for concern because PCPs have been linked to a number of forms of cancer and possibly to birth defects."

129. The correct answer is (A). This answer is based on these sentences in the last paragraph: "While it is reasonable to assume that salmon fish farming is here to stay, it is clear that the way salmon are farmed needs to be better monitored. Methods to reduce the water pollution caused by the farming must be developed and implemented on a worldwide scale."

130. The correct answer is (D). To be apprehensive can also mean anxious or fearful about the future. Choices (A), (B), and (C) are inaccurate.

131. The correct answer is (C). The correct answer is based on these sentences in paragraph 1: "These differences favor men, while women are penalized, overburdened, and limited to the confines of the home and family. Though the men work hard, 1950s and 1960s Puerto Rican society allows them time for recreation, while women work far harder with no time off at all." Choices (A), (B), and (D) are referred to in the passage as several differences.

132. The correct answer is (C). The answer is based on this sentence in paragraph 4: "The concept of *dignidad*, when men can look at women in whatever way they choose and whatever manner they want, reinforces such behavior."

133. The correct answer is (A). The answer is based on these sentences in paragraph 4: "Santiago learns early that double standards for the sexes are acceptable. 'Men's natures' are the reasons that men's infidelities are permitted and not considered shameful. Respectable women are expected to tolerate their men's indiscretions."

134. The correct answer is (D). The answer is based on the following sentences in paragraph 4: "Respectable women are expected to tolerate their men's indiscretions. Santiago uses the word *sinverguenza,* applying it to men who behave in ways that cause good women to suffer because such behavior is explained to the reader as 'men's natures.'"

135. The correct answer is (B). The answer is based on the following sentence in paragraph 5: "Santiago also relates how she was expected to behave once she becomes a *senorita,* a young woman. Her former tomboyish behavior and playing with boys is to be replaced with demure behavior among grown-ups and acting lady-like. She has to always sit with her legs together, learn the responsibilities of housework and cooking, and avoid acting improperly in public."

136. The correct answer is (C). The answer is based on the process of elimination. Choice (C) is supported by these sentences in paragraph 4: "Santiago discovers her father's continued unfaithfulness to her mother when he takes her to visit his mother for a week promising he would return to pick her up at the end of that time" and "Eventually, Santiago's father, having lived with Ramona for 14 years and fathered seven children with her, refuses to marry Ramona. Two months after Ramona and Santiago have left for New York, Pablo abandons four of his children Ramona has left with him to marry someone else." This sentence implies Pablo's disregard for caring for his wife and children. Choices (A), (B), and (D) are inaccurate statements.

137. **The correct answer is (A).** The correct answer is found in this sentence in paragraph 4: "Santiago learns early that double standards for the sexes are acceptable."

BIOLOGICAL SCIENCES

138. **The correct answer is (B).** The conversion of one amino acid to another (phenylalanine to tyrosine), also called transamination, occurs in the liver.

139. **The correct answer is (A).** Since the pigment melanin is derived from tyrosine, and PKU individuals produce lower levels of tyrosine, their hair and skin color may be lighter than normal individuals. The body's 24-hour circadian rhythms are influenced by melatonin.

140. **The correct answer is (D).** When carriers of a detrimental allele experience heterozygote advantage, this is referred to as a balanced polymorphism.

141. **The correct answer is (C).** Since tetrahydrobiopterin (THB) works as a cofactor with PAH to convert phenylalanine to tyrosine, a defect in the THB allele can result in the same symptoms as those exhibited by individuals with a defect in the PAH allele.

142. **The correct answer is (B).** By restricting the intake of phenylalanine, dangerous levels of phenylpyruvic acid cannot accumulate, even in PKU individuals who lack PAH.

143. **The correct answer is (B).** Phenylpyruvic acid interferes with myelination of neurons. Myelin is normally found on axons, not on dendrites or axon endings. Therefore, myelin would not be found within synapses either.

144. **The correct answer is (D).** Nitrification involves the conversion of ammonia/ammonium to nitrites and nitrates. Denitrification converts nitrites or nitrates to nitrogen gas. Ammonification refers to the conversion of organic nitrogenous molecules to ammonia/ammonium.

145. **The correct answer is (B).** Xylem tissue carries water, minerals, and other molecules from the roots upward. Phloem transports glucose and other organic molecules down from the leaves throughout the plant. Parenchyma and sclerenchyma are not transport tissues at all.

146. **The correct answer is (A).** In the absorptive state (during and immediately after a meal), there is a surplus of nutrients, including amino acids, and many are deaminated and converted to fat. During the post-absorptive state, glucose levels drop and gluconeogenesis takes place. This includes the deamination of amino acids for use as substitutes for glucose in cellular respiration.

147. **The correct answer is (C).** Ammonia is highly toxic and requires large amounts of water for its transport and subsequent excretion. This occurs primarily in aquatic organisms where water is not a limiting factor.

148. **The correct answer is (C).** See answer to question 144.

149. **The correct answer is (B).** Nitric oxide acts as a vasodilator that can increase local blood flow.

150. **The correct answer is (A).** The carbonyl group helps to distribute the negative charge associated with the carbanion through resonance. Although less acidic than the carboxyl hydrogens, α-hydrogens are more acidic than other hydrogens on the aldehyde or ketone and thus can form carbocations.

151. **The correct answer is (B).** In structure II the more electronegative O is carrying the charge. Unlike the carboxylate, the resonance structures are inequivalent.

152. The correct answer is (D). Two molecules of an aldehyde form a β-hydroxyaldehyde.

$$CH_3-\underset{\underset{H}{|}}{\overset{\overset{H}{|}}{C}}=O + H-\underset{\underset{H}{|}}{\overset{\overset{H}{|}}{C}}-\overset{\overset{H}{|}}{C}=O \xrightarrow{OH^-} CH_3-\underset{\underset{OH}{|}}{\overset{\overset{H}{|}}{C}}-\underset{\underset{H}{|}}{\overset{\overset{H}{|}}{C}}-\overset{\overset{H}{|}}{C}=O$$

aldol

153. The correct answer is (A). There are no α-hydrogens.

154. The correct answer is (B). The carbanion formed in the condensation attacks the carbonyl carbon on another ester molecule to form:

$$CH_3-\underset{\underset{OC_2H_5}{|}}{\overset{\overset{O^-}{|}}{C}}-CH_2COOC_2H_5$$

β-ketoester

However, because of the presence of the acyl group, the ethoxide is released and a nucleophilic substitution reaction occurs.

155. The correct answer is (D). In both cases addition initially occurs and a tetrahedral carbon is formed; in the case of acyl compounds, however, the carbonyl group is reformed to produce a substitution product.

156. The correct answer is (C). When body temperature is too low, superficial blood vessels constrict to reduce heat loss, and thyroxine is released to increase metabolic rate and heat production.

157. The correct answer is (D). Heat loss is minimized when arteries carrying warm blood from the core to the periphery give up heat to veins returning blood from the periphery back to the core. This helps keep the core organs warm.

158. The correct answer is (A). The pineal gland's hormone, melatonin, is associated with 24-hour (circadian) rhythms. Although serotonin has been associated with sleep-wake cycles in some organisms, it is not known to be released by either the pineal or anterior pituitary gland.

159. The correct answer is (A). Ectotherms like snakes and lizards bask in the sun to absorb heat until body temperature is high enough to go about their business. When it rises above homeostatic range, they will move to the shade or some other cooler location. If they remain in the heat, their body temperature will continue to rise to the level of ambient temperature.

160. The correct answer is (B). Pyrogens raise the hypothalamic set-point so that heat-conservation (constriction of superficial blood vessels) and heat-producing (release of thyroxine and shivering) mechanisms go into effect. Even though the resulting body temperature is higher than normal, the individual still feels cold because temperature is still below the new set-point.

161. The correct answer is (C). Excess sweating during prolonged exposure to heat leads to decreased blood volume and a resulting drop in blood pressure.

162. The correct answer is (B). The one gene–one enzyme hypothesis has been modified to one gene–one polypeptide. This is because many enzymes (and other proteins) have different polypeptide components encoded by different genes.

163. The correct answer is (B). The release of calcium from the sarcoplasmic reticulum is needed for skeletal muscle contraction. The movement of calcium into axon terminals causes the release of neurotransmitters from synaptic vesicles. Calcium is also needed for the activation of prothrombin to thrombin and fibrinogen to fibrin.

164. The correct answer is (C). Assuming no chromosomal interference, the frequency of recombinants resulting from a double crossover will be equivalent to the product of the frequencies of each separate single crossover ($0.20 \times 0.10 = 0.02$).

165. The correct answer is (A). The very basic ion can abstract H^+ and lead to elimination as well as substitution.

166. The correct answer is (A). The heart and skeletal muscles develop from mesoderm, the brain and adrenal medulla develop from ectoderm, and the pancreas develops from endoderm.

167. **The correct answer is (C).** Parathormone helps regulate calcium levels via negative feedback.

168. **The correct answer is (A).** Aldosterone release can be stimulated by both a decrease in sodium ions and an increase in potassium ions. Additionally, a drop in blood volume or blood pressure initiates the renin-angiotensin system, which also stimulates aldosterone.

169. **The correct answer is (D).** The adrenal cortex produces glucocorticoids; the adrenal medulla produces epinephrine and norepinephrine; and the anterior pituitary gland produces GH, TSH, and ACTH. Each of these hormones contributes to increased glucose levels in the blood. Oxytocin and ADH, released by the posterior pituitary gland, do not affect glucose levels.

170. **The correct answer is (B).** Sodium and calcium levels are influenced by antagonistic hormones from different sources (sodium: aldosterone/adrenal cortex and ANP/heart; calcium: parathormone/parathyroid glands and calcitonin/thyroid gland). Estrogen is regulated *synergistically* by different hormones from the same gland (FSH and LH/anterior pituitary gland). Only glucose is regulated in part by two antagonistic hormones from the same gland (insulin and glucagon/pancreas).

171. **The correct answer is (C).** Endometrial development is influenced by estrogen and progesterone from the ovaries, FSH and LH from the anterior pituitary gland, and releasing hormones (GnRH) from the hypothalamus. Metabolic rate is influenced by thyroxine (and T_3) from the thyroid gland, TSH from the anterior pituitary gland, and TSH-RH from the hypothalamus. Blood pressure is influenced by any hormones that affect sodium and water balance (aldosterone, ADH, ANP). Potassium levels are influenced by aldosterone and ANP.

172. **The correct answer is (A).** Epinephrine is released from the adrenal medulla in response to sympathetic nervous stimulation. Oxytocin and ADH are released by the posterior pituitary gland in response to stimulation from hypothalamic neurons.

173. **The correct answer is (C).** Except during pregnancy and nursing, the hypothalamus continuously produces PRL-IH to keep prolactin production low.

174. **The correct answer is (B).** Data from the table indicate that out of 180 liters of water that are filtered from the plasma, 178–179 are reabsorbed. Thus, 1–2 liters leave in the urine. $1/180 = .006$; $2/180 = .011$. These figures are read as slightly more than one-half of one percent and slightly more than one percent, respectively.

175. **The correct answer is (D).** An examination of the first two columns shows all constituents EXCEPT proteins have every gram (or mL) that is present in the plasma filtered into the filtrate.

176. **The correct answer is (C).** Any situation in which a wide vessel (or pipe) feeds fluids into an area that is drained by a narrower vessel will have fluid accumulate and pressure build up between them. Red blood cells in the filtrate is not a usual situation since they are too large normally to pass through the glomerulus. The countercurrent mechanism of the kidney refers to the directional flow of solutes and water around the loop of Henle.

177. **The correct answer is (C).** Without proper insulin function, plasma glucose levels are high in diabetics. Therefore, higher than normal quantities will be filtered into the nephrons. However, there are only the "normal" numbers of carrier molecules to reabsorb glucose into the peritubular capillaries, and the excess glucose continues through the kidney and leaves in the urine.

178. **The correct answer is (A).** If an individual's blood pH is too high (too alkaline), the urinary system can adjust by either retaining additional sources of H^+ or by allowing additional alkaline substances out in the urine. HCO_3- is such a basic ion. Reabsorption of HCO_3- or filtering acidic substances will only increase pH further. "Larger alkaline proteins" do not normally get filtered through the glomerulus.

179. **The correct answer is (C).** Knowledge of the variables that influence blood pressure, and the role of the adrenal cortex hormone aldosterone (increasing reabsorption of Na^+), are essential. An understanding of osmotic relationships is also required, i.e., increased levels of cells and solutes in the blood will osmotically attract additional water. This will raise blood volume, which in turn raises blood pressure (vasodilation lowers blood pressure).

180. The correct answer is (A).

$$\begin{array}{ccc}
\text{COO}^-\text{Na}^+ & & \text{COOH} \\
| & \xrightarrow{\text{H}_2\text{O/H}^+} & | \\
\text{CH}_2 & & \text{CH}_2 \\
| & & | \\
\text{CN} & & \text{COOH}
\end{array}$$

Malonic Acid

181. The correct answer is (C). Malonic acid, $HOOCCH_2COOH$, has one more carbon than oxalic acid, $HOOCCOOH$.

182. The correct answer is (D). The two –COOH groups become esters that can then react with other –COOH groups.

183. The correct answer is (B). Each amino group reacts with a –COOH group to form an amide linkage. Nylon is a polyamide.

184. The correct answer is (A). The second ionization of a diprotic acid always occurs less readily than the first because it involves separating a H^+ from an anion.

185. The correct answer is (C). Each –COOH becomes esterified.

186. The correct answer is (D). Since the genetic material of the tobacco mosaic virus is single-stranded RNA, Chargaff's rule does not apply. One cannot predict nucleotide base content resulting from complementarity if there is only one strand of nucleic acid.

187. The correct answer is (C). The spleen and liver are responsible for the removal of old and infected red blood cells. Lymph nodes and other lymphoid tissues would play a role as well.

188. The correct answer is (A). The actual withdrawal of the hand happens immediately and is the result of a three-neuron spinal reflex that does not involve the brain.

189. The correct answer is (C). Similar functional structures in species that are not closely related are the result of convergence and are referred to as analogous structures. The wings of birds and bats, because they are close in ancestry, are homologous.

190. The correct answer is (C). The three-membered ring of epoxides is highly strained due to the 60-degree bond angles. Carbon prefers the 109.5-degree angle when it is bonded to four groups and O also prefers a much larger angle. Thus, the bonds are considerably weaker than in most ethers.

191. The correct answer is (B). Since the daughter's phenotype is $Xg^{(a-)}$, her genotype must be $Xg^{(a-)} Xg^{(a-)}$. If the mother's phenotype is $Xg^{(a+)}$, she must be a carrier of the $Xg^{(a-)}$ allele.

192. The correct answer is (C). Alleged father 1 is ruled out because of his $Xg^{(a+)}Y$ genotype. Father 2 is ruled out because of his $Rh^- R h^-$ genotype. Father 4 is ruled out because of his ii genotype as well as his $Rh^- R h^-$ genotype.

193. The correct answer is (C). Since the mother has genotype MN, any of the alleged fathers could have produced children with genotype MN.

194. The correct answer is (B). The real father (father 3) must be heterozygous at the ABO locus ($I^B i$). He also must be heterozygous at the Rh locus (Rh^+Rh^-) to produce an Rh^- son (Rh^-Rh^-). The father's genotype at the $Xg^{(a)}$ locus is $Xg^{(a-)}Y$, but this is considered hemizygous.

195. The correct answer is (B). One can definitely rule out alleged father 1 at the $Xg^{(a)}$ locus and alleged father 4 at the ABO locus.

196. The correct answer is (D). The daughter cannot be $I^A I^A$ if father 3 is type B. She also cannot be Rh^+Rh^+ if her mother is type Rh^-.

197. The correct answer is (C). Treppe refers to the stronger contractions produced by muscle fibers in response to single stimuli as they warm up. Wave summation, a slight increase in the force of contraction, occurs when multiple stimuli are applied with time available between stimuli for partial relaxation.

198. The correct answer is (A). The "all-or-none" principle does not apply to whole muscles. Whole muscles can contract with varying degrees of force, depending on how many muscle fibers are being stimulated.

199. The correct answer is (C). Figure 2a shows that as load increases, the latency period prior to the onset of contraction increases as well.

200. The correct answer is (C). Figure 2a indicates that for a light load, the contraction and relaxation times are approximately the same. However, this does not appear to be the case for intermediate or heavy loads.

201. The correct answer is (D). Osteoblasts deposit bone, while osteoclasts break down bone.

202. The correct answer is (B). A correct list of characteristics associated with light (white) muscle fibers would be fast speed of contraction, low myoglobin content, high rate of fatigue, good for short-term intense activities.

203. The correct answer is (A). In addition to the usual motor output from CNS to muscles, there is a constant flow of sensory information from proprioceptors in muscles, tendons, and joints back to the CNS.

204. The correct answer is (D). The ethoxide base is able to extract the α-hydrogens because they are acidic.

205. The correct answer is (A). The electropositive alkyl group attacks the anion.

206. The correct answer is (B). The two alkyl groups add to the starting molecule.

207. The correct answer is (C). The methyl and n-propyl groups produce the product.

208. The correct answer is (A). The ease of decarboxylation can be attributed to the ability of the keto group to handle negative charge. Loss of CO_2 leaves a carbanion, which is resonance stabilized.

209. The correct answer is (D). Step 5 is the basic hydrolysis of an ester to form the parent acid.

210. The correct answer is (B). Surface molecules of infectious agents are recognized by the host's immune system as foreign antigens, thus activating the immune response.

211. The correct answer is (B). When old red blood cells are destroyed by the spleen and liver, the metabolism of heme produces bilirubin and biliverdin. Ultimately, the liver sends these pigments, along with bile salts, into the small intestine. They are subsequently eliminated from the body in feces.

212. The correct answer is (B). When the diaphragm contracts downward prior to inspiration, the volume of the lungs increases and the pressure drops below atmospheric pressure. This causes air to rush in during inspiration.

213. The correct answer is (D). All three events take place as part of the modification process that produces the final mRNA transcript.

214. The correct answer is (C). The O in alcohols deshields nearby protons due to its electronegativity. The greater the degree of H-bonding, the greater the chemical shift.

ANSWER SHEET

Physical Sciences

1. Ⓐ Ⓑ Ⓒ Ⓓ   40. Ⓐ Ⓑ Ⓒ Ⓓ
2. Ⓐ Ⓑ Ⓒ Ⓓ   41. Ⓐ Ⓑ Ⓒ Ⓓ
3. Ⓐ Ⓑ Ⓒ Ⓓ   42. Ⓐ Ⓑ Ⓒ Ⓓ
4. Ⓐ Ⓑ Ⓒ Ⓓ   43. Ⓐ Ⓑ Ⓒ Ⓓ
5. Ⓐ Ⓑ Ⓒ Ⓓ   44. Ⓐ Ⓑ Ⓒ Ⓓ
6. Ⓐ Ⓑ Ⓒ Ⓓ   45. Ⓐ Ⓑ Ⓒ Ⓓ
7. Ⓐ Ⓑ Ⓒ Ⓓ   46. Ⓐ Ⓑ Ⓒ Ⓓ
8. Ⓐ Ⓑ Ⓒ Ⓓ   47. Ⓐ Ⓑ Ⓒ Ⓓ
9. Ⓐ Ⓑ Ⓒ Ⓓ   48. Ⓐ Ⓑ Ⓒ Ⓓ
10. Ⓐ Ⓑ Ⓒ Ⓓ   49. Ⓐ Ⓑ Ⓒ Ⓓ
11. Ⓐ Ⓑ Ⓒ Ⓓ   50. Ⓐ Ⓑ Ⓒ Ⓓ
12. Ⓐ Ⓑ Ⓒ Ⓓ   51. Ⓐ Ⓑ Ⓒ Ⓓ
13. Ⓐ Ⓑ Ⓒ Ⓓ   52. Ⓐ Ⓑ Ⓒ Ⓓ
14. Ⓐ Ⓑ Ⓒ Ⓓ   53. Ⓐ Ⓑ Ⓒ Ⓓ
15. Ⓐ Ⓑ Ⓒ Ⓓ   54. Ⓐ Ⓑ Ⓒ Ⓓ
16. Ⓐ Ⓑ Ⓒ Ⓓ   55. Ⓐ Ⓑ Ⓒ Ⓓ
17. Ⓐ Ⓑ Ⓒ Ⓓ   56. Ⓐ Ⓑ Ⓒ Ⓓ
18. Ⓐ Ⓑ Ⓒ Ⓓ   57. Ⓐ Ⓑ Ⓒ Ⓓ
19. Ⓐ Ⓑ Ⓒ Ⓓ   58. Ⓐ Ⓑ Ⓒ Ⓓ
20. Ⓐ Ⓑ Ⓒ Ⓓ   59. Ⓐ Ⓑ Ⓒ Ⓓ
21. Ⓐ Ⓑ Ⓒ Ⓓ   60. Ⓐ Ⓑ Ⓒ Ⓓ
22. Ⓐ Ⓑ Ⓒ Ⓓ   61. Ⓐ Ⓑ Ⓒ Ⓓ
23. Ⓐ Ⓑ Ⓒ Ⓓ   62. Ⓐ Ⓑ Ⓒ Ⓓ
24. Ⓐ Ⓑ Ⓒ Ⓓ   63. Ⓐ Ⓑ Ⓒ Ⓓ
25. Ⓐ Ⓑ Ⓒ Ⓓ   64. Ⓐ Ⓑ Ⓒ Ⓓ
26. Ⓐ Ⓑ Ⓒ Ⓓ   65. Ⓐ Ⓑ Ⓒ Ⓓ
27. Ⓐ Ⓑ Ⓒ Ⓓ   66. Ⓐ Ⓑ Ⓒ Ⓓ
28. Ⓐ Ⓑ Ⓒ Ⓓ   67. Ⓐ Ⓑ Ⓒ Ⓓ
29. Ⓐ Ⓑ Ⓒ Ⓓ   68. Ⓐ Ⓑ Ⓒ Ⓓ
30. Ⓐ Ⓑ Ⓒ Ⓓ   69. Ⓐ Ⓑ Ⓒ Ⓓ
31. Ⓐ Ⓑ Ⓒ Ⓓ   70. Ⓐ Ⓑ Ⓒ Ⓓ
32. Ⓐ Ⓑ Ⓒ Ⓓ   71. Ⓐ Ⓑ Ⓒ Ⓓ
33. Ⓐ Ⓑ Ⓒ Ⓓ   72. Ⓐ Ⓑ Ⓒ Ⓓ
34. Ⓐ Ⓑ Ⓒ Ⓓ   73. Ⓐ Ⓑ Ⓒ Ⓓ
35. Ⓐ Ⓑ Ⓒ Ⓓ   74. Ⓐ Ⓑ Ⓒ Ⓓ
36. Ⓐ Ⓑ Ⓒ Ⓓ   75. Ⓐ Ⓑ Ⓒ Ⓓ
37. Ⓐ Ⓑ Ⓒ Ⓓ   76. Ⓐ Ⓑ Ⓒ Ⓓ
38. Ⓐ Ⓑ Ⓒ Ⓓ   77. Ⓐ Ⓑ Ⓒ Ⓓ
39. Ⓐ Ⓑ Ⓒ Ⓓ

Verbal Reasoning

78. Ⓐ Ⓑ Ⓒ Ⓓ   108. Ⓐ Ⓑ Ⓒ Ⓓ
79. Ⓐ Ⓑ Ⓒ Ⓓ   109. Ⓐ Ⓑ Ⓒ Ⓓ
80. Ⓐ Ⓑ Ⓒ Ⓓ   110. Ⓐ Ⓑ Ⓒ Ⓓ
81. Ⓐ Ⓑ Ⓒ Ⓓ   111. Ⓐ Ⓑ Ⓒ Ⓓ
82. Ⓐ Ⓑ Ⓒ Ⓓ   112. Ⓐ Ⓑ Ⓒ Ⓓ
83. Ⓐ Ⓑ Ⓒ Ⓓ   113. Ⓐ Ⓑ Ⓒ Ⓓ
84. Ⓐ Ⓑ Ⓒ Ⓓ   114. Ⓐ Ⓑ Ⓒ Ⓓ
85. Ⓐ Ⓑ Ⓒ Ⓓ   115. Ⓐ Ⓑ Ⓒ Ⓓ
86. Ⓐ Ⓑ Ⓒ Ⓓ   116. Ⓐ Ⓑ Ⓒ Ⓓ
87. Ⓐ Ⓑ Ⓒ Ⓓ   117. Ⓐ Ⓑ Ⓒ Ⓓ
88. Ⓐ Ⓑ Ⓒ Ⓓ   118. Ⓐ Ⓑ Ⓒ Ⓓ
89. Ⓐ Ⓑ Ⓒ Ⓓ   119. Ⓐ Ⓑ Ⓒ Ⓓ
90. Ⓐ Ⓑ Ⓒ Ⓓ   120. Ⓐ Ⓑ Ⓒ Ⓓ
91. Ⓐ Ⓑ Ⓒ Ⓓ   121. Ⓐ Ⓑ Ⓒ Ⓓ
92. Ⓐ Ⓑ Ⓒ Ⓓ   122. Ⓐ Ⓑ Ⓒ Ⓓ
93. Ⓐ Ⓑ Ⓒ Ⓓ   123. Ⓐ Ⓑ Ⓒ Ⓓ
94. Ⓐ Ⓑ Ⓒ Ⓓ   124. Ⓐ Ⓑ Ⓒ Ⓓ
95. Ⓐ Ⓑ Ⓒ Ⓓ   125. Ⓐ Ⓑ Ⓒ Ⓓ
96. Ⓐ Ⓑ Ⓒ Ⓓ   126. Ⓐ Ⓑ Ⓒ Ⓓ
97. Ⓐ Ⓑ Ⓒ Ⓓ   127. Ⓐ Ⓑ Ⓒ Ⓓ
98. Ⓐ Ⓑ Ⓒ Ⓓ   128. Ⓐ Ⓑ Ⓒ Ⓓ
99. Ⓐ Ⓑ Ⓒ Ⓓ   129. Ⓐ Ⓑ Ⓒ Ⓓ
100. Ⓐ Ⓑ Ⓒ Ⓓ   130. Ⓐ Ⓑ Ⓒ Ⓓ
101. Ⓐ Ⓑ Ⓒ Ⓓ   131. Ⓐ Ⓑ Ⓒ Ⓓ
102. Ⓐ Ⓑ Ⓒ Ⓓ   132. Ⓐ Ⓑ Ⓒ Ⓓ
103. Ⓐ Ⓑ Ⓒ Ⓓ   133. Ⓐ Ⓑ Ⓒ Ⓓ
104. Ⓐ Ⓑ Ⓒ Ⓓ   134. Ⓐ Ⓑ Ⓒ Ⓓ
105. Ⓐ Ⓑ Ⓒ Ⓓ   135. Ⓐ Ⓑ Ⓒ Ⓓ
106. Ⓐ Ⓑ Ⓒ Ⓓ   136. Ⓐ Ⓑ Ⓒ Ⓓ
107. Ⓐ Ⓑ Ⓒ Ⓓ   137. Ⓐ Ⓑ Ⓒ Ⓓ

Biological Sciences

138. Ⓐ Ⓑ Ⓒ Ⓓ   177. Ⓐ Ⓑ Ⓒ Ⓓ
139. Ⓐ Ⓑ Ⓒ Ⓓ   178. Ⓐ Ⓑ Ⓒ Ⓓ
140. Ⓐ Ⓑ Ⓒ Ⓓ   179. Ⓐ Ⓑ Ⓒ Ⓓ
141. Ⓐ Ⓑ Ⓒ Ⓓ   180. Ⓐ Ⓑ Ⓒ Ⓓ
142. Ⓐ Ⓑ Ⓒ Ⓓ   181. Ⓐ Ⓑ Ⓒ Ⓓ
143. Ⓐ Ⓑ Ⓒ Ⓓ   182. Ⓐ Ⓑ Ⓒ Ⓓ
144. Ⓐ Ⓑ Ⓒ Ⓓ   183. Ⓐ Ⓑ Ⓒ Ⓓ
145. Ⓐ Ⓑ Ⓒ Ⓓ   184. Ⓐ Ⓑ Ⓒ Ⓓ
146. Ⓐ Ⓑ Ⓒ Ⓓ   185. Ⓐ Ⓑ Ⓒ Ⓓ
147. Ⓐ Ⓑ Ⓒ Ⓓ   186. Ⓐ Ⓑ Ⓒ Ⓓ
148. Ⓐ Ⓑ Ⓒ Ⓓ   187. Ⓐ Ⓑ Ⓒ Ⓓ
149. Ⓐ Ⓑ Ⓒ Ⓓ   188. Ⓐ Ⓑ Ⓒ Ⓓ
150. Ⓐ Ⓑ Ⓒ Ⓓ   189. Ⓐ Ⓑ Ⓒ Ⓓ
151. Ⓐ Ⓑ Ⓒ Ⓓ   190. Ⓐ Ⓑ Ⓒ Ⓓ
152. Ⓐ Ⓑ Ⓒ Ⓓ   191. Ⓐ Ⓑ Ⓒ Ⓓ
153. Ⓐ Ⓑ Ⓒ Ⓓ   192. Ⓐ Ⓑ Ⓒ Ⓓ
154. Ⓐ Ⓑ Ⓒ Ⓓ   193. Ⓐ Ⓑ Ⓒ Ⓓ
155. Ⓐ Ⓑ Ⓒ Ⓓ   194. Ⓐ Ⓑ Ⓒ Ⓓ
156. Ⓐ Ⓑ Ⓒ Ⓓ   195. Ⓐ Ⓑ Ⓒ Ⓓ
157. Ⓐ Ⓑ Ⓒ Ⓓ   196. Ⓐ Ⓑ Ⓒ Ⓓ
158. Ⓐ Ⓑ Ⓒ Ⓓ   197. Ⓐ Ⓑ Ⓒ Ⓓ
159. Ⓐ Ⓑ Ⓒ Ⓓ   198. Ⓐ Ⓑ Ⓒ Ⓓ
160. Ⓐ Ⓑ Ⓒ Ⓓ   199. Ⓐ Ⓑ Ⓒ Ⓓ
161. Ⓐ Ⓑ Ⓒ Ⓓ   200. Ⓐ Ⓑ Ⓒ Ⓓ
162. Ⓐ Ⓑ Ⓒ Ⓓ   201. Ⓐ Ⓑ Ⓒ Ⓓ
163. Ⓐ Ⓑ Ⓒ Ⓓ   202. Ⓐ Ⓑ Ⓒ Ⓓ
164. Ⓐ Ⓑ Ⓒ Ⓓ   203. Ⓐ Ⓑ Ⓒ Ⓓ
165. Ⓐ Ⓑ Ⓒ Ⓓ   204. Ⓐ Ⓑ Ⓒ Ⓓ
166. Ⓐ Ⓑ Ⓒ Ⓓ   205. Ⓐ Ⓑ Ⓒ Ⓓ
167. Ⓐ Ⓑ Ⓒ Ⓓ   206. Ⓐ Ⓑ Ⓒ Ⓓ
168. Ⓐ Ⓑ Ⓒ Ⓓ   207. Ⓐ Ⓑ Ⓒ Ⓓ
169. Ⓐ Ⓑ Ⓒ Ⓓ   208. Ⓐ Ⓑ Ⓒ Ⓓ
170. Ⓐ Ⓑ Ⓒ Ⓓ   209. Ⓐ Ⓑ Ⓒ Ⓓ
171. Ⓐ Ⓑ Ⓒ Ⓓ   210. Ⓐ Ⓑ Ⓒ Ⓓ
172. Ⓐ Ⓑ Ⓒ Ⓓ   211. Ⓐ Ⓑ Ⓒ Ⓓ
173. Ⓐ Ⓑ Ⓒ Ⓓ   212. Ⓐ Ⓑ Ⓒ Ⓓ
174. Ⓐ Ⓑ Ⓒ Ⓓ   213. Ⓐ Ⓑ Ⓒ Ⓓ
175. Ⓐ Ⓑ Ⓒ Ⓓ   214. Ⓐ Ⓑ Ⓒ Ⓓ
176. Ⓐ Ⓑ Ⓒ Ⓓ

Writing Sample

NOTES

NOTES

NOTES

NOTES

NOTES

NOTES

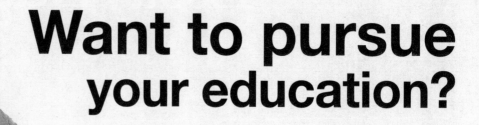